Well

For People Over 50

Advised ™

With 94 Illustrations and 87 Photographs

D1402293

Mosby Consumer Health

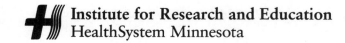
Institute for Research and Education
HealthSystem Minnesota

The material in this publication is for general information only and is not intended to provide specific advice or recommendations for any individual. Your doctor or other health professional must be consulted for advice with regard to your individual situation.

Mosby Consumer Health
263 Summer Street
Boston, MA 02210
(800) 729-5285

Institute for Research and Education
HealthSystem Minnesota
3800 Park Nicollet Boulevard
Minneapolis, MN 55416
(800) 372-7776

ISBN 1-56066-695-1

97 98 99 01 02/ 9 8 7 6 5 4 3 2 1

Introduction

Well *Advised for People Over 50* is about your health. We wrote this book to help you become an active member of your health care team. When you know more about your health, you can make better health decisions. This book will help you know which problems your doctor needs to treat and which problems you can treat at home with self-care. Throughout the book you will find easy-to-follow boxes called "What to do about...." They tell you when to call or see a doctor. They also tell you when you can use self-care. If a box suggests self-care, you will find an easy-to-follow guide with self-care tips. There are also guides on how to prevent illness and injury.

But this book does more than guide you in self-care and prevention. Your health problems today are not the same as the ones you faced when you were younger. This book looks at some of the most common health problems people over 50 face. It tells you about choices you can make that will affect your health.

Much of the advice in this book is based on health guidelines developed by a leader in healthcare and education research: the Institute for Research and Education, Health System Minnesota. We also relied on guidelines from the Institute for Clinical Systems Integration. This institute is made up of teams from Park Nicollet, Health Partners, and the Mayo Clinic. We also used published sources from the following agencies:

- The U.S. Preventive Task Force
- The Agency for Health Care Policy Research
- The U.S. Office of Technology Assessment
- The National Institute of Medicine

We use the word doctor throughout this book. But sometimes you may need to see a health care professional who is not a doctor. All of the following are important members of your health care team:

- nurses
- pharmacists
- psychologists
- dietitians
- health educators
- physical therapists
- occupational therapists

You may need to see one or more of them to be the healthiest you can be.

We hope you rely on this book to help you care for health problems. We hope it helps you make wise choices about health care. But don't use this book as a substitute for quality medical care. Always think of your own health history and condition when reading the advice in this book. Check with your doctor if you are not sure that the self-care tips apply to you. Also talk with your doctor if you try the self-care steps and find they are not working.

What the Symbols Mean

What to do about **Cramps and Spasms**	
Symptoms/Signs	**Action**
◆ Occasional cramps that come and go	Use self-care
◆ Muscle cramps or spasms that occur for several weeks	Call doctor

The "What to do about" boxes use symbols to show you what action to take for each symptom. This key helps you know what the symbols mean.

Use self-care

Use self-care. You can often treat these symptoms at home. Look for the self-care heading and follow the self-care tips. If the symptoms do not go away, call your doctor.

Apply first aid

Apply first aid. Look for the first aid heading. The information there will tell you what to do before medical help arrives.

Call doctor

Call doctor. Call your doctor's office for advice. You might be able to treat these symptoms at home. Or you might need to see your doctor. Your doctor will help you decide what to do.

See doctor

See doctor. Your doctor needs to see you to know what to do about your symptoms. When you call, your doctor will help you know how soon to come in.

Seek help now

Seek help now. These symptoms mean you need to see a doctor in less than two hours. Call your doctor if you are not sure where to go. Do not drive yourself. If you do not have a safe ride, call an ambulance.

Call ambulance

Call ambulance. These symptoms are signs of an emergency. They mean your life is at risk. You need medical treatment at once. Do not drive yourself.

Table of Contents

Introduction III

**SECTION ONE:
HEALTHY AGING**..........................1

**Chapter 1 ◆ What Is
"Normal" Aging?**.............................3
How Age Changes Your
   Immune System 3
How Age Changes Your Heart,
   Blood Vessels, and Lungs.................4
How Age Changes Your Brain and
   Central Nervous System...................4
How Age Changes Your Senses..........5
How Age Changes Your Bones,
   Joints, and Muscles.......................5
How Age Changes
   Your Digestive System....................6
How Age Changes Your
   Skin and Hair.............................6
How Age Changes Sexuality..............7
The Role of the Mind 7

**SECTION TWO: SELF-CARE
FOR COMMON CONCERNS**.............9

**Chapter 2 ◆ Digestive and
Urinary Concerns**...........................11
Digestive Concerns.......................11
Abdominal Pain...........................11
Black or Bloody Stools....................12
Colon Cancer.............................14
Constipation..............................17
Diarrhea..................................19
Diverticulosis and Diverticulitis.......21
Gallbladder Disease......................22
Gastritis and Peptic Ulcers.............23
Heartburn................................24

Hemorrhoids..............................25
Hiatal Hernia.............................26
Indigestion and Gas 26
Irritable Bowel Syndrome................27
Lactose Intolerance......................28
Rectal or Anal Pain......................28
Vomiting..................................30
Urinary Concerns.........................32
Urinary Incontinence.....................32
Urinary Tract Infections (UTIs).........34

Chapter 3 ◆ Ear Concerns...............39
Earaches.................................39
Airplane Ears 40
Earwax Buildup...........................41
Middle Ear Infections....................42
Swimmer's Ear............................42
Hearing Loss 44
Conductive Hearing Loss.................46
Sensory Neural Hearing Loss 47

Chapter 4 ◆ Eye Concerns..............49
Eye Irritations and Infections..........50
Burning, Dry, and Irritated Eyes 50
Foreign Object or
   Chemical in the Eye 52
Pinkeye (Conjunctivitis)..................54
Sties 55
Vision Problems..........................56
Cataracts.................................57
Diabetic Retinopathy.....................58
Glaucoma.................................58
Macular Degeneration....................59
Refractive Problems......................60
Specks and Floaters......................62

Chapter 5 ◆ Foot Concerns.............63
Foot Pain................................65
Bunions..................................67

Hammertoe 68
Heel and Arch Concerns................68
Morton's Neuroma.........................70
Stress Fractures 71
Skin Problems of the Feet.................**72**
Athlete's Foot................................74
Calluses...75
Corns...76
Plantar Warts.................................77
Ulcers on Your Feet 77
Toenail Concerns............................**78**
Ingrown Toenails 78
Toenail Fungal Infections...............79

Chapter 6 ◆ Heart and
Circulation Concerns.......................81
Chest Pain....................................**82**
Angina...84
Heart Attack..................................86
Edema (Swelling)...........................**88**
Heart Disease................................**89**
Atherosclerosis...............................90
Hypertension (High Blood Pressure)...90
Palpitations 93
Phlebitis..**94**
Varicose Veins **95**

Chapter 7 ◆ Lung Concerns............97
Asthma...98
Bronchitis......................................98
Colds...101
Fevers...102
Influenza......................................104
Lung Cancer.................................106
Pleurisy..107
Pneumonia...................................107
Pulmonary Embolism....................109
Wheezing......................................110

Chapter 8 ◆ Mind and Body.........111
Anxiety...112
Depression....................................114
Fatigue...117

Grief and Loss 118
Insomnia.......................................121
Loneliness.....................................123
Memory...126
Stress..128

Chapter 9 ◆ Mouth, Tooth, and
Throat Concerns...........................131
Mouth Concerns............................**131**
Bad Breath....................................132
Cancer of the Lip and Mouth........133
Dry Mouth....................................134
Mouth Sores.................................135
Tooth and Gum Concerns..............**136**
Dentures.......................................136
Lost Tooth....................................138
Periodontal (Gum) Disease...........139
TMJ (Temporomandibular
Joint) Problems..........................139
Toothaches...................................140
Throat Concerns............................**141**
Hoarseness and Laryngitis............141
Sore Throats.................................143
Throat Cancers.............................144

Chapter 10 ◆ Muscle and
Joint Concerns...............................145
Ankle Pain....................................**148**
Gout...149
Back Pain.....................................**150**
Compression Fractures..................155
Herniated Disk 155
Spinal Stenosis 156
Hip and Thigh Pain.......................**156**
Knee Pain **158**
Lower Leg Pain..............................**161**
Cramps and Spasms 162
Shinsplints....................................163
Periodic Limb Movements
(Restless Legs)............................164
Neck Pain.....................................**164**
Meningitis.....................................167
Whiplash.......................................167

Shoulder Pain 167
  Rotator Cuff Injuries 168
Wrist and Hand Pain 168
  Carpal Tunnel Syndrome................169
  Ganglions 170

Chapter 11 ◆ Nerve and Brain Disorders 171
  Alzheimer's Disease 171
  Bell's Palsy.......................174
  Dizziness........................175
  Headaches.......................178
  Parkinson's Disease.....................181
  Stroke.............................183
  Trigeminal Neuralgia 186

Chapter 12 ◆ Sexual Health Concerns 187
Physical Changes and Sex............187
  Changes in Desire and Intimacy....188
  Sexual Changes in Men.................189
  Sexual Changes in Women 191
  Medicines and Sexuality................192
  Illness and Intimacy......................193
Sexually Transmitted Diseases (STDs)....................193
  Acquired Immune Deficiency Syndrome (AIDS) and HIV............194
  Chlamydia 197
  Genital Herpes (Herpes Simplex 2 Virus) 197
  Gonorrhea.........................198
  Hepatitis B Virus (HBV)................199
  Syphilis.............................199

Chapter 13 ◆ Skin and Hair Concerns 201
  Age Spots.........................201
  Bruises 202
  Dry Skin 203
  Eczema (Dermatitis).....................203
  Hair Loss..........................205
  Hives..............................207

  Moles...............................208
  Poison Ivy, Poison Oak, and Poison Sumac.......................209
  Pressure Sores.....................211
  Rashes.............................213
  Scrapes and Abrasions..................214
  Shingles............................215
  Skin Cancer.......................216
  Sunburn............................218
  Wrinkles...........................220

Chapter 14 ◆ Special Concerns for Men 221
  Inguinal Hernias................221
Prostate Concerns....................222
  Benign Prostatic Hypertrophy (BPH)................223
  Prostatitis.........................224
  Prostate Cancer...................225

Chapter 15 ◆ Special Concerns for Women 227
  Menopause.......................228
  Hot Flashes.......................232
Vaginal Problems 232
  Vaginal Dryness...................232
  Irritation and Infections of the Vagina.......................234
Women's Cancers....................236
  Breast Cancer.....................236
  Cervical Cancer...................240
  Endometrial Cancer..................241
  Ovarian Cancer...................242

SECTION THREE: CHRONIC HEALTH CONCERNS....................243

Chapter 16 ◆ Living with a Chronic Illness 245
  When You Have Arthritis................245
  When You Have Cancer.................247
  When You Have COPD.................248
  When You Have Diabetes.................249

When You Have High
  Blood Pressure.................................253
When You Are Overweight............254
When You Have Osteoporosis 255

SECTION FOUR: TAKING CHARGE OF YOUR HEALTH....................257

Chapter 17 ◆ Your Role as a Health Care Consumer 259
The Role You Play................................259
You and Your Doctor......................261
  Finding a Doctor.............................261
  Getting Ready to See the Doctor.....265
  After Your Doctor Visit...................267
You and Your Drugstore 267
  Choosing a Drugstore.....................268
  Keeping Drugs Safe and Effective...269
  Choosing Over-the-Counter Drugs...270
You and the Hospital......................275
  If Your Doctor Tells You to
    Go to the Hospital........................275
  If Your Doctor Says You
    Need Surgery..............................276
  How to Review Your Hospital Bill...278

Chapter 18 ◆ Preventive Health Care 279
  Having the Screening
    Tests You Need.............................279
  Keeping Your Immunizations
    Up-to-Date..................................280
Recommended Preventive Services...282

Chapter 19 ◆ Making Healthy Lifestyle Choices..............285
  Alcohol Use and Alcoholism 285
  Eating for Your Health....................287
  Staying Active 291
  Staying Safe..................................294
  Quitting Smoking...........................299

Chapter 20 ◆ Your Future Health Concerns 301
Putting Your Affairs in Order..........302
  Advance Directives.........................303
Living at Home................................306
Living Away From Home..................308
  Assisted Living...............................309
  Continuing Care Communities......313
  Nursing Homes 315
Stay Informed About Your Choices 320

Chapter 21 ◆ Where to Get Help 321

SECTION FIVE: EMERGENCY CARE..327

Chapter 22 ◆ First Aid and Urgent Care 329
Preparing for an Emergency...........330
What to Do in an Emergency..........331
Emergency Situations 333
  Allergic Reactions 333
  Burns...335
  Carbon Monoxide Poisoning........337
  Chest Pain....................................339
  Choking..340
  Cuts and Wounds..........................342
  Fractures......................................345
  Frostbite and Hypothermia............347
  Head Injuries................................349
  Heat-Related Problems...................351
  Shock...353
  Stroke..354

Index..355
Credits..370
Tear-out forms..................................373
Color Plates 377

Healthy Aging

It has been said that age is a state of mind. Many people well past age 50 don't feel much different from when they were 20. They stay active and healthy, both physically and mentally. But others don't. Aging is a complex process, and people respond to it in different ways.

It is normal for your body to change as you age. Your vision and hearing may change. You may have more aches and pains. Many of your body's systems change. These changes can affect the way your body fights off disease. They can also make you more prone to injury and more likely to develop a chronic disease.

To stay well, most people need to take a more active role in their health care than they did in the past. This may mean focusing more on self-care than you have before. It is also important to stay connected to other people. Doing so can help you feel useful. When you feel useful, life is more satisfying. And that can help you stay well.

It seems clear that age alone does not make you sick. Age does not cause illness or physical and mental disabilities. That's good news. But you still need to take steps to stay as healthy as you can. Medicines and doctors may help you do this. But good health and good health care start at home.

The most basic step in good health care is to take care of your body. No matter how old you are, it is never too late to start taking care of yourself.

These are the most important steps you can take toward good health:

- Stay physically active.
- Eat a well-balanced diet that is low in fat.
- If you drink alcohol, be sure that you drink moderately.
- If you have a problem with alcohol, nicotine, or other drugs, get the help you need to take care of it.
- See your doctor for health screening and immunizations.

Taking these basic steps can help you avoid many diseases and chronic conditions.

The mass media are quick to tell us how to live longer. But what they tell us may change from month to month. Results from one study may be at odds with the next study. Then we don't know what to believe. The truth is, there is no fountain of youth. But we know more about health and have more options than ever before. To benefit from these options, you should understand what people mean when they talk about "normal" aging. This section tells you what you can expect as you get older.

The first part of this section describes the normal changes your body goes through as you age. Try not to think of these changes as problems. But be aware of them. Then you can be more prepared if you have a health problem. The second part of this section is about staying vital and involved in life. It looks at aging as a state of mind.

Chapter 1

What Is "Normal" Aging?

Why do some people look and feel younger than their age? Why do others seem to age early? Each of us ages at our own pace. Some people have gray hair and wrinkles as early as their 20s. Other people can pass for 40 when they are in their 60s. Even organs in the body may age at different rates. For instance, a 70-year-old man may have a heart as healthy as someone half his age. But he could have the bones and joints of someone who is 85.

There are many theories that try to explain why people age differently. For instance, age could be related to changes in our genes. Or it could be related to the buildup of waste in our cells. There are many other theories. But no one theory explains all the changes we go through. This section looks at the changes that take place in the body's systems as we age.

How Age Changes Your Immune System

Your body's immune system helps keep you well. Antibodies are special proteins your body makes. Both antibodies and white blood cells fight off things like bacteria and viruses. But as you age, your body does not make as many antibodies as it once did. This may be why you become more prone to infections, cancer, and other diseases. Your skin and mucous membranes change. (Mucous membranes include the moist parts of your eyes, nose, and mouth.) Your urinary tract and digestive system change. So does your respiratory system. These changes make it harder for your body to keep out bacteria. And they make preventive care even more important as you age. Preventive care includes such things as flu shots. It is care that can help your immune system fight off disease. To learn more about preventive care, see the chapter Preventive Health Care, which starts on page 279.

How Age Changes Your Heart, Blood Vessels, and Lungs

As you get older, your heart cannot speed up when you exercise as much as it did when you were younger. This change, though, does not cause any major problems.

Your lungs keep working the way they need to, despite getting older. No matter what age you are, aerobic exercise can benefit your lungs. Aerobic exercise builds endurance. As you build endurance, you can do more without running out of breath. A regular walking program builds endurance. You can slowly increase the number and pace of your walks as well as the amount of time you walk. Doing these things will make your lungs stronger and healthier. (SEE STAYING ACTIVE, PAGE 291.)

Smoking always hurts your lungs, no matter how old you are. Smoking speeds up the progress of many diseases. Even if you have smoked for years, quitting now may help prevent lung disease in the future. If you already have a lung disease, you should still quit smoking. Quitting smoking will slow the progress of the disease. (SEE HOW TO QUIT SMOKING, PAGE 300.)

How Age Changes Your Brain and Central Nervous System

From age 30 on, your brain loses nerve cells. This loss is normal. It does not affect how well you think and function. Nor does it affect your personality. It is a myth that you get more cranky as you age. The idea that you mellow with age is also a myth. But some of the changes that occur as you age do seem to affect the way your brain works. Those changes vary greatly from person to person.

Getting older does not mean you can't learn new things. After age 70, your ability to learn from reading does not decline. But your ability to learn from what you hear may. Also, it may take you longer to react to things around you.

The Baltimore Longitudinal Study of Aging began in 1958 and continues today. This study has shown some important things. For instance, short-term memory declines with age. But your ability to learn new things does not decline until after age 70. Even then, the decline is only in ability to learn new things through hearing. You can still learn from what you read. Your vocabulary stays constant too. But after age 70 your ability to respond to the world around you may slow. You may take a little longer to do certain things. The more complex the task, the longer it takes to react. To learn more, see the chapter on the nerves and brain that starts on page 171.

How Age Changes Your Senses

As you get older, you may not see as well as before. But with eyeglasses, most people can enjoy 20/20 vision for years. For most people, this lasts well past the age of 80. There may be other changes. For instance, it may be harder to adjust to changes in light. More or brighter lights may help. If you have concerns about your eyes, see the chapter Eye Concerns that starts on page 49.

You may not hear as well, either. Hearing loss may begin as early as in your 20s. But you may not notice it until after age 60. Loud background noises can make it hard for you to hear someone speak. This may be true even if you have no other major hearing loss. (SEE THE CHAPTER EAR CONCERNS, PAGE 39.)

Your sense of taste is affected by age too. You may not be able to taste salty and bitter flavors as well as you once could. You may not be able to tell the difference between smells. These changes can make it hard to tell one flavor from another. This may be especially true when you eat dishes that combine many flavors.

Though you can certainly still feel pain, you may respond to pain more slowly. You may not pull away from something painful as fast as you would have when you were younger.

How Age Changes Your Bones, Joints, and Muscles

You lose bone mass as you age. As your body takes the calcium it needs from your bones, your bones become weaker and more porous. Your joints begin to break down after years of hard use. Loss of muscle may not be a normal part of aging. It can occur when people use their muscles less as they get older. If you do nothing, these changes can lead to health problems such as osteoporosis. (SEE PAGE 255.) This is a disease that makes your bones become brittle.

But you can offset these changes. You can offset the loss of bone and muscle by doing weight-bearing exercises. Those are exercises in which your legs carry your body's weight. Walking and running are both weight-bearing exercises. Adding calcium to your diet will also help. Milk products, spinach, and canned salmon (with the bones) are high in calcium. The goal is not to have the shape of a 25-year-old bodybuilder. The goal is to have the strength, energy, and endurance to do the things you enjoy. Exercise and a healthy diet can help you stay independent and active, despite the changes in your body. (SEE THE CHAPTER ON LIFESTYLE CHOICES, PAGE 285.)

Body changes may make you lose height as you grow older. Between ages 40 and 80, most people shrink about two inches. Much of this loss comes from the flattening of your feet and compression of the disks in your vertebrae. Some diseases such as osteoporosis can also make you shorter.

How Age Changes Your Digestive System

Your digestive system does not change much with age. But your muscles lose tone and become less elastic. Then you may digest food more slowly. Changes in your liver keep medicines and alcohol in your body longer. Changes in weight may have more to do with your eating and living habits than with age. American men tend to gain weight until their mid-50s and lose it in their late 60s and 70s. Most women gain weight until their late 60s. Then they lose. But they do not lose weight as fast as men do. If you have concerns about your digestion, see the chapter on the digestive system that starts on page 11.

How Age Changes Your Skin and Hair

The most obvious signs of aging are the changes in your skin and hair. Hair turns gray when you lose pigment cells. Growth of scalp, pubic, and underarm hair slows down. If you are a man, you may grow more eyebrow and nostril hair. If you are a woman, you may have more facial hair.

With age, your skin gets thinner and less elastic. When skin is less elastic, it wrinkles. Sun-damaged skin wrinkles even more. Exposure to too much sunlight can cause skin cancer. The sun can also make your skin turn leathery, yellow, spotted, and rough. If you have concerns about your hair or skin, see the chapter on skin and hair that starts on page 201.

Despite the changes in your body, exercise and eating well can help you stay independent.

How Age Changes Sexuality

After middle age, your reproductive system changes. Some of these changes make you prone to certain medical conditions. For instance, as a woman gets older, her vagina becomes drier. This dryness increases the risk of infection. It can also make sex uncomfortable or less desirable. You can buy over-the-counter lubricants that will help. As a rule, older men and women stay interested and active in sexual relationships. To learn more about how age affects sexuality, see the chapter on sexual health that starts on page 187.

The Role of the Mind

Our bodies change as we age, and our minds do too. This is called psychosocial aging.

Some older people turn away from the world around them. They no longer seek out other people. They don't care about things they once enjoyed. Their minds are less alert.

Other people stay "young at heart." They stay involved with their families. They take part in church groups and social programs or do volunteer work. They tend to stay younger, in body and mind. A 75-year-old may volunteer, see friends and family, and take classes. This person is psychosocially young. If this same person shunned people and activities, he or she would be psychosocially old.

We all need to have meaning in our lives. Our minds and bodies stay more

Your need and desire for closeness are not likely to change with age.

healthy when we are giving to the world around us. When we connect with others, we feel needed. And others feel that they are needed as well.

The connection between feeling useful and being in good health was supported by a recent study. The goal of the study was to create more effective health care plans for older adults. In this study, some of the older adults set goals for each day and week. Each goal was supposed to improve the quality of their lives in some way. These goals included everything from social activities to household chores.

It turned out that the people in the study who set goals improved in both body and mind in just a few months. The most unique part of the study was that in setting goals, people planned to do things not just for themselves but for others. Doing for others gave them a sense of purpose that lifted their spirits.

No matter what your age, you need to have a sense of purpose. Once you retire, you may need to be more conscious about keeping meaning in your life. You may spend many years in retirement. On average, people who turned 65 in 1993 will live another 17.3 years.

These years are a new phase of your life. You might spend more time being retired than you did at any job. Even if you never worked outside the home, your family roles and duties change as you age. Planning for retirement means more than saving money. It means finding ways now to stay active and involved for the years to come.

You do, of course, need to be realistic. Don't set the goal of running a marathon with your grandson if you have bad knees. Instead, do something together that won't cause you pain. Playing catch or shooting baskets may

be a good choice. You need to be honest with yourself about things you can't do anymore. If you don't see well, you should not keep driving. To do so could put you and others in harm's way.

But there are many things you can do that are sensible, meaningful, and enjoyable. For ideas, see the chapter on the mind and body, which starts on page 111.

Doing the things you love helps to keep your mind alert.

Self-Care for Common Concerns

Do you want to make better choices about when to see a doctor? Self-care books such as this one can help you make better health decisions. Reading self-care books makes you more likely to see a doctor when you really need one. You are also more likely to use the right home treatment if you know about self-care.

The more you know about common health problems, the better prepared you will be to use the health care system. It's important to know when your symptoms are serious enough to need your doctor's attention. But seeing the doctor can be inconvenient and uncomfortable. It can also take time and cost money. So it is helpful for you to know when you or a family member has symptoms that can be treated at home.

This section helps you decide how to treat symptoms of common health problems. Self-care tips are offered when possible. For some health concerns, only a few self-care steps are listed. That may be all you need.

For a quick review of symptoms, use the guides that tell you "What to do about" your condition. Many of these guides tell you to call your doctor's office. Your doctor can often help you over the phone. You may save time and the cost of an office visit.

Remember that self-care steps cannot replace your doctor's advice. If you are not sure that these steps apply to you, call your doctor. If your symptoms do not seem better after self-care, you should also call your doctor. Consider your medical history and your current health. Then decide if self-care is a good idea.

Medical Supplies You Should Have

To care for health problems at home, you need the right supplies. Some of these supplies help you treat minor health problems. Others, like books, can help you make decisions about more serious problems. Then you can take care of those problems. The following is a list of basic medical supplies to keep at home.

- Medical and self-care books. Choose books that deal with your needs. For example, choose books that focus on health issues for older adults. If children live with you, choose books about childhood health.
- A first aid kit. Put together your own first aid kit. (SEE HOW TO MAKE YOUR OWN FIRST AID KIT, PAGE 330.) Or buy a kit at a drugstore.
- A thermometer
- A heating pad for treating sore muscles
- Adhesive bandages in different sizes. You can buy a box of bandages at a drugstore. The box should include butterfly-shaped bandages for closing cuts. Be sure to check your supply often. Always have enough bandages on hand.
- Sterile gauze pads to clean cuts and scrapes. You also need gauze pads to cover larger wounds.
- Paper tape for holding gauze pads in place. Paper tape does not hurt when you pull it off.
- An elastic bandage for wrapping sprained ankles or wrists. You can also use it to help treat injured, swollen, or sore knees.
- A cold-water vaporizer. Use it to relieve colds and coughs.
- A penlight for looking at sore throats
- Two pairs of tweezers. One pair of tweezers should have blunt tips. Use these tweezers for such things as taking an object from a child's nose. The other pair of tweezers should have pointed tips. Use these tweezers for taking out splinters.
- An ice pack. There are two kinds you can use. You can use the kind that holds ice cubes. You can also use the newer kind of ice pack that is filled with gel. You can keep this ice pack in the freezer.

Chapter 2

Digestive and Urinary Concerns

Most of us love to eat. We eat and digest thousands of pounds of food every year. This includes a variety of meats, fruits, vegetables, grains, and drinks. Your body works all the time to process these foods. It has been doing so for years.

As you grow older, the way you digest food may change. You need to know what is a normal change and what is not. This chapter describes common concerns with the stomach, intestines, kidneys, and bladder.

Digestive Concerns

You can treat many digestive problems at home. For instance, diarrhea and constipation respond well to self-care. You may need your doctor's help for some problems. For instance, you should call your doctor about painful hemorrhoids or repeated vomiting. Your doctor may refer you to a specialist. A gastroenterologist treats problems of the stomach and intestines.

Abdominal Pain

"I thought my pain was indigestion because I often had it after eating. When it got worse, I saw my doctor. To my surprise, I had gallbladder disease."
—Barbara

Your abdomen is the area between your chest and your hips. Pain in the abdomen is common. Pain can be caused by the following:

- constipation (SEE PAGE 17.)
- diarrhea (SEE PAGE 19.)
- gallbladder disease (SEE PAGE 22.)
- urinary tract infections (SEE PAGE 34.)

What to do about
Abdominal Pain

Symptoms/Signs	Action
◆ Mild pain that comes and goes for less than four weeks	 Use self-care
◆ Pain that comes and goes for more than four weeks	Call doctor
◆ Sudden abdominal pain with constipation and loss of appetite ◆ Sudden, intense pain that gets worse over a few hours ◆ Abdominal pain with any of these: fever, yellowish skin or eyes, dark urine, or pale, pasty stools	See doctor
◆ Sudden black, tarlike stools ◆ Constant intense abdominal pain after an injury ◆ Vomiting blood or a substance that looks like coffee grounds ◆ Abdominal pain and sudden, bright red rectal bleeding	 Seek help now

- vomiting with diarrhea, often called the stomach flu (SEE VOMITING, PAGE 30.)

If you often have pain in your abdomen, you may need to change what you eat. Or you may need to see your doctor. You could have a more serious problem.

Self-Care: Mild Abdominal Pain

- Avoid foods that you know have caused pain in the past. High-fat foods often cause problems. Rich desserts and fried foods are two examples of high-fat foods.
- Avoid alcohol, nicotine, caffeine, aspirin, and ibuprofen (Advil). Take acetaminophen (Tylenol) for pain relief.
- Take a warm bath. Or place a hot-water bottle on your abdomen. This may ease pain. Learn to relax. (SEE HOW TO RELAX, PAGE 129.)

Black or Bloody Stools

"I was glad to find out that the iron pills I was taking caused me to have black stools. I was scared that I had a serious illness."

—Jean

Normal stool color varies from dark brown to dark green. You should be concerned if your stools are tarlike, black, or bloody. Think about what you have eaten. You may have eaten

What to do about **Black or Bloody Stools**

Symptoms/Signs	Action	Symptoms/Signs	Action
◆ Pain, itching, and rectal bleeding, with symptoms that are worst when you move your bowels	See doctor	◆ Bright red rectal bleeding and abdominal pain with fever ◆ Black, tarlike stools that are unrelated to food you ate or medicine you took recently	Seek help now
◆ Black or bloody stools with history of an ulcer ◆ Black or bloody stools with history of Crohn's disease or ulcerative colitis ◆ Red blood in the stool when you are taking a blood thinner	Seek help now	◆ Black, tarlike stools and you feel dizzy, light-headed, and have a rapid pulse ◆ Sudden onset of heavy, steady, bright red rectal bleeding	Call ambulance

something that caused this change. Black stools may be caused by any of these:

- Pepto-Bismol
- iron pills
- foods that have a lot of iron, such as spinach

If you don't think any of these are the cause, see your doctor. These stools may be a sign of a serious illness.

Black or tarlike stools may be a sign of internal bleeding. They can also be a sign of serious bowel problems. These include:

- bleeding ulcers (SEE GASTRITIS AND PEPTIC ULCERS, PAGE 23.)
- colon cancer (SEE PAGE 14.)
- hemorrhoids (SEE PAGE 25.)
- ulcerative colitis

Ulcerative Colitis. With this condition, the colon and rectum are inflamed and have ulcers. It can cause loose, bloody stools. Other signs of the condition are:

- a need to have bowel movements more often
- stools that are covered with mucus
- fever and weight loss

- Avoid pain relievers such as ibuprofen (Motrin), aspirin, and naproxen sodium (Aleve). They may cause serious intestinal irritation and bleeding.

Colon Cancer

"My gynecologist gave me a kit to test for blood in my stools. There were three pieces of special tissue I had to drop in the toilet after three different bowel movements. If the paper turned blue, I was supposed to call the doctor's office. But I didn't have to call. The paper never turned color."

—Becky

The colon is also called the large intestine or the bowel. The last section of the colon is the rectum. (SEE DRAWING AT RIGHT.) That is why colon cancer is also called colorectal cancer. Colon cancer is the second most common cancer in the United States. It affects men and women in about equal numbers. At the next party or church group you go to, look around. If 16 people are in the room, chances are that 1 of them has colon cancer.

When found early, colon cancer can be treated. The problem is that too many people wait to see their doctor even when they have symptoms. Because so many wait, many people who could have been treated die. You can help prevent colon cancer by knowing the warning signs. (SEE BOX, PAGE 15.) You should also know if you are at risk. If you are at risk, screening tests are important. You should see your doctor every year so you can be screened.

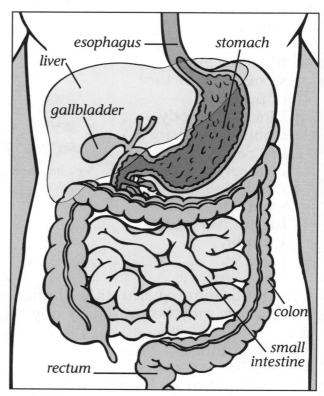

Problems can occur anywhere along the digestive tract. Heartburn affects the esophagus. Peptic ulcers affect the stomach. But other problems, such as diarrhea and constipation, are not in the stomach. You may call these problems "upset stomach." But the problem really is in the intestines.

Know the Warning Signs of Colon Cancer

Be smart. See your doctor if you have any of the warning signs below.

- a change in bowel habits
- blood in your stool or on it
- constant fatigue
- frequent diarrhea or constipation
- frequent gas pains
- weight loss with no known reason

- stomach cramps, bloating, or fullness
- stools that are thinner than normal, maybe as thin as a pencil

Having these symptoms does not always mean that you have cancer. You may have other problems. See your doctor to find out for sure.

Who Is At Risk for Colon Cancer?

If you answer "yes" to any of the following questions, you are at risk for colon cancer. See your doctor every year or so to be screened for this disease.

- Has someone in your family had colon cancer?
- Do you have polyps in your colon? Polyps are benign growths. They may be harmless now. But they can become cancerous over time.
- Are you older than age 65?
- Is your diet high in fat and low in fruits, vegetables, and fiber?
- Do you have ulcerative colitis? This means the colon and rectum are inflamed and have ulcers. (SEE PAGE 13.)

How to Prevent Colon Cancer

Eat foods that are high in fiber. This is one of the most important ways to help prevent colon cancer. Eat plenty of fruits, vegetables, and grains. (SEE THE FOOD GUIDE PYRAMID, PAGE 288.)

If you are at risk, have routine screenings. These screenings can find colon problems early. To learn more about routine screenings, see the Guide to Preventive Services on page 283.

Screening for Colon Cancer

Doctors have many ways to check for colon cancer. Three of them are:
- a digital rectal exam
- a sigmoidoscopy
- a stool test for blood

All of these tests may be mildly uncomfortable. But they are safe and easy for your doctor to perform.

Experts disagree about how often the colon should be examined. They also disagree about how well the tests find colon cancer in people who don't have symptoms. Talk with your doctor. Talk about your risk factors. You can decide together how often you should be screened. (SEE HOW TO MAKE THE MOST OF YOUR DOCTOR VISIT, PAGE 265.)

Digital rectal exam. For this exam, your doctor uses a finger to feel for lumps in your colon. Fewer than 13 percent of colon cancers are within the reach of a finger. The American Cancer Society suggests that adults over age 40 have this exam every year.

Sigmoidoscopy. For this test, your doctor gently inserts a slender tube into your rectum. This tube is called a flexible sigmoidoscope. The tube has a light at the end. With this tube, the doctor can see about 27 inches into your colon. The U.S. Preventive Services Task Force suggests that you have this test every three to five years beginning at age 50.

Stool test for blood. Another way to find colon cancer is to test the stool for blood. Cancers produce small amounts of blood that you may not be able to see. This blood is carried away in the stools. Tests such as Hemoccult can find blood in the stool.

Remember that these are only screening tests. They are not always accurate. If the result of any test is abnormal, your doctor will probably order more tests. If your test results are normal and you still have symptoms, see your doctor again. Be sure to see your doctor routinely even if your last test was normal.

How Colon Cancer Is Treated

There are three main ways to treat colon cancer. If cancer is found early, these treatments are very effective.

Surgery. Colon cancer is treated most often with surgery. The surgeon removes the part of the colon that has the cancer. This operation is called a colectomy.

Common Ways Cancer Is Treated

Surgery. Your doctor may remove the part of the body that has cancer in it.

Chemotherapy. This uses drugs to kill or control cancer. It is often used after surgery. You can take these drugs in more than one way. You may get an injection. Or you may take pills. The first time you take the drugs, your doctor may want you to stay in the hospital. That way you can be watched for side effects. Later,

you can probably take the drugs at home or as an outpatient.

Radiation. Radiation is also called X-ray therapy. This therapy aims radioactive particles at the spot where the cancer is. This helps kill cancerous cells. The radiation can come from a machine. It can also be put into the tumor with a needle. You can have this treatment without staying at the hospital.

Chemotherapy. After surgery, your doctor may prescribe drugs. (SEE BOX, PAGE 16.)

Radiation therapy. Your doctor may use this before surgery to shrink the cancer. (SEE BOX, PAGE 16.)

Constipation

"My mother always said we had to move our bowels once a day. Now I know that this isn't always necessary."

—Grace

Constipation is the passage of hard, dry, or infrequent stools. If you believe what you hear on TV, constipation is the curse of modern life. Ads tell you that laxatives are the only way to treat it. But constipation is easy to cure with self-care.

It should be fairly easy to empty your bowel. After all, the bowel sends a signal when it is ready to pass a stool. But if you ignore the signal, you can become constipated. If stools stay in the colon too long, they turn hard. The harder stools get, the more difficult they are to pass. The hardness of the stool or the amount of discomfort tells you if you are constipated.

The need for daily bowel movements is a common myth. Each person has his or her own natural schedule. Some people may move their bowels two or three times a day. Other people may have a bowel movement once

What to do about **Constipation**	
Symptoms/Signs	**Action**
◆ **Constipation without other symptoms**	 Use self-care
◆ **Increased discomfort, or symptoms that do not improve, after a week of self-care** ◆ **Constipation with vomiting or fever** ◆ **Constipation with cramps or gas** ◆ **Constipation with loss of appetite** ◆ **Constipation with abdominal pain** ◆ **Constipation that may be caused by a drug** (SEE SELF-CARE: CONSTIPATION, PAGE 18.) ◆ **Stools that are thin, like pencils**	Call doctor
◆ **An impacted bowel movement in the rectum that allows only mucus and fluids to pass**	See doctor

every three to five days. You don't need to worry about how often you move your bowels. You should be concerned only when your bowel habits change a lot from what they have been.

Constipation is fairly common among older people, but it's not always a part of aging. Sometimes more serious health problems can cause constipation. These include the following:
- an underactive thyroid
- diverticulitis (SEE PAGE 21.)
- irritable bowel syndrome (SEE PAGE 27.)

Call your doctor if your bowel habits change suddenly and do not return to normal with self-care. Your doctor can make sure that you don't have a more serious problem.

How to Prevent Constipation

You can often keep your bowels moving by following these tips.

Eat more fiber. Fiber relieves constipation and keeps your bowels moving. Fiber is the part of a plant that does not break down during digestion. It works as a natural laxative, adds bulk, and draws water to the stool. This makes the stool easier to pass.

You can easily add fiber to your diet. Eat fresh fruits, vegetables, and whole-grain breads and cereals. (SEE THE FOOD GUIDE PYRAMID, PAGE 288.)

Take fiber supplements like Metamucil. These help relieve and prevent constipation. When you add fiber or fiber supplements to your diet, drink extra fluids. Plain water and fruit juices are the best choices.

Do not make a habit out of using laxatives. Your body can begin to depend on laxatives. Then the bowel can "forget" how to work on its own.

Self-Care: Constipation

- If you have no other symptoms, relax and wait. It's not unusual to be a little irregular sometimes.
- Learn to heed the call. Your body will tell you when it is ready for a bowel movement. Don't ignore the message. Then take your time.
- Drink six to eight glasses of fluid each day. Plain water and fruit juices are best. Prune juice is very good for relieving constipation. Go easy on coffee and sodas that have caffeine. These can cause your body to lose fluids. And that can make your stools harder.
- Exercise more. Exercise helps your bowels move more freely. It also helps ease the stress that can make you temporarily constipated. To learn more about physical activity and exercise, see page 292.
- Use a stool softener, a mild laxative, or a fiber supplement only for relief of temporary symptoms. These include Colace, Metamucil, and Citrucel.

- Once your bowel movements are normal, keep eating high-fiber foods and keep exercising. Also keep trying to avoid stress. (SEE HOW TO RELAX, PAGE 129.)
- Follow the tips on page 18 about how to prevent constipation.
- Talk with your pharmacist or doctor. One of them can see if a medicine you take could be a cause of constipation. The following are some drugs that can cause it:
  —antacids
  —antidepressants
  —antihistamines
  —diuretics
  —drugs for Parkinson's disease
  —narcotic pain relievers
  —blood pressure medicines

Your doctor may change your medicine or advise you how to avoid constipation. Don't stop taking prescription drugs unless your doctor tells you to.

Diarrhea

"I had a mild case of diarrhea when I was on a business trip. I took Pepto-Bismol and felt better."
—Larry

People often get diarrhea when they travel. Of course, you can also get it at home. Most of us have it at times.

Diarrhea is frequent loose or watery stools. You may have it with cramps, vomiting, or fever. When you have diarrhea, stools move through the bowel much faster than normal. That means the body does not have time to absorb the water in these stools. This can be dangerous if you lose too much fluid.

Diarrhea can be caused by any of the following:
- bacteria
- food poisoning
- a virus
- stress
- certain drugs
- some long-term bowel diseases
- certain foods, if you are sensitive to them

Most diarrhea goes away by itself. With self-care it often stops within two days. A diet of clear liquids does not always help. Your doctor may prescribe a drug such as Lomotil. This makes your stools pass more slowly.

Bacterial infections of the colon can be serious. These can last longer than one or two days. Amebic dysentery is an infection of the large intestine that is caused by a bacteria. Diarrhea that lasts a long time may also come from giardiasis. This condition is caused by a parasite that is found in unclean drinking water.

How to Prevent Diarrhea
- Wash your hands after each bowel movement.
- Always wash your hands well before eating or fixing food.

What to do about **Diarrhea**

Symptoms/Signs	Action	Symptoms/Signs	Action
◆ Diarrhea that lasts less than 48 hours with mild cramps that are relieved by bowel movements	Use self-care	◆ Diarrhea with constant, intense abdominal pain for longer than two hours ◆ Abdominal pain or cramps that come and go and last 24 hours or more ◆ Signs of dehydration such as dry skin that does not spring back normally, or fever, dizziness, and confusion ◆ Diarrhea with difficulty breathing	Seek help now
◆ Diarrhea that lasts more than three days ◆ Blood streaking on toilet paper and you have no history of hemorrhoids ◆ Recent travel out of the country ◆ Drinking water from lakes, streams, or wells	Call doctor		
◆ Diarrhea if you have a chronic illness such as diabetes ◆ Mucus or blood appears on stool repeatedly ◆ Fever of 101 degrees or higher	See doctor	◆ Black, sticky, or dark red stools and you are sweaty, dizzy, have a fast heartbeat, or lose consciousness briefly	Call ambulance

- Always be sure to cook foods well. Undercooked fish, chicken, eggs, and meat can cause diarrhea and other digestive problems.
- Use warm, soapy water to wash everything. This includes cutting boards, pots, knives, forks, and hands that have touched uncooked meat.
- Don't eat dairy products unless they have been pasteurized.
- Keep hot foods hot and cold foods cold. If foods are left at room temperature too long, harmful bacteria can grow.

- Until your diarrhea and upset stomach are gone, don't work as a cook, waitress, or waiter. Don't work at any job where you may have to touch food.
- Before going to a foreign country, check to see that the water there is safe. Your state health department should have a list of countries with safe water. If the water is unsafe, use only boiled or bottled water. Use this even when you brush your teeth. Also, avoid all fresh vegetables there. Eat fruit only if it is peeled.

Self-Care: Diarrhea

- Cut out alcohol, caffeine, milk, and fruit juice. All of these can increase fluid loss.
- Don't eat if your stomach feels very upset or crampy.
- Drink only clear liquids such as water. Or drink flat, clear soda such as ginger ale, 7UP, or Sprite. Drink soda with sugar in it, not diet soda. The sugar in soda helps replace the calories you need. Drink clear beef or chicken broth or Gatorade. Sip a few ounces at a time all day long.
- Suck ice chips if you can't keep other liquids down. This keeps you from getting dehydrated.
- Eat bland foods. These include ripe bananas, rice, applesauce, white toast, cooked cereal, potatoes, turkey, chicken, and cooked carrots.

- Avoid foods that may upset your stomach. These include fresh fruits, green vegetables, and greasy or fatty foods like cheeseburgers or bacon. Also avoid alcohol and highly seasoned or spicy foods.
- Take over-the-counter drugs such as Pepto-Bismol, Kaopectate, or Imodium. Follow the instructions. Pepto-Bismol may turn your stools or your tongue dark.
- Call your doctor if you think your condition might be caused by a drug. Diarrhea is a common side effect of some drugs. These include pain relievers such as aspirin and ibuprofen, antibiotics, gold compounds, and antidepressants like Prozac, Zoloft, and Paxil.

Diverticulosis and Diverticulitis

"It seemed as if I was always constipated. Drinking prune juice did not help. My doctor did an exam and said I had diverticulosis."
—Margaret

Small pockets sometimes form on the inside wall of the large intestine. (SEE DRAWING, PAGE 22.) This is called diverticulosis. This condition often has no symptoms. It may cause pain in the lower left side of the abdomen. These pockets can become inflamed. Then the condition is called diverticulitis.

You can ease symptoms. You can also prevent diverticulitis. Drink a lot of fluids. Also, eat foods that are high in fiber. These include fruits, vegetables, and whole-grain breads. If you have this condition, your doctor will most likely prescribe antibiotics. Rest can also help.

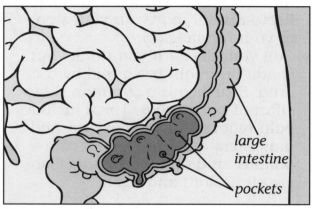

Diverticulosis occurs when pockets form in the large intestine. If they become inflamed, you have diverticulitis.

Gallbladder Disease

"I had an awful pain in my side. I called my doctor right away. She told me to go to the emergency room. It turned out that the pain was from stuck gallstones."

—Sally

The gallbladder is a small sac that stores bile from the liver. (SEE DRAWING, PAGE 14.) Bile helps you digest fatty foods. The gallbladder releases bile into the small intestine when it is needed. Gallstones can form in the gallbladder over time. They are made most often from cholesterol.

You can have gallstones without symptoms. These "silent" stones may be nothing to worry about. But some gallstones cause inflammation and infection. The stones can also get stuck in the duct that leads from the gallbladder to the intestine. Both of these problems can cause pain.

You feel pain most often in the upper right part of the abdomen, just below the ribs. Sometimes you feel pain in the back. Sharp pains may shoot through to the back and up to the right shoulder blade. You may vomit or have nausea or heartburn. In bad cases, fever, chills, and jaundice can occur. When people have jaundice, their skin and eyes turn yellow.

If you have symptoms only now and then, your doctor may tell you to watch and wait. Cutting out high-fat foods may help ease the symptoms. Your doctor may suggest surgery if any of the following is true:
- You often have symptoms.
- Your symptoms are severe.
- Your symptoms are getting worse.
- You have jaundice.
- You have an infection.

You may need to have your gallbladder taken out. This surgery is called cholecystectomy. The surgeon may use a laparoscope. This thin tube has a light and a tiny camera. It lets the doctor take out the gallbladder by making small incisions.

The laparoscope is not the best choice for some people. The surgeon may need to make a larger cut. Your doctor knows your symptoms, history, and the results of your tests. He or she can suggest the treatment that will be best for you.

Gastritis and Peptic Ulcers

"I was trying to lose weight. That's how I found out about my ulcer. When I waited too long to eat, my stomach really hurt. I knew then that I had a problem. It wasn't just my stomach's way of trying to make me cheat on my diet."

—José

Gastritis and peptic ulcers both cause pain in the upper abdomen. Both may be caused by bacteria. The bacteria are called *Helicobacter pylori* (Hp). No one knows how they get into the stomach.

Peptic ulcers and gastritis are treated with drugs that reduce acid. The drugs may form a protective coating. Antibiotics are very important for gastritis and ulcers caused by bacteria. They are taken for one to two weeks. Surgery is used less often now that there is drug treatment.

Gastritis. Gastritis is an inflammation of the stomach lining. Some symptoms of gastritis include vomiting and nausea. Eating can make gastritis pain worse. Bacteria can cause this problem. Drinking alcohol or taking some drugs can also cause it. Some of the drugs that cause it are:
- aspirin
- ibuprofen
- other nonsteroidal anti-inflammatory drugs (NSAIDs)

Peptic Ulcers. Peptic ulcers are sores in the stomach lining. They can also be in the small intestine. (SEE DRAWING, PAGE 14.) With peptic ulcers, you may have a burning or gnawing pain in your abdomen. You may belch, bloat, or lose your appetite. You may vomit, lose weight, or have nausea.

Bleeding ulcers can cause you to vomit blood. They can also cause black, tarlike stools. If you have these symptoms, seek help right away.

Self-Care: Gastritis and Ulcers

- If your doctor prescribes antibiotics, follow the directions exactly. Take all of your medicine. If you don't, the bacteria will come back.
- Don't drink alcohol if you have gastritis or ulcers. Cut out coffee, tea, and colas that have caffeine in them.

- If you are taking medicine that irritates your stomach, tell your doctor. Your doctor may want to change your drug.

Heartburn

"Every year I take my grandchildren to the fair. I get awful heartburn every time. I know it's because I eat stuff like fried dough and hot dogs with chili and onions. At the end of the day I always say, 'Never again.'"

—Forrest

What to do about Heartburn

Symptoms/Signs	Action
◆ **Taking a drug that may be causing your heartburn** (SEE SELF-CARE STEPS AT RIGHT.) ◆ **No relief after one week of self-care**	Call doctor
◆ **Heartburn with symptoms of heart attack, such as a feeling of heaviness, squeezing, pain, or pressure in the chest**	Call ambulance

Heartburn is a burning feeling behind the breastbone. It occurs when acid from the stomach backs up into the esophagus. The esophagus is the tube that connects your mouth to your stomach. (SEE DRAWING, PAGE 14.) At the end of it, a muscle opens and closes the opening to your stomach. This muscle may not close all the way. Then acid and bile from the stomach can wash back up the esophagus. The acid is what causes the "burn" of heartburn.

Most people get heartburn once in a while. Spicy or greasy foods and peppermint can cause it. Smoking can too. The pain can last for minutes or hours. Changing what you eat can ease heartburn. Over-the-counter drugs can also help.

Never ignore heartburn. Sudden heartburn could be the sign of a heart attack. (SEE PAGE 86.) Call an ambulance right away if you have symptoms of a heart attack. These include a feeling of heaviness, squeezing, pain, or pressure in the chest.

Self-Care: Heartburn

Do the following to help reduce the acid in your stomach. This will soothe the burning.

- Don't eat the foods that seem to give you heartburn. These may include chocolate, fried foods, and fruit juices.
- Don't eat too much at a meal. Eat smaller meals more often. This keeps you from being too full. A full stomach makes it easier for acid to push back up into the esophagus.

- Eat slowly and chew well. Make mealtime a time when you relax.
- Loosen tight clothes when you eat. Or change into loose clothes.
- Don't lie down just after you eat.
- Don't eat when you will go to bed in just a few hours.
- Raise the head of your bed a few inches. This makes it hard for acid to flow up from the stomach when you sleep.
- Don't smoke. If you smoke, get help to quit. (SEE HOW TO QUIT SMOKING, PAGE 300.)
- Lose weight if you need to. (SEE WHEN YOU ARE OVERWEIGHT, PAGE 254.) Losing weight will reduce the pressure on the esophagus.
- Avoid aspirin and all nonsteroidal anti-inflammatory drugs (NSAIDs) such as Advil and Aleve. Take acetaminophen (Tylenol) for pain.
- Take an over-the-counter antacid to ease heartburn. Antacids include Alka-Mints, Mylanta, Tums, or Maalox.

Hemorrhoids

"I have had hemorrhoids for years. I had them first when I had babies. Then I had them when I got older. When my daughter-in-law got pregnant, I didn't want her to have that pain. I put a basket together for her. It had a pregnancy diary and a book of babies' names. It also had Metamucil, fruit, and a big, pretty glass for water."

—Marge

Hemorrhoids are often caused by straining to have bowel movements. They can be inside the anus, at the opening of the anus, or outside the anus. The anus is the bottom of the rectum. It is where stools leave the colon.

Hemorrhoids can cause pain, itching, and rectal bleeding. Symptoms are worst during bowel movements. If you have hemorrhoids, you may see bright red blood on your toilet paper after wiping. Or you may see bright red blood on the stool itself. You may also have a discharge of mucus.

Home care can ease most anal pain and itching. But if you have bleeding often, see a doctor. Only the worst hemorrhoids need surgery. When hemorrhoids are removed, you probably won't need to stay at the hospital.

Self-Care: Hemorrhoids

- Use an over-the-counter rectal ointment. Ointments include Anusol-H.C. and Preparation H. These may help for a while. Don't use Nupercainal if you are allergic to novocaine.
- Soak in a warm bath for 10 to 15 minutes. Do this three times a day. Soaking helps ease pain. It also helps clean and heal the area.
- Place Tucks pads on the anal area twice a day and after each bowel movement.
- To ease pain, take acetaminophen (Tylenol). If pain is bad, call your doctor.

- Follow the self-care tips for constipation. (SEE PAGE 18.) Constipation can irritate hemorrhoids.
- Do not scrub the area.

Hiatal Hernia

"I used to belch a lot after I ate. I almost cried from embarrassment. I didn't want to talk about it. But then I had heartburn so often that I told my doctor. She found out that I had a hiatal hernia. When I read up on it, I found out that it caused the belching too."

—Nora

A hernia occurs when an organ bulges through a weak spot in a muscle or tissue. A hiatal hernia is caused by a weak spot in the diaphragm muscle.

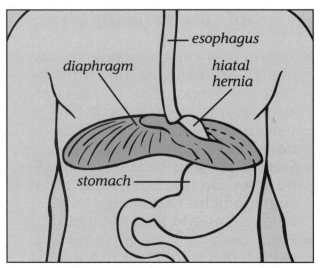

When you have a hiatal hernia, your stomach pushes up through a weak spot in the diaphragm.

(SEE DRAWING BELOW.) The stomach pushes up through that weak spot and into the chest.

These hernias are not often painful by themselves. However, food or acid may pass back into the esophagus. When that happens, you may have heartburn, indigestion, and pains in your chest. You may also hiccup and belch after meals.

Self-care can often ease the symptoms of a hiatal hernia. See your doctor if you think you have one, if symptoms get worse, or if you find it hard to swallow. Your doctor may advise you to have surgery to fix the hernia.

Self-Care: Hiatal Hernia

- Take an antacid when you need it. Tagamet or Pepcid AC can help. You can buy these drugs over the counter.
- Follow the self-care steps for heartburn. (SEE PAGE 24.)

Indigestion and Gas

"Who said that food can't bite back? What you eat and how much you eat can bite back with gas, heartburn, or indigestion."

—Nutritionist

Some foods can cause indigestion. Too much food can also cause it. Indigestion can cause pain in the abdomen. It can give you nausea and make you feel bloated. It may also give you heartburn. (SEE PAGE 24.)

The foods that cause indigestion may differ from person to person. If you have indigestion often, try to find out what foods cause it. Make a list of what you ate and drank before the symptoms began. Once you know what foods or drinks bother you, don't eat them.

Vegetables in the cabbage group can cause gas. Some of these are cabbage, collard greens, broccoli, cauliflower, and brussels sprouts. Beans and bran can also cause gas. When gas builds up in the intestines, it can cause pain and bloating. You need to keep eating foods like these even if they cause gas. Don't stop eating them. Just eat smaller portions.

If you change what you eat and still have indigestion, talk with your doctor. Your indigestion may be caused by a more serious problem, such as peptic ulcers or gastritis. (SEE PAGE 23.) Indigestion can be a sign of gallbladder disease. (SEE PAGE 22.)

How to Prevent Indigestion and Gas

- Eat a balanced diet that is high in fiber and low in fat. Eat vegetables, fresh fruits, and whole-grain breads and cereals. (SEE THE FOOD GUIDE PYRAMID, PAGE 288.)
- Try over-the-counter drugs such as Gas-X and Phazyme. These may ease the symptoms of gas.
- Try a product called beano. You add it to bean dishes and other foods to reduce gas.
- Exercise often. (SEE STAYING ACTIVE, PAGE 291.)
- Drink six to eight glasses of water every day.
- Alcohol may bother your stomach. Don't have more than one or two drinks a day. Or don't drink alcohol at all.
- Avoid tea, colas, coffee, and other drinks that have caffeine.
- Read the labels of all over-the-counter and prescription drugs you take. Some may cause indigestion. Be careful to follow the directions.

Irritable Bowel Syndrome

"I had diarrhea, then constipation. When I started eating foods with a lot of fiber, my system seemed to calm down. I eat bran cereal for breakfast every day."
—Oliver

Irritable bowel syndrome is also called IBS or spastic colon. If you have IBS, you may find that stress can cause spasms that lead to diarrhea. The diarrhea may be followed by constipation. You may also have cramps, bloating, and gas.

IBS is not caused by a disease. IBS is caused by a problem with the way the bowel works. IBS does not cause ulcerative colitis, cancer, or ulcers.

Your doctor may prescribe drugs to ease symptoms. Self-care can often help.

- Eat a balanced diet.
- Eat foods high in fiber. Try vegetables, fresh fruits, cereals, and whole-grain breads and cereals.
- Find ways to cope with stress. (SEE HOW TO RELAX, PAGE 129.)
- Exercise often. (SEE STAYING ACTIVE, PAGE 291.)

Lactose Intolerance

*"Milk upsets my stomach.
So now I take Lactaid pills. I
take them when I drink milk.
It makes a big difference."*
—Fran

As you age, you might not be able to drink milk or eat milk products. You may not have the enzyme that breaks down the sugar called lactose in cow's milk. That enzyme is called lactase. Do you often get cramps, gas, bloating, or diarrhea after you drink milk or eat ice cream? If so, then you may have lactose intolerance. Self-care can often help with the symptoms.

Self-Care: Lactose Intolerance

- Eat dairy foods only with other foods or beverages. Don't eat them by themselves.
- Eat smaller servings of dairy foods. Or eat yogurt and processed cheeses, like wrapped slices of American cheese.
- Buy acidophilus milk. It has been processed to help digestion.
- Ask your doctor if you can use an over-the-counter drug called Lactaid. Lactaid is an enzyme. Some milk, such as the milk called Lactaid, has been treated with it. Lactaid also comes in pills. When you take the pills with meals, they help you digest foods that are made with milk.
- If you cut down on milk products, eat more foods that are rich in calcium. Eat dark-green leafy vegetables, canned salmon with bones, and tofu. Ask your doctor if you should take extra calcium in the form of a pill.

Rectal or Anal Pain

*"When someone has anal itching,
they don't want to talk about
it. Luckily, in this case, the TV
ads are right. Tucks pads work.
They can soothe the itch."*
—Nurse

Long-term diarrhea or constipation may cause anal pain. Bowel infections may also cause anal pain. The anus is the bottom of the rectum where stools leave the colon. (SEE DRAWING, PAGE 14.) Anal pain may be mild. Or it may occur with intense itching, fever, and bloody stools.

What to do about **Rectal Pain**

Symptoms/Signs	Action
◆ **Pain or itching that lasts less than one week**	 Use self-care
◆ **Itching with pain or bleeding** ◆ **Pain that lasts for more than one week of self-care**	Call doctor
◆ **Intense pain and pain with fever** ◆ **Heavy or dark-colored bleeding**	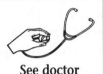 See doctor
◆ **Heavy bleeding with signs of the onset of shock, which may include: shallow breathing and weak pulse, nausea and vomiting, pale or clammy skin, shivering, or cold limbs** (SEE SHOCK, PAGE 353.)	 Call ambulance

Two of the main causes of anal pain are the following:

- hemorrhoids, which are badly swollen veins in the anal area (SEE PAGE 25.)
- fissures, which are cracks in the skin around the rectum

Self-Care: Rectal Pain

Following these self-care tips can help ease symptoms as well as prevent anal itching.

- Try not to strain when you move your bowels.
- Clean anal area well after each bowel movement. Do not scrub. Use Tucks pads instead of toilet paper. Or use Tucks after you use toilet paper. You can also use a soothing lotion like Balneol on the toilet paper.
- Use soft, white, unscented toilet paper to reduce irritation.
- Try dusting the anal area with cornstarch or talcum powder.
- Use zinc oxide ointment. It will decrease chafing and absorb excess moisture.
- Don't sit for too long at one time.
- Raise your legs when you sit. If you are obese, this takes pressure off the buttocks.
- For pain, apply a cold, wet cloth for 10 minutes, four times a day. Ice packs, Tucks pads, and witch hazel on a cotton pad will soothe too.
- After you use a cold, wet cloth, take a warm bath to soothe and cleanse.
- Take aspirin or use medicated suppositories, such as glycerin suppositories or Dulcolax. These can ease pain. You can buy them over the counter.
- Wear cotton underwear. Wear loose clothing made from natural fabrics.

- Drink a lot of water. Also eat high-fiber foods. This will soften stools and help you avoid constipation. (SEE PAGE 17.)
- Avoid spicy or acidic foods. They may irritate rectal tissue. Coffee, alcohol, and chocolate may also cause irritation.
- Some ointments and suppositories contain novocaine. If you are allergic to novocaine, read the labels on over-the-counter products, or ask your pharmacist for help.

Vomiting

"When someone is vomiting, fever or loss of fluids or appetite can lead to major problems. It is important to keep enough fluids in the body. Take frequent, small sips of clear liquids. Then you can make sure that you are getting enough fluids."
—Family practice doctor

Vomiting often results from an infection anywhere from the stomach to the colon. The following are common causes of vomiting:
- Foods that have been left at room temperature for too long. Hot foods must stay hot. Cold foods must stay cold. Otherwise, bacteria may form.
- A blockage in the intestinal tract
- Alcohol and other drugs
- Motion sickness
- Too much sun (SEE HEAT RELATED PROBLEMS, PAGE 351.)

- Medicine
- Nervousness, stress, excitement, or tension

Vomiting can be a symptom of a disease, including some kinds of cancer.

You need to prevent dehydration when you have been vomiting. Dehydration is a loss of fluids. It is a major concern for older adults who are weak and frail. A person who is dehydrated needs medical attention. The following symptoms are early signs of dehydration. If you have any of these symptoms, call your doctor:
- dark circles around the eyes
- dry mouth
- less urination than normal

Late signs of dehydration are:
- dry skin that does not spring back when you pinch it between your thumb and index finger
- being dizzy or confused
- fever

If you have any of the above symptoms, call your doctor.

Self-Care: Vomiting

- Over-the-counter drugs may not help you recover faster. But they may make you feel more comfortable as you recover.
- Let your stomach rest. Don't eat for several hours. Then slowly add liquids as the nausea stops.

What to do about **Vomiting**

Symptoms/Signs	Action	Symptoms/Signs	Action
◆ Possible motion sickness ◆ Vomiting after you drank too much alcohol ◆ Vomiting that may be related to stress or tension	Use self-care	◆ Vomiting when you have diabetes ◆ Vomiting with a yellowish look to your skin or the whites of your eyes ◆ Vomiting with early signs of dehydration, such as dark circles around the eyes, dry mouth, and less urination than normal	Call doctor
◆ Vomiting or diarrhea with light stools ◆ Taking drugs that may be making you vomit ◆ Vomiting with a fever of 101 degrees or higher for more than 24 hours ◆ Vomiting, with listlessness or less energy than normal ◆ Vomiting with constant, intense pain	Call doctor	◆ Late signs of dehydration, such as dry skin that does not spring back when you pinch it, fever, dizziness, or confusion	See doctor
		◆ Vomiting blood or a substance that looks like coffee grounds	Seek help now

- Drink clear liquids for the first full day after you vomit. Drink a little liquid at a time. Sip water, clear soup, broth, or flat clear soda. Don't drink diet soda.
- Add bland foods on the second day after you vomit. Choose foods like bananas, rice, applesauce, dry toast, soup, crackers, or dry cereal without milk. Eat small amounts of these foods as often as you can tolerate them.
- Get plenty of rest.
- Don't drink milk or eat milk products. You should also avoid alcohol, cigarettes, coffee, tea, and colas with caffeine. All of these products may upset your stomach.

Urinary Concerns

Some pain in your abdomen is caused by problems in your urinary tract. You can use self-care for mild problems with incontinence or for mild infections. Sometimes you need drugs or other help from your doctor. In some cases your doctor may refer you to a specialist. A urologist treats problems of the bladder and kidneys.

Urinary Incontinence

"I leak urine when I sneeze or cough. I have been doing this for more than 20 years. It has gotten worse lately. I use special pads and try not to drink a lot of liquid. Sometimes I wish I could talk to my doctor about this, but I'm just too embarrassed."

—Joyce

Many people can't control urine loss. This is called urinary incontinence. It affects millions of older adults. A lot of people are ashamed to talk about it with their doctor.

You can get help. This problem can be treated. Most often it gets better. Sometimes it can be cured.

What Causes Incontinence?

To treat incontinence you need to know the cause. Some drugs are to blame. These include diuretics, such as Lasix, Dyazide, and Maxzide. Some illnesses or conditions can make it hard for you

What to do about **Urinary Incontinence**	
Symptoms/Signs	**Action**
◆ **Occasional symptoms that you can control**	Use self-care
◆ **Symptoms that don't improve with self-care**	Call doctor
◆ **Urine loss you can't control that is frequent and interferes with your life**	See doctor

to get to the bathroom. For instance, you may be in a wheelchair. If you have arthritis, you may walk slowly. You may lose urine in the time it takes you to get to the bathroom.

There are three types of incontinence. Each has its own symptoms and causes.

Urge Incontinence. This is also known as detrusor instability. The bladder wall is a muscle called the detrusor muscle. (SEE DRAWING, PAGE 37.) This muscle may contract more often and more strongly than it should. That can cause a sudden need to urinate. The contractions may be strong enough to cause urine loss before you reach the bathroom.

Stress Incontinence. This can occur when you cough, sneeze, laugh, lift heavy things, exercise, or even get up from a chair. Sometimes the muscles that hold the bladder in place are weak. Then the muscle that controls the flow of urine may not be able to do its work.

In a woman, the muscles that control the opening to the bladder can weaken. When a woman gives birth, these muscles are stretched. Then urine

How to Keep Track of Urine Leakage

Keep a list of your symptoms. It can help your doctor find the exact problem. Then your doctor can suggest the right treatment.

- For several days, make a note of each time you drink fluids.
  —Write "D" for drink.
- Note each time you urinate. Also mark each time you leak urine, even during the night.
  —Write "U" for urinate.
  —Write "L" for leak.

- Note the time of day or night next to each letter.
- For every "L," note what else happened. You might write "while coughing" or "couldn't get to the bathroom in time."
- Bring this list with you when you see your doctor.

Pelvic-Floor (Kegel) Exercises for Women

These exercises can strengthen the muscles that hold up the bladder. If your muscles are stronger, you will be less likely to leak urine.

1. Start the exercises the first time you urinate after waking. While your bladder is full, start and stop the flow of urine. Let out only small amounts of urine at a time. Start and stop the flow of urine in this way until your bladder is empty. Pay attention to the muscles that you use to do this exercise. They are called the pelvic-floor muscles.

2. Exercise your pelvic-floor muscles all day long. You don't have to be in the bathroom. Squeeze the muscles around the anus and urethra. Hold for a few seconds, then relax them. Repeat 20 times. Do these exercises while you wash dishes, brush your teeth, or read the paper. If you do a set of 20 exercises three to five times a day, it should help within a few months.

loss can become a problem. It may also be a problem if you are overweight or going through menopause.

Overflow Incontinence. This occurs when the bladder does not empty all the way. With this problem, you can leak small amounts of urine all day long. You may feel the need to go to the bathroom. But you can urinate only a little. You may not feel completely "empty" after you finish. This may be more common at night. Men have this problem more than women. An enlarged prostate is often the cause. It can block the flow of urine. (SEE BENIGN PROSTATIC HYPERTROPHY, PAGE 223.)

How Incontinence Is Treated

Incontinence can be treated. Self-care may be all you need. Some people get help from drugs. For women who have gone through menopause, estrogen may help. These drugs can lessen the contractions of the detrusor muscle. (SEE DRAWING, PAGE 37.)

Surgery can help some types of incontinence. For women, surgery can reduce how much urine is leaked. For men, an operation can take out the part of the prostate gland that blocks urine flow.

Self-Care: Urinary Incontinence

- If this problem is worse for you at night, don't drink after dinner.
- Don't drink alcohol, especially after dinner.

- Cut out drinks with caffeine, such as coffee, tea, and colas. These drinks can increase the flow of urine.
- Practice Kegel exercises. (SEE BOX, PAGE 33.)
- Use Depend or another brand of absorbent undergarment. They are made for both men and women.
- Keep a list of your symptoms. This will help your doctor find the exact problem. (SEE HOW TO KEEP TRACK OF URINE LEAKAGE, PAGE 33.)

Urinary Tract Infections (UTIs)

"The pain I had from UTIs was bad. I wanted to have medicine in the house if it happened again. So I saved the last few pills. When my doctor found out, I got an earful. She said I had to take every pill. She told me if I had the pain again, all I had to do was call her. She promised to get me a prescription right away."

—Kaye

Urinary tract infections are called UTIs. They are more common after the age of 50. UTIs are often caused by the bacteria *E. coli*. These bacteria are common in the bowel. From there they can enter the urethra. (SEE DRAWING, PAGE 36.) If they do, they can spread to the bladder and kidneys.

The infection may be only in the urethra. This is called urethritis. It is called cystitis if the bladder is affected. This is also called an uncomplicated

What to do about Urinary Tract Infections

Symptoms/Signs	Action	Symptoms/Signs	Action
◆ Pain and burning when you urinate ◆ Frequent urge to urinate ◆ Symptoms that last more than 48 hours ◆ Blood in urine ◆ For men: frequent, burning, urgent urination, with or without fever ◆ Urinary tract infection, and you have diabetes	Call doctor	◆ Urinary tract infection with changes in mental state, such as confusion ◆ Urinary tract infection with nausea, chills, and fever ◆ Four or more urinary tract infections in the past 12 months ◆ Urinary tract infection when you have a weak immune system (HIV infection or recent radiation or chemotherapy treatments) ◆ Urinary tract infection with kidney disease or kidney stones	See doctor
◆ For women: frequent, burning, urgent urination with fever of 101 degrees or higher	See doctor		

UTI. The infection may reach the kidneys. Then it is called pyelonephritis. A kidney infection can cause fever, chills, and pain or tenderness in the lower back. If it is not treated, this infection may cause lasting kidney damage.

These are the symptoms of an uncomplicated UTI:
- frequent or urgent urination, especially at night
- a hard time urinating
- pain or burning when you urinate
- blood in the urine
- pressure in the lower abdomen
- urine that is dark or cloudy, or that smells very bad

As we age, our bodies may react differently to a UTI. Even the bacteria that causes the infection may be different. Older adults with a UTI may have these symptoms:
- nausea and vomiting
- confusion or other changes in mental state
- tenderness in the abdomen
- a hard time breathing
- lack of fever

Who Is Likely to Get UTIs?

Do you have diabetes or kidney disease? If so, you are more likely to get UTIs. If you have a urinary catheter, you are also at risk for infections. Women get UTIs more often than men do. Women are likely to get them because a woman's urethra, vagina, and rectum are so close together. (SEE DRAWING ON LEFT.) Bacteria from stools can cause infections in the urethra. Bacteria can be spread during sex. This can cause infections as well.

UTIs are more common in women who have gone through menopause. This is due to changes in the vagina. After menopause, the vagina can be drier and less acidic. This gives bacteria a good place to grow. If they reach the urethra, you may get an infection. Estrogen creams can help. These are inserted in the vagina. Estrogen pills can also help. (SEE HORMONE REPLACEMENT THERAPY, PAGE 230.)

Women who have sex with a new partner may be at higher risk for UTIs. So too are women who have stress incontinence. (SEE PAGE 33.)

UTIs are very rare in men who are young and middle aged. But men who are around the age of 60 are more likely to get them. This may be due to prostate disease or an enlarged prostate. (SEE PROSTATE CONCERNS, PAGE 222.) These problems can stop the bladder from emptying all the way. (SEE DRAWING ON RIGHT.) Then bacteria can grow in the urinary tract.

Female and Male Urinary Tracts

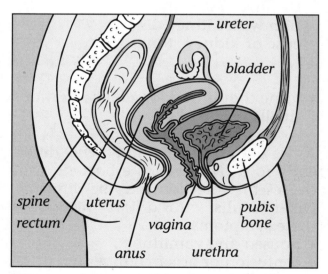

Women: *As you get older, the muscles that hold the bladder in place may weaken. This can make it hard to control the flow of urine.*

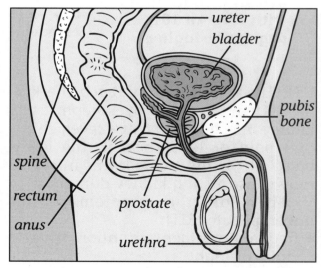

Men: *The prostate gland surrounds the urethra. An enlarged prostate can make it difficult to urinate.*

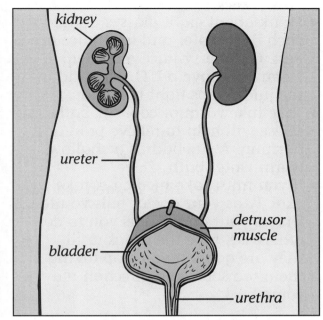

Your kidneys take waste and water out of your blood to make urine. Urine is stored in the bladder. If your bladder is working well, it tells you when it is full. You feel the urge to urinate. Urine then leaves your body through the urethra. Muscles at the base of your bladder hold the urethra closed. When the muscles relax, the urethra opens.

How to Prevent UTIs
- Drink a lot of water. Try to drink at least eight glasses of water a day. But if you have kidney disease, you should check with your doctor. Ask him or her how much water you should drink.
- Urinate as soon as you can after you have sex.
- Wear clean cotton underwear. Cotton underwear will help you avoid UTIs. Cotton underwear allows air to flow. When air flows, it is harder for bacteria to grow.

- Women should wipe from front to back when they use the toilet. This prevents bacteria that is in the vagina or rectum from spreading to the urethra.
- Don't use bubble bath, perfumed soaps, and douches. These products can cause irritation. The irritation can lead to infection.

Treatment of UTIs
If you think you have a UTI, your doctor may want a urine sample. Your doctor will check it for bacteria. You will be asked for a "clean catch" urine sample. The doctor or nurse will tell you how to collect the urine. This test may show right away if you have an infection. Or the results can take one or two days.

Your doctor may have you take antibiotics for the infection. Tell your doctor if you are allergic to any drugs. Some women who have an uncomplicated UTI need to take the medicine for only three days. Older women may need to take it longer. This is true when they have frequent infections or kidney infections. Men may also need longer treatment. After you have finished the medicine, you may need to give one more urine sample.

Symptoms often go away within two days after you start the medicine. But you should take all of the medicine and drink more fluids.

A follow-up urine test may show that bacteria are gone. But you may still have some bacteria in your urine even if you don't have symptoms.

If you have UTIs often, your doctor may keep you on a low dose of an antibiotic. You may need to take it for more than one month.

Self-Care: Urinary Tract Infections

You can't treat a UTI on your own. When you have symptoms, see your doctor. Use these tips to help ease the symptoms and aid recovery.

- Cut out caffeine, alcohol, and spicy foods. They can make your symptoms worse.
- Drink about eight glasses of fluid each day. Water and fruit juice are best. Cranberry juice may help when you have a UTI. The acid in the juice helps fight bacteria.
- Take lukewarm or cool sitz baths. These will help to relieve pain and burning. A sitz bath is a shallow, warm water bath.
- If you must take medicine, take it exactly as your doctor tells you to. Unless your doctor tells you to do otherwise, take the drugs until they are gone. If you stop taking them too soon, the infection may come back.

Chapter 3

Ear Concerns

The ear picks up sound waves in the air and turns them into electrical signals. Then it sends those signals across nerves to your brain. The brain tells you that you are hearing speech, music, or a train whistle.

As you age, you are more likely to lose some hearing than any other sense. Almost one-third of people older than 65 say they have hearing problems. One-half of people who are age 85 say the same thing.

Your family doctor can treat most ear problems. If you have hearing problems, your doctor may want you to see an ear, nose, and throat doctor (ENT). This doctor is also called an otolaryngologist. These doctors work with audiologists, who are not doctors. They have special training in hearing or speech therapy. They cannot treat ear infections or other diseases.

This chapter talks about these ear-related problems:
- earaches
- hearing loss

Earaches

Two things cause most ear pain. One is water in the ear. This can lead to a condition called swimmer's ear. The other main cause of ear pain is colds. It is common for people to get an ear infection after a cold. Then, if they travel by plane, they may also get airplane ears.

Airplane Ears

"It never fails. When I have to take a trip by plane, my ears get plugged. I used to be in agony during landings. Then I talked to my doctor. She told me to try a decongestant or nasal spray. Now I'm not afraid to fly, no matter how I feel."

—Martha

The pilot says that you are landing. Your ears don't feel right. Sound is muffled, and your ears ache. You have aerotitis media, also called airplane ears. Here is what happens when a plane lands: The air pressure outside your ears is greater than the pressure inside your ears behind the eardrum. (SEE DRAWING, PAGE 41.) This makes a vacuum inside your ears. Your eardrums may be pulled inward. This can hurt, and your ears may feel plugged.

Allergies or a head cold can make it very painful when your plane starts to land. Some doctors may suggest that you don't fly when you have these health problems.

Normally, airplane ears cause only brief discomfort with no lasting harm. But if you still don't hear well after you have landed, or if your ears hurt, call your doctor.

What to do about Earaches

Symptoms/Signs	Action	Symptoms/Signs	Action
◆ **Ear stuffiness** (SEE SELF-CARE: AIRPLANE EARS, PAGE 41.) ◆ **Mild wax buildup** (SEE SELF-CARE: EARWAX BUILDUP, PAGE 42.)	Use self-care	◆ **Blocked or stuffed ear that does not respond to self-care within three days** ◆ **Fever higher than 101 degrees** ◆ **Itchy outer ear that hurts when the ear is moved up and down** ◆ **Earwax that will not come out easily** ◆ **Severe, constant ear pain**	See doctor
◆ **Symptoms of middle ear infection, such as pain in ear, swollen glands, or fluid that seeps from the ear** (SEE MIDDLE EAR INFECTIONS, PAGE 42.) ◆ **Hearing loss** (SEE HEARING LOSS, PAGE 44.)	See doctor		

Self-Care: Airplane Ears

- To clear your ears, swallow, yawn, or chew gum.
- Pilots use the following trick. If it works, you will feel your ears pop.
  1. Squeeze your nostrils shut.
  2. Take a big gulp of air.
  3. Shut your mouth tightly.
  4. Try to blow the air out against your closed mouth and nose.
- Stay awake when the plane starts to land. You don't swallow as often when you are asleep.
- If you want to sleep, ask a flight attendant to wake you when the plane begins to land.
- If you must fly when you have a cold or the flu, be prepared. Take an oral decongestant, such as Sudafed (pseudoephedrine). Take it about two hours before landing to give it time to work.
- Before landing, use a nasal decongestant spray such as Afrin or Dristan. Spray once in each nostril. Do this one hour before landing, and repeat 5 to 10 minutes later. Don't use nasal decongestant sprays if you have high blood pressure or angina.
- Don't use nasal sprays for more than three days. Your nose gets used to the effect of the spray. Then your nose may start to depend on it.
- Don't use an oral decongestant and a nasal decongestant at the same time. This may be harmful.

Earwax Buildup

"A buildup of wax in your ear can cause slight hearing loss. It's not serious. With help, you can remove the wax."
—ENT doctor

When wax builds up in your ear canal, your ear may feel plugged. (SEE DRAWING BELOW.) Earwax helps keep dust and dirt out of your middle ears. Earwax can form a plug and block your ear canal. This stops sound from reaching the eardrum. Your doctor can remove earwax by flushing the wax out. If you often have earwax buildup, you may want to buy an irrigation kit. Then you can flush your ear. Ask your pharmacist to help you choose a kit. You can buy one over the counter.

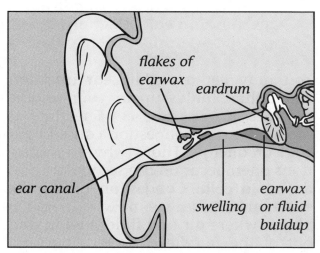

If too much wax builds up in the ear canal, it can form a plug. See your doctor about removing excess wax. This drawing also shows where swelling and fluid are in swimmer's ear. (SEE PAGE 42.)

Self-Care: Earwax Buildup

- If earwax has built up, do not probe the ear with swabs such as Q-Tips. A swab can push wax deeper into your ear. This can cause more problems.
- Squeeze warm water into your ear to remove wax. Use a soft-tipped syringe. Don't do this if you know that you have a broken eardrum. And don't use a syringe if fluid is draining from your ear.

Middle Ear Infections

"To avoid ear infections, don't smoke or be around smoke. Cigarette smoke irritates breathing passages. It can increase the chance of congestion and ear infections."
—Family practice doctor

You may get a middle ear infection when fluid builds up in your middle ear. (SEE DRAWING, PAGE 43.) The fluid is most often the congestion caused by a cold or allergy. That's why ear infections often occur on the second or third day of a cold. Congestion blocks the eustachian tube. (SEE DRAWING, PAGE 43.) This is where air and fluid pass in and out of the middle ear. Once bacteria reach this fluid, it becomes infected.

You will know if you have an infection. You will most likely feel pain. But you can help prevent middle ear infections. Wash your hands often. Stay away from people who have colds. If you think you have a middle ear infection, see your doctor. You cannot cure it at home. Your doctor will most likely prescribe antibiotics.

Self-Care: Middle Ear Infections

- You can't cure this kind of earache yourself. Untreated ear infections can cause major problems.
- If your doctor has prescribed an antibiotic or other drug, take it as directed. Even if your symptoms have gone away, don't skip a dose. If you do, the infection could come back. Store all ear medicines as directed.
- Follow your doctor's orders for follow-up exams and any other steps you should take. This can help prevent future ear problems.
- To ease pain, take aspirin or acetaminophen (Tylenol).
- To ease pain, place a warm cloth on the ear.

Swimmer's Ear

"Wear a bathing cap when you swim. I cannot think of a better way to help prevent swimmer's ear."
—Family practice doctor

Swimmer's ear is an infection of the outer part of the ear canal. (SEE DRAWING, PAGE 41.) Swimmer's ear is most often caused by bacteria in water that gets into the ear. The symptoms include

How We Hear

The ear has some of the smallest parts in the human body. The eardrum is only a half-inch across and less than one-fiftieth of an inch thick. The bones known as the hammer, anvil, and stirrup are tiny. Together these three bones fit into a space about the size of a baked bean.

These bones carry vibrations from the eardrum toward the inner ear. There the vibrations are changed to electrical impulses. The impulses travel to the brain along the auditory nerve. The brain recognizes the impulses as sounds. The inner ear may go a little out of tune over time.

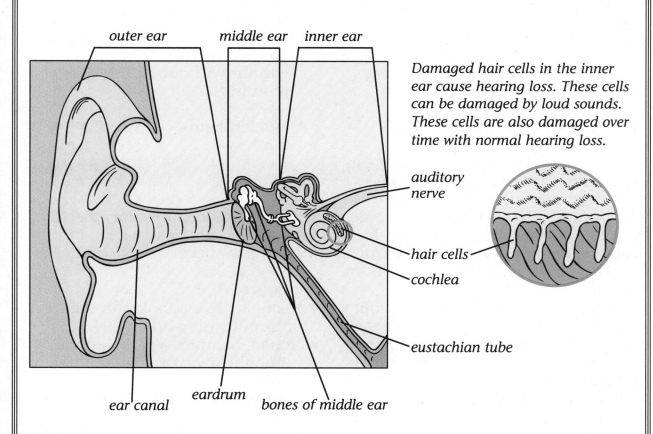

outer ear   middle ear   inner ear

Damaged hair cells in the inner ear cause hearing loss. These cells can be damaged by loud sounds. These cells are also damaged over time with normal hearing loss.

auditory nerve

hair cells

cochlea

eustachian tube

ear canal   eardrum   bones of middle ear

Problems in the outer ear include swimmer's ear (SEE PAGE 42) and conductive hearing loss (SEE PAGE 46). Problems in the middle ear are usually earaches, such as the pain that comes from airplane ears (SEE PAGE 40) or middle ear infections (SEE PAGE 42). Problems in the inner ear can cause hearing loss. Problems in the inner ear may also lead to a dizzy feeling. (SEE DIZZINESS, PAGE 175.)

itching, swelling, and redness of the outer ear. Sometimes the ear produces yellowish-green pus. It may hurt to touch the ear. If you get swimmer's ear, your doctor will treat it with eardrops that contain a corticosteroid. Your doctor may also prescribe an antibiotic.

How to Prevent Swimmer's Ear
- After swimming, dry your ears with a clean towel or hair dryer.
- Ask your doctor about drying eardrops like Swim-EAR. You can buy these over the counter.

Hearing Loss

Not all older people suffer from hearing loss. But as you age, you may not be able to hear high-pitched sounds as well. Almost 3 out of 10 people older than age 65 lose some hearing. Men are at greater risk than women because they are more likely to have been exposed to loud noise.

Hearing loss can affect the quality of your life. When you don't hear well, people may think you are confused. They may think that you are not paying attention. In fact, people often mistake symptoms of hearing loss for senility. When your hearing isn't good, you may find it hard to talk with someone. Being in a room with many people or a lot of background noise can be frustrating. If you cannot hear well, you may feel embarrassed, depressed, or even

What to do about **Hearing Loss**	
Symptoms/Signs	**Action**
◆ **Ringing in the ears** (SEE BOX, PAGE 47.)	Call doctor
◆ **Heavy earwax buildup** (SEE PAGE 41.) ◆ **Trouble hearing with or without pain in the ears**	 See doctor
◆ **Sudden hearing loss**	 Seek help now

scared. It is hard to remember things that you did not hear clearly. But there are simple ways to treat hearing loss.

Signs of Hearing Loss
- steady noise or ringing in the ear, or tinnitus (SEE BOX, PAGE 47.)
- trouble hearing over the phone
- tilting the head or leaning forward to hear better
- frequent need to ask others to repeat what they said
- complaints that other people are mumbling or talking too softly
- a need to turn up TV or radio volume louder than others want
- a hard time hearing in noisy rooms

There are two main kinds of hearing loss. One is conductive hearing loss. (SEE PAGE 46.) The other is sensory neural loss. (SEE PAGE 47.) Your doctor is likely to give you an ear exam and hearing test to diagnose hearing loss. Your doctor may suggest other tests to find the cause.

Listening Devices

Many devices can help people hear better. These devices are called assistive listening devices (ALDs). You can use them alone or with hearing aids. ALDs include the following:

- Telephone amplifiers. These devices help you hear voices on the phone.
- Television listening systems. These systems amplify the sound of a TV.

- One-to-one personal communicators. These devices make it easier to communicate. They make your companion's voice louder than the other noises around you. Then you can hear the person who is talking to you.
- Alerting devices. These are devices such as a flashing light or vibrator. For instance, one device tells you when a smoke detector goes off. Another one lets you know when the doorbell rings.

How Hearing Loss Is Treated

Treatments for hearing loss include earwax removal, surgery, and hearing aids. If you need treatment, you will work with both your doctor and an audiologist.

Types of Hearing Aids

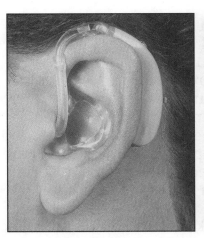

One popular kind of hearing aid is the type that fits behind the ear. That is why it is called BTE.

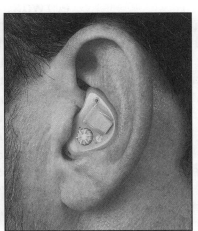

The in-the-ear hearing aid is probably the most common type. It is called an ITE for short.

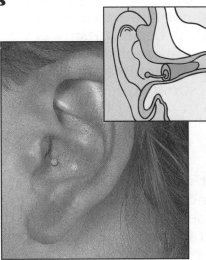

The completely in-the-ear hearing aid fits into the ear canal. (SEE INSET.) You can't see it by looking at the ear.

An audiologist may do these things:
- give you a hearing test
- counsel you about hearing problems
- teach you ways to listen better
- fit you with a hearing aid
- help you select the best hearing aid

Hearing Aids. When you choose a hearing aid, think about your lifestyle, budget, activity level, and physical condition. You may want to think about how you want the hearing aid to look. (SEE PHOTOS, PAGE 45.) A hearing aid helps by making sounds louder. It can help people who have conductive hearing loss or sensory neural hearing loss. There are different kinds of hearing aids. All hearing aids work in about the same way. They have the same basic parts:

A positive attitude about your hearing aid will help you make the best of it.

- a microphone that picks up sounds
- an amplifier that makes the signals stronger
- a receiver that turns the signals back to sound
- a battery

It will take time to get used to a hearing aid. All hearing aids need adjustment. So keep all follow-up visits with your doctor and have routine checkups. Follow the instructions for taking care of your aid. A positive attitude about your hearing aid will help you make the best of it.

Conductive Hearing Loss

"I thought I was losing my hearing. Each day it seemed that I could hear less and less. I started turning up the TV and the radio. Then I had to see the doctor for a cold and fever. When she looked in my ears, she saw that they were blocked with earwax. She cleaned them out, and now my hearing is fine."
—Bart

Conductive hearing loss comes from problems that occur in the outer or middle ear. (SEE DRAWING, PAGE 43.) These problems block sound waves. Things that can block sound waves include the following:
- packed earwax. (SEE EARWAX BUILDUP, PAGE 41.) About one-third of older people have a problem with packed earwax.
- a swollen ear canal from an infection such as swimmer's ear (SEE DRAWING, PAGE 41.)
- a punctured eardrum
- fluid behind the eardrum
- stiffness in the three middle ear bones: the hammer, the anvil, and the stirrup. This stiffness can come from repeated ear infections or a condition called otosclerosis.

When you know the cause of the blockage, conductive hearing loss can often be treated. In most cases, hearing comes back after treatment.

Sensory Neural Hearing Loss

"For years I operated a drill for the highway department. Ear protectors were required. They were annoying sometimes, but they may have saved my hearing."
—Harold

Sensory neural hearing loss comes from problems deep in the ear. These problems may affect the hair cells in the cochlea or the auditory nerve. (SEE DRAWING, PAGE 43.) There are three main causes of this type of hearing loss:

- changes in the ear from aging
- damage to the ear from loud noises
- certain medicines

Sensory neural hearing loss can run in families. It can seldom be reversed.

Hearing Loss From Changes That Occur With Aging

As you age, your inner ear may not work as well as it once did. You may not be able to hear high-pitched sounds. You might have trouble understanding speech.

Sensory neural hearing loss that comes with aging is called presbycusis. This loss happens over time. It does not cause complete deafness.

Hearing Loss From Loud Sounds

Long-term exposure to loud sounds can lead to hearing loss. Many people

---

Tinnitus (Ringing in the Ears)

Tinnitus, or a steady noise in the ear, is associated with sensory neural hearing loss. Tinnitus is often called "ringing in the ears." With tinnitus, you hear a ringing or buzzing sound in your ears. You hear this ringing when no true sound has caused it. The sound you hear may be a high-pitched whine or a low-pitched machine sound. Or you may hear a sound like blowing wind. Tinnitus is strongly linked to hearing loss and is most likely caused by the hearing loss.

Millions of people get tinnitus. Here are the most common causes:

- It can be a normal part of hearing loss that often comes with age.
- It can come from anxiety.
- In rare cases, heart disease, hyperthyroidism, or a noncancerous growth on the auditory nerve can cause it.

If you hear steady noises inside your ears, see your doctor. In most cases, tinnitus is not an emergency. It is rarely life-threatening. Some people find it helpful to listen to music when they have tinnitus. Music can cover up the sound that results from the tinnitus.

have been exposed to loud noises at work. Working around any of the following can cause hearing loss: power tools, firearms, tractors, or heavy equipment. Working in some factories can also cause damage.

If you spend a long time around loud sounds, they can damage the hair cells in the inner ear. (SEE DRAWING, PAGE 43.) This damage causes hearing loss. Noise-related hearing loss cannot be reversed. You can protect your ears in noisy places by wearing earplugs. You can buy earplugs at a drugstore.

Hearing Loss From Medication

In rare cases, certain drugs cause hearing loss. These include some antibiotics and diuretics. These drugs can damage the parts of the inner ear that turn sound waves into electrical signals. This type of hearing loss can't be reversed. High doses of aspirin and arthritis medicine can cause short-term hearing loss. This can happen if you take 6 to 12 aspirin a day. You may have ringing in your ears and even hearing loss. Hearing improves and ringing stops when you stop taking aspirin.

Chapter 4

Eye Concerns

Imagine a black and white world. Imagine how hard it would be to drive if you could not read street signs. Fortunately, vision problems like these are not that common. Most people see fairly well into their 80s. Very few people lose all their vision.

You can help keep your vision by seeing an eye specialist. You should see an eye specialist once every two years. You can choose an optometrist or an ophthalmologist.

An optometrist does not have a medical degree. Optometrists have studied at a school of optometry. They have an O.D. or a D.O.S. after their names. An optometrist can check your vision, prescribe glasses, and check your eyes for diseases. If an optometrist finds that you have an eye disease, he or she will probably refer you to an ophthalmologist.

An ophthalmologist can do everything an optometrist can and more. Ophthalmologists have more training in eye diseases. They went to medical school and are medical doctors. They prescribe medicines and perform eye surgery.

Eye doctors can find many eye problems before you notice symptoms. If you wait until you have symptoms before you see an eye doctor, your condition may be harder to treat. Sometimes not seeing an eye doctor right away can cause permanent damage to your eyes. Many vision problems can be corrected with glasses. Sometimes minor surgery may be needed.

In this chapter, you'll learn what to do about some common eye problems. You will learn what kind of problems you can treat yourself and when you should see a doctor. The chapter is divided into two main types of problems: eye irritations and infections, and vision problems.

Eye Irritations and Infections

Many things can irritate your eyes. We all know what it feels like when something gets stuck on the eye, even a tiny eyelash. A larger object or a chemical can cause serious damage.

As you get older, your eyes may get more irritated. You may have more eye infections. This is because the mucous membranes in your eyes change. You produce fewer tears. Tears can help wash objects and bacteria out of the eyes.

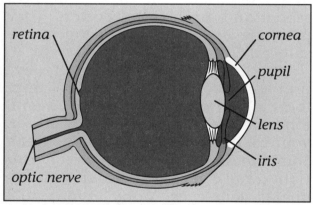

Your eye works like a complex camera. The cornea helps it focus. Light passes through the cornea and through the pupil. The pupil opens and closes to adjust to light. The lens changes shape to help the eye focus. The focused light strikes the retina. The retina changes the light into nerve impulses. These impulses travel through the optic nerve to the brain. The brain helps you identify pictures, shapes, and symbols.

Burning, Dry, and Irritated Eyes

"When I get allergies, my eyes get red and itchy. I rub them and that irritates them even more. I found that if I use eyedrops, it helps soothe my eyes."
—Harold

Smoke and pollen are just two things that can make your eyes burn. Burning and itching usually stop when you get away from the cause. Some other causes of burning eyes are not so easy to avoid.

A virus can cause your eyes to itch, burn, water, or redden. Even colds and flus can cause these symptoms. Some diseases, such as rheumatoid arthritis, can make your eyes dry. If your eyes are dry, they may feel irritated.

An infection can make your eyelids itch and burn. If you have discharge from the eye and it is red, you may have an infection. (SEE PINKEYE, PAGE 54.)

You can easily burn your eyes from sunlight reflected off water, sand, or snow. Tanning lamps and welding arcs also give off ultraviolet (UV) rays. These rays can damage the eye's cornea or the retina. (SEE DRAWING AT LEFT.) Burned eyes swell, and so does the skin around the eyes. Sometimes you won't feel pain until hours after you burn your eyes. Taking preventive steps can keep you from burning your eyes.

What to do about
Burning Eyes

Symptoms/Signs	Action
◆ **Irritated, burning, dry, and itchy eyes**	 Use self-care
◆ **Irritation that does not respond to self-care** ◆ **Pain and swelling from sunburned eyes that last longer than 24 hours**	Call doctor
◆ **Loss of vision** (SEE PAGE 52.) ◆ **Whitish or cloudy look to colored parts of eyes** ◆ **Discharge from the eye**	 See doctor

How to Prevent Burning, Dryness, and Irritation

- Wear glasses or sunglasses to shield your eyes against dust and irritations.
- Always wear sunglasses with UV protection.
- Wear goggles to protect your eyes from chlorine when you swim in a pool.
- If your eyes are irritated by certain cosmetics, do not use them.

Self-Care: Burning, Dry, and Irritated Eyes

- If your eyes are irritated and watering, try to find the cause. If you find it, then avoid it. Smoke or chemical fumes can bother your eyes. So can cosmetics and pollen.
- Put a cool, damp cloth, or a compress, on sunburned eyes. Stay out of the sun until the swelling is gone.
- If your eyes are dry, use lubricating eyedrops or artificial tears. You can buy these over the counter at most drugstores. One brand is Hypo Tears.

To put lubricating drops into your eye, pull down the lower lid and look up. You may want to lie down to put in the eyedrops.

Foreign Object or Chemical in the Eye

"Don't rub your eye when something is in it. Rubbing could damage the clear tissue that covers your eye. This is called the cornea."
—Ophthalmologist

Pain in your eye can signal that you need treatment. Get treatment soon to prevent lasting damage to the eye.

Always wear protective glasses or goggles when you work with harsh chemicals. Chemical products such as paint thinner, lye, toilet cleaner, drain cleaner, or gasoline can burn your eyes. Chemical burns are painful and need emergency medical care. Flush the eye with water and call an ambulance.

If you feel something in your eye, don't rub it. Rubbing can damage the cornea. The cornea is the clear tissue that covers the eye. It is important to know when you need emergency care. Seek medical attention right away if:

- You have a piece of glass or metal anywhere on your eye.
- You have an object that is stuck anywhere on your eye.
- You have a floating object anywhere in your eye and cannot remove it.

If any of these things are in your eye, protect your eye with a patch. Be careful not to put any pressure on the eyeball. The patch should be loose. See a doctor right away.

What to do about Foreign Objects in the Eye

Symptoms/Signs	Action
◆ **Object is on the white part of the eye.**	 Use self-care
◆ **Self-care methods don't remove the object.** ◆ **Pain continues after the object has been removed.**	Call doctor
◆ **Eye becomes red, warm, swollen, more painful, and discharges a yellow-green pus.** ◆ **Object is on the colored part of the eye.** ◆ **Eye is bleeding.**	 See doctor
◆ **Embedded object is a piece of metal or glass.** ◆ **Vision is impaired.**	 Seek help now
◆ **Eye was burned with a chemical.** (START FLUSHING EYES WITH WATER RIGHT AWAY.) ◆ **Object is embedded in the eyeball.** ◆ **Object is stuck to the eye.**	Call ambulance

Self-Care: Foreign Object or Chemical in the Eye

You can safely remove most small objects from the white part of the eye. If an object is in your eye, wash your hands first. Then you should take the following steps:

- Wash your eye with water from a clean eyedropper, squeeze bottle, or eyecup. Water may wash the object or chemical away.
- Roll the corner of a clean handkerchief, napkin, or tissue to a point. Dampen the point with a little water. Then use the point to gently push the object out of your eye. You may need someone to help you. (SEE DRAWING BELOW.)

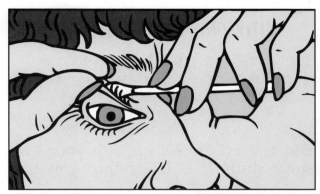

Use a cotton swab to help you hold up your upper eyelid. Then you can look for an object under the upper lid.

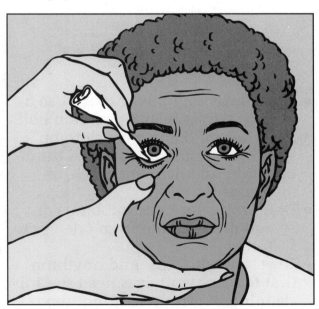

Another person can use the point of a dampened and rolled handkerchief or tissue to push a small object from your eye.

- Never use a toothpick, matchstick, tweezers, or other hard, sharp object to remove something from your eye.
- To remove an object stuck on the surface under your upper eyelid, use a moistened cotton swab. Or use the corner of a clean cloth, handkerchief, or tissue. Take care not to brush the cornea. The cornea is the clear layer over the colored part of the eye.
- If you are not sure whether an object is stuck in your upper or lower lid, follow the steps below. You can look in the mirror or have someone help you look at your eyes.

For the lower lid: Look up and pull your lower lid down. Look for an object under your lower lid.

For the upper lid: Look down and pull the upper lid up. Do this by pulling gently on your eyelashes. A cotton swab can help you hold the upper lid. Look for an object under your upper lid. (SEE DRAWING ABOVE.)

Pinkeye (Conjunctivitis)

"Washing your hands often is one of the best ways to keep from getting or spreading pinkeye."
—General practice doctor

Did you ever wake up with your eyes stuck shut? It is likely that you had conjunctivitis. This is also known as pinkeye. Pinkeye is an infection of the eyelid's lining. This infection can produce a sticky pus. An eye with pinkeye is red and swollen and feels irritated. It may feel as if you have sand in your eyes. You may have discharge from your eye or nose.

Pinkeye can be caused by a virus or bacteria. You can get pinkeye in three ways. You can get pinkeye from someone who has it. You can get it if the person touches his or her eye then touches you or something you touch later. You can also get it from an upper respiratory infection that can get in your eyes. Or you can get it from allergies, pollution, or other irritants. This is called allergic pinkeye. It does not spread from person to person.

What to do about Conjunctivitis	
Symptoms/Signs	**Action**
◆ **Infection that is mild and lasts less than two days**	 Use self-care
◆ **Sensitivity to light** ◆ **Pinkeye with cold sores on lip and/or on eyes**	Call doctor
◆ **Pus from eye that is thick and yellow or greenish** ◆ **Pinkeye after recently injuring your eye or having a foreign object in your eye** ◆ **Symptoms that get worse after two days** ◆ **Blurred vision** ◆ **Intense pain in the eye (not just irritation)** ◆ **One pupil that is bigger than the other one**	See doctor

Self-Care: Pinkeye

- Wipe away any pus or crust. Use a warm, wet washcloth or cotton ball.
- Put a warm, damp washcloth on your eyes. Doing this soothes the irritation and itching and clears discharge.
- Don't rub your eyes. Rubbing can spread the infection from one eye to the other.
- Towels, washcloths, and anything that touches your eyes need special cleaning. Wash these things separately in hot water.
- Wash your hands often when you care for someone who has pinkeye or are near someone who has it.

Sties

"I have gotten sties for years. Now when I get one, I'm pretty sure one of two things caused it. Either I went to bed without washing off my makeup, or it's time to buy new mascara."

—Maria

What to do about Sties

Symptoms/Signs	Action
◆ Red, swollen, itchy lump on eyelid	Use self-care
◆ Painless lump on eyelid	Call doctor
◆ Sty that hurts and lasts for a week or more ◆ Sty that will not go away	See doctor

A sty is a red, tender bump on your eyelid. It can cause the lid to swell and itch. Sties form when an oil gland at the base of an eyelash gets clogged. Most sties are smaller than a pebble. But they can feel huge because of the pain and swelling. After a few days, the sty usually comes to a head, like a pimple. It will drain on its own. A sty may last for weeks without coming to a head. Your doctor may open and drain the sty.

To prevent sties, wash your face daily. This can keep oil glands from clogging and forming sties.

Some growths on the eyelid are not red and painful. These are usually cysts, called chalazion. Most eyelid cysts are harmless and do not need removal. Cysts often go away in a month or two without treatment. But have your doctor check any unusual lump or growth.

Self-Care: Sties

- Place a clean washcloth in hot water. Do not use scalding water. Wring out the cloth and put it on your eye. Keep the cloth on your eye for 5 to 10 minutes. Do this three or four times each day. It helps a sty come to a head and drain.
- If pus comes out of a sty, carefully clean the whole area with warm water. You may see pus when using a warm washcloth.

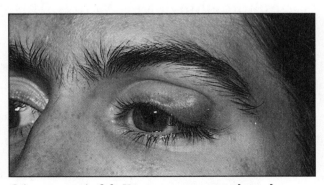

Sties are painful. You may prevent them by washing your face every day.

Vision Problems

Many people think that vision loss is a normal part of aging. This is not true. Most people see fairly well, even in their 80s. Very few people lose all their vision. Many types of vision loss can be corrected with the use of glasses or surgery.

How to Prevent Vision Problems

- If you're older than 50, have an eye exam at least every two years. Age makes you more likely to get conditions such as glaucoma (SEE PAGE 58), cataracts, and macular degeneration (SEE PAGE 59). Because it is better to catch these conditions early, your doctor or eye specialist may ask you to have eye exams more often. Prompt treatment can prevent problems from getting worse and may even prevent blindness.
- If you have diabetes or high blood pressure, talk with your doctor about regular eye exams. These conditions can cause eye problems.
- Wear sunglasses that protect your eyes from ultraviolet (UV) rays. This is very important when you are in bright sunlight or near water, sand, or snow. Too many UV rays may cause cataracts or may sunburn the eye.
- Make sure you have bright lights at home. Place lights where you read and climb stairs. Keep your kitchen well lit. Good lighting helps you to see better and can prevent accidents.

What to do about **Vision Problems**	
Symptoms/Signs	**Action**
◆ **Decreased vision that began while taking medicine** ◆ **A change in the type or number of spots or flashes you see** ◆ **Decreased or blurred vision** ◆ **Constant itching and burning, or redness** ◆ **Increased or heavy discharge from tear ducts** ◆ **Pain or swelling in an eye or eyelid**	 Call doctor
◆ **Tunnel vision or loss of side vision**	 See doctor
◆ **Sudden loss or blurring of vision** ◆ **Loss of vision from injury to the head or eyes** ◆ **Flashing lights or black spots**	Seek help now

Cataracts

"I didn't realize how much my vision had changed until I had my lens replaced. My cataracts had kept me from seeing birds in the yard and from reading my favorite magazines."
—Stella

The lens in your eye is normally clear. A cataract makes your lens "fog up." (SEE PHOTOS BELOW.) As a result, your vision becomes cloudy or blurry. You may have a cataract if:

- Your eyes are sensitive to light when you drive.
- You often need stronger glasses.
- You need brighter lamps when you read.

Despite what many people may think, a cataract may not cause a visible "film," or whiteness, on the eye. This is especially true in the early stages of a cataract. Cataracts do not cause pain.

Most cataracts come from aging. People can get cataracts as early as age 40. You can also get cataracts from eye injuries, certain drugs like prednisone, and diseases such as diabetes. Too much direct sun on the eyes can also cause cataracts. Smoking has also been linked to cataracts.

The treatment for a cataract depends on how bad it is. A cataract may cover just a small part of the lens. You may be able to see well enough for normal activities. In that case, there may be no need to remove the cataract. Your doctor may prescribe special eyeglasses or contact lenses. Or you may need reading glasses that have magnifying lenses, or handheld magnifying glasses. Filters, visors, and sunglasses cut down on glare and can help you see better.

How Cataracts Affect Vision

People who have cataracts may see things with a "ghost," or double image.

People who have cataracts often see images as blurry, like this photo.

People with cataracts often see a cloud over everything. Things look "fogged up."

If the cataract starts to bother you, you may need to think about surgery. Cataract surgery is the only effective way to take out the cloudy part of the lens. This surgery is also called lens replacement. A surgeon removes the cataract and puts a plastic lens in its place. This can often be done in day-surgery, without admission to a hospital. More than 90 percent of cataract surgery patients regain useful vision.

Diabetic Retinopathy

"When I found out I had diabetes, my biggest fear was that I would go blind. My doctor said as long as I follow my treatment plan and have my eyes checked every year, I should be able to keep my sight."
—James

Diabetic retinopathy is an eye problem related to diabetes. (SEE WHEN YOU HAVE DIABETES, PAGE 249.) It happens when small blood vessels do not feed the retina properly. These blood vessels may leak blood and impair vision. As the condition gets worse, new vessels can grow and release blood in the eye's center, causing a more serious loss of vision. These blood vessels may break and cause the retina to swell. Or the blood vessels may block the retina.

If retinopathy is not treated, it can lead to severe vision loss or blindness. It can start without symptoms. So, get eye checkups every year. If found early, diabetic retinopathy can be treated with a laser.

Glaucoma

"I don't wear glasses, but I still have my eyes checked every two years because glaucoma runs in my family."
—Edward

Glaucoma is caused by pressure from built-up fluid in the eye. This pressure harms the optic nerve. (SEE DRAWING, PAGE 50.) Glaucoma does not cause pain. It does cause blind spots that you may not notice at first. You may also see halos around lights.

Finding glaucoma early is important. The damage it causes often cannot be reversed. If glaucoma is not found and treated early, it can cause blindness.

You may be able to prevent nerve damage or blindness. The best way is

People with glaucoma may have a blind spot in their side vision, or they may have only "central" vision.

to be checked for glaucoma every two years. Glaucoma runs in families. African-Americans have a greater chance of getting it. If someone in your family has had glaucoma, tell your doctor.

If you develop glaucoma, your doctor may treat it with eyedrops or pills. Medicine can often keep any damage from getting worse. Your doctor may suggest laser treatment or surgery.

If you have glaucoma, tell every doctor you see. Many drugs can make it worse. These include:

- allergy pills
- antihistamines
- tranquilizers
- cortisone
- some stomach medicines

Macular Degeneration

"I was having trouble reading, and I didn't know why. The letters looked blurred. But I could see fine when I did other things. I finally went to an eye doctor. He told me that this was a normal process of aging. He told me to get large-print books and said I should get a bright reading lamp. It is much easier to read now."

—Juan

Macular degeneration is the main cause of permanent vision loss in older people. With this condition, the macula becomes damaged. The macula is the center part of the retina. The macula is where vision is the most sharp.

Macular degeneration causes gradual loss of vision.

You may see a blurred or dark area in the center of your vision. But you may still be able to see clearly around this area. (SEE PHOTO BELOW.) Some people have problems in only one eye at first. The other eye may see well for years. This can make it harder for you to know that there is a problem. If both eyes are affected, you could have trouble reading close-up and seeing things.

There is no cure for this condition. Have an eye exam at least every two years. The exam can help your eye doctor find this condition early, before you have symptoms. If you have macular degeneration, your eye doctor can help prevent more eye damage. Or your doctor can help you adjust to the

People with macular degeneration may have a blind spot in the center of their vision. The surrounding area is clear.

condition. Magnifying devices, eyeglasses, closed-circuit TV, and special lamps may help. Your doctor may also suggest large-print books and newspapers.

Refractive Problems

"I've always thought bifocals were for old people. So of course I didn't want them. But now that I have them, I don't know why I waited so long. I felt much older not being able to read than I do wearing bifocals."

—Joe

The eye has a complex and exact way of letting you see. The lens of the eye bends when light hits it. Then rays of light come to a sharp focus on the retina. If the shape of the eye is not perfect, the lens cannot bend properly to have the ray hit the right spot. Then things look blurry.

Changes in the shape of your eyes cause refractive problems. Refractive is a word that describes how the lens bends to focus light. These problems are common. You may know them by their common names: nearsightedness and farsightedness. These problems can often be corrected with eyeglasses or contact lenses.

How to Use the Yanuzzi Card

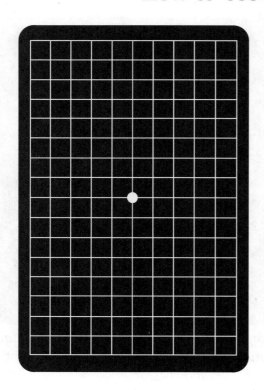

The Yanuzzi card shows how much your vision has been affected by macular degeneration. You can ask your eye doctor for one and test your vision at home.

Here's how to use the chart:
1. Sit in a well-lit area.
2. Hold the chart at eye level, about 10 to 14 inches from your eyes.
3. If you wear glasses, keep them on, but cover one eye completely.
4. With your uncovered eye, stare at the center dot.
5. Notice what happens to the lines surrounding the dot.
6. Make an appointment with your eye doctor if you see blurry, distorted, or curvy lines or holes or spots on the card.

Farsightedness (Hyperopia). This problem makes objects that are close to you look fuzzy. You may have a hard time reading. You may need to hold the book away from your eyes. This problem occurs when the eyeball is shorter than normal. (SEE DRAWING BELOW.) That means the lens of your eye cannot bend correctly so that light falls on the retina. Eyeglasses can correct this.

Nearsightedness (Myopia). When you are nearsighted, you have a hard time seeing objects that are far away. You may have a hard time reading road signs or squint when you read a menu that is posted on a wall. This problem occurs when the eyeball is longer than normal. (SEE DRAWING BELOW.)

When the eyeball is longer than normal, the lens cannot bend correctly for light to hit the retina. Being nearsighted runs in families. It can often be corrected with eyeglasses or contact lenses. Radial keratotomy is a new surgery to correct this problem. Excimer laser surgery can also correct this problem. Ask your doctor if these treatments might help you.

Presbyopia. This problem is also called "aging eyes." This is not caused by the shape of your eye. It is caused by a hardening of your lens.

As you age, your eye lenses get hard and the lens muscles get weak. That makes it harder for the lens to bend light. When you have this problem, it

How the Shape of Your Eye Affects Your Vision

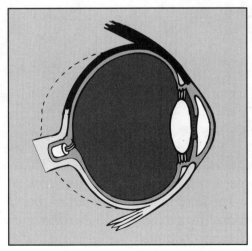

When you are farsighted, you have problems seeing objects up close. Your eyeball is shorter than normal. The dotted lines show the normal shape of an eye.

When you are nearsighted, you have problems seeing objects that are far away. Your eyeball is longer than normal. The dotted lines show the normal shape of an eye.

is hard to focus on nearby objects. It is harder to read small print. You may have to hold a book at arm's length to read it. No known treatment can prevent presbyopia. But you can correct most cases with special eyeglasses for reading, bifocals, or contact lenses.

Your eyes are likely to age the most between the ages of 50 and 65. You may need new glasses more than once during these years. Refractive problems rarely change vision after age 65.

Specks and Floaters

"Specks look like bits of dust across the eye. They may bother you less if you look from side to side or up and down."
—General practice doctor

Specks or "bugs" that move in your field of vision are called floaters. (SEE PHOTO AT RIGHT.) You may see floaters when you look at a plain background. For instance, you may see floaters against a clear sky or a white wall. Nearsighted people often have floaters. Floaters are also common after cataract surgery.

Floaters are small clumps of gel in the fluid inside your eye. Between the lens and the retina, there is a jellylike substance. This gel is called vitreous humor. The gel starts turning to liquid as you age. When that happens, you see floaters.

For the most part, floaters are just a part of aging. Floaters are harmless. You may notice them less over time. If floaters annoy you, try moving your eyes from side to side or up and down.

See your doctor right away if you have either of the following:
- floaters that occur with flashes of light when your eyes are closed
- floaters with loss of vision to the sides (peripheral vision)

People with specks or floaters see dark, wavy lines. The lines move in and out of their field of vision. You should see an eye doctor if you develop new floaters.

Chapter 5

Foot Concerns

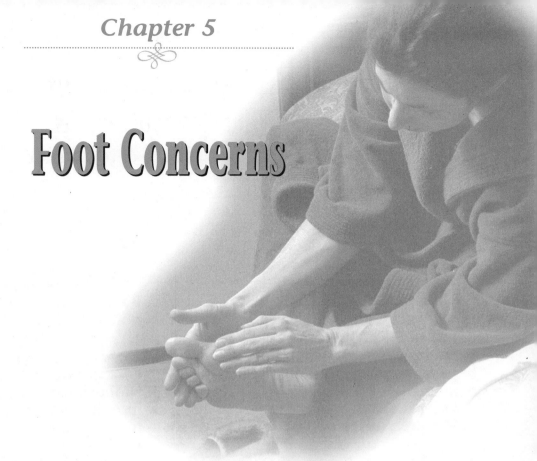

Your shoes may no longer fit. The style and size that used to feel great may hurt now. Did you ever wonder why? It's often because your feet change over the years. They have supported your body's weight every day of your life. As you age, muscles and tendons in your feet change. As a result, the bones in your feet spread apart. You may find that you wear a new shoe size. Or you may need a shoe style that has more room for your toes.

The shape of your feet is not the only thing that changes. As you age, the padding on the heels and balls of your feet becomes thinner. This padding works like a shock absorber. It shields your feet from injury. When there is less padding, your feet are less protected from things that can cause them pain.

The skin on your feet changes too. Aging skin is more likely to get infected by bacteria or fungus. Even toenails get harder to take care of as you age. They can develop problems that cause pain and infections.

You can prevent most foot problems. Treat foot problems right away so they don't get worse. A special branch of medicine is devoted to treating feet. It is called podiatry, or the study of the foot. A podiatrist is a doctor who treats foot problems. This chapter discusses foot pain, problems with the skin on your feet, and toenail concerns.

Diabetes and Your Feet

"I have diabetes. I have to make sure I don't get a cut or sore on my feet. If I did, it could get seriously infected. So I take extra care with my feet. My niece cuts my toenails for me. And I pamper myself with lotion after each bath."

—Maud

Diabetes can damage blood vessels in your feet. Your blood vessels carry oxygen. If the blood vessels in your feet are damaged, your feet don't get enough oxygen. Then your feet may be more prone to injury or infection.

Why Foot Care Is Important When You Have Diabetes

Diabetes can also cause nerve damage in the feet. This damage is called neuropathy. Nerve damage in your foot can prevent you from feeling pain. Then you might not realize if you have a cut, sore, or blister on your foot. If an injury is not treated, it could get infected. You may not notice the infection. Without treatment, an infection can cause a lot of damage.

If you have diabetes, work with your doctor to control it. (SEE PAGE 249.) That way you may be able to prevent damage to your nerves and blood vessels. Pay close attention to your feet every day. See the prevention and self-care sections in this chapter. Both of these sections have special notes about diabetes.

How to Improve Circulation in Your Feet

Diabetes can cause poor circulation in your feet. To improve the circulation in your feet, try these tips:

- When you are sitting down, put your feet up.
- When you have to sit for a long time, stand up and stretch every half hour or so. This will keep the blood moving in your feet and legs.
- Don't cross your legs when you sit. This can cut off the flow of blood to your feet.
- Don't smoke. Smoking makes problems with circulation worse. For help quitting, see page 300.
- Be sure to stay active. Walking and other activities help blood circulate through your body and move to your feet. (SEE STAYING ACTIVE, PAGE 291.)

Foot Pain

You don't have to put up with sore feet. In fact, you shouldn't. Sore feet are not a price you pay for getting older. Foot pain is a sign of problems that need care. When you take care of your feet, you protect your health.

If you don't take care of your feet, they can become the source of major health problems. For instance, foot pain can make walking difficult. This may keep you from getting the exercise you need. Lack of exercise, in turn, will affect your overall health. And when foot pain keeps you from walking, you may become isolated and dependent. Here's another way foot pain can affect more than your feet. Suppose foot pain makes you stand differently. Just changing your stance can cause pain

What to do about Foot Pain

Symptoms/Signs	Action	Symptoms/Signs	Action
◆ Pain from overuse or an injury, but feet can still support body weight	Use self-care	◆ Inability to move foot or support body weight after a blow to the foot or a fall ◆ Swelling at the top of the foot that gets worse with pressure	Call doctor
◆ Pain in heel or arch, especially when you wake ◆ Tender points on bottom of foot between heel and ball ◆ Bunions (SEE PAGE 67.) ◆ Hammertoe (SEE PAGE 68.) ◆ Pain, burning, tingling, or numbness in the toes, between the toes, and at the ball of the foot	Call doctor	◆ Pain from plantar fasciitis or heel spurs that does not respond to self-care in three to six weeks (SEE PAGE 69.) ◆ Pain on top or bottom of foot, with swelling	See doctor

as far up as your back. Then you may have pain in your foot and pain in your back.

How to Prevent Foot Pain

Proper shoes help prevent foot pain. Shoes should support your arch. They should also cushion the heel, ball, and outside area of your foot. To make sure that your shoes don't make foot pain worse, follow these tips:

- Have your feet measured when you buy shoes. Your feet can change size.
- Don't wear shoes that pinch your feet or toes. Don't wear shoes that are too big. Your feet should not slide around in them. Loose shoes can rub and cause blisters and other problems.
- Look for shoes that have a low heel. Heels between $1/2$ and $1^1/2$ inches are the best height. Higher heels can strain the feet and legs.
- If your shoes need extra support or cushioning, buy arch supports or cushioning for soles.
- Break in new shoes. For the first few days, wear new shoes for one to two hours. Then increase the time you wear them by an hour each day. You should always check your feet after wearing new shoes. Shoes should not cause blisters or irritate your feet. If you have diabetes, it is important to break in your shoes. This will help prevent foot problems that could become serious.
- Ask your doctor about buying sneakers or running shoes instead of orthopedic shoes. Special orthopedic shoes can be expensive.
- Do not walk around barefoot. Wear shoes around the house and yard to prevent injury. Even at the beach, wear sandals, thongs, or "beach socks." Broken glass, shells, hot sand, and other objects can injure your feet.
- Before you put on your shoes, check inside for any objects. This is important if you have lost the feeling in your feet.

Self-Care: Foot Pain

- Make sure you don't have any foot injuries.
- Check your shoes to make sure they fit properly. Shoes that fit poorly are a major cause of foot pain. Are your shoes the right size? Are they too loose or too tight?
- Take a pain reliever, such as aspirin, ibuprofen (Advil), or naproxen sodium (Aleve). These help pain and reduce swelling when your foot is inflamed.

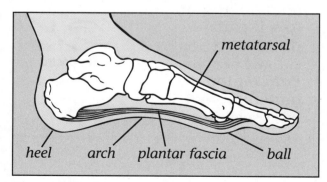

Parts of the foot

Bunions

"Some people think a bunion is just an extra bone on their foot. It isn't. A bunion means something is wrong with the way the foot is working."
—Podiatrist

A bunion is an enlargement of the joint on the side of your big toe. A bunion is not a growth of bone, as some people believe. Bunions are a sign that your foot may not be working the way it should.

Flat feet often cause bunions. Flat feet can lead to poor muscle alignment. That, in turn, can cause your big toe to slant toward your other toes. Then the joint where the big toe connects to the foot will poke out. A bump may appear in this spot. A bunion can become inflamed and sore. It can be irritated when it rubs against the inside of your shoe.

A "tailor's bunion" causes similar problems and can form on the outside of the foot by the small toe.

If self-care does not relieve the pain from a bunion, see your doctor. He or she may suggest a special insole for your shoe. The insole will take pressure off your big toe. Your doctor might also suggest steroid injections or surgery.

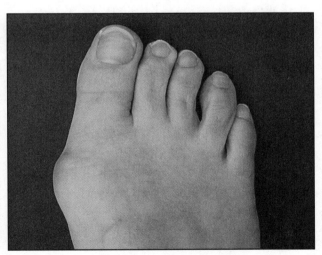

A bunion is usually on the inner side of the foot near the big toe. Bunions can also form on the outside of the foot near the little toe.

Self-Care: Bunions

- Choose a shoe with a larger toe box. The toe box is the part of a shoe that surrounds the toes. Look for a shoe that has a squared or rounded toe. These shoes give your toes more room so the bunion will not rub.
- Place padding around the bunion. Padding will ease pressure and rubbing from shoes. Moleskin and bunion pads can be found at most drugstores.
- Cut a hole in an old pair of shoes to wear around the house. Cut the hole where the bunion would rub against the shoe.
- Try using an arch support. An arch support can keep bones from rubbing together. It can prevent the metatarsal (SEE DRAWING, PAGE 66) and the big toe from pressing together. This jamming can cause a bunion.
- See your doctor if pain keeps you from walking or does not go away with self-care.

Hammertoe

"I had a painful corn where my hammertoe pressed against my shoes. It helped when I wore a protective felt pad on my foot."
—John

With a hammertoe, one of your toes buckles. This buckling causes the middle joint of the toe to poke above the other toes. You might think your toe looks like a claw. A hammertoe may also cause your toe to bend sideways at the middle joint. This bending will turn the toe in toward the toe next to it.

Tight shoes can rub and put pressure on the raised portion of your toe. This pressure can cause a corn. (SEE PAGE 76.) Hammertoes may cause no problems at all. Or they can cause pain, especially if you wear shoes that are too tight or shoes that fit poorly. If self-care does not relieve pain, your doctor might suggest surgery. A surgeon can straighten the toe or remove the bony part that sticks out.

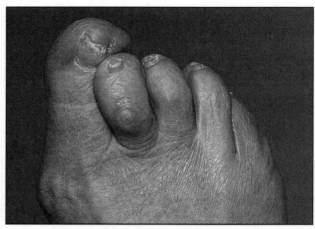

A hammertoe can cause your toe to bend sideways. Or like the second toe in this picture, a toe may buckle. This picture also shows a corn (SEE PAGE 76) on the hammertoe and fungus in the nail (SEE PAGE 79).

Heel and Arch Concerns

"I had never heard of putting arch supports in slippers until my doctor suggested it. My feet hurt so bad in the morning that I thought I would try it. Now I put my slippers on as soon as I get up."
—Joanne

Self-Care: Hammertoe

- Wear shoes with toe boxes that don't put pressure on the hammertoe. The toe box is the part of a shoe that surrounds the toes.
- Treat corns by soaking feet, then rubbing with a nail file or pumice stone. (SEE SELF-CARE: CALLUSES AND CORNS, PAGE 76.)

Some people have flat feet or high arches and don't have any problems. For others, flat feet or high arches cause pain in the feet, knees, and even hips. When your foot's arch is too high or too low, your leg and parts of your feet have to work harder. This can cause added stress and put extra weight on your feet. It can affect the way you walk. Your feet may feel tired and painful. They can become inflamed.

Putting arch supports in your shoes can help relieve many problems caused by weak arches. These arch supports are called orthotics. Some exercises can stretch and strengthen your lower leg and the arch in your foot. The exercises can also help make your feet feel better. (SEE DRAWING, PAGE 70.)

Two other problems often cause heel and arch pain. They are plantar fasciitis and heel spurs.

Plantar Fasciitis. This condition causes most heel and arch pain. The plantar fascia is a strong band of tissue on the bottom of your foot. It runs from the heel to the base of your toes. (SEE DRAWING AT RIGHT.) The plantar fascia helps support your arch. It also works like a shock absorber to protect your feet. Problems occur when this band is overstretched. It may become strained and inflamed where it connects to your heel bone.

If you have plantar fasciitis, you may notice a dull ache in the arch. Or you might feel pain in your heel. The pain will be worst when you have not put pressure on your foot for a while. It may hurt most after you wake up or after you sit for a long time. It might hurt to walk right away. Once the plantar fascia is warmed up, the pain may lessen. Any of the following can cause plantar fasciitis:
- increasing foot activity
- standing and walking for a long time on a hard surface, such as concrete
- gaining 10 pounds or more

- switching from high heels or cowboy boots to flat shoes or athletic shoes
- wearing shoes that don't have good arch support

Heel Spurs. Plantar fasciitis can also cause heel spurs. A heel spur is a bone growth on the heel where it meets the plantar fascia. The plantar fascia is a strong band of tissue on the bottom of your foot. When the plantar fascia is pulled and stretched, it pulls the heel bone's lining away from the main bone. This causes a bony growth, or spur, to form.

Heel spur pain occurs when the plantar fascia tissue pulls on the bone. The spur does not always have to be removed. Self-care and rest may relieve pain. If symptoms don't go away, or if pain is bad, see your doctor. Your doctor may have you take steroids to ease the pain. Surgery is needed only in serious cases.

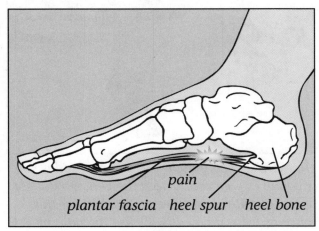

pain

plantar fascia   *heel spur*   *heel bone*

A heel spur is a bone growth on the heel where the bone meets the plantar fascia. You may feel more pain along the arch than at the heel.

Self-Care: Plantar Fasciitis and Heel Spurs

- Rest your feet. Avoid high-impact activities for three to six weeks. These include running and basketball. Walk or swim instead.
- Put ice on your heel two or three times a day. Ice reduces swelling and eases pain.
- Support your arches. This protects them from stretching and tearing. Use arch supports, even in your slippers. Put them on when you first get out of bed.

To exercise a sore arch, use a can of soda. Roll the ball of your foot across the can. Do this for a few minutes or for five or six rolls. Do this once or twice a day. It will ease the pain of plantar fasciitis and heel spurs.

Morton's Neuroma

"I felt as if I was walking on a lump. It turned out I had Morton's neuroma."
—George

The long bones in your feet are called metatarsal bones. (SEE DRAWING, PAGE 71.) They have nerves that run between them. When one of those nerves is squeezed between the bones, it can become enlarged. Doctors call this condition Morton's neuroma.

Morton's neuroma can come from wearing narrow, tight shoes. Stress from repeated motions such as climbing ladders, kneeling, and running can also cause it. Morton's neuroma usually occurs between the bones that lead to the third and fourth toes. Or you may have it between the bones that go to the second and third toes.

If you have Morton's neuroma, the area will feel tender. You may feel as if you are walking on a lump. You will notice this feeling most when you go barefoot.

Your pain may spread to the toes or toward the heel. When you apply pressure, the pain will get worse. If the pain is constant, you may notice numbness, burning, and tingling in your toes. You may also notice these feelings between your toes or at the ball of your foot.

Self-care often helps Morton's neuroma. If not, your doctor may suggest a cortisone shot or surgery.

Self-Care: Morton's Neuroma

- Avoid any activity that causes pain. Avoid high-impact activities for three to six weeks. These include running and dance aerobics. Don't do any activity that seemed to cause the pain you first felt. Wait until your discomfort is gone.
- Try wearing shoes that have a wider toe box. (The toe box is the part of your shoe that surrounds the toes.) This will help to ease pressure on the nerve.

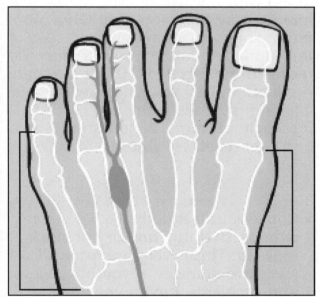

Morton's neuroma occurs when the nerves that run between the metatarsal bones are squeezed or enlarged. The pain from this condition is most often felt between the third and fourth toes. The brackets show the metatarsal bones of the big and little toes.

Stress Fractures

"My foot really hurt. It didn't occur to me that it could be broken. But when the pain got really bad, I called my doctor. He said I had a stress fracture, and I needed to give my foot time to heal."
—Julia

Stress fractures to the foot occur most often in the metatarsal that connects to the second toe. (SEE DRAWING AT LEFT.) When your feet pound against a hard surface over and over, it can cause a stress fracture. Running can cause stress fractures. So can high-impact aerobics. Stress fractures can occur if you jump and land wrong.

Stress fractures are common a few weeks after starting a new physical activity. At first, pain may be mild enough to ignore. But after a while, this pain becomes intense. Both the top and bottom of your foot may be tender.

If you are a woman who has gone through menopause, you are at greater risk for stress fractures. The reason for this high risk is osteoporosis, which makes bones more brittle. (SEE WHEN YOU HAVE OSTEOPOROSIS, PAGE 255.) If you have osteoporosis, your bones can break more easily. Osteoporosis is more common in women than in men. Women or men who have had long-term steroid therapy are also at greater risk for stress fractures.

Time is the main treatment for stress fractures. It usually takes at least one month for the bone to heal. You don't usually need a cast. Your doctor may have you wear a special shoe with a wooden sole. The shoe will allow the fracture to heal.

A stress fracture in the bone that connects to the little toe can be serious. That bone heals slowly. With this kind of fracture, you may need a cast. You may need to use crutches for six weeks, or even several months. Your doctor may say that you need surgery.

Self-Care: Stress Fractures

- Avoid high-impact activities, such as running. Switch to low-impact or nonimpact activities. Swimming is an example of a nonimpact activity. The exercise you do should be weight-bearing exercise. That means exercise in which the legs carry the body's weight. Weight-bearing exercises make bones stronger and help prevent bone loss. Walking is an example of a low-impact, weight-bearing exercise.
- Go back to regular activities slowly. Wait until the fracture heals and pain is gone.
- Take a pain reliever, such as aspirin. See your doctor if pain doesn't go away after a week or two of this treatment. Always call your doctor if pain gets worse.

Skin Problems of the Feet

Calluses, corns, and infections from fungus and bacteria can cause a lot of pain. So can plantar warts and ulcers. Don't ignore these problems.

Most drugstores sell over-the-counter remedies for corns, calluses, and plantar warts. The main ingredient in these products is salicylic acid. This acid can dissolve healthy skin along with unhealthy skin. When you lose healthy skin, you may have more pain. You also increase your risk of infection. So these products may do more harm than good. Don't use these products unless you check with your doctor first. Follow the self-care steps for each of these conditions. If you don't get relief, see your doctor.

How to Prevent Skin Problems of the Feet
- Check your feet daily. Look for sores, redness, swelling, and dry or cracking skin. This is very important if you have diabetes. If you have vision problems, have someone else check your feet. Also ask for help if you can't move your feet enough to see both top and bottom.
- Wash your feet daily with warm, soapy water. Do not use hot water. Dry your feet well. Be sure to dry the skin between your toes.

- Use a moisturizing lotion. Don't put lotion between your toes. Keep this area dry to help prevent fungal infections. Fungus lives only in wet, dark places.
- Wear shoes with leather uppers. Leather lets air circulate around your feet. When air circulates, you can avoid skin problems. Leather also stretches to match the shape of your feet. When weather permits, sandals are a good choice of footwear.

- Don't wear tight socks or hosiery. Wear socks made of natural fabrics, such as cotton or wool. These fabrics allow air to move around your feet.
- Keep your feet dry. Take off wet shoes and socks as soon as you can.
- Don't expose your feet to the cold. If you go out in cold weather, wear warm boots or shoes.
- Take off boots when you go inside. Let your feet air out. Bacteria and fungus breed in warm, damp places.

What to do about Skin Problems of the Feet

Symptoms/Signs	Action	Symptoms/Signs	Action
◆ **Corn or callus that does not hurt** (SEE SELF-CARE: CALLUSES AND CORNS, PAGE 76.) ◆ **Red, itchy, burning, pimply rash or peeling skin, especially between toes** (SEE SELF-CARE: ATHLETE'S FOOT, PAGE 74.)	Use self-care	◆ **Corn or callus that is painful or that does not go away with self-care** ◆ **Plantar wart that is painful or is spreading new warts** ◆ **Open sore, with or without pus, that is surrounded by red, inflamed skin** ◆ **Sores, calluses, corns, or warts when you have diabetes, nerve damage, or circulation problems**	See doctor
◆ **Red, hot sores filled with pus that may be from bacterial infection** ◆ **Area with fungal infection that hurts when it is touched**	Call doctor		

Athlete's Foot

"I had a patient who could not figure out why his athlete's foot kept coming back. I suggested he use an antifungal powder in his shoes. That cleared it up."
—Family practice doctor

The inside of a shoe is warm, dark, and sometimes sweaty. That makes it a good place for fungus to grow. Athlete's foot is one kind of infection caused by a fungus. It can cause your skin to peel, itch, or burn. Athlete's foot can cause a rash of red, pimply blisters. The most common place for fungus infections is between your toes. To help prevent fungus infections, keep your feet clean and dry.

Self-Care: Athlete's Foot

- Use an over-the-counter antifungal cream, ointment, or spray. Buy one that contains clotrimazole (such as Lotrimin or Mycelex). Apply the medicine twice a day for two to four weeks. The infection should go away within four weeks. If it does not go away, see your doctor.
- A hydrocortisone cream or ointment, such as Cortaid, may help relieve itching. But it will not kill the fungus.
- Use an antifungal spray or powder inside your shoes. This will kill fungus and keep you from getting the infection again. If you have infections from fungus often, use an antifungal powder on your feet every day.
- After bathing, dry your feet well. Be sure to dry between your toes. Fungus does not thrive in dry areas.
- Allow your feet to air out. Take off your shoes and socks when you sit down or rest at home. Or wear sandals around the house. If your feet get cold easily, wear cotton or wool socks under sandals. Cotton and wool allow air to circulate.

If fungus is not treated, it can create a break in your skin. Bacteria may then enter and cause an infection. An infection from bacteria may be red, hot, painful, and filled with pus.

Infections from bacteria should be treated promptly. Use the self-care steps on the next page. When you treat such infections, you can keep them from getting worse. If you wait to treat an infection that comes from bacteria, it will take longer to heal.

If you have diabetes or problems with circulation, a foot infection can be serious. (SEE BOX, PAGE 64.) You should see

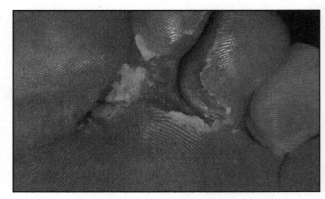

Athlete's foot occurs most often between the toes. The skin can burn, itch, and peel.

your doctor. Infections from bacteria can cause gangrene, which is the death of tissue. It is a serious condition.

Self-Care: Infections From Bacteria

Athlete's foot or another fungus infection may lead to a bacterial infection. Take these steps to treat a bacterial infection on your feet:

- Use an over-the-counter antibiotic ointment to treat small or mild infections. Signs of minor infection include increased pain, redness or swelling, and warmth or heat at the site of infection. Use ointments that contain bacitracin, neomycin, polymyxin B, or a combination of all three. Neosporin and Mycitracin are examples of this type of ointment.
- Keep the affected area clean.
- Soak your feet in a solution of Epsom salts or soapy water every day. After soaking, make sure that you dry your feet well.
- See your doctor if the infection gets worse or does not go away after two to three days of self-care.

Calluses

"Some of my patients want to ignore calluses. They say they have had them for years with no problems. But as you get older, calluses can be more serious. So we work together to take care of them."
—Registered nurse

A callus is a thickened area of skin caused by repeated rubbing. Shoes that do not fit properly can rub. Your feet may have more calluses as you get older. This is because the padding on the bottom of your feet is thinner. Calluses are called corns when they form on top of the foot. Corns are discussed in the next section.

You may have ignored calluses when you were younger. But as you age, it's more important to treat them. If you ignore a callus, it can get thicker. This can irritate the tissue under the callus. Then a sore may form under the callus. In bad cases, a cyst may also form. Doctors call this kind of cyst an adventitious bursa.

If a callus is painful, see your doctor. Otherwise, use self-care. (SEE SELF-CARE: CALLUSES AND CORNS, PAGE 76.)

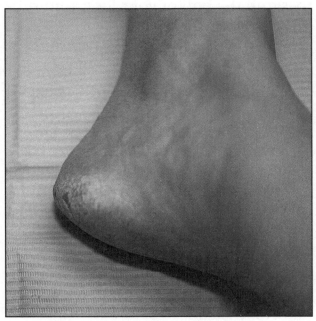

It is important to treat calluses as you get older. They can lead to more serious problems.

Corns

"My doctor said I would have fewer problems with my feet if I wore a bigger shoe size. So I got shoes that were a half size bigger. Now I don't seem to have as many corns."

—George

Corns are yellowish growths that are similar to calluses. Corns form on the tops of your toes. This happens in spots where shoes rub against your toes. If your shoes rub against a corn, it can become red, inflamed, and painful. Hammertoes are likely to have corns. (SEE HAMMERTOE, PAGE 68.)

The best way to prevent corns is to wear shoes with a large toe box. (The toe box is the part of a shoe that surrounds the toes.) This will keep your toes and the ball of your foot from rubbing against the shoe.

Self-Care: Calluses and Corns

- Soak your feet in a solution of Epsom salts and water for 15 minutes every day. Dry your feet well. Apply lotion. Rub the corn or callus with a clean towel, nail file, or pumice stone. Use a side-to-side motion when rubbing. Follow these steps until the corn or callus is gone. If you have diabetes or problems with circulation, do not use a file or pumice stone. See your doctor instead.

- Use a nonmedicated corn pad to ease pressure on the area.
- Wear shoes that do not rub on the corn or callus. Use insoles in your shoes to ease pressure on calluses.
- If a corn or callus becomes red or painful, see your doctor. Also see your doctor if the area around the corn or callus becomes red or painful.
- Never cut away corns or calluses. It is especially bad to cut them away with a razor blade or knife.

Soak your feet in a solution of Epsom salts to help soften corns and calluses. (SEE SELF-CARE STEPS, THIS PAGE.) This can also help treat a bacterial infection on your feet.

Plantar Warts

"I had a wart on my foot. My doctor said that it would go away, but it could take a long time. I decided to have it removed. He used liquid nitrogen to freeze it off."

—Julia

The word "plantar" refers to the sole of your foot. Plantar warts are warts that grow on the soles of your feet. The warts are caused by a virus. Since your body's weight puts constant pressure on your feet, the warts can grow inward. When they do, you get a painful lump on the bottom of your foot. The lump makes you feel as if you are walking on a pebble.

A plantar wart looks like a round, whitish growth. The area around it looks as if it is surrounded by a callus. As the wart grows larger, the area may look bumpy. Some warts have little black dots in the center of the bump. The wart may turn red if it is irritated.

It is hard to treat plantar warts. A slow approach is best. If left alone, some plantar warts go away on their own. But it may take as long as a few years for this to happen.

Do not try to remove a wart. Plantar warts can bleed badly when cut. If plantar warts hurt when you walk, see your doctor. He or she can remove them. Also see your doctor if plantar warts spread. Warts can be removed with medicine, laser technology, or surgery.

Ulcers on Your Feet

"I check my feet every day. I have diabetes and can't always feel when I have a sore. My doctor said an open sore could be dangerous for me. Since I wouldn't be able to feel one, it is likely to become infected."

—Richard

An ulcer is an open sore. It has red, inflamed skin around it. An infected ulcer may be filled with pus. Ulcers often come from repeated pressure or rubbing. This pressure can come from wearing shoes that do not fit properly. Ulcers can also form in places that stay moist or wet. Look between toes that overlap or curve into each other. Also check for ulcers underneath tightly curled toes. (SEE HAMMERTOE, PAGE 68.) You may be able to prevent ulcers by keeping the area between your toes dry.

If you have diabetes or poor circulation, check for ulcers every day. When your feet don't get enough blood, it's easier for ulcers to form. If you have nerve damage, you may not feel an ulcer.

Ulcers are serious. Always have ulcers treated by a doctor. Doctors treat ulcers in a number of ways. They may use an antibiotic to clear up the infection. They may also clean away bad tissue. Or a doctor may suggest that you wear an insole or special shoe. This will help relieve pressure.

Toenail Concerns

Your toenails can tell you a lot about your health. Changes in your toenails can be signs of certain diseases. This includes changes in the following:

- color
- curve or ridges
- growth rate
- strength (or brittleness)
- thickness

The following conditions can cause changes in your toenails:

- anemia
- heart and circulation problems
- psoriasis
- thyroid disease

The most common toenail problems are ingrown nails and fungal infections.

Ingrown Toenails

"I never paid attention to how I cut my toenails. One time my big toe got very tender and then turned red along the side of the nail. I had an ingrown toenail. I soaked my toe in warm water. That made it feel better. Now I trim my nails straight across."
—Michael

An ingrown toenail cuts into the skin at the side of the nail. It can cause redness and pain. It may even become infected.

Most ingrown toenails are on the big toe. But you can have an ingrown toenail on any toe. If your nails curve inward instead of being flat on top, you may be more prone to ingrown toenails. Shoes with tight or pointed toes can also cause ingrown toenails.

How to Prevent Ingrown Toenails

- Don't trim your nails too short. Keep nails level with the end of the toe. This gives the nail space to grow.
- Trim your toenails straight across. Don't trim your nails at an angle. Round the nails gently. If it is hard to see or reach your toenails, have someone trim them for you. Your doctor can do this.
- Use a nail file to soften the corners and smooth rough edges. If you have diabetes or circulation problems, don't use a nail file. Talk with your doctor about caring for your toenails.

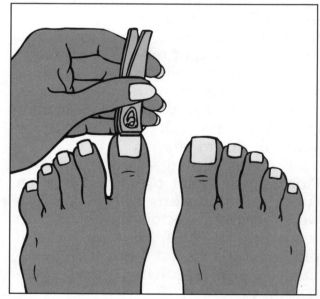

Trim toenails straight across and not too short. This can prevent ingrown toenails.

What to do about
Toenail Concerns

Symptoms/Signs	Action
◆ **Pain and redness from an ingrown toenail** ◆ **Brown, thickened toenails** (SEE SELF-CARE: TOENAIL FUNGAL INFECTIONS, PAGE 80.)	 Use self-care
◆ **Toenail problems that don't respond to self-care** ◆ **Sudden pain in toenails with no known cause** ◆ **Sudden change in how toenails look, other than symptoms of fungal infection**	Call doctor
◆ **Bruising or unusual color under the toenail that does not go away** ◆ **Bruising or unusual color under the toenail for no known reason** ◆ **Ingrown toenails or signs of fungal or bacterial infection when you have diabetes, nerve damage, or problems with circulation**	See doctor

Self-Care: Ingrown Toenails

- Place a piece of cotton or gauze under the corner of the toenail to ease the pain and pressure.
- Watch for signs of infection, such as hotness, redness, and pus.
- If symptoms of infection appear, soak your toe in warm soapy or salty water. Soak it every day for about 15 minutes. Make sure to dry your foot well.
- After soaking, apply an over-the-counter antibiotic ointment. Cover with a bandage. The infection should clear up in two to three days. If it does not clear up, see your doctor.
- See your doctor if you have diabetes or problems with circulation. Your doctor may prescribe antibiotics.
- If an ingrown toenail causes a lot of pain and frequent infections, see your doctor. He or she may suggest surgery or other treatment to stop the nail from growing.

Toenail Fungal Infections

"One day I saw that my toenails were getting darker and very thick. My pharmacist said it was a fungal infection."

—Peter

Brown, thick toenails are a sign of fungal infection. With this kind of infection, the nail may crumble. It may also pull away from the nail bed.

Self-Care: Toenail Fungal Infections

- Use an over-the-counter antifungal cream, ointment, or spray, such as Lotrimin or Mycelex. Apply the medicine twice a day for two to four weeks. If the infection does not go away in four weeks, see your doctor.
- Use an antifungal spray or powder inside your shoes. This kills fungus and can keep you from getting another infection.
- If you have frequent fungal infections, use an antifungal powder on your feet daily.
- Let your feet air out. Take off your shoes and socks when you sit down or are resting at home. Or wear sandals around the house. Wear cotton or wool socks with sandals if your feet are cold.
- If you have diabetes, see your doctor.
- If the problem continues after self-care, see your doctor.

Chapter 6

Heart and Circulation Concerns

Your heart and blood vessels make up your circulatory system. They pump blood to all parts of your body. Blood carries the oxygen and nutrients your body needs to stay well.

You may have minor problems with circulation at any age. For instance, you may have swelling in your legs or have an uneven heartbeat.

But as you get older, you have more risk for major problems. One is heart disease. That's why you need to know what your symptoms mean. A symptom may mean that something serious is wrong. Or it may not. For instance, chest pain may be a sign of a heart attack. But a pulled muscle can cause chest pain too. Use the charts that tell you "What to do about" a condition. The charts can help you respond to symptoms and may save your life.

Your doctor can treat many heart and blood vessel problems. At times, your doctor may refer you to a cardiologist. This is a doctor who treats heart problems.

This chapter covers the following problems:
- chest pain
- edema (swelling)
- heart disease
- palpitations
- phlebitis
- varicose veins

Chest Pain

Many things can cause chest pain. Heart problems cause some chest pain. Three common heart problems that cause chest pain are:
- angina (SEE PAGE 84.)
- heart attack (SEE PAGE 86.)
- pulmonary embolism (SEE PAGE 109.)

The following types of chest pain are rarely serious:
- a sharp pain after a deep breath
- a sharp pain that lasts only a few seconds
- pain from exercise
- pain from a fall
- pain from a coughing spell

Heartburn is one kind of chest pain that your heart does not cause. (SEE PAGE 24.) Here are some other types.

Muscle Pain. Answer these questions. If you say "yes," your pain is most likely in a muscle. It is probably not a sign of a heart problem.

What to do about Chest Pain

Symptoms/Signs	Action	Symptoms/Signs	Action
◆ Chest pain after exercise, a fall, or a coughing spell	Use self-care	◆ Chest pain that wakes you up ◆ Chest pain or pressure with uneven or rapid heartbeat, with shortness of breath, nausea or vomiting, sweating, light-headedness, anxiety, or fainting	Call ambulance
◆ Chest pain after eating that requires repeated use of antacids ◆ Chest pain that improves with rest	Call doctor	◆ Sudden, severe chest pain with shortness of breath or with bloody cough	
◆ Chest pain or pressure that feels crushing or that spreads to the shoulder, back, neck, or jaw ◆ Chest pain that lasts longer than 15 minutes and is not relieved by rest	Call ambulance	◆ Pain that feels like heartburn but is not relieved when you take antacids	

- Is your pain very sharp? Is it worse when you press on the painful spot?
- Does the pain feel worse when you move around?

Panic Disorder. This can cause chest pain. (See Anxiety, page 112.) Panic attacks can also cause any of the following:
- anxiety
- a fast, strong, or uneven heartbeat
- fear of dying
- shortness of breath

Ulcers. These may cause pains that spread in your chest. Ulcer pains are worse if your stomach is empty. This pain is relieved by antacids. (See Gastritis and Peptic Ulcers, page 23.)

Gallbladder Problems. These can also cause pains that spread in your chest. These pains often occur in the upper right side of the body and tend to be worse after you eat a fatty meal. (See Gallbladder Disease, page 22.)

Don't try to diagnose your own chest pain. And don't wait too long to get help. Call your doctor if you don't know what is causing your chest pain or other symptoms.

Self-Care: Chest Pain

- To ease a muscle strain in the chest, take an anti-inflammatory drug. Two types are ibuprofen (Advil) and aspirin.
- Apply heat and get rest.

Types of Chest Pain

Heart attack: Severe crushing pain in the center of chest, sometimes spreading to jaw, arms, neck, or back. This is often accompanied by sweating, shortness of breath, anxiety, dizziness, nausea or vomiting, and an irregular or rapid heartbeat. (See page 86.)

Angina: Pressure or pain in the heart that is often brought on by exertion or stress. It is relieved by rest. Angina is a warning sign that the heart is not getting the oxygen it needs. (See page 84.)

Heartburn: Burning pain behind the breastbone (See page 24.)

Muscle pain: Chest pain that is worse when you press on the affected area

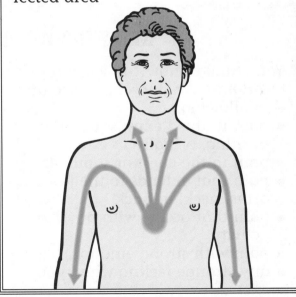

Angina

"I thought I was having a heart attack. We were hiking and taking a slow, easy route. After an hour, I felt pressure and squeezing in my chest and neck. I sat on a rock to rest. In a few minutes, the pain was gone. But I was scared. I called the doctor when we got home. The next day I had an EKG. The day after that I had a stress test. I found out that I have angina."

—Paul

Angina causes chest pain. One or more blood vessels that supply the heart can become blocked. This causes angina. These blockages are usually caused by plaque that has built up on the blood vessel walls. Plaque is made mostly of cholesterol. (SEE DRAWING, PAGE 86.) Angina is a sign that your heart is not getting enough oxygen. (SEE BOX BELOW.)

Angina may feel like a heart attack, but it is different. Most angina attacks last about 15 minutes. This is because the blood supply is reduced, but not cut off. Heart attacks occur when the blood supply is cut off. So a heart attack feels like an angina attack but lasts longer and may be more severe. The pain from a heart attack lasts longer than 15 minutes.

How to Prevent Angina

To prevent angina and other heart problems, keep cholesterol from building up in your blood vessels. Take steps to lower your cholesterol and keep your blood vessels clear. (SEE HOW TO PREVENT HEART DISEASE, PAGE 89.)

How Angina Is Diagnosed

Some chest pain feels like angina but is not. If you have chest pain, you should know what causes it. After your doctor checks you and asks about your

---

Know the Warning Signs of Angina

You should know the warning signs of angina. Angina can cause any of the following:
- pain that is heavy, squeezing, burning, or tight
- pain in the chest or shoulder
- pain that extends to the jaw, arms, neck, or back
- pain that occurs with physical activity
- pain with strong emotion
- any strange feeling when you exercise

Do you ever feel any of these symptoms? Does the pain go away with 15 minutes of rest? If so, you may have angina. If you have never had this type of pain before, don't try to diagnose yourself. Call your doctor or an emergency room for advice. (SEE WHAT TO DO ABOUT CHEST PAIN, PAGE 82.)

If pain is not relieved after you rest for 15 minutes, you may be having a heart attack. Call for an ambulance.

---

pain, he or she may order some tests. Tests may include blood tests and an electrocardiogram (EKG).

An EKG tells how well your heart is working while you rest. Your doctor may also want you to have an exercise stress test. This test shows how well your heart is working when you are being active.

Your doctor may suggest a heart catheterization. This test shows what part of your heart is blocked. The doctor guides a thin plastic tube through an artery in your arm or leg. This tube is called a catheter. The doctor slides the tube until it reaches the arteries of your heart. Then the doctor injects a dye and takes an X-ray. The X-ray shows where the dye can and cannot flow. This tells the doctor where the heart is blocked.

How Angina Is Treated

You can often control angina with drugs and lifestyle changes. (SEE HOW TO PREVENT HEART DISEASE, PAGE 89.) You will most likely need to take medicine.

Nitroglycerin is the drug prescribed most often to ease angina. (SEE BOX BELOW.) The drug most often comes in tiny pills that you put under your tongue. You may need to take up to three nitroglycerin pills to ease angina pain. Talk with your doctor about how many pills you can take safely before you should call him or her.

Medicine does not always control angina. Your doctor may also suggest a procedure such as angioplasty or bypass surgery.

Angioplasty. In this procedure, a doctor inserts a long tube into an artery in your arm or leg. Then a second tube with a balloon tip is threaded through the first tube. When the tip reaches the blockage, the doctor inflates the balloon. This pushes the plaque against the walls of the artery, opening up the blockage. Once the artery is opened up, more blood can flow through it. Then the doctor deflates the balloon and takes out both tubes.

Bypass Surgery. This surgery fixes arteries that are badly blocked. The surgeon takes a vein from another part of the body. A vein from the leg is often

If You Take Medicine for Angina

- Know what side effects the drug can have. Talk with your doctor if side effects bother you.
- Always keep nitroglycerin pills in the container they came in. Keep it closed tight. Don't store pills in a damp place. The pills often come in a brown bottle. Once you have opened the bottle, pills lose their strength quickly. You should replace an open bottle every six months.
- Don't run out of your medicine. Keep a good supply on hand. Always have your medicine with you.

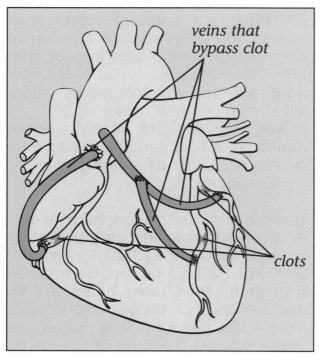

veins that
bypass clot

clots

*In coronary bypass surgery, a surgeon uses part
of a vein from somewhere else in your body to
bypass the blockages in your heart. This drawing shows three blockages that are bypassed
with "new" veins.*

used. The surgeon uses that vein to go
around the blocked artery, or bypass it.
(SEE DRAWING ABOVE.) This creates a new
route for blood to travel. Then blood
can flow freely again.

Self-Care: Angina

Take these steps when you feel angina
pain. You should also follow your doctor's advice.
1. Sit down before you take your
   medicine. Nitroglycerin may make

you dizzy. Let the pill fully dissolve
under your tongue. Don't swallow
the pill. If you have a spray medicine, spray once inside your cheek.
2. If you still have chest pain after five
   minutes, take another pill. Or spray
   inside your cheek again.
3. If you still have chest pain after
   another five minutes, take a third
   dose. Remember to let the pill dissolve fully.
4. After three doses in a 15-minute
   period, your chest pain should be
   relieved.
5. If you still have chest pain, you
   could be having a heart attack.
   Call for an ambulance.

Heart Attack

"Sometimes patients call to tell me
they have had an awful pain in
their chest for two hours or more.
My advice is always the same. Call
for an ambulance. Get to the emergency room. When you have chest
pain, don't wait to get help."
—Internist

A heart attack almost always causes
chest pain. This pain may be mild or
severe. Pain from a heart attack does
not go away as quickly as pain from
angina. (SEE PAGE 84.) The pain often
lasts longer and is much worse. It may
seem to go away, but then it comes
back. Rest and drugs won't ease the
pain completely. (SEE WHAT TO DO ABOUT
CHEST PAIN, PAGE 82.)

Are You At Risk for a Heart Attack?

Answer the questions below to help you find out your risk of heart attack. Each question relates to a risk factor. Each time you answer "yes," your risk is higher. You can change some risk factors. You can't change others. The first set of questions relates to things you can't change. The next set of questions relates to things you can do something about. Do what you can to reduce your risk of heart attack.

Things you cannot change:
- Did anyone in your family have heart disease before age 50?
- If you are a woman, are you post-menopausal or older than 65?
- If you are a man, are you older than 55?
- Are you African-American?

Things you can do something about:
- Do you smoke? Smoking may cause your cholesterol to rise. It also raises your blood pressure. Both of these problems can lead to a heart attack. Even secondhand smoke puts you at higher risk for a heart attack. (SEE HOW TO QUIT SMOKING, PAGE 300.)
- Do you have high blood pressure? (SEE HYPERTENSION, PAGE 90.)
- Is your cholesterol level too high? (SEE BOX, PAGE 91.)
- Do you have diabetes? Diabetes makes you more likely to have high cholesterol and to have other blood vessel problems. (SEE WHEN YOU HAVE DIABETES, PAGE 249.) Both of these increase your risk of a heart attack.

Know the Signs of a Heart Attack

You may be having a heart attack if you have chest pain with any of these symptoms:
- shortness of breath
- nausea or vomiting
- sweating
- anxiety
- light-headedness
- pain that spreads to the back, neck, or jaw
- chest pain that lasts more than 15 minutes

Call for an ambulance at once. Do not drive yourself to the emergency room.

Be Prepared for a Heart Emergency

If you are close to someone who has heart disease, learn CPR. (SEE PAGE 332.) Be ready to use it in an emergency. You may save a life. Call the American Red Cross or American Heart Association to find out about classes near you.

- Do you weigh more than you should? Extra weight raises your chance of diabetes and hypertension. Both increase your risk of heart attack. (SEE WHEN YOU ARE OVERWEIGHT, PAGE 254.)
- Do you lead an inactive life without much exercise? Lack of exercise is a risk factor for heart disease. Start slowly, and don't do too much at first. Slowly work up to at least 30 minutes of moderate exercise each day. Walk. Swim. Ride a bike. Do yard work. These are all good forms of exercise. (SEE STAYING ACTIVE, PAGE 291.)
- Do you have a lot of stress? (SEE HOW TO RELAX, PAGE 129.)

You may think you can't do anything about a chronic disease such as diabetes or high blood pressure. But you can work with your doctor to control it. Then you can lower your risk for heart problems.

Edema (Swelling)

Mild swelling in both legs is common. It often occurs at the end of the day. Sitting or standing for a long time is the most likely cause. Varicose veins also cause swelling. (SEE PAGE 95.)

In most cases, swelling goes down by itself overnight. But swelling may be a sign of a major problem.

For instance, congestive heart failure can cause your legs and ankles to

What to do about Edema (Swelling)

Symptoms/Signs	Action
◆ Swelling in legs or feet that does not cause problems at the end of the day	 Use self-care
◆ Swelling that does not respond to self-care ◆ Swelling in the legs while taking testosterone, estrogen, blood pressure drugs, or corticosteroids	Call doctor
◆ Ankle or leg swelling when you have a problem with your liver, lung, kidney, or heart	See doctor
◆ Painful and sudden swelling in only one leg ◆ Painless swelling in one or both legs or ankles, with shortness of breath or feeling as if you can't breathe	 Seek help now

swell. So can lung, kidney, and liver diseases. Fatigue can cause swelling too. If you have sudden swelling, or if swelling does not go down with self-care, call your doctor.

Some drugs may cause your legs to swell. If you use any of these drugs and have swelling, call your doctor:

- testosterone or estrogen
- drugs that control blood pressure
- drugs for arthritis (including ibuprofen)
- corticosteroids (prednisone or cortisone)

Self-Care: Swelling in the Legs

- Raise your legs if they feel swollen or heavy. Keep them up. This helps send blood back toward your heart.
- Don't sit or stand still for long stretches of time. Get up and walk often. When you can't get around, wiggle your toes and feet. That will help keep the blood flowing.
- Wear support stockings. The pressure they put on your legs will ease the swelling.
- Eat less salt. Too much salt can make water build up in your body. This may cause swelling.
- Don't cross your legs when you sit. Sit straight with your feet flat on the floor. When you cross your legs, you can cut off blood flow. This can make your legs swell.

Heart Disease

Heart disease is the main cause of death among Americans older than 65. You can do a number of things to lower your risk. Your diet and your habits both affect your risk. You can lower your risk by following the tips below. Also see the chapter Making Healthy Lifestyle Choices, starting on page 285.

This section describes these types of heart disease:

- atherosclerosis
- hypertension (high blood pressure)
- high blood cholesterol
- palpitations

How to Prevent Heart Disease

- Eat low-fat, low-cholesterol food. (SEE WHAT YOU SHOULD KNOW ABOUT HIGH BLOOD CHOLESTEROL, PAGE 91.) Keep your cholesterol in the proper range.
- If you have high blood pressure, follow the plan your doctor suggests. (SEE HYPERTENSION, PAGE 90.)
- Lose weight if you need to. (SEE WHEN YOU ARE OVERWEIGHT, PAGE 254.)
- Quit smoking. Avoid secondhand smoke too. Smokers are more likely to get all types of heart disease. (SEE HOW TO QUIT SMOKING, PAGE 300.)
- Exercise every day. Ask your doctor how much and what kinds of exercise are right for you. (SEE STAYING ACTIVE, PAGE 291.)
- Try to avoid stress in your life. (SEE HOW TO RELAX, PAGE 129.)
- Cut out caffeine.

Atherosclerosis

"When I was in my 50s, my doctor told me to change my diet. I ate too much fat. Now people my age are having heart attacks. I'm just glad I took the doctor's advice."
—Peter

One of the most common forms of heart disease is atherosclerosis. This term refers to the hardening of the inner walls of your arteries. Most doctors agree that high cholesterol is the main cause of this condition. High levels of cholesterol in the blood form plaque. The plaque sticks to the artery walls. (SEE DRAWINGS ON THE LEFT.) Over time, the plaque clogs the arteries. Then all of your body may not get the blood it needs.

By the time you notice symptoms, this hardening may have already damaged your body. You may have mild symptoms, such as cramps in your legs when you exercise. But the first sign of a problem is often a stroke (SEE PAGE 183), kidney failure, angina (SEE PAGE 84), or heart attack (SEE PAGE 86).

It may take years for symptoms to show. So the best approach is to prevent atherosclerosis and slow it down. One way to do this is to cut down on the amount of cholesterol you eat. Cutting back on the fat you eat will also help. (SEE WHAT YOU SHOULD KNOW ABOUT HIGH BLOOD CHOLESTEROL, PAGE 91.) Some people need medicine to control their cholesterol.

Normal Arteries and Clogged Arteries

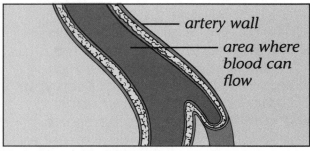

Blood flows freely through a normal artery.

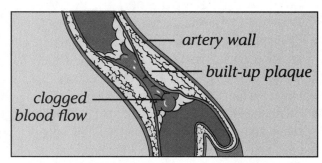

Built-up plaque narrows the path that blood can flow through in an artery. Clogged arteries lead to conditions such as angina (SEE PAGE 84), atherosclerosis, and hypertension.

Hypertension (High Blood Pressure)

"Of all the illnesses I treat, high blood pressure is one of the hardest. My patients who have it don't feel sick. So it's hard for me to convince them to take their medicine."
—Internist

Each time your heart beats, it pumps blood. As the blood flows through your body, it puts force on your arteries. Blood pressure is how that force is measured. Your blood pressure is affected by the strength of your heart and the health of your blood vessels. If your heart has to work hard to pump blood, you could have high blood pressure. If your blood vessels are clogged, you could have high blood pressure. High blood pressure is also called hypertension.

High blood pressure is the most common chronic illness among adults in the United States. Most people who

What You Should Know About High Blood Cholesterol

Your body needs cholesterol to make hormones and to digest fat. Your liver most often makes all the cholesterol you need. But you can increase your level with the foods you eat. When you have high blood cholesterol, you are at risk for heart disease.

What Is a Safe Level?
A simple blood test shows your total cholesterol level. A result below 200 is safe. A result above 200 is too high.

Who Needs to Be Tested?
All people over the age of 50 should know what their cholesterol level is. If it is too high, try to lower it.

How Can You Help to Lower Your Cholesterol?
You don't have to make drastic changes all at once. Change things over time, and make changes you can live with. It takes time for plaque to build up in your arteries. It can also take time to change your routine.

- Eat less fat. Saturated fat is in dairy products and meats. It can be related to higher blood cholesterol levels. Eat low-fat dairy foods and lean meats. Unsaturated fat is in vegetable oils and nuts. It is better for your health. But eat less of all kinds of fat.
- Eat fewer high-cholesterol foods. Food that has cholesterol comes from animals. This includes fish, chicken, beef, pork, eggs, and dairy products. Egg yolks and organ meats, such as liver, are very high in cholesterol.
- Eat more foods that are high in carbohydrates and fiber. (SEE THE FOOD GUIDE PYRAMID, PAGE 288.)
- Exercise routinely. Being active can decrease the level of fats in your blood.
- Stay at a healthy weight. If you eat more calories than you need, your levels can increase.
- Take any drugs your doctor prescribes to lower your cholesterol.

How Your Blood Pressure Is Taken

Having your blood pressure taken is painless. Here is what happens:

1. Your doctor or nurse puts a cuff around your arm above the elbow.
2. He or she pumps air into the cuff until it is tight enough to stop the flow of blood.
3. The doctor opens a valve and lets the air out of the cuff. While the air escapes, he or she listens with a stethoscope. Your blood makes a sound as it goes through your arteries.
4. The doctor hears the first sound and notes the number on the gauge. This is your systolic pressure. It is the top number.
5. The sound last heard is recorded as your diastolic pressure. This is the bottom number.

What Is High Blood Pressure?

You have high blood pressure if your top number is always 140 or higher. You also have high blood pressure if your lower number is always 90 or higher.

What It Means if You Have a High Reading

If your blood pressure is too high, your doctor will ask you to come back. Your doctor will want to take more readings before saying that you have high blood pressure. Blood pressure can go up or down from one minute to the next. Many things can affect a blood pressure reading. They can include any of these:
- pain
- anxiety
- caffeine
- a full stomach

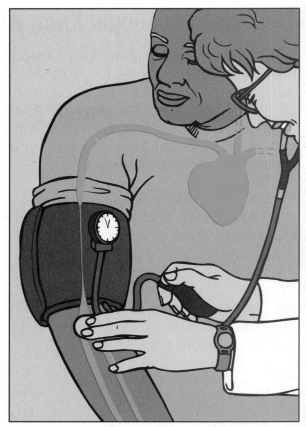

Your blood pressure reading is written like a fraction. For instance, it may be 130/85. Your doctor will say this as "130 over 85." The goal is to keep your blood pressure below 140/90. (SEE WHEN YOU HAVE HIGH BLOOD PRESSURE, PAGE 253.)

have it don't know they do. A heart attack or stroke can be the first sign of high blood pressure. That is why high blood pressure is often called "the silent killer." This also explains why all adults should have their blood pressure checked routinely. Your risk of high blood pressure goes up as you get older. So it is even more important, as you get older, to have it checked.

You can help lower your blood pressure by eating less fat, losing weight, drinking less alcohol, and exercising routinely.

How Hypertension Is Treated
Lifestyle changes can help control blood pressure. If you have high blood pressure, your doctor may ask you to do any of the following:

- change what you eat
- drink less alcohol
- exercise more
- lose weight
- take prescription drugs

Many drugs can help lower your blood pressure. Some types of drugs are diuretics, beta-blockers, calcium antagonists, and ACE inhibitors. Each drug has its own side effects. You need to work with your doctor to find the right drug for you. (SEE WHEN YOU HAVE HIGH BLOOD PRESSURE, PAGE 253.)

If high blood pressure is not treated, it can damage your heart. It can also damage your blood vessels, kidneys, and other organs.

Palpitations

"For years, I've drunk about 20 cups of coffee and smoked two packs of cigarettes a day. One day when I was mowing the lawn, my heart started to pound. Then it would skip a beat. I thought I was having a heart attack. When I got to the emergency room, they did an EKG. It was normal. Then the doctor asked about coffee and cigarettes. Once he heard my answers, he said they were the likely cause of my palpitations. I stopped smoking, and cut way back on coffee. I have never had another problem with it."

—Greg

What to do about
Heart Palpitations

Symptoms/Signs		Action
◆ **Occasional feeling that your heart skips a beat or races**		Use self-care
◆ **Persistent heart palpitations or a rapid heart rate**		Call doctor
◆ **Palpitations and dizziness, shortness of breath, or sweating** ◆ **Palpitations and chest pain** (SEE CHEST PAIN, PAGE 82.)	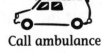	Call ambulance

You may have had the feeling that your heart skipped a beat. This is called heart palpitations. When your heart beats normally, its two upper chambers contract. Then the two lower chambers contract. This makes the two-thump heartbeat sound. If you have palpitations, your heart may seem to beat out of step, to skip beats, or to race. Common causes for this condition include the following:

- alcohol
- caffeine
- nicotine
- stress

Avoiding these things may correct your heartbeat. You can't get rid of stress, but you can learn to handle it. (SEE STRESS, PAGE 128.)

Palpitations are rarely dangerous. In fact, most people have them from time to time. But if you notice palpitations, tell your doctor. If you have them often, tell your doctor that too. Your doctor may say that you need some tests. This will depend on your history and risk factors. Or your doctor may be able to set your mind at ease.

Self-Care: Palpitations

- Stop smoking. Get help to quit. (SEE HOW TO QUIT SMOKING, PAGE 300.)
- Cut out caffeine and alcohol.
- Exercise. Warm up slowly and cool down at the end. This helps your heart return to its normal rate. (SEE STAYING ACTIVE, PAGE 291.)

- Find ways to lower your stress or anxiety. Meditation or yoga may help you. (SEE HOW TO RELAX, PAGE 129.)

Phlebitis

Phlebitis is also called thrombophlebitis. It is the term for inflammation in a vein. There may also be a clot in the vein. This problem can be close to the skin or deeper in the body. When it is close to the skin, it is called superficial phlebitis. It often occurs in only one leg. This problem is rarely serious. It can be caused by a long bed rest. It can occur after surgery or even after a long car ride or airplane trip. It is more common in people who have varicose veins.

Clotting or swelling can affect a vein close to the skin. Then a red, hard, and tender bump or cord may form under the skin. Your doctor may tell you to use heat on the sore spot. The doctor may also advise you to raise your leg. To ease the pain, take an anti-inflammatory drug such as aspirin or ibuprofen (Advil).

The more serious type of phlebitis is in the deep veins of the leg. This problem is most often caused by sitting too long with your legs crossed. This kind of phlebitis can cause the following:

- aching
- fever
- swelling
- tenderness
- a warm feeling in your calf

Seek medical help right away if you have any of these symptoms. Sometimes a part of the clot travels to the lungs. That can kill you. (SEE PULMONARY EMBOLISM, PAGE 109.)

You will need to stay in the hospital if you have phlebitis in the deep veins. Your doctor will have you take anticoagulants. These drugs are also called blood thinners.

Varicose Veins

Blood goes back to your heart from your legs and feet. The valves in your leg veins help move the blood upward. If those valves leak, the pressure in your veins goes up. This increased pressure makes the veins bulge on the surface of your skin. Those veins are called varicose veins.

Varicose veins are not attractive. They appear most often behind your knees, calves, or thighs. You may have had them for many years. They are common during pregnancy. They are also common in people who must stand for a long time at work. A family history of varicose veins is a major risk factor for getting them.

The most common type of varicose vein is a spiderlike vein. (SEE PHOTO, PAGE 96.) These veins are small and most often red or purple. Another type is called a rope vein. Rope veins are long and seem twisted. (SEE PHOTO, PAGE 96.) Varicose veins can make your legs ache. But they are almost never life-threatening. In a few bad cases, a clot may form in the vein. That can lead to phlebitis. If varicose veins get bad enough, they can make your legs swell and damage the skin. Your skin may get a sore, or you may have ulcers on your legs.

Varicose veins can be treated with an injection into the vein. Surgery may be a better choice for you if any of the following is true:
- Your skin is very painful, has ulcers, or is likely to bleed.
- You have phlebitis.
- You want to improve how your legs look.
- Your veins bother you and don't respond to self-care.

What to do about **Varicose Veins**	
Symptoms/Signs	**Action**
◆ **Small purple or red veins on the legs** ◆ **Long, twisted veins with no pain or discomfort**	Use self-care
◆ **Long, twisted veins with redness, swelling, and tenderness** ◆ **Skin around the vein that becomes irritated** ◆ **Sore that forms on skin near vein**	Call doctor

Even after injections or surgery, new varicose veins can form. Both treatments are costly. Many health plans do not cover this cost. This is often the case when the purpose is only cosmetic.

Self-Care: Varicose Veins

Most varicose veins do not need a doctor's care. Taking these steps may help:

- Exercise. Walking is a good choice. It improves your blood flow and makes your legs stronger. (SEE HOW TO START A WALKING PROGRAM, PAGE 294.)
- Lose weight if you are too heavy. This will take some stress off your veins. (SEE HOW TO LOSE WEIGHT SENSIBLY, PAGE 254.)
- Raise your feet when you can. This shrinks the swelling in your legs and ankles.
- Ask your doctor about support stockings. Men can wear support stockings too. Wearing them will lower the pressure in your veins. Elastic stockings are best. Your doctor may suggest knee-high stockings or custom-made, waist-high ones. What you wear will depend on how bad your veins are. When you wear stockings, be sure the elastic band at the top does not bind or bunch up. This can block blood flow. That is why most doctors almost never suggest thigh-high stockings. If your doctor tells you to wear them, they should be custom-fitted and worn with a garter belt.

Types of Varicose Veins

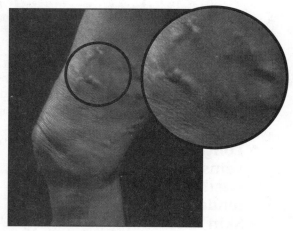

Rope veins are long and seem twisted. Although these look bad, they rarely cause pain. If they do, call your doctor.

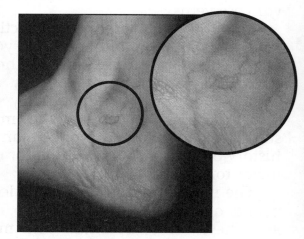

Spiderlike veins are the most common type of varicose veins. They are small and are most often red or purple.

Chapter 7

Lung Concerns

Each year, you breathe nearly eight million times. With each breath, your lungs expand. They take in oxygen and other gases from the air. Your lungs filter the air and move oxygen into your bloodstream. From there, oxygen goes to each cell and organ in your body. At the same time, your lungs remove carbon dioxide from your blood. Carbon dioxide leaves your body when you breathe out.

You might not pay much attention to your lungs unless you are sick. Your lungs work all the time. The wear and tear of constant use can cause lung problems. Some problems are minor. Bacteria and viruses can infect your lungs. Allergies can make it hard to breathe. Sometimes you may need to see a doctor for these conditions.

Some lung problems are serious. Chronic bronchitis, pneumonia, emphysema, and asthma can damage your lungs over time. So can air pollution and cigarette smoke. This damage can make it hard to breathe.

It is important to keep your lungs healthy. This chapter lists self-care steps that may help. Sometimes you should seek your doctor's advice right away. Remember, your body needs your lungs to survive. If you have a problem with your lungs, your doctor may send you to a lung specialist.

This chapter helps you know what to do about these lung concerns:
- asthma
- bronchitis
- colds
- fevers
- influenza (the flu)
- lung cancer
- pleurisy
- pneumonia
- pulmonary embolism
- wheezing

Asthma

"Whenever I get near my grand-daughter's cat, my asthma starts to act up. I start to cough and find it hard to breathe."
—Rick

Asthma is a chronic illness. Chronic means long-term. Once you are diagnosed with asthma, it is likely to come back again and again. One symptom of asthma is a chronic cough. You may cough when you rest or after you have been active. Other symptoms include shortness of breath, tightness in your chest, and wheezing. (SEE PAGE 110.) If you have these symptoms, see a doctor. If you have asthma, talk with your doctor. Learn how to recognize signs of an asthma attack.

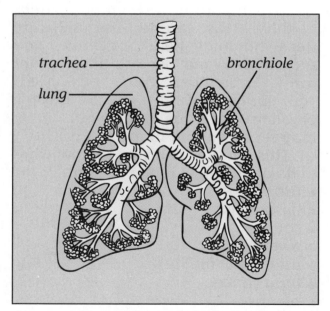

Air comes into the lungs through the trachea. In the bronchioles, oxygen is absorbed. Carbon dioxide is expelled.

Self-Care: Asthma

- Avoid air pollution.
- Avoid cigarette smoke. If you smoke, get help to quit. (SEE HOW TO QUIT SMOKING, PAGE 300.) Try to stay away from secondhand smoke too. Ask friends and relatives not to smoke around you.
- If allergies are causing your asthma attacks, try to find out what you are allergic to. Then stay away from it. Dust, some plants and grasses, and dander from animal fur or feathers can cause attacks. (SEE DO YOU HAVE AN ALLERGY? PAGE 334.)

Bronchitis

"I had the flu a month ago. The aches and pains went away, but the cough did not. Each morning when I woke up, I felt as if I were drowning! I tried to get back to my normal life, but I was worn out. I went to my doctor. He said I was lucky I didn't have pneumonia. He said I had acute bronchitis. The medicines he gave me really helped. Next time, I won't wait so long to see him!"
—Roberta

Sometimes you bring up mucus when you cough. When you do, the cough is called productive. Most coughs that bring up clear, thin mucus are not serious. This is especially true if you have a cold or the flu. But sometimes a cough lasts after other symptoms go away. You may have bronchitis if your cough becomes dry and hacking. Bronchitis may produce a thick yellow or gray mucus.

Bronchitis is a broad term. It means the lining of the tubes that lead to your lungs is inflamed. These tubes are called bronchioles. (SEE DRAWING, PAGE 100.) These tubes can be irritated by viruses, bacteria, smoke, dust, and fumes. If the tubes are irritated, your body makes more mucus than normal. When coughing does not clear out the extra mucus, you may develop bronchitis. Bronchitis can be chronic or acute.

If you have bronchitis, you need to see a doctor. If you are not treated, you could get pneumonia.

Chronic Bronchitis. A chronic illness is one that comes and goes again and again over time. You may have chronic bronchitis if you say "yes" to either of the following questions:

- Do you have bronchitis most days of the month?
- Have you had bronchitis for three months in a row? Has this gone on for two years in a row?

Acute Bronchitis. Acute means brief. This is what most people mean when they say bronchitis. Viruses and bacteria are the most common causes of bronchitis in healthy people. If you have bronchitis, you should see a doctor. If you are not treated, you could get pneumonia.

What to do about
Acute Bronchitis

Symptoms/Signs	Action
◆ **Cough that brings up phlegm after a cold or the flu, without fever**	 Use self-care
◆ **Cough that gets worse or lasts longer than one week** ◆ **Fever of 101 degrees or higher, with a cough or a fever lasting longer than three days** ◆ **Symptoms of bronchitis and you have chronic obstructive pulmonary disease** (SEE WHEN YOU HAVE COPD, PAGE 248.)	Call doctor
◆ **Blood in phlegm** ◆ **Cough that lasts longer than four weeks** ◆ **Shortness of breath and heavy coughing** ◆ **Cough and you have asthma** ◆ **Cough that gets abruptly worse or shortness of breath with fever**	See doctor

Who Is At Risk for Acute Bronchitis?

As you get older, your body is less able to fight off viruses and bacteria. You are more likely to get bronchitis. If you have asthma, you are more likely to have bronchitis after a cold or the flu.

Older adults who have bronchitis are more likely to get pneumonia. Bronchitis is closely related to pneumonia. It can be hard to tell them apart. You should call your doctor if your symptoms get worse or last more than a week. (SEE PNEUMONIA, PAGE 107.)

Even with treatment, bronchitis can often last for weeks. You can wheeze or cough for even longer.

Even with your doctor's care, bronchitis often lasts one to two weeks. You may wheeze or have a dry cough for up to six weeks. If self-care doesn't help, tell your doctor. See your doctor if your symptoms get worse. If your symptoms last more than four weeks after treatment starts, see your doctor.

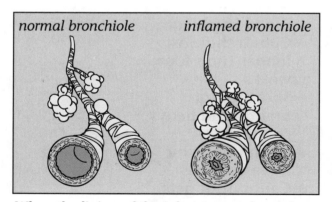

normal bronchiole   inflamed bronchiole

When the lining of the tubes to your lungs becomes inflamed, you have bronchitis. The tubes may fill with mucus and make it harder for you to breathe.

Self-Care: Acute Bronchitis

- Drink six to eight glasses of clear liquid a day. This is the best treatment for bronchitis. It keeps mucus from clogging your bronchial tubes.
- Avoid milk. Drinking it can cause the body to make more mucus. This mucus may be thicker than normal. It is easier to cough up thin, watery mucus.
- Avoid alcohol and caffeine. Both make you lose fluid. You need fluid to keep the mucus thin.
- Get a lot of rest. You may be able to stick to your daily routine. Listen to your body, and don't overdo it.
- For a nagging cough, buy a cough syrup with the cough suppressant dextromethorphan. The bottle may say DM.
- If it is hard to cough up mucus, try a product that has guaifenesin in it. It is an expectorant. It thins the mucus so that you can cough up more of it.
- Don't take products that have antihistamines. You do not need these for bronchitis. They may thicken your mucus.
- Call your doctor if you have signs of pneumonia. (SEE PAGE 108.)
- Avoid smoke, dust, and cold, dry air. These can make you cough.
- Suck on cough drops or hard candy to soothe your throat.

Colds

"When it comes to colds, a doctor's advice is not much better than your mother's. You can try cold remedies, but I don't think you can do better than chicken soup. If you have a sore throat, gargle with warm water mixed with a little salt. Protect others by washing your hands often. And cover your mouth when you cough or sneeze."
—Infectious disease specialist

You know the signs of a cold. You have a runny nose, congestion, a fever, and a cough. You may have headaches too. It is normal to lose your appetite. It may be hard to sleep. You may have a yellow or greenish discharge from your nose. These symptoms do not always mean you have a serious infection.

There are many myths about colds. A walk in the rain cannot give you a cold. Being out in cold weather or sitting in a draft cannot give you one. Colds are viral infections. The only way to catch a virus is to have contact with it. Most people catch colds by being with someone who has a cold.

It is easy to catch colds from people who have them. You can stand close to them and breathe in germs. You can shake hands and spread germs. You can touch what they touch and catch a cold. You can avoid a cold by avoiding people who have one. If you are around someone who has a cold, wash your hands afterward.

Cold symptoms come on fast. Symptoms are often worst the first three to

five days. Then they slowly improve. A cold often lasts 7 to 14 days, no matter what you do. You may still cough a bit for two to three weeks after other symptoms go away.

Bacterial infections make some colds worse. These are the bad colds—the ones that last so long that you call your doctor.

What to do about **Colds**	
Symptoms/Signs	**Action**
◆ **General aches** ◆ **Congestion, post-nasal drip, or runny or stuffy nose** ◆ **Scratchy throat, mild hoarseness, and cough** ◆ **Fever of 101 degrees or lower that lasts less than three days**	 Use self-care
◆ **Symptoms that get worse after three to five days** ◆ **Symptoms that don't improve after seven days** ◆ **Symptoms that last more than 14 days** ◆ **Fever with symptoms that get worse**	Call doctor
◆ **Wheezing or difficulty breathing**	 Seek help now

Bronchitis & Colds

LUNG CONCERNS **101**

Self-Care: Colds

There is no cure for the cold. But you can treat the symptoms. And over-the-counter drugs may make you feel better. You rarely need to see a doctor when you have a cold.

- Raise the humidity in your home. Steam helps clear your nose and lungs. It can ease the pain from coughing. Sit in the bathroom and turn on the shower. Use a humidifier or a vaporizer. Set the vaporizer on the cool-mist setting. If you use a humidifier, empty and clean it each day. Follow the instructions. Bacteria love warmth and moisture. Washing your humidifier keeps these germs from growing and spreading.
- Drink extra fluids. Don't drink alcohol. Drinking clear fluids thins your mucus. This eases congestion. Warm fluids soothe your throat. Fluids also help when you have a fever.
- Gargle with warm salt water. Mix 1/4 teaspoon salt in 8 ounces of warm water. Or you can buy a product like Chloraseptic.
- Suck on cough drops and lozenges to soothe your sore throat. Examples are N'ICE and *HALLS*. Hard candy works as well as these drops.
- Use an extra pillow. Sleeping with your head raised clears your nose. This helps you breathe better.
- Wash your hands often. Washing keeps you from spreading germs to other people.
- Get plenty of rest. It will help you get better faster.
- Do not smoke. Smoking makes a cough worse. Smoking also puts you at greater risk of getting bacterial pneumonia.
- Talk with your pharmacist when you choose over-the-counter drugs. Your pharmacist knows what drugs you should not take together. (SEE HOW TO USE OVER-THE-COUNTER DRUGS SAFELY, PAGE 271.)
- Decongestants can clear a runny or stuffy nose. These include Dristan and Sudafed.
- Robitussin or a generic cough syrup can ease coughs.
- Cold medicines like NyQuil or Comtrex may ease coughs and minor aches.
- Treat a headache, sore muscles, and fever by taking aspirin, acetaminophen (Tylenol), or ibuprofen (Advil or Nuprin).
- Try saline nose drops or sprays to clear your nose. Examples of nose sprays are Ocean and Salinex.

Fevers

"Watch fevers closely as you get older. Any fever of 101 degrees or higher is cause for concern. Many folks older than 65 don't get fevers at all with colds or the flu. If you feel dizzy, restless, or confused when you are sick, see your doctor, even if you don't have a fever."

—Lung specialist

What to do about Fevers

Symptoms/Signs	Action
◆ Fever of less than 101 degrees for less than three days without other symptoms	 Use self-care
◆ Fever with sore throat, earache, or frequent cough ◆ Fever with vomiting	Call doctor
◆ Shaking or teeth-chattering chills ◆ Fever with back pain or painful urination ◆ Fever of 101 degrees or higher ◆ Fever and sudden confusion in an older person ◆ Fever with stiff neck ◆ Lower abdominal pain and fever for more than two hours	 See doctor

What is normal body temperature? Normal does not mean 98.6 degrees for everyone. This is only an average. A person's body temperature goes up and down all day. It may be 97.5 degrees in the morning. Later in the day, 99.5 degrees may be normal. Many older adults have temperatures that are lower than average.

A fever raises your body temperature above 99.5 degrees. Most doctors are not troubled by a fever unless it is above 101 degrees. A fever can mean that your body is fighting an infection.

As you age, you are less likely to get a high fever when you are ill. You can still be sick without a fever. A low fever in an older adult can cause the same symptoms as a high fever in a younger person.

Some older adults with other signs of an infection may not have a fever. Call your doctor if you have headaches or feel dizzy, restless, or confused. Call even if you have no fever.

Fever can be a problem if you have heart disease or lung disease. You will need to watch for signs of fever. A fever above 101 degrees can put a lot of stress on a weak heart. The stress can lead to heart failure.

Self-Care: Fevers

- If fever is your only symptom and you are uncomfortable, you can take aspirin or acetaminophen (such as Tylenol).
- Drink eight glasses of fluid a day. Don't drink alcohol. A fever may make you sweat. Losing body fluid can cause dehydration. If you drink extra fluids, you can keep from getting dehydrated.

Influenza

"Many of my older patients don't want to get a flu shot each year. They tell me, 'I got the shot once. It made me sick for a week. I'll never make that mistake again!'

I tell them that this does not happen much anymore. The newer vaccines are much better. Older adults, especially those with chronic illnesses, should worry more about the effects of the flu and not about the effects of the shot."

—Internist

You may use the word "flu" to mean more than one illness. When some people say "flu," they mean stomach flu. Stomach flu is an upset stomach or diarrhea. Other people mean influenza.

With influenza, you have a fever and muscle aches. You may have cold symptoms. But this flu comes on faster than a cold and lasts longer. The flu affects the nose, mouth, breathing tube (trachea), and lungs. It can cause chills and a moderate to high fever. You may have a headache and muscle aches. You may feel tired. You may also have a dry cough, a sore throat, hoarseness, and a runny nose. At first you may think you only have a cold. The flu starts suddenly and gets worse faster than a cold. The flu lasts longer than a cold. Not everyone has the same symptoms. Older adults may not have high fevers. If you have no other complications, the flu usually lasts 7 to 14 days.

What to do about **Influenza**	
Symptoms/Signs	**Action**
◆ **Fever, scratchy throat, a feeling of soreness when breathing, cough, aches all over** ◆ **Fever of less than 101 degrees that lasts less than three days**	 Use self-care
◆ **Cough that produces a thick yellow or green mucus** ◆ **Symptoms that don't improve after seven days** ◆ **Fever of 101 degrees or higher with chills or muscle aches** ◆ **Symptoms that get worse**	Call doctor
◆ **Wheezing or difficulty breathing**	 Seek help now

When you have the flu, your body is less able to fight infections caused by bacteria. If you cannot fight infection well, you can get sicker. You can get bronchitis (SEE PAGE 98), pneumonia (SEE PAGE 107), or an ear infection (SEE PAGE 42). The flu can also cause problems that can be fatal.

What You Need to Know About the Flu Shot

You can avoid the flu by getting a flu shot. A flu shot can make flu season less dangerous.

Who Should Get the Shot? You should always get one if:
- You are older than 65.
- You have a chronic disease. These include heart disease, emphysema, asthma, kidney disease, bronchitis, or diabetes.

Who Should Not Get It? The flu vaccine comes from viruses that are grown in eggs. You should not get a flu shot if you are allergic to eggs. This allergy is rare. If you can eat eggs without getting ill, you don't need to worry. You can safely get a flu shot. Do not get a flu shot if you are allergic to thimerosal.

When to Get the Shot. The flu virus varies from year to year. So does the vaccine that fights it. That is why you have to get a flu shot every year. The fall is the best time to get it. Having it then will protect you for most of the flu season.

Side Effects. Some people do not get a flu shot because they think it will give them the flu. This is not true. Like any vaccine, the flu shot can cause some side effects. These include:
- pain where you received the shot
- general muscle aches
- a mild rash
- a slight fever

Side effects do not last as long as the flu. If you have a reaction to the shot, it is likely to start 6 to 12 hours after you get the vaccine. It may last for just a day or two.

These side effects are a lot like flu symptoms, so some people think the shot gave them the flu. They may not get a flu shot the next year because of this. But the vaccines have improved. The side effects of the newer shots are milder.

Self-Care: Influenza

There is no cure for the flu. But you can reduce the discomfort that it brings.
- Spend most of your time in bed. It is one of the best ways to deal with the flu. Make sure your room is warm and gets plenty of air. Stay there until you feel better. That will help you get the rest you need. And it keeps you from spreading the flu.
- Some antiviral drugs can ease the symptoms and prevent complications of the flu. These drugs may also keep you from catching the flu if you did not get a flu shot. Your doctor may prescribe these drugs.
- Follow the self-care steps for colds on page 102.

Lung Cancer

"I started smoking in 1935. Everyone smoked then. We didn't know it caused cancer. When they told us that it did, I smoked three packs of cigarettes a day. I smoked at work, at home, even at the movies. Quitting was the hardest thing I have ever done. It was also the smartest."

—Joe

Know the Warning Signs of Lung Cancer

The lungs are large organs. Cancer can invade the lungs and grow for many years before it is found. It can even spread outside the lungs without any obvious symptoms. If you have any of the these signs, talk with your doctor.

- Persistent cough. This is the most common symptom.
- Pain in the chest, back, or shoulder
- Shortness of breath or wheezing
- Fatigue
- Repeated pneumonia or bronchitis
- Coughing up blood
- Hoarseness
- Swelling of the neck and face
- Pain and weakness in the arm, shoulder, and hand. These may be present if a tumor is pressing on nerves in the lung.

Lung cancer is the widespread growth of abnormal cells in the lung. Today lung cancer kills more men and women in the United States than any other form of cancer.

Lung cancers are most often one of two types: nonsmall-cell lung cancer and small-cell lung cancer. The terms "small" and "nonsmall" refer to the size of the cells, not the size of the tumor. Lung cancer can spread to other parts of the body, such as the bones, brain, or liver.

How to Prevent Lung Cancer

- Don't smoke. Cigarette smoking is the number one cause of lung cancer. Even if you have smoked heavily for years, quit. For tips to help you quit, see page 300. You may be able to prevent lung cancer and other diseases if you quit. Many lives could be saved each year if no one smoked.
- Stay away from other people's tobacco smoke.
- Avoid things that cause cancer, such as radon and asbestos. You can do this if you pay attention to warnings in buildings and at work sites.

How Lung Cancer Is Diagnosed

If your doctor thinks that you may have lung cancer, he or she will advise you to have a series of tests. These tests will tell you if you have the disease. They can also tell how much the cancer has spread. The only way the doctor can know for sure if you have lung cancer is by examining some cells taken from your lung.

How Lung Cancer Is Treated

The way lung cancer is treated depends on many factors. Your doctor will suggest treatment based on your age and health history. Treatment also depends on the size and type of tumor. You may have more than one type of treatment. You may have surgery. Or you may have radiation or chemotherapy. (SEE COMMON WAYS CANCER IS TREATED, PAGE 16.)

Pleurisy

"I thought my bronchitis was over. I had stopped coughing. I felt less tired. But it hurt to breathe. The pain was gone, but I felt breathless. My wife took me to the doctor. I had fluid around my lungs. My doctor called it pleural effusion. She said it was one stage later than pleurisy."
—Milton

Your lungs are covered with a double membrane. The membrane is called the pleura. Normally, a thin layer of fluid fills the space between the two pleurae. This fluid moves inside the pleurae as you breathe. It protects the lungs. If you have an infection, the pleurae can become inflamed. This inflammation causes pain that limits the movement of your lungs. As a result, you may feel short of breath. You may have pain when you breathe. This is the condition doctors call pleurisy. If you have pleurisy, deep breathing may be very painful.

Pleurisy can occur after an injury, pneumonia, or some other serious lung infection. Since you are more likely to get these conditions as you age, you are also more likely to get pleurisy.

Pleurisy often clears up on its own. But if you think you have pleurisy, see your doctor. If you have it, your doctor may have you take an antibiotic.

Pleural Effusion. This may happen if pleurisy is not treated. Then excess fluid can build up between your lung and chest wall. You might not feel pain anymore. But you may feel short of breath. Pleural effusion is more serious than pleurisy. You may need to have the fluid drained.

Self-Care: Pleurisy

- You can ease the pain from pleurisy with a pain reliever such as acetaminophen (Tylenol) or ibuprofen (Advil).
- Apply heat to your chest to relieve discomfort.

Pneumonia

"Older adults can give themselves two gifts. One is the yearly flu vaccine and the other is the pneumonia shot."
—Internist

Pneumonia is an infection of the lungs. It is caused by a virus, bacteria, or fungus. In older adults, pneumonia often follows the flu, bronchitis, or a cold. It

What to do about **Pneumonia**

Symptoms/Signs	Action
◆ **Cough that lasts three weeks or more after a cold, the flu, or bronchitis** ◆ **Cold, flu, or bronchitis symptoms that last more than seven days** ◆ **Cold, flu, or bronchitis symptoms that suddenly get worse** ◆ **Coughing that produces green, yellow, or red-tinged mucus**	 Call doctor
◆ **Fever higher than 101 degrees with colored mucus, shortness of breath, or pain when breathing**	 See doctor
◆ **Cold, flu, or bronchitis with difficulty breathing**	 Call ambulance

can also develop when food or liquid enters your breathing tubes and travels to your lungs. Pneumonia is more common in older adults than in other age groups. It is the fifth leading cause of death in people age 65 and older.

Know the Warning Signs of Pneumonia

Symptoms of pneumonia include:
- coughing that produces white, yellow, green, or blood-streaked mucus
- fever with shaking and chills
- shortness of breath, chest pains, and pain when breathing
- extreme tiredness or weakness

Some people may not have any of these symptoms.

Older adults who are infected with pneumonia often get the illness quickly. A sudden change in mental alertness is sometimes the first obvious symptom.

Get medical care right away if you think you have pneumonia. If it takes you a long time to get better when you have the flu or bronchitis, see your doctor. Your doctor will listen to your chest and order a chest X-ray if needed. Antibiotics are the most common treatment for bacterial pneumonia. You may also have to spend a few days in the hospital. Get plenty of bed rest and drink extra fluids to help you recover from pneumonia.

How to Prevent Pneumonia

A pneumonia shot can prevent some kinds of pneumonia. This vaccine protects you against the most common causes of bacterial pneumonia. Talk with your doctor about this shot. (SEE BOX, NEXT PAGE.)

Pneumonia often follows a case of the flu. So you can get a yearly flu shot to help prevent pneumonia. (SEE BOX, PAGE 105.)

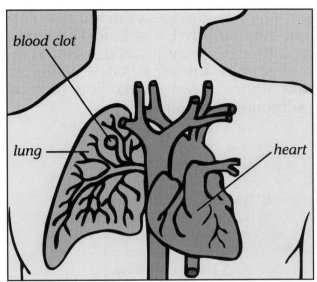

A blood clot may form in your leg. But it can travel through your heart. Then it may lodge in your lung. This kind of clot is called a pulmonary embolism.

What You Need to Know About the Pneumonia Shot

Who Should Get It? You should get this shot if:

- You are between the ages of 50 and 64 and have a chronic disease.
- You are older than 65, regardless of your health.
- You may need a booster. Ask your doctor.

When to Get It. Unlike the flu vaccine, the pneumonia vaccine lasts for many years. You may need to get the shot only once.

Side Effects. Side effects from the pneumonia vaccine are rare. The shot may cause your arm to swell and feel tender. Sometimes you may get a fever or rash.

Pulmonary Embolism

"After I had my car wreck, I was in the hospital for two weeks. Two nights before I was supposed to go home, I had chest pain. It got worse with each breath. Then I started coughing. My husband recognized the signs of an embolism and called the nurse. She told me I was lucky that he did."

—Irene

A clot may block the flow of blood in one of your blood vessels. This is called an embolism. A clot in your lung is called a pulmonary embolism.

These are the symptoms of a pulmonary embolism:

- sudden shortness of breath
- chest pain that gets worse when you take a deep breath
- a bloody cough
- anxiety, sweating, rapid heart rate
- pain and swelling in the calf (SEE PHLEBITIS, PAGE 94.)

Pulmonary embolisms are not rare. They occur most often in people who have to stay in bed. They may also occur in people who sit in one place too long. You should get up and move around as soon as you can after you have any type of surgery. This can help prevent blood clots. Embolisms can also happen after a stroke. They may also be caused by heart disease. They are always an emergency. Call an ambulance if you think you have a pulmonary embolism.

Wheezing

"An older patient came in for a routine visit. She had a cold and had been wheezing for several days. She did not seem to be in distress. She told me that her friend has asthma and often wheezes. Her friend is not alarmed by the wheezing. So my patient decided her wheezing was not serious. But it was. Her X-rays showed that she had pneumonia."

—Family doctor

If you hear a whistling sound from your chest when you breathe out, you are wheezing. Wheezing happens when the airways in the lungs get narrow. It is a sign that you are having a hard time breathing. Wheezing is a common symptom of asthma. (SEE PAGE 98.) It can also be caused by bronchitis, allergies, pneumonia, or even an object trapped in the airways. Wheezing is also caused by smoking, exposure to chemicals or pollution, and chronic diseases such as emphysema, lung cancer, or congestive heart failure.

You may already see your doctor for one of these conditions. You and your doctor may have decided on a plan of action. If the plan works, you don't

What to do about **Wheezing**	
Symptoms/Signs	**Action**
◆ **Mild bouts of wheezing if you have asthma** (SEE SELF-CARE: ASTHMA, PAGE 98.)	 Use self-care
◆ **Wheezing that lasts or gets worse after self-care and you have asthma** ◆ **Any new wheezing**	Call doctor
◆ **Wheezing and shortness of breath**	 Seek help now
◆ **Wheezing caused by an object lodged in the throat** (IF THE PERSON IS UNABLE TO BREATHE, TRY THE HEIMLICH MANEUVER. SEE PAGE 340.)	Call ambulance

need to run to the doctor's office each time you start to wheeze. Just follow your doctor's earlier advice.

If you don't have asthma or other chronic conditions and you start to wheeze, call your doctor. You may need medical care to avoid a major or chronic illness. Even if you think you know why you are wheezing, call your doctor. Call even if you think the problem is not serious.

Chapter 8

Mind and Body

We don't know all there is to know about how the mind affects our health. We are just finding out how important a healthy mind is when a person is sick. Research shows that a healthy mind affects treatment and recovery. And a person needs a healthy mind to have a good quality of life. It's clear that taking care of your mind is as important as taking care of your body.

Many conditions can affect your mind and body. Sometimes you can help yourself through anxious or sad feelings. But if you feel so anxious or depressed that you can't function normally, see your doctor. Your doctor may want you to see a mental health professional.

A psychiatrist is a medical doctor who has training in how to diagnose, treat, and prevent mental disorders. A psychologist is not a medical doctor but has at least a master's degree in psychology. A psychologist can test and counsel people who have mental or emotional problems.

This chapter covers some common problems that affect the mind and body. If you want to know more about these topics, talk with your doctor. You can also contact the groups listed at the end of this book. (SEE WHERE TO GET HELP, PAGE 321.)

Anxiety

"At one point I worried all the time. I worried about my job. I was afraid that my kids did not have what they needed. My doctor said that all that worrying was hurting my health. So I took a class to learn how to relax. Now I take 30 minutes each day to do exercises that help me relax."

—Peg

Everybody worries at times. You might worry about paying your bills. Crime might worry you. Or you might worry about getting sick and having to depend on your children. Some worry can be good. It may make you take steps to protect your health and safety. But for some people, worry can get in the way of doing day-to-day things. When this happens, doctors say the person has an anxiety disorder.

An anxiety disorder disrupts your daily life. It can make you think too much about little things that you don't need to worry about. For instance, you might spend all your time worrying about money. You may do this even if money is not a problem. You may worry about what you would do if you had no money. Likewise, an anxiety disorder may make you want to stay home when you don't need to. You may fear what might happen if you leave the house. You may be so full of fear that you can't enjoy life. You may not be able to visit friends or go on a trip. Anxiety can change the quality of your life. It can also go hand in hand with depression. (SEE PAGE 114.)

Generalized Anxiety Disorder

If you have generalized anxiety disorder, you may feel fearful and not know why. You may have this feeling for more than a month. Agitation may come with anxiety. When you are agitated, you can't stop moving. You might pace or be unable to sit still. You may also be anxious about certain things, such as becoming sick.

Anxiety makes you worry about things you have little or no reason to worry about. You may have trouble doing day-to-day chores such as grocery shopping. You may have problems relating to other people. Symptoms can include any of the following:

- being easily fatigued (SEE PAGE 117.)
- being irritable
- feeling keyed up, or on edge
- feeling restless
- having a hard time concentrating
- feeling that your mind has "gone blank"
- feeling muscle tension
- being unable to fall asleep or stay asleep
- having sleep that is not satisfying

Anxiety From Drugs or Certain Conditions

Some drugs can make you anxious. These include drugs for heart disease, thyroid problems, depression, and asthma. Over-the-counter drugs can make you anxious. A normal dose of the decongestant pseudoephedrine (Sudafed), for instance, can also cause anxiety. Caffeine can cause anxiety. Sometimes withdrawing from a drug can make you anxious. You may feel anxious when you stop drinking alcohol for instance. Quitting tranquilizers, such as Valium or Ativan, may have the same effect.

Some medical problems can cause anxiety. These conditions include:

- Alzheimer's disease
- asthma
- some kinds of cancer
- chronic constipation
- heart disease (congestive heart failure, irregular heartbeat, and others)
- incontinence
- lung disease
- motor problems that keep you from walking without help
- thyroid problems
- vision loss or hearing loss
- vitamin B12 deficiency

Panic Attacks

People who have anxiety may also have panic attacks. A panic attack is an episode of intense fear. It comes on "out of the blue" and builds to a peak, most often within 10 minutes. During a panic attack, you may have one or more of these symptoms:

- chest pain or discomfort
- chills, hot flashes, or sweating
- dizziness or fainting
- feeling as if you are choking
- feeling as if you need to escape
- numbness
- pounding or rapid heartbeat, or heart palpitations
- shortness of breath
- trembling

When you have a panic attack, you may fear that you are losing control.

You might think that you are going crazy, or even dying. Treatment can ease and prevent panic attacks.

Treatment for Anxiety Disorders

If you have an anxiety disorder, your doctor may tell you that you need to relax. You may need counseling. If you are so anxious that you can't cope with your daily tasks, you may need drugs. You may also need drugs if anxiety makes other health problems worse. For instance, it could make your high blood pressure even higher.

Your doctor may think that you need drugs if they have helped you in the past. The drugs used most often are Xanax and Ativan. Another drug used for general anxiety disorder is buspirone (BuSpar). This drug is not used for panic attacks.

Self-Care: Anxiety

- Talk with your doctor if you are so anxious that you can't get on with your daily life.
- Call your doctor if the symptoms last more than one week. Also call if you have had an anxiety disorder before.
- Tell your doctor about all the medicines you take. Tell him or her about over-the-counter drugs and herbal medicines. Some conditions and drugs can cause anxiety or make it worse. Your doctor may want you to change drugs or stop taking a certain drug.

- Get help for problems that may make you feel anxious. For instance, if you are losing your hearing, wear a hearing aid. (SEE HEARING AIDS, PAGE 45.)
- Learn relaxation techniques. (SEE HOW TO RELAX, PAGE 129.) Do them as part of your routine. Also do them when you feel anxious. Your doctor may know where you can learn more.
- Learn how to deal with stress. (SEE SELF-CARE: STRESS, PAGE 130.) You can learn to worry less and relax more.
- Don't eat chocolate or drink coffee, tea, or cola. The caffeine in them can make you more anxious.
- Don't use over-the-counter drugs that contain ephedrine. This drug is found in some over-the-counter decongestants and antihistamines. It can make you feel anxious. So can pseudoephedrine. This drug is found in Sudafed, NyQuil, and other products.

Finding new ways to handle stress can make you feel less anxious. Doing things with other people may help.

Depression

"I used to wish that I were dead. Even seeing my kids on the weekend did nothing to help. I thought they did not need me anymore. My doctor said I should take an antidepressant. I said no at first, but she convinced me that it might help. Now I wonder why I waited so long."
—Rosa

Everyone feels blue from time to time. Stress can make you feel sad. Bad news or bad weather can make you sad. You may even feel sad for no reason at all. Adjusting to retirement can cause mood changes. So can grieving over the death of a loved one or moving out of your home. These feelings are normal. But sad feelings that last for weeks or months are more than just "the blues."

When sadness gets in the way of normal living, it is called depression. Depression is not a blue mood that comes now and then. It affects your whole body. It also affects your feelings, thoughts, and actions. Depression is not a sign of weakness. You can't will it or wish it away. Truly depressed people are not able to just "snap out of it" and get better.

The following four facts about depression could save your life. If you know them, you might also help save someone else's life.
1. Major depression is a medical illness. It is not a character flaw.
2. If not treated, depression can lead to suicide.

Know the Signs of Depression

Depression can cause one or more of these symptoms:
- excessive crying
- feeling guilty, worthless, or helpless
- inability to enjoy life
- loss of appetite or weight loss
- mood change (feeling cranky, anxious, sad, or all of these)
- poor concentration
- sleep problems, such as waking early in the morning or over-sleeping (SEE INSOMNIA, PAGE 121.)
- suicide attempt or thoughts of death or suicide
- tiredness (SEE FATIGUE, PAGE 117.)
- vague aches and pains, such as headaches, backaches, or stomachaches
- weight gain

If you think you are depressed, or if your symptoms don't go away in a week or two, see your doctor. Depression can be treated and cured. Without treatment, your symptoms may not improve. And they could get worse.

3. Most people can be helped. Treatment almost always works.
4. The goal of treatment is not just to get better, but to stay well.

Many people think that it is normal for older people to get depressed. It is not. Severe depression is more common in younger people than in older people. But depression seems to take a bigger toll as we get older. When you are depressed, it takes you longer to recover from an illness or pain. Depression can lead to suicide. Older white males are at particularly high risk for suicide. Feeling depressed and anxious at the same time is common. (SEE ANXIETY, PAGE 112.)

Who Is At Risk for Depression?

Depression can run in families. And people who have been depressed before are more likely than others to be depressed in the future. Many other factors can lead to depression. Those factors include:
- alcohol use
- an uneven balance of chemicals in the brain
- poor self-image, or viewing yourself in a negative way
- feeling that the challenges in your life are too great
- a major loss, problems in a relationship, or sudden life changes
- some drugs, such as steroids or drugs for high blood pressure

Some health problems make you more likely to be depressed. Some common illnesses that occur with depression include:
- alcoholism
- Alzheimer's disease
- chronic illness
- heart disease
- Parkinson's disease
- strokes, even small ones from which you have recovered

How Doctors Treat Depression

Treatment for depression can include counseling, drugs, or both. People who are treated with drugs take them each day. Most people start to feel better within 4 to 6 weeks. It is most common to take these drugs for at least 6 to 12 months.

Counseling can give you support. A counselor helps people work on their problems. If you are depressed, you might see a counselor by yourself. Or you may see a counselor as part of a group or with your spouse or family.

Self-Care: Depression

- Don't expect to snap out of your depression all at once. Most people don't get better right away. It takes weeks and even months for treatment to work. Give yourself time. Don't blame yourself for not being "up to par."
- It may help to talk about what you are going through with people you feel close to.
- If you take antidepressant drugs, take them the way your doctor tells you to. When you start to feel better, don't stop taking the drugs. Your doctor will tell you when to stop.
- Tell your doctor about any drug side effects. Tell your doctor if you find it hard to lead a normal life.
- Keep all follow-up visits you have with your doctor. Don't miss a visit, even if you feel better that day.

- Don't set goals you can't meet. If big projects are too much to handle, don't take them on.
- Break large tasks into small ones. Do the most important things first. Don't be hard on yourself if you can't get them all done.
- Do things that make you feel better. Try some exercise. Or go to an art show or a movie you have wanted to see.
- Do things with other people so that you don't cut yourself off from the world.
- Don't drink alcohol. Don't take drugs unless your doctor prescribes them. Some drugs can make you feel more depressed.

Exercise can ease depression. It may seem strange, but sometimes if you do more, you will have less fatigue. Regular exercise can help you feel more energetic. It can also help prevent insomnia. (SEE PAGE 121.)

- Make sure to tell any doctor you see that you are depressed. Then if you need to take a drug, your doctor can prescribe the right one.
- If you feel so bad that you want to kill yourself, seek help right away.

Fatigue

"I laughed when my son told me that I should get out of the house more. He said I should volunteer in some way. I could barely do my own housework. But one day I took his advice. I offered to read to children at the library. Now I stay busy all the time. And I have more energy than I ever did."

—Connie

Fatigue is an overwhelming sense of being tired. It makes you too tired to move. If you don't have enough variety in your day, you may feel bored and tired. Most fatigue is brought on by hard work or exertion. This kind of fatigue can be cured if you get enough sleep and eat healthy meals. But when rest and good food don't help, your body is sending you a message. The fatigue you feel may mean that something else is wrong.

Depression (SEE PAGE 114) and anxiety (SEE PAGE 112) can cause fatigue. Both can be treated. You may have fatigue with any of the following illnesses:
- alcoholism
- anemia
- cancer
- diabetes
- heart disease
- hepatitis
- hypothyroidism
- rheumatoid arthritis
- sleep disorder
- urinary tract infection
- viral infection

Drugs can also cause fatigue. Over-the-counter drugs that cause problems include these:
- allergy remedies
- cough and cold medicines
- motion sickness pills
- pain relievers
- sleeping pills

Some prescription drugs can cause fatigue too. These include:
- drugs to reduce blood pressure
- muscle relaxants
- sedatives
- tranquilizers

Self-Care: Fatigue

You can try many things to reduce your fatigue. Managing stress is one way to ease fatigue. (SEE SELF-CARE: STRESS, PAGE 130.) If these steps don't help, call your doctor.

Get enough rest. Use your energy wisely.
- Most people need five to nine hours of sleep each night. If you can, go to bed and wake up at the same time every day.

- Keep a record of how you feel. Make note of when you have the most energy and when you feel tired. Plan activities for times that you have the most energy.
- Save your energy. When you have too much to do, ask others to help you. Learn how to say no when you have enough to do.
- Make some changes in your routine. They may help you find new energy and be less bored.

Make healthy choices.
- Exercise. You should exercise three to five times a week. If you are not used to exercising, start slowly. Then build up to 20 to 30 minutes each time. Move around as much as you can during the day. (SEE THE ACTIVITY PYRAMID, PAGE 292.)
- Avoid late-night activities. They can disrupt your sleep and make you tired in the morning.
- Lose weight if you are overweight. Eat balanced meals and avoid crash diets.
- Quit smoking. (SEE PAGE 300.) Smoking steals some of your body's oxygen. With less oxygen in your blood, you have less pep. However, nicotine is a stimulant. If you quit smoking, you may feel tired while your body withdraws from nicotine. In time, though, you should have more energy.
- Watch less TV. Watching too much TV can make you lazy. Read a book or take a walk. When you stimulate your mind and body, you have more energy.

Think about what and when you eat and drink.
- Drink less caffeine and alcohol. Alcohol slows you down and makes you feel tired. At first, caffeine boosts your energy. But when the effect wears off, you feel more tired than you did before you drank it.
- Eat at the times of day that are best for you. Some people feel best when they eat a light lunch. Others need to make lunch their biggest meal of the day.
- Eat foods that are low in fat. Your body takes longer to digest fat. Too much fat will slow you down.
- Eat less at each meal, but eat more often.

Grief and Loss

"When my wife died, it felt as if my whole world had ended. Friends helped, but it took a long time for me to get over her death. One thing I had to learn was to let myself cry. I still miss her, but now I am able to smile when I think about the good times we had."
—Roger

The longer you live, the more likely you are to lose people you love. The death of a spouse or partner is one of the hardest things you can go through. It is hard no matter how good or bad the relationship was. As you grow older, you may also lose parents, brothers and sisters, and friends. Losing an adult child is extremely hard. Even the death of a pet can be painful.

Grief is personal. People with the same kind of loss may grieve in different ways. How long and hard you grieve may be different from how others grieve. The way you grieve may even change from one loss to another.

The Causes of Grief

When people hear the word grief, they most often think of death. But death is just one kind of loss you may face. Any change is a kind of loss. Even a good change is a loss. And each loss has to be mourned. Besides death, losses that may cause grief include the following:

- Loss of friends or changes in friendships. You may feel this loss when a friend moves far away. People who are widowed often feel ignored by couples who were once their friends.
- Loss of a home. You may feel loss when you move to a smaller place, a retirement community, or a nursing home. Even moving in with a family member can feel like a loss.
- Loss of health. People who learn that they have a terminal illness go through grief. A terminal illness is one that has no cure and that will result in death. You may also feel this loss if you find out that you have a chronic illness. A chronic illness is one you will always have, such as emphysema, arthritis, or heart disease.
- Loss of freedom or mobility. You might grieve when you can't do even small things you once could.

You might grieve for any kind of loss. People don't grieve only about death. For instance, losing your ability to walk is a loss you may grieve.

- Changes in relationships and family roles. Some people grieve if they feel they have become like a child to their own children.
- Loss of a dream or failure to reach a goal. People may feel this loss when they retire before they reach a career goal.
- Loss of social life. Many people feel this loss when they quit work.

What to Expect When You Grieve

The process of grieving is called bereavement. Grief does not follow any set rule or order. And there are no rules about how long each phase should last.

You may not feel grief all of the time. Grief is more likely to come in waves. Sometimes you will feel saddened by a sight, a sound, a smell, or a place. These things can make you think about your loss or about the person who died. Sometimes you will have strong and painful feelings but won't know why.

Feelings that come from grief should fade with time. Some people have constant sadness, anger, despair, or other feelings for more than six months. If this happens to you, talk with your doctor or a counselor. You may be going through depression. (SEE PAGE 114.)

Self-Care: Grief

- Don't hold back your feelings. It is OK to cry. It is OK to be angry. As long as you are moving from one feeling to another, your grief is normal.
- Share your memories. They can help you heal from grief. Make a long-distance call if you have to. It may help to share your memories with a friend or relative who cares.
- If you are stuck thinking for weeks and weeks of nothing but your loss, get help to move on. You may be angry for so long that it gets in the way of your daily life.

  If you are stuck, join a grief support group or talk with a counselor. A counselor can help you find a support group. Or call the American Association of Retired Persons. (SEE PAGE 322.) It sponsors such groups, and there may be one near you. Talk with a member of the clergy. This can be a comfort at any point in your grief.

- Take care of your health. Eat a balanced diet. Try to get a good night's sleep. Take time out each day for a walk or other exercise.
- Keep in mind that alcohol and sedatives do not truly ease your grief. If you use them, you may end up needing more time to grieve. Alcohol can also lead to depression. Get help if you need it. It is important to face your loss. To be well emotionally, you need to grieve.
- In the first few months after the death of a spouse, don't make major life changes. For instance, don't move to a new place. Don't sell or give away the things you love. Don't sell your home or move in with family. Don't have someone move in with you permanently.

  Wait before you change things in ways that you can't change back. Take time to think about what you want. If someone moves in with you, make sure that he or she knows it is only for a short while. Take time to decide where and how you want to live.

- When you feel ready to make your own choices, thank your family and friends for their help. But don't feel guilty about saying what kinds of help you don't want. Clearly tell them what you need. This will help avoid frustration and hard feelings.
- If your family has a hard time solving problems, have a family meeting. Ask a counselor or a member of the clergy to be there. Otherwise the meeting may do more harm than good.

- If you are worried about money, get financial advice. If health is a concern, ask your doctor, a social worker, or a nurse about support services.
- For more ways to help you through grief, see sections on stress (SEE PAGE 128), loneliness (SEE PAGE 123), and depression (SEE PAGE 114).

Insomnia

"When I was younger, I never had a problem going to sleep. About a year ago, I would lie in bed with my eyes wide open. I started taking a walk every day. Walking seems to help. I don't have so many sleepless nights anymore."
—Beverly

When you have trouble sleeping, doctors call it insomnia. Insomnia may be caused by normal changes as you age. It can also be caused by changes in your routine, your health, or the drugs you take.

As you age, the way you sleep may change. You may have heard that you need less sleep as you get older. This is not true. Your body needs just as much sleep as it always has. For an adult, that is five to nine hours each day. But your need for sleep spreads out over the course of the whole day. You can't stay up as late as you once could. You may have more trouble falling asleep at night. You may wake up more during the night. You may not feel as rested as you once did after sleeping. If you don't get all the sleep you need, you may feel drowsy during the day and take more naps. These changes may be a bit annoying, but they are normal.

Excitement or anxiety can cause insomnia. (SEE ANXIETY, PAGE 112.) You may have trouble sleeping when there are big changes in temperature. A new bed, loud noises, or too much light can wake you or keep you awake. Changes in your routine can cause sleep problems. So can losing a spouse or a friend. (SEE GRIEF AND LOSS, PAGE 118.) Eating too much or drinking alcohol or caffeine can cause sleep problems.

Drugs can affect your sleep. The nicotine in cigarettes can cause problems. Taking diuretics may cause you to get up to urinate. If you take a drug that interferes with your sleep, your doctor may want you to take a different drug. Talk with your doctor if you have a hard time sleeping and take drugs for any of the following conditions:
- arthritis
- asthma
- colds or flu
- depression
- emphysema
- high blood pressure
- kidney disease
- Parkinson's disease

Illnesses can disturb sleep. If you are sick, you may not exercise. When you don't get enough exercise, it can be hard to sleep. Talk with your doctor if you think one of these conditions interferes with your sleep:
- angina
- arthritis
- asthma

- congestive heart failure
- heartburn
- migraines
- ulcers
- urinary tract infection

Sleep problems can be a sign of depression. (SEE PAGE 114.) If you think you may be depressed, talk with your doctor. Your doctor can treat depression, and that treatment might cure your insomnia.

Self-Care: Insomnia

When your normal sleep pattern is disturbed, it may take a few weeks to form a new one. Or it may take time to return to your normal sleep pattern. Try the following steps to get a better night's sleep. If these steps don't help, you should call your doctor. Your doctor may want to evaluate your problem. Then he or she can help you find ways to sleep better.

Use routines to help you sleep.
- Get up and go to bed at the same time each day. Keep the same schedule on weekends. Your body has an internal clock. It works best when you stick to a daily routine.
- Clear your mind of worry before you go to bed. Set aside 30 minutes early in the evening. Use that time to work on problems that might keep you up later. Make lists and plan ways that you can work out your problems the next day.

- Take a warm bath an hour or two before bedtime. A bath can soothe tense muscles. It can also make you sleepy. A bath right before bed may not work because it may rouse you. Try different times to see what works for you.
- Read in bed for a while. Reading can help you relax and make you feel drowsy.
- Picture yourself in a pleasant place. Imagine that you hear relaxing sounds as you drift off to sleep.

Plan activities each day that will help you sleep.
- Be physically active during the day. Activity will help ease tension and clear your head. It will also tire you out so that you can sleep better. (SEE THE ACTIVITY PYRAMID, PAGE 292.)
- Avoid hard physical activity in the four hours before bed. This kind of activity can keep you awake.
- Get some exposure to daylight. Go outside in the morning and in the afternoon. This will help adjust your internal clock. You will see nighttime more as a time for sleep.
- Don't take long naps late in the day. A nap that lasts 20 minutes or less can be refreshing. Longer naps and naps after 4 P.M. may upset your sleep patterns. These naps can make it harder to fall asleep at bedtime.

Think about what and when you eat and drink.
- Avoid caffeine, or cut down on it. Caffeine stays in your system for

12 to 24 hours. Caffeine is in coffee, chocolate, and many colas and teas. If you think caffeine causes your sleep problems, don't have any caffeine for at least 12 hours before you go to bed.

- Don't eat a big meal right before you go to bed. A full stomach may keep you awake. Try a light snack instead.
- Many people drink a glass of warm or cold milk before bed. If you don't like plain milk, add a bit of honey, cinnamon, or vanilla. Milk has a substance in it that can promote sleep.
- Don't drink alcohol at night. It can keep you from deep sleep. Even though you may fall asleep quickly, you may wake up suddenly and often.

Avoid over-the-counter drugs that can keep you awake.

- Some over-the-counter drugs can keep you awake. These include decongestants, such as Sudafed. Pain relievers that contain caffeine can also keep you awake. For instance, Extra Strength Excedrin has caffeine.
- Some cold medicines have phenylpropanolamine. This drug can be as bad for sleep as caffeine. Before taking a drug, ask your pharmacist if it might keep you awake. If it might, ask your pharmacist what drug may help you instead.

Make your bedroom a restful place.

- Keep your bedroom cool. A temperature between 60 and 65 degrees is best for sleeping.

- Use a firm, comfortable mattress. It will help you get a good night's sleep.
- Your bedroom should be quiet and dark. If noise is a problem, try using earplugs when you sleep. Or you might try "white noise." The sound of a fan or an air conditioner helps many people.

Loneliness

"I like craft fairs, and it seems I can always find one somewhere. I go with two or three friends. We have fun, and sometimes we get new ideas for hobbies."
—Ben

If you stay active and stay involved with others, you may live longer. If you are lonely and isolated, you can get depressed. (SEE PAGE 114.) Loneliness can also cause anxiety. (SEE PAGE 112.) If you are grieving, loneliness can make you feel worse. Staying in touch with other people is important for your good health.

It is not always easy to fight off loneliness and stay active. As you get older, your family and social networks change. After you retire, you may fall out of touch with people you have known for years. Your friends may move to be closer to their children. You may do the same. Some of your friends and relatives may die.

Health problems can also lead to isolation and loneliness. For instance, if you have trouble walking, you may lose touch with your friends. Hearing loss may make it hard for you to talk with family and friends. This can frustrate and isolate you.

Self-Care: Loneliness

Everyone feels lonely once in a while. But if you feel lonely most of the time, you can do something about it. Take action that can improve your emotional, mental, and physical health. To stay involved, take some of the following steps.

Strengthen your network.
- Routinely call or see people you like.
- Look up old friends. Find ways to make new ones. New friends can add spice to your life. The friendship can satisfy both of you.
- Seek out events and social gatherings in your neighborhood. Look for chances to go to art displays and craft shows. Attend lectures and plays. Go to yard sales and block parties. Check newspapers and bulletin boards to find out what events are planned.
- Invite people to your home.
- Make a date to share meals with a friend or neighbor who is also alone.
- Take care of health problems that isolate you. If it is hard for you to hear, get a hearing aid. Or talk with your doctor about how to increase your mobility.
- Share experiences and feelings with your friends. Be a good listener. Help your friends and let them help you.

- Make an effort to stay in touch. Write letters and use the phone. Send greeting cards to stay in touch with people you care about. If you have access to a computer, you might like the Internet.
- Get a pet. A pet can ward off loneliness. It can also help lower your blood pressure, decrease anxiety, and prevent or ease depression. If space or cost is a problem, a bird makes a good pet.
- Go for a walk with a neighbor every day, or as often as you can.
- Stay positive. Stay away from negative people.

Be a volunteer or a mentor.
You have a lifetime's worth of skills, knowledge, and wisdom. Share those riches with others. When you give your time, you get back a feeling that you are needed. You may make friends. You also get the joy that comes from helping.
- Find ways to volunteer where you live. Check the White Pages of your phone book under United Way. This group has a telephone referral service called First Call for Help. It can help you find an agency that needs your skills.
- Call a local chapter of the American Red Cross. Or call the volunteer coordinator at any of these places: American Cancer Society, American Arthritis Foundation, or Courage Centers. You can find their numbers in the phone book.
- Donate some time to a local hospital or nursing home.

- Offer your time to your place of worship.
- Volunteer at a museum, theater, library, or historical society.
- Serve as a mentor through the Service Corps of Retired Executives (S.C.O.R.E), a local chapter of the Optimist Club, or a similar group. This kind of group may want you to advise others on career or personal issues.

Build friendships across generations.
People who live long, active lives have friends of all ages. Many older adults find that being with children is a source of energy and joy. If you live in a retirement community, you may need to make a special effort to have contact with people of other ages. Here are some things you might do:

- Spend time with grandchildren. If you don't have any, "borrow" some from a friend or relative. Offer to baby-sit or take the children for an outing.
- Donate your time at a local school or day-care center.
- Become involved in mixed-age groups or clubs. Join a book club. Go to a religious study group. Join a political or community group. Play sports or help out in a neighborhood league.

Continue to work.
Retiring from your job does not mean that you have to stop working. A part-time job can help keep you from being lonely and bored. From serving fast food to consulting, you can do something to keep busy. Find out how much money you can earn without losing your retirement benefits.

Be a lifelong learner.
When learning is a lifelong habit, life seems more rewarding. You build new skills. You challenge your mind. You understand things better. Most important, you keep growing and changing. You also have more to talk about with other people. That can make you a more interesting friend.

- Study a foreign language.
- Learn to play a musical instrument. Or relearn one that you once played.
- Take some college or community education courses in a field that has always interested you. Or get a college degree.
- Read books, newspapers, and magazines.
- Join a Toastmasters International club. Learn public speaking.
- Join an Elderhostel program. That way you can travel and see the world.

Life seems more rewarding when you keep learning. Playing an instrument is one way to keep your mind active.

Memory

"I pride myself on my good memory. I am sure it comes from all the crossword puzzles and word games I do. But my memory goes to pot when I have too many distractions."
—Sylvia

Your memory changes as you age. You may not recall bits of information, such as "to-do" lists. You may forget a name. Or you may forget the reason you came into a room.

How Your Memory Works

This is how your memory works: Your brain receives signals, and it processes them in three ways. It encodes information, stores it, and retrieves it.

Encoding. When your brain encodes, it translates what you see, hear, feel, smell, or taste into a form it can store as memory. For instance, the first time you heard a bird sing, someone told you what it was. In your mind, you put together the sound you heard and how the bird looked. Then you attached the idea of a bird to them.

Storing. Then you stored this information. That means that you saved this message in your brain. Birds became a part of your memory.

Retrieving. Each time you see or hear a bird, your brain retrieves the stored information. It finds the information it stored long ago. Your brain tells you that what you see or hear is a bird.

Things That Affect Your Memory

How well you can remember depends on the following things:

How focused you are. If you are distracted, stressed, or tired, it may be hard to encode or retrieve memories.

How sharp your senses are. If you have trouble seeing or hearing, it may be hard to understand information. In turn, you may have trouble remembering. Treating your sensory problem will help your memory improve.

How well you store information. This depends on whether you have healthy brain cells. Alzheimer's disease, a stroke, and other illnesses can destroy brain cells. If a storage problem causes memory loss, it can't be treated and it won't improve.

What disorders or conditions you have. Depression can cause memory loss. So can poor nutrition and hypothyroidism. When diagnosed, this type of memory loss can be treated and reversed.

Memory Loss Versus Dementia

A term doctors use for permanent memory loss is dementia. Dementia is a brain disease. It is not a normal part of the aging process. Its effects can't be reversed. Alzheimer's disease is the most common form of late-life dementia. (SEE PAGE 171.) It is a progressive dementia. That means it gets worse over time. A type of progressive dementia can be caused by strokes. (SEE MULTI-INFARCT DEMENTIA, PAGE 186.) It can also be caused by lack of oxygen or trauma. These may not be progressive.

Self-Care: Memory

To keep your memory sharp, give it a workout by doing these things:
- Make reading a habit. Read books, magazines, or the newspaper. When you read, you challenge your mind and sharpen your memory. Try to learn a new fact each day.
- Organize, don't memorize. Make lists rather than trusting your memory. Make a special place for those things you always lose, such as your wallet, car keys, or watch. Always put them in that place when you are not using them.
- Do mental gymnastics. Play bridge, Scrabble, or cribbage. Fill out crossword puzzles. These things will make your mind more lively.
- Have your eyes and ears checked. You will not remember things that you don't see or hear. Wear your hearing aid or glasses when you need to.

How to Remember New Information

For better recall of new information try these methods. Here we use the example of remembering a new name. But you could use the same method for other new information, such as the title of a book.
- Focus on the new information. To remember a new name, for instance, focus your attention and listen carefully. Ask to have the name repeated if you do not hear it well the first time.
- Repeat the information. Say the name right away. Repeat the name three or four times within the next few minutes.
- Link the new information to something you already know. What rhymes with the name? What does the name make you think of? What about the person seems to fit with the name? Remember the name, the person, and the setting where you met. Say them aloud.

- Associate. Link new information with visual images. For instance, if you have just met Bill Swanson, think of a "swan" holding a dollar "bill." (SEE HOW TO REMEMBER NEW INFORMATION, ABOVE.)

Stress

"I used to feel a lot of stress all the time. Once I had chest pains that I thought were a heart attack. That's when I decided I wasn't going to do that to myself anymore. Now I always exercise. And I always take time to relax. I even do deep breathing exercises every day."

—Wilt

Some stress is good. Stress can drive you to do the things you need to do. It can make life interesting. But too much stress can be bad for your body and your emotions.

The following signs may mean that you have too much stress:
- backache
- change in sleeping habits
- cold hands and feet
- eating more or less than usual
- feeling nervous or tired
- headache
- tight muscles and stiffness in and around the neck

Many things can cause stress. Retiring can be stressful. Caring for a sick spouse or parent is stressful. So is grieving the death of a loved one. Stress can come from money worries, loss of a job, or moving to a new home.

These things don't even have to happen for you to feel stress. Just thinking about them can cause stress. And dealing with day-to-day hassles can cause as much stress as larger events.

Too much stress or stress over a long time can make you feel anxious, angry, grouchy, or even depressed. You may feel a lack of interest in life. When faced with stress, some people quit eating or eat too much. Others find it hard to think clearly, or they make more mistakes than usual. They even make mistakes while doing simple tasks. Too much stress can make you more likely to get colds or the flu.

Smokers often smoke more when they are stressed. People who have quit may start smoking again. Some people turn to alcohol or other drugs. These habits often create more problems.

You may not be able to change a stressful situation. But you may be able to change how you think about it and react to it. Think about whether it makes sense to feel the amount of stress you are feeling. Some things may be serious. Other things may not be worth the worry. Practice the self-care steps for stress. (SEE PAGE 130.) Learn new ways to relax. (SEE BOX.) If you take these steps, you may learn to manage stress better.

If you feel you can't function in your daily life, see your doctor or a counselor. A counselor may be a social worker, a psychologist, or another mental health professional. Seek help if you start to feel helpless or depressed. Read the sections on depression (SEE PAGE 114), anxiety (SEE PAGE 112), grief (SEE PAGE 118), loneliness (SEE PAGE 123), or caregiving (SEE PAGE 307). These sections give more information about things that cause stress.

How to Relax

Here are two relaxation exercises you can try. If you take medicine or have a health condition, talk with your doctor before you try either exercise.

Technique 1: Mental Imagery

1. Sit comfortably. (You can learn to do this technique while you stand too. Then you can do it while you wait in line.)
2. Take a deep breath through your nose. Hold it as you count to five slowly.
3. Exhale slowly through your mouth and tell all your muscles to relax.
4. Repeat steps 2 and 3 several more times to relax even more. Do this until you can feel your breathing slow down.
5. If you get stuck on one thought, quietly tell it "no." Move on to other thoughts.
6. Think of something pleasant and positive. Picture a pleasant scene such as a calm lake or a mountain stream. Use all of your senses to picture the scene. See it in your mind. Think about how your calm spot sounds. Think about how it smells and how you feel while you are there.
7. Once your pleasant scene starts to replace your thoughts, let it fade. Then picture a gray or black "nothingness."
8. Let blue colors drift into your mind. You might see patches of blue.

When you see the blue, you often have no muscle tension left in your body. Both your body and mind may feel more relaxed.

9. Tell yourself something positive. For instance, say, "I am able to relax. I can handle this."

Technique 2: Deep Breathing

1. Choose a quiet spot and get comfortable.
2. Gently blow out all the air that is in your lungs.
3. Slowly count to four while you inhale through your nose. Count "1-and-2-and-3" and so on.
4. Hold your breath for another count of four.
5. Exhale through your mouth slowly as you count to four.
6. Do slow, rhythmic breathing again for a few minutes. Take as much time to breathe in as you do to breathe out. Breathe deeper than you usually do. If you are breathing as you should, your chest will barely move. This means that you are breathing from your diaphragm. Your abdomen will expand and contract.
7. Repeat these steps until you feel relaxed.

A good belly laugh is one of the best stress busters. Look for humor in life. Spend time with people you enjoy.

Self-Care: Stress

- Breathe deeply and slowly. The more deeply you breathe, the more oxygen you will take into your body. Oxygen gives you energy.
- Take a break from your daily tasks. If you have not had a vacation in a while, take one. Or just set aside a quiet time to relax at home.
- Find ways to calm yourself. Listen to music or relaxation tapes. Repeat a word, phrase, or prayer that gives you a sense of peace. Picture yourself on a beach, at the mountains, or in a favorite quiet spot. (SEE BOX, PAGE 129.)
- Exercise regularly. (SEE THE ACTIVITY PYRAMID, PAGE 292.) Walk, swim, or do other activities that make you breathe harder and increase your heart rate. These are great stress relievers. Gentle stretching can also help. It loosens the tight muscles that stress can cause.
- Make a list of things in your life that cause stress. Put a check mark next to things you can do something about. Then make a plan for dealing with the things you can change.
- Look for ways to bring balance to your life. Find time for family, friends, work, play, and spirituality. Do the things that bring you meaning and pleasure.
- Don't try to do everything by yourself. Share your work with others. A shared burden is easier to carry. You may make new friends or learn other ways to solve problems.
- Look for humor in your day. Laughing is one of the best ways to deal with stress. Even the most stressful problem may be funny in some way. Add humor to your life. Watch a funny movie or read a humorous book or the comics.
- Take time to have fun. Spend time with friends. Work on a favorite hobby. Start a new one. Listen to relaxing music. Or simply soak in a nice warm bath.
- Organize your time. Don't put things off. Focus on the steps you should take to get a job done. Do one step at a time.
- Talk with a friend or a family member. Your thoughts and fears will be less of a burden if you share them.
- Avoid caffeine. It can increase your sense of stress.

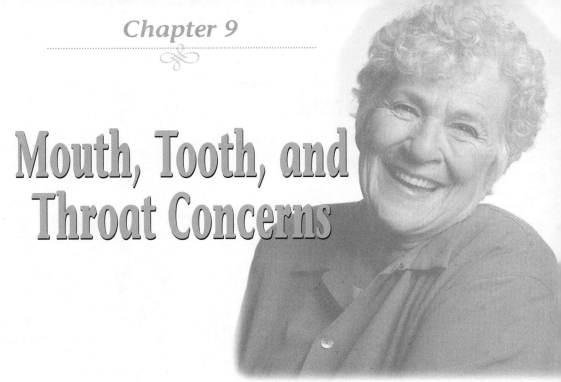

Chapter 9

Mouth, Tooth, and Throat Concerns

Many things can affect the health of your mouth, teeth, gums, and throat. Luckily, most of these types of problems are not serious. You can take steps to get rid of bad breath, to keep your teeth healthy, and to ease a sore throat. But at times you may need help from a doctor. For instance, if bacteria have caused a sore throat, it must be treated with antibiotics. You should also see your doctor for sores on the mouth that don't heal or lumps that don't go away.

Your doctor can treat many of the conditions you will read about here. For some problems, your doctor may refer you to a specialist. A periodontist is a dentist who deals with gum disease. An otolaryngologist treats ear, nose, and throat concerns. An oncologist treats cancer.

This chapter has three parts. One part is about mouth concerns. The next part covers tooth and gum concerns. The third part covers throat concerns.

Mouth Concerns

Keep your mouth clean and healthy. Doing this will help your appearance. It will help prevent bad breath. And it may prevent health problems later.

How to Keep Your Mouth Clean
To keep your mouth clean, follow these steps:
- Brush your teeth after every meal or at least twice a day.
- Drink water that has fluoride in it. Call your local water department and ask if your water has fluoride. If it does not, ask your dentist if you need a fluoride supplement.
- Eat healthy foods. (SEE EATING FOR YOUR HEALTH, PAGE 287.)
- Floss your teeth every day. (SEE DRAWING, PAGE 132.)
- See your dentist for routine cleanings and checkups. Ask him or her how often you should do this.

Bad Breath

"In the past, people seemed to back away when I talked to them. I figured out that I had bad breath. The dental hygienist who cleans my teeth says that brushing won't stop bad breath. She told me to floss at least once a day and brush after every meal."

—Murray

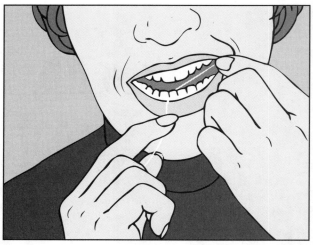

Place the floss between two teeth. Hold both ends of the floss. Curve the floss around one tooth. Start at the bottom of the tooth. Move the floss back and forth against the tooth as you move up from the gum. Curve the floss against the next tooth to floss it.

What to do about **Bad Breath**	
Symptoms/Signs	**Action**
◆ **Most cases of bad breath**	Use self-care
◆ **Bad breath that does not improve with self-care**	Call doctor
◆ **Bad breath caused by tooth or gum disease** (SEE PERIODONTAL DISEASE, PAGE 139.)	See dentist

Doctors call bad breath halitosis. Many people have bad breath but don't know it. Most people don't like to tell you if your breath is bad. But you can find out if you have bad breath. One way is to ask someone to tell you. You can also check your breath. To check your breath, cup your hands over your mouth. Then exhale into your hands. Sniff what you have exhaled. If it smells bad, you have bad breath. You can also use dental floss to see if you have bad breath. Take a piece of floss and floss between your back teeth. Smell the floss when you are done. If it smells bad, you probably have bad breath.

Some types of medicine can cause bad breath. These include diuretics, antihistamines, and tranquilizers. Colds, sinus infections, tonsillitis, and pneumonia can also cause bad breath. The bacteria that cause the illness can also cause bad breath. Or the illness may cause you to breathe with your mouth open. That can lead to dry mouth (SEE PAGE 134), which can cause bad breath.

Self-Care: Bad Breath

- Avoid foods that have a strong smell. Onions and garlic can give you bad breath. Your breath can smell for a day or so after you eat these foods.
- Take self-care steps if you have a dry mouth. (SEE SELF-CARE: DRY MOUTH, PAGE 134.) A dry mouth can cause bad breath.
- Don't eat breath mints made with sugar. The bacteria that cause bad breath thrive on sugar.
- Brush your tongue at least once a day. Doing so will help get rid of food odor.
- Chew fresh mint leaves. Or use mouthwash or mouth spray. Any of these can hide bad breath for a while. But none will totally get rid of the problem.
- Eat raw vegetables and fruit. The rough texture of apples, oranges, lettuce, and carrots can clean your teeth. Plaque is a sticky white film that builds up on your teeth. (SEE PERIODONTAL DISEASE, PAGE 139.) Bacteria feed on old food and plaque that cling to your teeth, gums, and tongue. Some bacteria cause bad odor.
- Follow the tips for how to keep your mouth clean. (SEE PAGE 131.)
- If you smoke, get help to quit. The tar and nicotine in cigarettes coat your teeth, your tongue, and the inside of your mouth. This makes your breath smell bad.

Cancer of the Lip and Mouth

"My mouth had been sore for a while. I finally went to the dentist. She found a small lump under my tongue. I was scared. She sent me to an oral surgeon, who gave me some Novocain. Then he took a bit of tissue from the lump and sent it to a lab. It turned out I had mouth cancer. I am glad my dentist caught the problem early. I had the lump taken out. Now I feel fine. I was very lucky."

—Godfrey

Cancer of the lip and mouth is found most often in people older than 45. Oral cancer often makes a lump form on your lip, on your gums, or in your mouth. Another sign of oral cancer is a mouth sore that does not heal. If you have fair skin and have spent a lot of time in the sun, you are more likely to get cancer on your lip. If you chew tobacco or smoke a pipe, you are also at risk for oral cancer.

If you think you might have oral cancer, see your doctor. He or she will look at your mouth closely. The doctor may also take a biopsy. This means that a small piece of tissue will be removed and checked for cancer. The tissue is sent to a medical lab where someone tests it for cancer cells. If you have cancer, you may need surgery. Oral cancer can often be cured when it is found early.

Dry Mouth

"My pharmacist told me that having a dry mouth might be a side effect of my blood pressure medicine. Before long, it was clear that she was right. I can really tell the difference if I go out and forget to bring water with me."

—Letty

What to do about **Dry Mouth**

Symptoms/Signs	Action
◆ **Your mouth feels drier than normal.** ◆ **Your mouth feels dry and your lips are chapped.** ◆ **Your mouth feels dry and scratchy, or feels as if it is burning.**	Use self-care
◆ **Your mouth feels dry all the time.**	Call doctor

A dry mouth can make it hard to eat, swallow, taste, and speak. A dry mouth may make you feel as if your mouth is burning. Doctors call a dry mouth xerostomia. The following things can cause you to have a dry mouth:

- breathing or sleeping with your mouth open
- chemotherapy
- dehydration
- diabetes
- over-the-counter drugs such as Sudafed and antihistamines such as Benadryl
- prescription drugs you take to get rid of excess water, such as diuretics
- prescription drugs you take for high blood pressure or depression
- radiation therapy
- smoking
- talking a lot
- too much caffeine or alcohol

If self-care steps don't ease your dry mouth, talk with your doctor. A dry mouth can be a sign of a more serious problem.

Self-Care: Dry Mouth

- Avoid soft drinks, caffeine, alcohol, and tobacco. These can dry your mouth more.
- Avoid spicy and salty foods.
- Chew sugarless gum. The act of chewing can help make more saliva. But avoid any gum that has sugar in it. Sugar helps bacteria grow. And bacteria can cause bad breath.
- Drink plenty of water. Always keep some near you. Take a water bottle with you when you go out for a walk. Sip from it often.
- Suck on mints or hard candies that don't have sugar. This can help keep your mouth moist.

Mouth Sores

"I have gotten cold sores since I was a kid. They are ugly and they burn like crazy. Now I protect my lips with Carmex. I use it every time I go outside. These days I get sores less often."
—Barbara

The most common types of mouth sores are canker sores and cold sores. Both can be painful, ugly, and slow to heal. Most mouth sores will go away in a couple of weeks with self-care. You can use sunscreen to help prevent chapped lips.

Canker sores form on the inside of your mouth, lips, or cheeks. They are red or yellowish-white sores with a red border. (SEE PHOTO BELOW.) They can form on your gums. No one knows what causes canker sores.

Cold sores often form on the outside of your mouth or on and around your lips. They have a bright red border and a gray center. (SEE PHOTO, PAGE 136.) They are also called fever blisters. Cold sores can start before or during a

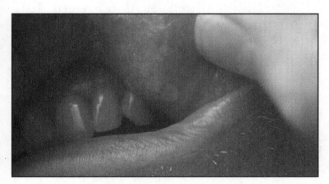

Canker sores form inside the lips. You may also have them on the gums or inside your cheeks.

What to do about **Mouth Sores**

Symptoms/Signs	Action
◆ **Red craterlike sores inside your mouth, on your gums, or on the insides of your lips or cheeks** ◆ **Cold sore on your lips or on the skin around them**	 Use self-care
◆ **Mouth sores caused by dentures that don't fit well**	Call dentist
◆ **Mouth sores that keep coming back**	Call doctor
◆ **Small white sores in your mouth that look like lace** ◆ **Creamy yellow patches in your mouth that may or may not hurt** ◆ **Large painful open sores on your gums that bleed** ◆ **Mouth sores that don't heal in three weeks**	See doctor

cold or the flu. Your lips may itch, burn, or tingle before the cold sore appears. Cold sores are caused by the herpes simplex virus type 1. Some cold sores can cause fever and chills.

Cold sores can spread easily. It is not wise to kiss someone who has a cold sore. And if you are under physical or emotional stress, you may be more likely to get a cold sore.

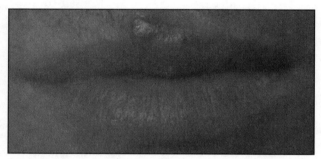

Cold sores form on or around the mouth. They are also called fever blisters.

Self-Care: Mouth Sores

- To ease the pain of canker sores, use a medicine like Anbesol.
- To ease the pain of cold sores, use an over-the-counter medicine like Carmex or Campho-Phenique.
- Avoid foods that have a lot of acid. These include oranges and tomatoes. They can make a mouth sore feel worse.
- Avoid foods that have a lot of salt, spice, or vinegar. They can bother your sores.
- Avoid food like potato chips that have sharp edges. They can cut your sores and irritate them more.

Tooth and Gum Concerns

You might take your teeth and gums for granted. Healthy gums hold your teeth firmly in place. You need your teeth so you can eat the foods that keep you healthy. This part of the chapter tells you how to deal with tooth and gum problems you may have. It also tells you how to avoid problems.

Dentures

"It took me a while to get used to my dentures. They would slip and food would stick to them. I got so mad that I would take them out. My dentist told me to keep them in so that my mouth would get used to them. After a while, they felt like my own teeth."

—Esther

Many adults older than 65 wear full or partial dentures. Proper dental care is important if you wear dentures. Your jawbone is slowly shrinking all the time. This is normal. If your dentures don't fit well, they can cause tissues in the mouth to shrink. So be sure to have your dentures checked. Ask your dentist how often you should have this done.

It is normal for new dentures to feel loose until you get used to them. But see your dentist if your dentures make it hard to chew.

What to do about **Tooth and Gum Concerns**

Symptoms/Signs	Action
◆ **Pain when you chew, bite, talk, or swallow** (See Self-Care: TMJ Problems, page 140.)	Use self-care
◆ **A sensitive tooth** (See Self-Care: Toothaches, page 141.)	Use self-care **+** Call dentist
◆ **Pain in teeth or jaw when you open your mouth** ◆ **Chipped tooth**	Call dentist
◆ **Lost tooth** (See Self-Care: Lost Tooth, page 138.)	Use self-care **+** See dentist

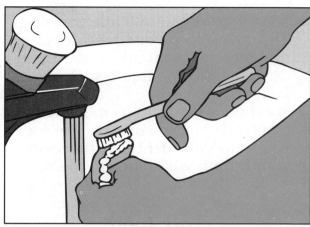

To clean dentures, wash them under running water with toothpaste or a denture cleaner such as Dentu-Creme. Also soak them overnight in a denture cleaning liquid such as Polident.

- Brush your dentures once a day with a denture care product such as Dentu-Creme. This will help keep them clean and free of odor. Don't use scouring powder.
- Cut your food into small pieces to make it easier to chew.
- Eat soft foods until you get used to your dentures. Soft food won't stick to them. Some soft foods are eggs, cheese, pasta, and chicken. Avoid sticky foods like peanut butter until you are used to your dentures.
- Massage and brush your gums and the roof of your mouth every day. Use a soft toothbrush or a washcloth. This helps stimulate circulation in the tissue and keeps food from settling between your gums and your dentures.
- See your dentist every six months if you wear partial dentures. See your dentist every year if you wear full dentures.

Self-Care: Dentures

- Don't use too much denture adhesive. It can irritate your gums and mouth. If your dentures don't stay in place without the adhesive, see your dentist.

- Soak your dentures while you sleep. This helps keep your dentures clean and gives your mouth a rest. Use a denture cleaning liquid such as Polident.
- Wear your dentures as much as you can while you are awake. The more you wear your dentures, the sooner your mouth will adjust to them.

Lost Tooth

"My grandson is going to be a great pitcher. One day I was playing catch with him. The ball hit me in the mouth and knocked out one of my teeth. I put my tooth in a glass of salt water and went to the dentist. She was able to put my tooth back in."
—Jeremy

Teeth can be knocked out by accident. You should act quickly if you lose a tooth. If your tooth is out of its socket for less than 30 minutes, there is a good chance that your dentist can put it back in your mouth to stay. But the longer your tooth is out of your mouth, the harder it is for a dentist to put it back in place.

Self-Care: Lost Tooth

To help prepare your tooth to go back into your mouth, take the following steps before you see your dentist. First

What to Do If You Chip a Tooth

A chipped or broken tooth may annoy you. But it is not likely to cause any real trouble. See your dentist as soon as you can after you chip a tooth. Your bite may have changed. Your bite is the way your upper teeth line up with your lower teeth. An incorrect bite can cause more serious problems.

protect your tooth. Then see your dentist right away.
- Don't touch the root of your tooth. Pick it up by the crown only so you don't damage the root.
- If the tooth is dirty, rinse it in a bowl of tap water as soon as you can. Don't hold it under running water. Don't scrub it.
- Put your tooth gently back into the socket it fell out of. Hold it in place with either a wet tea bag or a piece of gauze. Doing this will also apply pressure to the injured area to slow the bleeding.
- If you can't get your tooth into the socket, put it in a glass of milk or salt water. (Add about half a teaspoon of salt to eight ounces of water.) If you don't have milk or salt water, wrap the tooth in plastic wrap or in a wet towel. Or put the tooth in a glass of water. Don't let the tooth dry out.

Periodontal (Gum) Disease

"My toothbrush turned pink every time I brushed my teeth. When I saw my dentist for a checkup, she told me that I have gingivitis. After she treated me, she told me to use a Water Pik at home before I brush."
—Abdul

Periodontal disease is the most common cause of tooth loss in adults older than 40. Periodontal means "around the tooth." Periodontal disease is also called pyorrhea or gum disease.

Inflammation of the gums is called gingivitis. Inflamed gums may bleed when you brush your teeth. If you have gingivitis and don't see your dentist, you could get gum disease. This disease can make your teeth become loose. It can leave a bad taste in your mouth. When gums are infected, there may be pus. The pus can lead to a loss of bone in your jaw. This loss of bone can make your teeth fall out.

Gingivitis and gum disease are caused by too much plaque on your teeth. Plaque is a sticky white film. Your saliva hardens the plaque and turns it into tartar. Tartar can build up between your teeth and gums. Too much tartar can cause your gums to become infected. This makes them swell and bleed.

To treat gum disease, your dentist will clean and scrape tartar from your teeth and just under the gums. If you have more advanced gum disease, your dentist may suggest surgery.

Self-Care: Gum Disease

To help prevent and treat gum disease, take the following steps:
- Brush with a tartar control toothpaste at least twice a day.
- Floss every day. (SEE DRAWING, PAGE 132.)
- Have your teeth cleaned routinely by a dental hygienist. Talk with your dentist to find out how often you should have this done.
- Rinse your mouth twice a day with an antiplaque mouthwash such as Plax. Do this after you brush and floss.
- Use a special device to wash out your mouth before you brush. A gadget like the Water Pik shoots water into your mouth. The force of the water flushes out plaque. This can slow the buildup of tartar.

TMJ (Temporomandibular Joint) Problems

"When I open my mouth, my jaw hurts. I hear little clicking noises when I eat. My dentist said that I have a TMJ disorder. He told me to use both sides of my mouth when I chew. He also gave me a mouth guard to wear at night."
—Earl

The joint where your lower jaw meets your skull is called the temporomandibular joint, or TMJ. (SEE DRAWING AT

RIGHT.) If the joint is inflamed, you might have a TMJ disorder.

When you talk, bite down, chew, or swallow, you use this joint. If you hear a clicking noise when you chew, you may have a TMJ problem.

Chewing on only one side of your mouth can cause a TMJ problem. A TMJ problem can also come from grinding and clenching your teeth. Chewing gum may also add to your chance of having a TMJ problem. People may also have rheumatoid arthritis or osteoarthritis (SEE PAGE 146) in this joint.

A dentist can treat most TMJ problems. Your dentist can look at your bite. This is the way your upper teeth line up with your lower teeth. To fix your bite, you may need to have a filling replaced. Or you may need a splint or mouth guard to keep you from grinding your teeth. If these treatments don't work, your dentist may refer you to an oral surgeon.

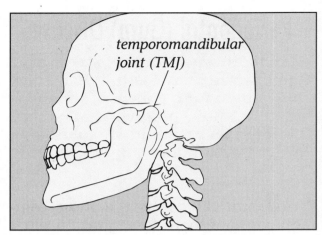

You can feel your temporomandibular joint (TMJ) with your hand. Put your finger on the hard, fleshy triangle right in front of your ear. Move your finger toward your mouth just a bit. You should be able to feel a small dent between the bones that meet there. Your TMJ is where those bones meet.

Self-Care: TMJ Problems

- If chewing causes pain, avoid hard, chewy foods and chewing gum.
- Chew on both sides of your mouth.
- Don't clench or grind your teeth. Both clenching and grinding add to discomfort in your mouth.
- Exercise your jaw. Bring your lower teeth out in front of your upper teeth. Do this 10 times. Do this exercise four times a day.

Toothaches

"I woke up one morning with an awful toothache. My dentist said that she could not see me until later that afternoon. She told me to rub some Orabase on the sore spot and that ibuprofen would ease the pain. Both helped. When I saw her, she said a huge cavity was causing my pain."
—Gustav

Tooth decay causes most toothaches. A cracked tooth can cause you to have stabbing pain. Food that is stuck between your teeth can also cause pain. Inflamed sinuses can make your upper teeth hurt. Brushing and flossing well

What to do about **Toothaches**

Symptoms/Signs	Action
◆ **Toothache and earache** ◆ **Toothache and fever** ◆ **Swelling on the gum near the sore tooth**	 Call dentist

can help prevent toothaches. Also see your dentist routinely. (SEE HOW TO KEEP YOUR MOUTH CLEAN, PAGE 131.)

Self-Care: Toothaches

- Try to find the cause of your tooth pain. Look for food that might be stuck between your teeth. Try to remove the food by flossing. If you can't get it out, call your dentist. Don't try to remove a piece of food that is badly stuck. You could hurt your gums.
- To ease pain, take acetaminophen (Tylenol) or ibuprofen (Advil or Nuprin). Don't rub the pill on the sore area. This could cause acid burns in your mouth.
- Use oil of cloves to reduce pain. You can buy it over the counter at a drugstore. Rub a small amount on your tooth. You can also try an over-the-counter gel with benzo-caine that numbs the pain. Rub

the gel on the sore spot. One brand is Orabase with benzocaine.
- Use a toothpaste for sensitive teeth (such as Sensodyne). This may make your teeth less sensitive.
- If your gums swell, you might have an infection. Call your dentist. To ease pain, apply a cold pack to the outside of your cheek. Use ice cubes wrapped in a towel if you don't have a cold pack. You can even hold a can of cold soda to your cheek.

Throat Concerns

Everyone gets a sore throat or laryngitis now and then. This part of the chapter covers the causes of hoarseness and sore throats. It can also help you decide when you should see a doctor for a throat problem.

Hoarseness and Laryngitis

"It seemed that every time I had to talk for an hour or two, I would lose my voice. My doctor told me to stop smoking, drink lots of water, and rest my voice once in a while. Now I don't lose my voice anymore."
—Lenore

Laryngitis is an inflammation of your larynx. Your larynx is also called your voice box. Your voice box can become swollen or irritated. Then your vocal

What to do about **Hoarseness and Laryngitis**	
Symptoms/Signs	**Action**
◆ **Losing some or all of your voice from too much use, a cold, or the flu**	 Use self-care
◆ **Hoarseness with no cold or flu symptoms**	Call doctor
◆ **Hoarseness that lasts more than one month** ◆ **Hoarseness if you are a smoker**	See doctor

flu (SEE PAGE 104), and sinus infections can cause this.

- Smoking, alcohol, and air pollution can dry out your vocal cords. When your vocal cords get dry, you may become hoarse.
- You can lose your voice by using it too much. This can happen if you sing, shout, or talk for long periods of time.

Most hoarseness caused by overuse or a virus will go away by itself within two weeks. If you are hoarse all of the time, you should see your doctor. The hoarseness may mean that you have a more serious condition. (SEE THROAT CANCERS, PAGE 144.)

Self-Care: Laryngitis

- Drink a lot of fluid. Water is a good choice because it helps carry oxygen and important nutrients through your body.
- Don't smoke. Don't drink alcohol. Smoking and drinking can both dry out your vocal cords.
- Rest your voice. Talk and whisper only when you must. Both talking and whispering can strain your vocal cords.
- Keep a pen and paper near you. Write down what you need to say. Sometimes you can make your point with hand signals.
- Use a humidifier. It will make the air in your house moist. This can help your throat.

cords can't vibrate the way they should. When your vocal cords don't vibrate the way they should, your voice may sound husky or hoarse. It may sound raspy, harsh, or grating. Or you might lose your voice. It may be painful to swallow when you have laryngitis. Any of the following things can cause laryngitis:

Most hoarseness caused by overuse or a virus will go away by itself within two weeks.

- You can lose your voice if you have a viral infection in your voice box. Colds (SEE PAGE 101), sore throats, the

Sore Throats

"I get sore throats a lot. My house is heated by forced hot air and that dries everything up. A piece of hard candy can often make my throat feel better. But one time, the candy did nothing. My throat was really red and my glands were swollen. My doctor took a throat culture. It turned out that I had strep throat and needed antibiotics."

—Agnes

Your throat can get sore if you don't drink enough fluids or if you smoke. Winter dryness can also bother your throat. A sore throat is often the first symptom of a cold (SEE PAGE 101) or the flu (SEE PAGE 104). A sore throat often goes away in a few days. But it can last for 7 to 10 days. Most sore throats are caused by a viral or bacterial infection.

A virus can cause a sore throat. You may or may not have a fever. You might have trouble swallowing. You may have swollen glands.

Bacterial infections are more serious than the viral types. Strep throat is caused by streptococcal bacteria. Signs of strep throat often include the following:
- fever higher than 101 degrees
- a very red throat
- white patches or pus on your throat
- swollen tonsils
- swollen neck glands

Call your doctor if you have a sore throat and you have been exposed to someone with strep. To find out if you

What to do about Sore Throats

Symptoms/Signs	Action
◆ Sore throat with no fever, or a fever lower than 101 degrees ◆ Cough that comes and goes ◆ Dry, sore, or itchy throat ◆ Sore throat with cold symptoms (SEE PAGE 101.)	 Use self-care
◆ Sore throat with a cough that gets worse	 Use self-care **+** Call doctor
◆ Red throat with white patches or pus ◆ Swollen glands ◆ Fever higher than 101 degrees that lasts more than 48 hours ◆ Sore throat that turns into chest pains, and cough that gets worse	See doctor
◆ Difficulty breathing ◆ Inability to swallow saliva	 Call ambulance

have strep, your doctor is likely to do a throat culture. A throat culture tests the mucus from your throat to see if there are bacteria. To collect cells for the culture, a nurse or a doctor gently brushes a long cotton swab on the back of your throat. If you do have strep throat, you will need to take antibiotics to treat it.

Self-Care: Sore Throats

- Don't smoke or chew tobacco. If you do, get help to quit. Talk with your doctor about what to try.
- Drink at least eight glasses of fluid each day. The fluid will soothe your throat. It will also loosen mucus.
- Gargle with warm salt water. Add about half a teaspoon of salt to eight ounces of warm water. Warm salt water will ease the soreness. Mouthwash does not prevent or soothe a sore throat.
- Suck on hard candy or cough drops. These may soothe your throat.
- To reduce fever or pain, take aspirin or acetaminophen (Tylenol).
- Take a hot shower. The steam will make your throat moist.
- Use a steam vaporizer on the cool mist setting. This will add moisture to the air. Keep the vaporizer clean. If it is dirty, it can grow mildew that can carry germs.

Throat Cancers

"In the past, my laryngitis always went away in a few days. But when it lasted a while, I went to my doctor. She saw a growth on my vocal cords. A biopsy showed that it was cancer. I had surgery to remove the lump. But at least my doctor found the cancer early."
—Toby

Cancers of the throat are most common in people around the age of 60. They are 10 times more common in men than in women. Cancer can occur in several parts of the throat. With cancer of the vocal cords, hoarseness is the only early symptom. Difficulty or pain when you swallow could be a sign of other throat cancers. A large swelling in the neck may also be a symptom.

People who smoke or who routinely drink alcohol are at greater risk of throat cancers.

If your doctor thinks you might have throat cancer, he or she will do a laryngoscopy. This lets your doctor look closely at your larynx. This procedure may be done in your doctor's office. In some cases you may need to be in the hospital.

Throat cancer can often be cured with radiation therapy or surgery. (SEE COMMON WAYS CANCER IS TREATED, PAGE 16.) You may need to have your larynx (voice box) removed.

Chapter 10

Muscle and Joint Concerns

One of the best things you can do for your muscles and joints is to use them. Activity can keep you moving with ease. Many aches and pains are a result of poorly conditioned muscles. Or pain can come from injury or overuse.

If you can, tell your doctor what happened before the pain started. Your doctor can give advice and treatment for most muscle and joint problems. If you need special care, your doctor may refer you to one of the following:

- a physical therapist, who works with you to help ease pain and to bring back normal movement and strength
- an orthopedist, a doctor who treats muscle and bone problems
- a physiatrist, a doctor who treats muscles, tendons, and bones but does not perform surgery
- a rheumatologist, a doctor who treats joints and arthritis

This chapter covers muscle and joint problems in each main area of the body except the foot. Problems with the foot are covered in Foot Concerns. (SEE PAGE 63.) Some problems may affect more than one part of the body. These problems include bursitis, tendinitis, osteoarthritis, and sprains and strains. These problems are explained first, before the discussion of problems that are specific to a joint or bone.

Bursitis

Bursitis is caused by an inflamed bursa. Bursas are the small fluid-filled sacs that are in and near the joints. They cushion and lubricate areas around both the joints and the tendons. Bursitis will make a soft, fluid-filled lump in the joint. This lump will cause pain, tenderness, and swelling in the joint. A sudden increase in activity can cause bursitis. Sitting in one position for too long can also cause it. To prevent bursitis, avoid sitting for a long time. Get up and move around each half hour. Acute bursitis often heals in 7 to 10 days with self-care. Call your doctor if you don't feel better in 10 days.

Tendinitis

Tendons attach muscles to bones. You have tendons around every joint. Doing the same motion over and over, moving quickly, and moving too much can inflame tendons. These things can lead to tendinitis. This is also called an overuse injury. Tendinitis causes pain, swelling, and stiffness. Pain from inflamed tendons can vary. It may be constant, or you may feel pain only when you move a certain way. Ice, heat, anti-inflammatory drugs, and splints can all be used to treat the problem.

Self-Care: Bursitis and Tendinitis

- Take an anti-inflammatory drug such as aspirin or ibuprofen. (SEE WHICH PAIN MEDICATION IS RIGHT FOR YOU? PAGE 272.)
- Use the RICE method.
- Be less active until you feel better.
- Apply heat to the painful area before activity. Do not apply heat if there is swelling.
- Ice the painful area after you are active.
- If your symptoms don't improve after 10 to 14 days, call your doctor.

Osteoarthritis

Osteoarthritis is also called degenerative joint disease. It breaks down the cartilage that cushions the joints. Some experts say that it comes from wear and tear. Bone spurs and arthritis can lead to osteoarthritis. Bone spurs are bony deposits that can irritate the nerves. Osteoarthritis usually affects people older than 65. Osteoarthritis most often affects the joints of the hands, knees, hips, neck, and back. Osteoarthritis causes pain, swelling, and stiffness. Joints that have been injured before are the most likely ones to be affected.

Self-Care: Osteoarthritis

- Control your weight. Extra weight can stress your joints. This stress will cause more pain and do more damage.
- Exercise routinely. Swim, walk, or use a stationary bike. These exercises put less stress on your joints than others do. Exercise will help you move freely and with less pain. Be patient. It may take a while to feel better.
- Take an anti-inflammatory drug such as aspirin or ibuprofen. (SEE WHICH PAIN MEDICATION IS RIGHT FOR YOU? PAGE 272.)
- Use heat or cold treatments. Heat relaxes muscles. A hot shower, for instance, can relieve pain and stiffness. Apply an ice pack or even a bag of frozen vegetables to the area. This will numb pain and decrease swelling.

The RICE Method

The RICE method often helps joint and muscle injuries. RICE stands for Rest, Ice, Compress, and Elevate. The method will ease pain and help speed recovery. The RICE method is very helpful if you use it right away after an injury.

Rest

- For most injuries, rest the hurt area for 24 to 72 hours until the pain decreases.
- For sore muscles, stretch gently. Stretching will ease stiffness.
- Hold the stretch for 60 seconds. Then rest and repeat 5 to 10 times.
- Stretch several times a day.

Ice

Ice is the best way to reduce inflammation, pain, and swelling. The cold helps keep blood and fluid from building up in the injured area.

- Use ice as soon as you can after an injury. You should use ice even if you are going straight to the doctor.
- To speed recovery and ease pain, raise the injured area. Apply ice packs for 20 minutes every two to three hours. Don't use ice while you sleep.
- For best results, use crushed ice in a moist towel. This is called an ice pack. Hold the pack in place with an elastic bandage (such as Ace).
- For the first 48 to 72 hours, don't use heat on an injury. Don't apply heat if there is any swelling. Heat makes more blood flow to the area. This makes swelling and pain worse.

Compress

- For at least 48 hours, wrap the injured area with an elastic bandage (such as Ace) between icings. Wrapping will help control the swelling. It also gives you better support.
- Always start wrapping the injury at the point farthest from the body. For instance, if you have pain in the ankle, start at the toes and wrap to the calf.
- Don't wrap too tightly or you will cut off blood flow to the area.
- Don't sleep with the wrap on unless your doctor says you should.
- If the wrap causes pain, numbness, or tingling, take it off. Then wrap the bandage more loosely. Do the same thing if your fingers or toes are cool or pale.

Elevate

- Raise the injured area above your heart. This helps drain excess fluid and reduces swelling.
- Place a pillow under the area to support and raise it. Raise it whenever you can until the swelling goes down. If this causes more pain and swelling, lower the limb. If the limb still does not feel better, call your doctor.

Sprains

Ligaments connect bone to bone. When you tear or stretch a ligament, you have a sprain. You can sprain any joint. But most sprains are likely to be in the ankles, knees, wrists, or fingers. When you have a sprain, you will have the following symptoms: swelling, pain, and bruising.

Strains

Tendons connect muscle to bone. You can stretch or tear a muscle beyond its normal range of motion. When you do, you have a strain. Some people call a strain a pulled muscle. Signs of a strain include pain, swelling, muscle spasm, and limited movement.

Self-Care: Sprains and Strains

You can usually treat a sprain or strain at home. You should see your doctor if the injured part looks deformed. Call your doctor if the pain keeps you from using the injured part.

- Take an anti-inflammatory drug. (SEE WHICH PAIN MEDICATION IS RIGHT FOR YOU? PAGE 272.)
- Use the injured area as little as possible until the swelling stops. This often takes about 24 to 48 hours.
- Use crutches if it hurts you to stand or walk.
- Use the RICE method. (SEE PAGE 147.)
- If swelling lasts more than three days, follow these steps for a total of 15 to 20 minutes. Stop if you see more swelling:

—Soak the injured part in cold water for one minute. Use water that is 45 to 60 degrees.
—Soak in warm water (100 to 105 degrees) for two to three minutes.
—Go back to the cold water.
- As the swelling and pain decrease, do gentle exercises. This will stretch and strengthen the injured part. It will help you regain your range of motion. It will also make muscles around the joint stronger. Your doctor or physical therapist can show you the right exercises to do.

Ankle Pain

If you injure an ankle, take it seriously and treat it properly. Strains and sprains are the most common injuries. Bursitis (SEE PAGE 145), tendinitis (SEE PAGE 146), and fractures (SEE PAGE 345) can also occur.

Achilles tendinitis. This condition affects the tendon that attaches the calf muscle to the heel. If you have pain in the calf and ankle, you may have Achilles tendinitis. This pain is worse when you first get up. The pain usually gets better as your ankle warms up with use. You don't have to be an athlete to have this problem. You can get it from wearing shoes that fit poorly or shoes that fail to provide enough support or cushioning. Such shoes can inflame tendons and bursas in the ankle.

What to do about **Ankle Pain**

Symptoms/Signs	Action	Symptoms/Signs	Action
◆ Swelling, pain, and bruising from a sudden twist or force (SEE SELF-CARE: SPRAINS AND STRAINS, PAGE 148.)	Use self-care	◆ Pain and swelling that increase 24 hours after injury ◆ Ankle that cannot bear any weight after you hear or feel a pop, snap, or crack ◆ Swelling and pain in only one ankle or leg, with no injury ◆ Red, warm, or swollen ankles, with fever, with feeling ill, or after a recent illness with sore throat or skin infection ◆ Pain on inner side of ankle, and it twisted inward when you injured it	See doctor
◆ Pain at back of ankle that begins slowly and may be worse when you wake up (SEE SELF-CARE: BURSITIS AND TENDINITIS, PAGE 146.)	Use self-care **+** Call doctor		
◆ Tendinitis symptoms that don't improve in 10 to 14 days	Call doctor		
◆ Chronic swelling in ankles, feet, or lower legs, and difficulty breathing	See doctor		

Gout

"My big toe blew up like a balloon. The pain was so intense that even the sheets hurt it."
—Steve

Gout often begins in the big toe, but it may move to the ankle and knee. If uric acid builds up in the body, it can cause gout. Uric acid is a waste product. It is left over after your body metabolizes food. Symptoms of gout may show up in a joint. They include:
- sudden pain or extreme tenderness
- swelling
- redness

If you have symptoms of gout, raise your legs. Apply ice if you can stand it. Don't take aspirin. Aspirin makes your body excrete uric acid more slowly. Call your doctor as soon as you can. He or she may prescribe a drug to treat gout.

Back Pain

Anyone can get a backache. It can be caused by inflammation of joints, muscles, or ligaments. Poor posture, obesity, or lifting something the wrong way can also cause back pain. Pain can also come from sitting or standing too long, physical or mental stress, or lack of exercise.

Some back pain comes from problems in other parts of the body. This pain is called referred pain. For instance, a foot problem may change the way you

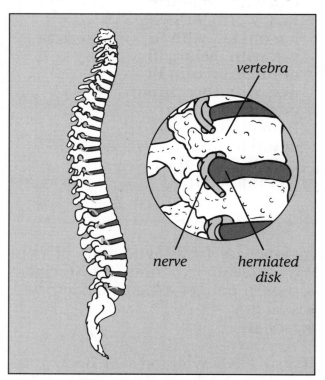

The spine is made up of bones called vertebrae. Between the vertebrae are gel-like disks that form cushions. The inset shows a herniated disk. (SEE PAGE 155.) The center of the disk bulges and puts pressure on the nerve.

walk. This change can lead to back pain. For the same reason, pain in your hip or leg may lead to back pain.

After middle age, your disks tend to dry up. When your disks become dry, they can be squeezed together more easily. This can cause pain.

These are some of the conditions that often cause back pain in people older than 50:

- osteoporosis (SEE PAGE 255.)
- disk compression (SEE COMPRESSION FRACTURES, PAGE 155.)
- osteoarthritis (SEE PAGE 146.)

In rare cases, back pain can be caused by infection, cancer, or other diseases. Doctors describe back pain as either acute or chronic.

Acute Lower Back Pain

If you have lower back pain but no pain below the knees for six weeks or less, you may have acute back pain. People often think that acute back pain can be caused only by a single event, such as lifting a heavy object. But most back pain is from ongoing problems such as poor posture, muscle weakness, or years of overuse. Acute back pain can be severe, but it usually improves after a few days of simple treatment. (SEE THE RICE METHOD, PAGE 147.)

Your doctor may prescribe muscle relaxants for the first few days. Muscle relaxants will help ease muscle spasms. These drugs can often make people drowsy. Doctors rarely prescribe narcotic painkillers for acute back pain. They rarely prescribe these drugs because they can be addictive.

What to do about Back Pain

Symptoms/Signs	Action	Symptoms/Signs	Action
◆ Pain or soreness from tension or poor posture ◆ Usual back or neck soreness	Use self-care	◆ Pain that travels below the knee ◆ Paralysis or numbness of a lower limb ◆ Back pain and difficulty walking ◆ Significant pain after a fall	See doctor
◆ Pain in upper to middle back, with no known muscle strain ◆ Pain that lasts for several days ◆ Back pain and painful or frequent urination, vaginal bleeding, or stomachache ◆ Back pain and fever above 100 degrees that last longer than 48 hours ◆ Back pain and nausea, vomiting, or diarrhea	Call doctor	◆ Back pain with loss of bowel control or bladder control	Seek help now
		◆ Paralysis, confusion, or signs of shock: cold and clammy skin, weak pulse, dizziness, or rapid, shallow breathing (SEE PAGE 353.)	Call ambulance

Sciatica. Sciatica is pain that extends from your back through your buttocks and down to your legs. Mild stretching and a warm bath may ease the pain. It can take as long as six weeks to heal.

Chronic Back Pain
Chronic back pain is pain that lasts longer than six weeks. It may be mild or severe. If your back pain lasts this long, your doctor may want you to have some tests. Your doctor may also want you to see a specialist who treats chronic back pain.

How to Prevent Back Pain
● Stay active. A regular walking program or any activity that keeps you moving is key to preventing lower back problems. (SEE HOW TO START A WALKING PROGRAM, PAGE 294.)

Exercises to Keep Your Back Fit

It is important to keep your back flexible and strong. Back exercises can help prevent back problems and improve posture. Regular activity helps prevent and treat lower back pain. Aerobic exercise such as walking, swimming, and biking can help.

Start the exercises below as soon as you can tolerate the pain. You may have some discomfort the day after you exercise. But this discomfort should not disrupt your daily activity. Start by doing each exercise two to four times. Slowly work up to 10. If your back hurts when you increase the number, stop. Next time, do only as many as you did without pain.

Pelvic Tilt

Lie flat on your back. Bend your knees. Keep your feet flat on the floor and relax your body. Tighten the muscles in your abdomen. Press the small of your back until it is flat on the floor. Your pelvis will tilt up. Tighten the muscles of the buttocks. Hold for 10 seconds and then relax.

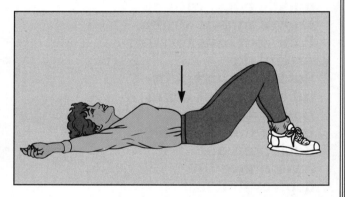

Knee Raise

Lie flat on your back with your knees bent. Keep feet flat on the floor. Do a pelvic tilt (SEE ABOVE) and raise one knee slowly to your chest. Hug the knee gently and hold for a count of 6 to 10. Let go, then lower your foot slowly back to the floor. Don't straighten your knees. Repeat this with the other knee.

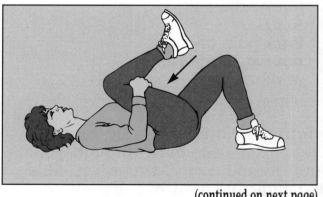

(continued on next page)

- Sleep on a firm mattress or put a board under a soft mattress.
- Stay at an average weight. If you are overweight, you will put more stress on your lower back.
- Try not to reach for objects that are above your head. Use a step stool or a device that helps you reach ob-

Exercises to Keep Your Back Fit (continued)

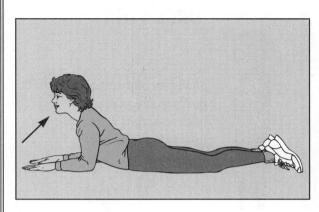

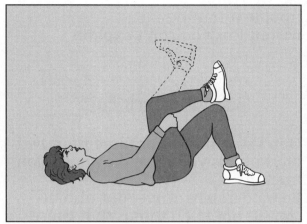

Partial Press-Up

Lie facedown on a soft, firm surface, such as a bed. Rest for a few minutes, and relax completely. Staying in the same position, bend your elbows and raise your upper body enough to lean on your forearms. Relax your lower back and legs as much as you can. Hold this position for 30 seconds at first. Slowly work up to two minutes.

Hamstring Stretch

Lie on your back with your left leg bent. Grab the back of your right knee. Pull your toes toward you. Slowly straighten your leg. Feel the stretch in the back of your thigh or behind the knee. Hold for a count of five. Switch to your left leg and repeat.

jects on higher shelves. If you can, store items that you use a lot on lower shelves. These may include dishes and food.

- Avoid lifting children. Ask a child to climb onto your lap instead.
- When you sit or stand for a long time, change positions often.
- Avoid repeated bending and twisting.
- Do exercises that will strengthen your back.

- Sleep right. Try lying on your back with a pillow under your knees. Or lie on your side with a pillow between your knees.
- Practice the postures that prevent back pain. (SEE BOX, PAGE 154.)

Is Your Back Pain a Serious Problem?

Some back pain is a sign of disease. Tell your doctor right away if you have back pain and any of the

following symptoms:
- constant pain at night
- fever
- leg weakness
- trouble urinating
- weight loss you can't explain

Self-Care: Back Pain

- Don't stay in bed for more than two days unless you have a compression fracture.
- Be moderately active. But also be careful not to do things that cause the pain in your back to get worse.
- Return to work or normal daily activity in a few days or even sooner. You should limit your hours, though, or have lighter duties. Stay active but use a slower pace. This is an important part of your recovery. You will feel some discomfort. But your back will not lose its flexibility and strength.
- Use an anti-inflammatory drug, such as ibuprofen or aspirin, to help ease pain and swelling in the lower back. (SEE WHICH PAIN MEDICATION IS RIGHT FOR YOU? PAGE 272.)
- Learn relaxation techniques (SEE BOX, PAGE 129) and other ways to manage stress. (SEE SELF-CARE: STRESS, PAGE 130.) Money worries, family problems, and other stress can affect back pain.
- Follow the guidelines for preventing back pain in the future. (SEE PAGE 151.)
- Follow the steps for the RICE method. (SEE PAGE 147.)

Postures That Prevent Back Pain

Stand straight. Good posture keeps your body's weight aligned and takes stress off your back muscles.

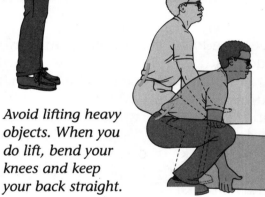

Avoid lifting heavy objects. When you do lift, bend your knees and keep your back straight.

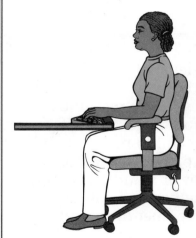

Choose a chair that has good support for your lower back.

Compression Fractures

"My mother was cleaning windows when she felt a sharp pain in her back. She found out that she had a compression fracture. She also found out that she had osteoporosis."

—Joanie

When you have a vertebral compression fracture, one or more of your vertebrae are crushed. Osteoporosis can cause this. (SEE PAGE 255.) But this type of fracture often occurs when you lift something with your arms stretched out. This kind of movement causes fractures more easily if you have osteoporosis. Even opening a window or lifting a bag of groceries can do it.

This kind of fracture can be quite painful. You may need bed rest and prescription pain relievers. A back brace may ease the pain. A brace also gives your back more support. The pain goes away slowly as the bone heals. Be sure to follow all of your doctor's advice.

A compression fracture can cause a loss of height. It can also cause kyphosis. This means a curving of the spine, or a hunchback. People with kyphosis have less space for their lungs and digestive organs. Less space may cause them to have long-term discomfort and other problems.

After the fracture heals, exercise can help you move more normally. Exercises that stretch the spine can also slow kyphosis, ease pain, and reduce muscle fatigue. You can ask your doctor or physical therapist to teach you these exercises. Your exercise program may include regular walking. (SEE PAGE 294.)

Herniated Disk

"My lower back bothers me now and then. But I know why. I always forget to bend my knees whenever I lift something. That means I can count on my back going out. My doctor tells me that after all these years I should know better."

—Jerri

A herniated disk occurs when a disk between the vertebrae bulges and extends into the spinal canal. (SEE DRAWING, PAGE 150.) The exact cause of a herniated disk is often not clear. Most disk problems are in the lower back.

A herniated disk can press on nerves and cause pain. It can also cause numbness and tingling. Treatment for back pain from this problem often includes rest for a day or two. After you rest, you can go slowly back to your normal routine. You can use ice to ease the pain. Your doctor or physical therapist may also show you exercises you can use to ease the pain.

Sometimes the pain from a herniated disk can keep you from moving. It can also lead to a problem called sciatica. (SEE PAGE 151.)

Spinal Stenosis

*"My back used to kill me when-
ever I walked. But when I sat
down, the pain would go away.
My doctor told me that I have
spinal stenosis. I also have osteoarthritis. My doctor said that people with osteoarthritis often have
a problem with spinal stenosis."*
—Mimi

Spinal stenosis is also known as narrowing of the spinal canal. It occurs
when the spaces between the vertebrae
become narrow. This narrowing is the
result of the disks being squeezed between the vertebrae. (SEE DRAWINGS ON THIS
PAGE.) Then the nerves are pinched,
which causes you to feel pain. The
most common symptom of spinal
stenosis is pain that you feel when you
walk. That pain goes away when you
sit. The irritated nerves can lead to
sciatica. (SEE PAGE 151.)

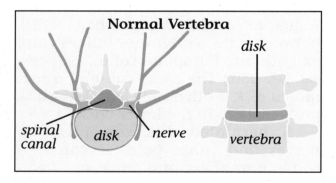

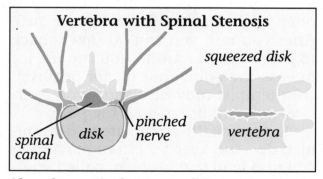

*If you have spinal stenosis, disks get squeezed
between the vertebrae. This can cause pain,
especially when you walk.*

Hip and Thigh Pain

The hip is one of the most stable joints
in the body. The hip is called a "ball
and socket" joint. It is surrounded by
large muscles and a deep socket. Because it is so stable, few problems occur
before middle age. Until that time, most
pain in the hip and thigh comes from
injury to muscles, tendons, or bursas.
For instance, a fall, a blow, or overuse
can cause pain in the hip or thigh. (SEE
BURSITIS, PAGE 145, AND TENDINITIS, PAGE 146.)

Pulled hamstring. The hamstring is a
group of muscles at the back of your
thigh. The hamstring runs from your
pelvis to your knee. Injuries here can
occur in the center of the muscle or just
under the buttocks. Exercise can help
the healing process and prevent further
injury. (SEE BOX, PAGE 158.) Exercise makes
the hamstring strong.

Groin pull. This is a pull of the muscles
on the inside of your thigh. Groin pulls
are common among tennis players. A
slip on the ice can also cause this. Symptoms of a groin pull include pain, tenderness, and stiffness deep in the groin.

What to do about Hip and Thigh Pain

Symptoms/Signs	Action	Symptoms/Signs	Action
◆ **Pain from overuse or injury that lasts less than 7 days** (SEE SELF-CARE: BURSITIS AND TENDINITIS, PAGE 146, AND SELF-CARE: SPRAINS AND STRAINS, PAGE 148.) ◆ **Pulled or torn muscle that causes stiffness, pain, or tenderness to the touch** (SEE SELF-CARE: SPRAINS AND STRAINS, PAGE 148.)	Use self-care	◆ **Swelling, pain, or stiffness after a blow to the thigh** ◆ **Any of the above symptoms that don't improve in 7 to 10 days** ◆ **Dull pain in hip and groin while you walk or climb stairs** ◆ **Severe pain in buttocks when you exercise, and pain stops when you stop exercising** ◆ **Pain that wakes you**	See doctor
◆ **Difficulty walking, running, or climbing stairs** ◆ **Pain on outside of the hip, perhaps down to the knee**	Call doctor	◆ **Severe pain after a fall or blow**	Seek help now

Hip fracture. Your chance of breaking a hip increases with age. Women are twice as likely to break a hip as men are. The main symptom of a hip fracture is pain deep in the groin that is worse when you stand, walk, or climb stairs. You may be able to walk even though your hip is broken. It depends on the type, location, and degree of the fracture.

If you do break a hip, make sure that you follow your doctor's advice carefully. Doing so helps make sure that you will regain use of your hip. Your doctor may refer you to a physical therapist. The therapist can teach you exercises that will help you rebuild muscle strength and reduce stiffness. This will allow you to walk again.

Hip replacement. Your doctor may suggest this treatment if your hip deteriorates and causes severe pain. Or you may need a hip replacement if you find it hard to walk or are disabled in some other way. During a hip replacement, a surgeon removes the damaged bone. Then your hip is replaced with an artificial hip.

Quadriceps Stretch

1. Lie on your right side on a bed.
2. Bend your right knee slightly.
3. Bend your left knee and grasp your ankle or pant leg. (If this is too hard, place a towel around your ankle and hold onto the ends as shown in the circle.)
4. Gently pull your heel toward your buttocks.
5. To feel the stretch more, slowly pull your leg backward. Don't raise the bent leg. Keep your knee at the same level as your hip.
6. Hold for a count of 5 to 10. Relax.
7. Repeat the stretch four to six times on each side.

How to Prevent Hip Pain

- Lose weight if you need to. Excess body weight puts more stress on the hip joint. (SEE PAGE 254.)

- Do regular exercise like walking, swimming, or biking.
- Do stretching exercises routinely.

Knee Pain

Runners and skiers are not the only people who hurt their knees. Anyone can do it. Knees are easy to injure. They can be injured over time by squatting, stooping, kneeling, or lifting. Here are some common ways that knee injuries happen:

- osteoarthritis (SEE PAGE 146.)
- a fall or a sudden twist or blow to the knee
- overuse, such as too much gardening (SEE BURSITIS, PAGE 145, AND TENDINITIS, PAGE 146.)

Housemaid's Knee (Prepatellar Bursitis)

Housemaid's knee is common in people who spend a lot of time on their knees. Symptoms include pain, stiffness, and a squishy, swollen area in front of the kneecap. In severe cases, swelling may go above and beside the knee. An inflamed bursa may break on its own. If this happens, the body absorbs the excess fluid. Then the swelling and inflammation usually stop. To prevent this problem, wear knee pads or use a gardening pad. Use these when you work on your knees for a long period of time. You can buy knee pads and gardening pads at a discount store.

What to do about **Knee Pain**

Symptoms/Signs	Action	Symptoms/Signs	Action
◆ **Pain or swelling after sudden twist or blow to side of knee. Leg can bear weight, but you may limp slightly.** (SEE SELF-CARE: SPRAINS AND STRAINS, PAGE 148.) ◆ **Inflamed tendon below kneecap that hurts when you climb stairs or jump** (SEE SELF-CARE: BURSITIS AND TENDINITIS, PAGE 146.) ◆ **Soft, squishy swelling in front part of knee, with pain and stiffness but without redness.** (SEE SELF-CARE: BURSITIS AND TENDINITIS, PAGE 146.)	Use self-care	◆ **Pain around or under kneecap that gets worse when you climb stairs or sit for a long time** ◆ **Signs of infection, such as local heat, redness, increased swelling, pain, and tenderness**	See doctor
◆ **Symptoms that do not improve within 7 to 10 days**	See doctor	◆ **Pain or swelling after sudden twist or blow to side of knee, and you can't bear weight** ◆ **Severe blow or injury to knee that causes severe swelling and has a deformed look, or you can't move the knee**	Seek help now

Roughing of Kneecap (Chondromalacia Patella)

Roughing of the kneecap is a frequent cause of knee pain. Activities that place stress on the knee can cause this condition. Wearing shoes that give you poor support can make it worse. With this condition, the kneecap rubs against the thigh bone. That rubbing causes wear and tear on the cartilage behind the kneecap. When that happens you may have any of the following symptoms:

● aching and swelling around the kneecap or behind the knee, especially during or after activity

Exercises to Strengthen the Knee

Push one leg against the other.

Leg Curl

First, lie on your stomach. Then bend your legs at the knees, and cross your legs at the ankles. With your left leg, push down on your right leg. Resist the push with your right leg until you slowly straighten it. Switch legs.

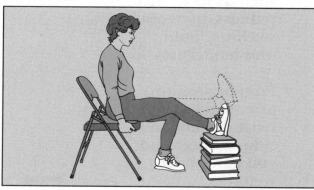

Leg Extension

Sit on a chair with your knees bent at a 90-degree angle. Straighten one leg so that it is parallel to the floor. Hold for a count of five. Then slowly bend the leg and rest it on a stool or pile of books. Switch legs. Once this becomes very easy, you can add leg weights. Start with one or two pounds.

- pain when you squat or sit for a long time with your knee bent
- grinding or popping as the knee bends and straightens

Exercises that help strengthen your knee may be helpful if you have this condition. (SEE BOX ABOVE.)

Osteoarthritis in the Knee

Years of minor knee injuries can lead to osteoarthritis. (SEE PAGE 146.) Torn cartilage and ligament injuries are problems that can lead to osteoarthritis in the knee. But you may be able to prevent the damage from getting worse or disabling you. Routine exercise is a major part of treatment for this condition. It can make the difference between being able to move and not being able to move. If exercise does not help, you may need medicine, physical therapy, or surgery.

Joint mice. These are loose bits of cartilage or loose bits of bone that float between the knee bones. Once cartilage is torn, the knee may click or lock without warning. This can damage the ligaments and damage tendons around the knee.

Knee replacement. If osteoarthritis disables you, your doctor may advise you to have your knee replaced. With this surgery, the knee is replaced with an artificial joint. An artificial knee joint is made from plastic and metal. This is also called a knee prosthesis.

Your new knee won't bend as far as your natural knee once did. But your doctor can show you how far you can safely move it.

Lower Leg Pain

Several things can cause pain in the lower leg. You may have injured your leg through overuse, overexertion, or trauma from a fall or blow. You can also have pain in your lower leg from problems with circulation. These problems include blood clots, congestive heart failure, and inflamed veins in the legs. (SEE PHLEBITIS, PAGE 94.) The main symptom of such conditions is swelling in the legs and feet. This is called edema. (SEE PAGE 88.) If you have chronic swelling in both legs but no pain, you should raise your legs. Then call your doctor.

The conditions covered on the next few pages are common causes of lower leg pain.

What to do about Lower Leg Pain

Symptoms/Signs	Action
◆ **Pain from overuse or a blow, but legs can bear weight** (SEE THE RICE METHOD, PAGE 147.) ◆ **Blow to shin area with bruising but no swelling** (SEE THE RICE METHOD, PAGE 147.) ◆ **Pain along the front or inner edge of the shinbone** (SEE SELF-CARE: SHINSPLINTS, PAGE 163.)	 Use self-care
◆ **Shinsplints that do not get better in two to three weeks** ◆ **Slow increase in shin or ankle pain that gets worse during or after activity**	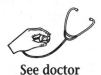 Call doctor
◆ **Painful and sudden swelling and redness in only one leg**	See doctor
◆ **Swelling and pain after a blow to the front of the leg** ◆ **Numbness or tingling in foot after a blow to the shin**	 Seek help now

Cramps and Spasms

"I can be sitting quietly by the fire, reading the daily paper. Nothing is bothering me. Then all of a sudden I get the worst cramp in my leg. I just can't sit still. I walk on it. And I rub it. Sometimes nothing works. It just has to go away by itself."

—Ken

Few things can get you out of bed faster than a muscle cramp in the middle of the night. You get cramps when a muscle suddenly contracts. No one knows why we tend to get cramps in the middle of the night.

What to do about Cramps and Spasms	
Symptoms/Signs	**Action**
◆ Occasional cramps that come and go	Use self-care
◆ Muscle cramps or spasms that occur for several weeks ◆ Neck or back spasm with numbness, tingling, or weakness	Call doctor
◆ Heaviness and pain with swelling, redness, or warmth	See doctor

Being active or inactive can lead to cramps and spasms in the lower legs. Muscles that you use too much may cramp. Muscles that you don't use enough may also cramp. This can happen when you sit in the same position for a long time.

How to Prevent Cramps and Spasms

- Eat more foods that have calcium and potassium in them. You can eat low-fat milk products to add calcium to your diet. These foods have a lot of potassium: bananas, citrus fruits, dried apricots, lentils, dried peaches, fresh vegetables, and whole grain cereal.
- Drink a lot of fluids all day. Water is best. Other drinks without caffeine or alcohol are fine.
- Avoid drinks with caffeine, such as coffee, tea, or colas. They can lead to dehydration.
- Warm up before you exercise. Cool down after you finish.

Self-Care: Cramps and Spasms

- Find the muscle that is cramping. Then massage the cramp gently but firmly.
- Stretch out the cramped muscle. For a leg cramp, sit with your leg flat on the floor. Pull your toes toward you. For a foot cramp, walk on that foot.
- To ease any pain that stays after the cramp is gone, take aspirin or acetaminophen (Tylenol).

Exercises for Your Lower Legs

Calf Stretch

Stand an arm's length away from a wall. Bend your right leg at the knee. Bring it toward the wall. Keep your right knee bent and your foot flat on the floor. Keep your left leg straight and your heel flat on the floor. Keep your back straight. Lean forward. You will feel a stretch in midcalf. Hold this position and count to 10 slowly. Repeat with the other leg.

Toe Taps

Sit on a chair. Keep your feet flat on the floor. Tap both of your feet on the floor 30 to 40 times or until your shin muscles feel tired. Do this whenever you have time during the day.

Shinsplints

"I used to think shinsplints meant a broken shinbone. I found out the hard way what they really are."
—Gary

Shinsplints happen where the muscle connects to the shinbone. The membrane there becomes inflamed and swells. Shinsplints cause pain along the front of the shinbone. You get them by overusing the shin muscles. There is often no swelling, redness, or bruise. The ache may start suddenly or build slowly.

Runners and other athletes often get shinsplints. People who stand all day on hard concrete floors often get them. The most common causes of shinsplints are the following:

- Muscle imbalance. The calf muscle is much stronger than the shin muscles.
- Not enough shock absorption during high-impact exercise. Or your shoes may not give you enough support for long hours of standing. Buy new shoes if the heels are broken down and the soles are worn unevenly.
- A tight Achilles tendon. This tendon is at the back of the heel and ankle.
- Running or walking on the balls of the feet without letting your heel touch the ground
- Doing too much activity too fast
- Flat feet

Self-Care: Shinsplints

- Massage your shins with ice four times a day.

- Rest the leg for three to six days.
- Do Achilles tendon stretches and exercises to strengthen the front of your legs. (SEE BOX, PAGE 163.)
- Wrap your ankle and shin for support when you exercise. Also wrap the leg if your daily activities cause you pain.
- After aching eases, go back slowly to your normal routine. To stay flexible, be sure to stretch routinely. You can also try biking, walking, and swimming.

Periodic Limb Movements (Restless Legs)

"My husband's legs started jerking at night. I thought something was really wrong and called our doctor. But our doctor told us this jerking movement was normal. She said not to worry about it unless it caused us to lose a lot of sleep."
—Muriel

Harmless twitching in the legs occurs in half of all people older than 65. It is most common at night. Your legs may twitch off and on for one to two hours at a time. The twitching rarely wakes you completely. But the twitching can make it hard for you to get a good night's sleep.

Twitching can occur when you are awake. Some people even have a crawling feeling in their calves or thighs when they sit or lie down. It may help you to walk or to move your legs. It might also help you to stretch your calves. Doctors may prescribe medicine for this condition.

Neck Pain

The neck is called the cervical spine. The neck is the most flexible part of the spine. It has a wide range of motion. The neck is easy to injure because it can move in so many directions. The most common sources of neck pain are stress, poor posture, trauma, and wear and tear from overuse and aging.

The neck and upper back muscles are often the first muscles to tense up when you are stressed. When these muscles stay tight for a long time, they may ache. This tension may also cause headaches.

There are more serious causes of neck pain. Both osteoarthritis (SEE PAGE 146) and sprains (SEE PAGE 148) can cause problems. A direct blow to the neck can also make disks bulge or break. This can cause problems similar to those caused by osteoarthritis.

Osteoarthritis in the neck. Osteoarthritis (SEE PAGE 146) can cause painful muscle spasms in the neck. The nerves become irritated, and then you may feel numbness and a tingling in your arms and fingers.

How to Prevent Neck Pain
- Sleep right. Do you often wake up with a crick in your neck? If so, the

What to do about **Neck Pain**

Symptoms/Signs	Action
◆ **Stiff, sore neck when you wake up** ◆ **Muscle tension and pain, especially when under stress**	 Use self-care
◆ **Pain after a sudden twist or blow or after the head is thrown forward or backward**	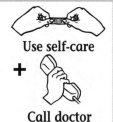 Use self-care **+** Call doctor
◆ **Pain that does not improve after 7 to 10 days of self-care**	 See doctor
◆ **Loss of feeling in shoulder after a trauma that causes the neck and shoulder to twist in opposite directions at the same time** ◆ **Stiff, sore neck with fever and headache** ◆ **Burning, shooting pain or weakness in shoulder**	 Seek help now
◆ **Any severe trauma or blow to the head or neck**	 Call ambulance

cause may be a soft mattress or poor pillow. A pillow may force your neck into an awkward angle or uncomfortable position.

—Position your spine correctly. A cervical-support pillow or a rolled towel under your neck can help.

—Try not to sleep on your stomach.

—If you sleep on your side, use a pillow that lets your head rest so that it is centered between your shoulders.

—If you sleep on your back, make sure that your pillow doesn't push your chin toward your chest.

- Stand and sit correctly. (SEE DRAWING, PAGE 154.) Your spine curves in at the neck, out at the upper back, and in again at the lower back. To improve your posture, stand up straight to keep the natural curve in your lower back. This helps pull the rest of the spine into place. Your shoulders and head will straighten as well. But when you straighten up, make sure your chin and abdomen don't stick out. Avoid slumped shoulders, a drooping head, and slouching or rounding of the lower back.

- Keep your briefcase or purse as light as you can. Switch it from one hand to the other. That way your neck and shoulders get a brief rest. If you have a lot to carry, you should carry the weight evenly on each side of your body. You may want to use a waistpack or backpack.

- Don't bend over your work. Hold what you read at eye level. Place computer screens at eye level too. Don't hold the phone on your shoulder.

Self-Care: Neck Pain

- If you often wake up with a sore neck, try one of the following:
  —Sleep in a different position.
  —Buy a cervical pillow.
  —Put a 3/4-inch plywood board between your mattress and box spring for extra support. If this does not help, you may want to get a new mattress and box spring.
- Stretch. Stretching is important for the neck. You will reduce stiffness and soreness. You will also gain motion and strength. (SEE DRAWINGS AT RIGHT.)
- Take an anti-inflammatory drug for pain. (SEE WHICH PAIN MEDICATION IS RIGHT FOR YOU? PAGE 272.) If pain continues, your doctor may prescribe medicine.
- Ice a sore neck for 10 to 15 minutes several times a day. This will relieve pain and inflammation. A bag of frozen peas or corn makes a good cold pack for the neck.
- If your muscles are sore after two days, apply mild heat for 20 minutes. Do this three times a day. Try switching between heat and ice.
- Rest when pain is at its worst. Lie flat on your back for an hour or so with a fairly flat pillow. Don't rest too long. Too much bed rest can make neck problems worse. This is because muscles get weak when you don't use them.
- Ask a friend to rub your neck or

Exercises for the Neck

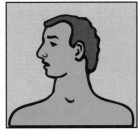 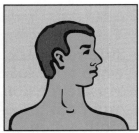

Turn right and hold for two counts. Turn left and hold for two counts.

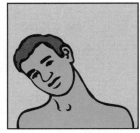 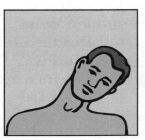

Tilt right and hold for two counts. Tilt left and hold for two counts.

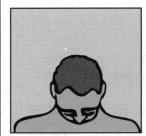 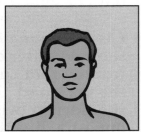

Put your chin down and hold for two counts. Then repeat.

upper back for a few minutes. This will help if your muscles feel tight and sore, especially from stress.
- Try not to move your head quickly. Don't move your head in any way that causes pain.

Meningitis

"I had a stiff neck, a bad head-ache, and a fever. I couldn't bend my neck without severe pain. I'm glad I went to the emergency room. I had meningitis."

—Bob

Membranes cover the brain and spinal cord. Meningitis is an infection or inflammation of these membranes. Symptoms include a very stiff neck, fever, and headache. Nausea, vomiting, or delirium may develop quickly. There are two basic kinds of meningitis: bacterial and viral. Bacterial meningitis can kill you if it is not treated at once with antibiotics. It is most common in children but can strike at any age. Viral meningitis is more common and less serious.

Whiplash

"I was driving in heavy traffic when a car hit me from behind. Thankfully, I had my seatbelt on. But I still injured my neck. I had whiplash."

—John

Whiplash is a neck sprain or strain. It happens when your neck is jerked forward, backward, or both. With this condition, the neck hurts and is stiff the day after the injury. Whiplash is most often caused by rear-end car crashes. But a fall or sudden twist can cause the same kind of pain. Pain from neck sprains and strains may spread to your shoulders, upper back, and arms. The pain may reach your legs. Exercise may ease your neck pain. Following the self-care steps for neck pain may also help.

Shoulder Pain

Your shoulder can move in all directions. That is what makes it unstable. Most of the shoulder's support comes from the rotator cuff muscles. They give the shoulder a wide range of movement. You may have pain from overuse as well as from a fall or a blow.

Muscle aches and tightness around the shoulder are often caused by muscle imbalance. This occurs when one side of the body is much tighter than the other. Strength training can prevent imbalance.

You can use self-care to treat many injuries from overuse and muscle imbalance. Stretching and applying ice can help ease the pain. (SEE SELF-CARE: SPRAINS AND STRAINS, PAGE 148, AND SELF-CARE: BURSITIS AND TENDINITIS, PAGE 146.)

Call your doctor if you feel sudden pain with no known cause. If you injure your shoulder, see a doctor as soon as you can.

If you feel sudden pain in your left arm, tightness in your chest, shortness of breath, or pain in your jaw with no known cause, call for an ambulance. You could be having a heart attack.

What to do about **Shoulder Pain**	
Symptoms/Signs	**Action**
◆ **Shoulder pain after activity that is limited to only certain movements** (SEE SELF-CARE: SPRAINS AND STRAINS, PAGE 148.)	 Use self-care
◆ **Overuse injury that does not improve after 7 to 8 days of self-care**	Call doctor
◆ **Inability to raise your arm**	See doctor
◆ **Trauma with any of these: a sudden pain, a pop, a snap, a cracking sound, a lump or deformity, or inability to move shoulder**	 Seek help now
◆ **Sudden pain in right or left shoulder with no injury, and you can move arm without making pain worse**	 Call ambulance

Rotator Cuff Injuries

"I played quarterback in high school and messed up my shoulder. I have to be careful now or the old injury flares up."
—Jim

Rotator cuff injury describes more than one problem. It refers to damage to the tendons or other parts of the shoulder.

The causes, symptoms, and treatment of these injuries are similar. These injuries may come from a fall or a blow to the shoulder. They are often caused by repetitive overhead motions such as throwing a softball, painting a ceiling, or swimming. Symptoms include shoulder pain at night and when you raise or lower your arm between waist and shoulder. If your tendons are compressed, pain may be worst when the arm is raised with the palm turned down. Your arm or fingers may also tingle or feel numb.

Wrist and Hand Pain

The wrist, hand, and fingers can move in a number of ways. The small muscles in your hand control fine movements. The forearm muscles allow you to write. They also give strength to the hand and fingers.

The wrist and hand don't have much protection. They are more likely to fracture than other bones. Many older adults break their wrists when

What to do about **Wrist Pain**

Symptoms/Signs	Action
◆ **Pain, tenderness, and minor swelling with limited motion** ◆ **Tingling or numbness in fingers that occurs during the day or that wakes you at night**	 Call doctor
◆ **Pain and limited movement after you fall on your hand** ◆ **Pain and fever or rapid swelling in joint** ◆ **Shooting pains** ◆ **Pain that spreads up from wrist to elbow, shoulder, or neck** ◆ **Wrist pain with neck stiffness** ◆ **Weakness or trouble holding objects** ◆ **Clicking, popping, or grinding sounds in your wrist**	 See doctor
◆ **Visible deformity after a fall**	 Seek help now

they use their hands to break a fall. Some causes of wrist and hand pain are discussed in this section.

Self-Care: Wrist and Hand Pain

- Take aspirin or another NSAID to ease pain and swelling.
- Apply ice right away after an injury.
- If you hurt your hand while wearing rings, remove them right away. Take the rings off before swelling can start.
- Rest the painful hand for a few days. Then begin to exercise it gently.

Carpal Tunnel Syndrome

"I type at a keyboard most of the day. At night I love to knit. The pain in my forearm and wrist kept me up at night. My doctor showed me how to ease the stress on my arms. He also thought I should take up a new hobby—at least on some nights."
—Marsha

Carpal tunnel syndrome is caused by doing the same thing over and over. This problem often occurs when you repeat a certain motion, such as throwing, squeezing, lifting, pushing, or pulling. Long periods of overuse can even cause joint damage. The injury that results may be a mix of bursitis (SEE PAGE 145), tendinitis (SEE PAGE 146), or trauma to specific tissues.

With carpal tunnel syndrome, your hands may feel weak in the morning. You may have numbness and tingling in your fingers. This feeling can wake you up at night. Shaking the hand will often ease the tingling and numbness.

The thumb, index finger, and middle finger often feel the worst. You may lose strength in your hand, causing you to drop things.

Carpal tunnel syndrome can be caused by anything that puts repeated pressure on the median nerve. This is the central nerve that runs down your forearm and through your wrist into your hand. If you often use the same hand and arm movements at your job, you are at risk. Those at risk include hairdressers, carpenters, mechanics, secretaries, and factory and farm workers. Some hobbies can lead to carpal tunnel syndrome too. These include needlework, knitting, woodworking, canoeing, golf, and tennis. Anyone can get this condition. It is most common in people in their 40s and 50s. Women have it more often than men.

Treatment for this condition depends on how severe the symptoms are. Your doctor may tell you to use a splint. This keeps the wrist straight while you sleep or while you do things such as typing. Corticosteroids or NSAIDs may ease pain and inflammation. If these methods don't work, your doctor may suggest surgery to relieve pressure on the nerve. You can often have this done without staying in the hospital.

Self-Care: Carpal Tunnel Syndrome

- Limit or stop the repeated motion. You should switch often from one task to another. Ask someone else to do any work that is painful for you.
- Apply cold and then heat. Switch between cold and heat every three minutes. Do this for 10 to 20 minutes at a time.
- Take anti-inflammatory drugs such as ibuprofen. These drugs will help ease the pain and swelling. (SEE WHICH PAIN MEDICATION IS RIGHT FOR YOU? PAGE 272.)
- Ask your doctor about physical therapy or exercises you can do.
- Try not to put direct pressure on your wrists. If you lean on your desk, change positions often. Work with your wrists straight, not bent.

Ganglions

"I have this bubble on my knuckle. It doesn't hurt. My doctor said it is a ganglion cyst, and I don't need to worry unless it grows."
—Emmett

Ganglions are soft, fluid-filled cysts. They form on the sheath of a tendon or on a joint capsule. They can be as small as a marble or as big as a golf ball. They are usually harmless. They may or may not cause discomfort.

A ganglion may go away by itself. If you are bothered by a ganglion, your doctor may drain it with a needle. Or you may have surgery to remove it. The risks of surgery may be greater than the benefits of removing the ganglion. Your doctor may prefer that you watch for any changes.

Chapter 11

Nerve and Brain Disorders

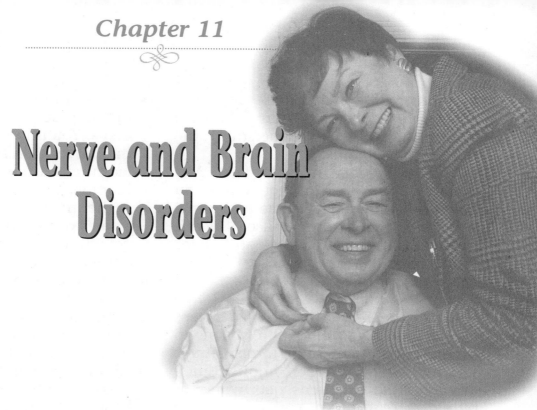

Your nervous system is a network made of billions of cells. All of those cells work together to keep you informed about your body and the world. For instance, your nerves tell your brain if you burn your hand. Then your brain tells your muscles to move your arm away. This happens so fast that you are not even aware of the signal.

Because the nervous system is so complex, there are many places for a problem to occur. For instance, a blocked blood vessel could reduce the supply of oxygen to your brain. This can cause a stroke. Other problems can result from the breakdown of nerve cells. This happens in both Alzheimer's disease and Parkinson's disease.

This chapter describes some of the conditions that affect your nerves and brain. They include:
- Alzheimer's disease
- Bell's palsy
- dizziness
- headaches
- Parkinson's disease
- stroke
- trigeminal neuralgia

Alzheimer's Disease

"My dad was always forgetful when I was a kid. Last year, he started losing his keys and wallet more often. We didn't think much about it. But one day the police called. They found him five miles from home. He was confused about where he was. He had only gone out for the paper."
—David

Alzheimer's disease is a form of dementia. Dementia changes the way you act and think. Alzheimer's affects the brain. It impairs thinking, memory, and behavior. This disease can also affect your personality, your judgment, and your ability to understand the world around you.

You are more likely to get Alzheimer's disease as you age. Once you have it, it slowly gets worse over time. It is the fourth leading cause of death in older adults. But people can live for many years with this disease.

Signs of Alzheimer's Disease

Some of the first signs of Alzheimer's are problems we all have from time to time. For instance, we all forget things. We may even have odd habits. But if any of these problems gets worse or puts you in danger, you could have Alzheimer's disease. It can cause any of the following problems:

- Abstract thinking problems. If you have Alzheimer's you might forget what the numbers in your checkbook mean.
- Daily activity problems. You might find it hard to walk, talk, or use the toilet in later stages of this disease.
- Decision-making problems. You might not dress properly if you have Alzheimer's. You might wear underwear on top of your clothes. You might wear a raincoat on a sunny day.
- Language problems. If you have Alzheimer's, you might forget common words or use the wrong words. Your sentences may not make sense.

- Losing things. You might put things in odd places if you have Alzheimer's. You might put your mail in the freezer. You might put your coffee cup in a closet.
- Memory problems. If you have Alzheimer's you might often forget names or numbers. You may forget what someone said 10 minutes earlier.
- Motivation problems. You may withdraw if you have Alzheimer's. You might not care about your hobbies or daily activities. Or you may begin to avoid your close friends.
- Changes in personality. You might become scared, wary, confused, or hostile if you have Alzheimer's. You might also have mood swings. You might be happy and then sad without knowing why.
- Time and place problems. You might forget what year it is if you have Alzheimer's. You might not always know where you are, even in your own neighborhood.

Alzheimer's disease affects people in different ways. The symptoms may be easy to see in some people, but not in others. The disease can also advance at different rates.

How Your Doctor Knows If You Have Alzheimer's Disease

Doctors don't know what causes Alzheimer's disease. Some think that age and family history are important.

Common Ways the Brain Is Examined

If you have symptoms that could be related to your brain or nerves, your doctor may order tests to look at your brain. Two common tests are the CT scan and the MRI. Each test can provide your doctor with a picture of your brain.

CT Scan is short for computerized tomography. It produces a picture by using a combination of computers and X-rays. Your doctor may use a CT scan to look at any organ in your body, not just your brain. The CT scan can detect tumors, cysts, displaced bone, and abscesses. A CT scan is so sensitive that it can tell if a tumor is benign (which means harmless) or malignant (which means it is cancerous and may spread). The CT scan is painless. The risk involved is the same as for any X-ray, which is very low.

MRI is short for magnetic resonance imaging. An MRI is safe because it does not use radiation. Instead, it uses a magnet and radio waves to make a picture. Your doctor may use an MRI to look at any part of your body. But an MRI is especially good for viewing the brain or spinal cord. It can find tumors, give information about strokes, and detect inflammation or infection. An MRI is painless and safe. But if you have a pacemaker or use a hearing aid, be sure to tell your doctor. An MRI can cause a problem with these devices.

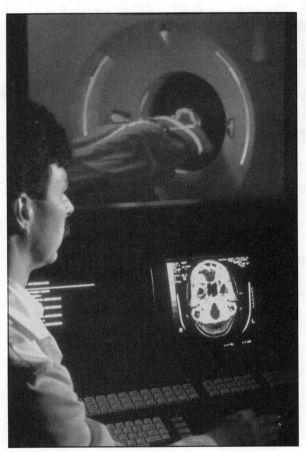

A CT scan works by sending out a thin X-ray beam that is rotated around the entire body. As the X-ray passes through your tissues, it sends readings to a computer. The computer interprets the readings and displays them on a screen.

Other doctors say that causes may include head injuries, viruses, or problems with the immune system or diet. Some doctors think that exposure to poisons might be a cause.

There is no special test to diagnose Alzheimer's. Your doctor will want to be sure that there is no other reason for your symptoms. Your doctor may check your hearing to see if that is a problem. Some doctors use memory tests and IQ tests. Many do X-rays, CT scans, or MRIs to look at your brain. (See Common Ways the Brain Is Examined, page 173.)

How Alzheimer's Disease Is Treated

There is no cure for Alzheimer's disease. Some doctors prescribe medicine to treat behavior problems. Antidepressants, antipsychotic drugs, or mild sedatives may help. In low doses, these drugs can improve the quality of your life.

Bell's Palsy

"I woke up one morning and I could not close my eye. Nothing like that had ever happened to me. I called my doctor. He did a neurological exam. He thought I might have had a stroke. But the doctor said that I had Bell's palsy. He said it will probably go away."
—Dwayne

Bell's palsy occurs most often between the ages of 30 and 60. Bell's palsy paralyzes muscles on one side of your

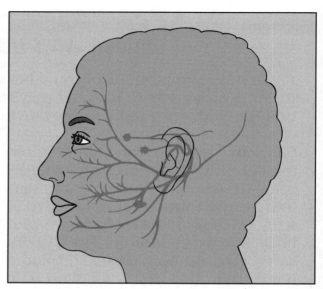

The facial nerve runs just under your ear and spreads along the face muscles. Damage to this nerve can lead to Bell's palsy.

face. That means you can't control the muscles of your face on that side. Your face might sag or feel weak. You might not be able to close one eye.

Bell's palsy is the result of damage to a nerve in your face. There is a nerve on each side of your face that starts in the brain and extends under your ear to reach your face. (See drawing above.) Doctors do not know how damage to the facial nerve occurs. Some doctors think a viral infection can cause the damage. Others think the damage may come from middle ear infections. (See page 42.)

As a rule, Bell's palsy needs no treatment. It can go away in two or three weeks. Some doctors use drugs to reduce the swelling in the nerve. They might give you a steroid like prednisone. Other doctors say that physical therapy will help keep the muscles active.

Dizziness

"If I get up from a chair too fast, I get dizzy. Even turning my head makes me feel woozy at times. My doctor says I have an inner ear problem. It's not serious. I just need to remember to get up slowly."

—Ethel

Feeling dizzy can mean many things. It can mean that you have a poor sense of balance. It can also mean that you are about to faint. You may feel light-headed. You may feel as if things are spinning. It can be unsettling to feel dizzy. But the feeling often lasts just a short time. And it is harmless most of the time.

What to do about Dizziness

Symptoms/Signs	Action	Symptoms/Signs	Action
◆ Dizzy feeling when you stand up or get out of bed	Use self-care	◆ Dizzy feeling with a headache ◆ Dizzy feeling with a tingling feeling in any part of body ◆ Dizzy feeling with a sudden loss of hearing, blurred or double vision, slurred speech, or a hard time swallowing ◆ Dizzy feeling with a loss of bladder control or bowel control	Seek help now
◆ Dizzy feeling that lasts for more than three days	Call doctor		
◆ Dizzy feeling with nausea, vomiting, or fainting ◆ Dizzy feeling with black or bloody stools ◆ Dizzy feeling with fever of 101 degrees or higher	See doctor	◆ Dizzy feeling with symptoms of shock, such as pale, clammy skin or shallow breathing (SEE SHOCK, PAGE 353.) ◆ Dizzy feeling with chest pain or pressure	Call ambulance
◆ Dizzy feeling with ear pain ◆ Dizzy feeling with numbness or weakness in an arm or leg ◆ Dizzy feeling after a head injury	Seek help now		

Dizziness with other symptoms may be a sign of another problem. Dizziness with other symptoms may even be a sign of an emergency. Feeling dizzy and slurring your speech, for instance, could be signs of a stroke. (SEE WHAT TO DO ABOUT STROKE, PAGE 183.) Being dizzy and having chest pain may mean that you are having a heart attack. (SEE KNOW THE SIGNS OF A HEART ATTACK, PAGE 87.)

If being dizzy makes it hard to do the things you always do, talk with your doctor. Also let your doctor know if you are dizzy and have trouble hearing. Your doctor can find out the reason for your dizziness. He or she can then help you learn how to control it. You can also use the self-care steps to help control the feeling. (SEE PAGE 178.)

Types of Dizziness

Many things can make you dizzy. Anxiety can make you dizzy. So can inner ear problems. Heart and blood pressure problems can make you dizzy. So can being dehydrated. The rest of this section explains specific kinds of dizziness.

Balance Problems. You may not be able to walk straight if you have a balance problem. You may feel as if you are going to fall. Balance problems can be dangerous. You could fall and hurt yourself. (SEE HOW TO PREVENT FALLS, PAGE 294.) Any of the following can cause poor balance:
- arthritis (SEE PAGE 245.)
- damaged nerves in your legs or feet (SEE DIABETES AND YOUR FEET, PAGE 64.)

- hearing problems (SEE PAGE 44.)
- poor vision (SEE PAGE 56.)

Even if balance is a problem, you can stay more steady. Use a cane or a walking stick to help keep yourself steady. Leaving a light on at night will help keep you from falling.

Light-headedness. You may feel confused if you feel light-headed. You might feel as if you will pass out. Some people feel light-headed when they get up from a chair or bed too quickly. Doctors call this kind of light-headed feeling postural, or orthostatic, hypotension. This problem comes from a drop in your blood pressure when you stand up. This feeling of being dizzy can pass quickly.

Take these steps to avoid light-headedness:
- Before you get up from sitting or lying down, sit still for a minute. This will keep you from rising too quickly.
- Tighten your leg muscles as you stand up. When you tighten your leg muscles, more blood will flow upward. It will keep your blood pressure from dropping.

High blood pressure, heart problems, and anxiety can make you feel light-headed. If you take a drug for high blood pressure and sometimes feel dizzy, tell your doctor.

Vertigo. Vertigo is the feeling that things are spinning. You might feel sick to your stomach.

Positional vertigo is the most common form of dizziness in older adults. This type of vertigo occurs when you change position. You may feel it when you look up or down or from side to side. You may also feel it when you roll over in bed. The dizzy feeling from positional vertigo often lasts less than a minute. You might have this feeling of being dizzy only once or twice a day. But some people experience vertigo each time they move their head.

Positional vertigo may be caused by a virus in your inner ear. (SEE DRAWING, PAGE 43.) Or it can start on its own. It may also occur after a head injury. Most people don't need treatment. But attacks of positional vertigo can come and go for life.

Labyrinthitis is another type of vertigo. If you have this kind of vertigo, you may not be able to control the direction in which your eyes move. You may have nausea and vomiting. For some people, the symptoms appear all at once during the day. Other people have symptoms when they wake up. This kind of vertigo may last a few days and then go away. But sometimes the other symptoms last for a few months, even after the vertigo is gone.

This kind of vertigo is caused by an infection of the inner ear. (SEE DRAWING, PAGE 43.) There are two kinds of labyrinthitis. The viral form clears up on its own. Your doctor may want you to take a prescription antihistamine such as meclizine to ease the symptoms. The

What Causes Fainting?

When you faint, you lose consciousness. Some people call this passing out. People faint when their blood pressure is too low. When your blood pressure is too low, your brain doesn't get enough blood. Fainting may be a way your body reacts to stress. For instance, you may faint when you see blood. Fainting may also be a sign of problems with your heart or with your blood pressure. Fainting is also dangerous because it can cause you to fall.

Dizziness caused by inner ear problems rarely makes people faint. If you feel dizzy and faint, you should see your doctor right away.

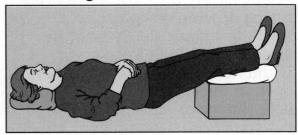

First aid for fainting:
1. *If the person is not breathing or has no pulse, get help right away. If you know CPR, use it.*
2. *If the person is breathing, lay the person on his or her back and raise the feet above the head.* (SEE DRAWING ABOVE.)
3. *Loosen clothes that are tight.*
4. *When the person revives, decide whether or not he or she needs to go to the doctor.*

bacterial form is treated with antibiotic drugs to wipe out the infection. Sometimes your doctor might tell you to try an over-the-counter drug to reduce the dizzy feeling. For instance, Dramamine can ease the spinning feeling and the nausea. This kind of drug works best during the first week, when the vertigo is often the worst. Talk with your doctor about the best way to use these drugs.

Self-Care: Dizziness

- Avoid driving. You could have a hard time controlling your car.
- Drink more fluids to prevent dehydration. Drinking fluids also helps you keep the right blood pressure.
- Get up slowly after you have been sitting or lying down.
- If you feel dizzy, slowly sit or lie down so you don't fall.
- If you have vertigo, keep your eyes open and focus on an object that does not move.
- Put your head between your knees if you feel faint or if your vision starts to go dark.
- Do not put yourself into positions that make you feel dizzy.
- When you want to change your position, move slowly.
- Use relaxation techniques to calm yourself. (SEE PAGE 129.)

Headaches

"Every now and then I get a really bad headache. I used to lie down, but that would not always help. Now I take two pain relievers and a long warm shower. Then I do some deep breathing. This seems to help me a lot."
—Donald

Headaches are a common health complaint among people of all age groups. Your head may seem to be pounding. You might feel pain in your forehead, cheeks, or the top of your skull. Some headaches make only one side of your head hurt. Others cause pain on both sides, the top, the front, or the back of the head.

People have headaches for many reasons. Tension headaches and migraine headaches may occur for no reason. Or they may be triggered by any of the following:
- physical or emotional stress
- certain foods
- very high blood pressure
- eye, ear, and nose infections
- problems with your teeth or jaw
- swollen muscles or sinuses

More serious causes of headache include stroke, infection or bleeding in the brain, and rupture of an aneurysm. (An aneurysm is an abnormal swelling of a blood vessel.) A head injury can also cause headaches.

What to do about **Headaches**

Symptoms/Signs	Action	Symptoms/Signs	Action
◆ Headache with pain on both sides of your head ◆ Headache with mild to severe steady pain, but no significant disability ◆ Headache that does not get worse with activity ◆ Headache with no nausea or vomiting	Use self-care	◆ Headache and nausea ◆ Headache with pain on one side of the head	Use self-care + Call doctor
◆ Headache and sensitivity to light and noise ◆ Headache pain that gets worse with activity	Use self-care + Call doctor	◆ Headache with fever and stiff neck ◆ Severe headache that you never had before ◆ Headache that gets worse over time	See doctor
		◆ Headache and sudden loss of vision ◆ Headache and loss of body functions	Seek help now
		◆ Sudden severe headache that starts with no warning	Call ambulance

Cluster Headaches

Cluster headaches often occur with no warning. You might feel a steady, sharp pain in or around one eye. Your eye may be red and watery. These headaches are called cluster headaches because they occur in groups, or clusters. Cluster headaches often start at the same time of day. The pain gets worse quickly and lasts from a half hour to two hours. You may have a series of these headaches each day. You may have them off and on for weeks or months. Cluster headaches are a chronic condition. But they don't cause lasting harm.

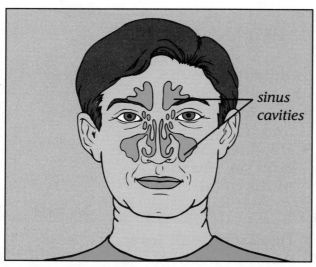

sinus
cavities

A sinus infection can cause headaches that last for days or even weeks. They will go away after the infection is treated with antibiotics.

Aspirin and acetaminophen don't stop the pain of cluster headaches. Your doctor may prescribe a drug or suggest oxygen therapy.

Migraine Headaches

Migraines tend to come less often as you get older. They can often cause intense, throbbing pain on one side of your head. You might also vomit or feel nauseated. Light and noise might make you feel worse. Movement can also make you feel worse.

Migraine headaches often start when you make changes in your routine. If you sleep more or less than normal, you might get a migraine. You might also get a migraine if you change what you eat or drink. Drugs that have estrogen in them, such as Premarin, can cause migraines too.

Some migraines respond to self-care. If self-care methods don't work for you, talk with your doctor. He or she may prescribe a drug to relieve the problem.

Tension Headaches

Most headaches are tension headaches. A dull pain in your scalp, temples, or back of the neck is a sign of a tension headache. With a tension headache both sides of your head are likely to hurt but not throb. Nausea and vomiting are rare in tension headaches. Physical activity will not affect the pain.

Many things can cause tension headaches. Stress, depression, and anxiety can all lead to a headache. Strain or poor posture can also cause headaches. Your doctor may want to do some tests if your headaches don't get better. Your doctor might ask for vision tests, sinus and skull X-rays, or CT scans. (SEE COMMON WAYS THE BRAIN IS EXAMINED, PAGE 173.) Your doctor will also ask about your mental state. Some people need to be treated for depression (SEE PAGE 114) or use relaxation therapy to get rid of their headaches.

Over-the-counter pain relievers, such as aspirin, ease many tension headaches. (SEE WHICH PAIN MEDICATION IS RIGHT FOR YOU? PAGE 272.). But overuse of these drugs can cause problems. Problems can include liver and kidney damage and stomach irritation. Try not to use them more than three days a week. Overuse can also make it hard for your doctor to find out what may be causing your headaches. Sometimes, routine exercise can help prevent and ease tension headaches.

Self-Care: Headaches

- Keep a "headache calendar." Use your calendar to keep track of your headaches and your daily routine. When you do, you may see a pattern or learn what causes your headaches. To track your headaches, write down these things:
  —how well you slept the night before the headache
  —what you did the day before the headache and on the day you had the headache
  —when your headache started
  —how you felt right before it started
  —how long it lasted
  —what made it better
  —what you ate and drank for the 24 hours before your headache started
- Rub your head where it hurts.
- Do exercises that help you relax. Relaxation techniques (SEE PAGE 129) can help ease tension headaches. Ask your doctor to show you some of these. Or call your local hospital to see if there are classes near you.
- Take a hot or cold shower to ease tension.
- Ask your doctor about over-the-counter drugs such as aspirin and acetaminophen. Take one or two tablets when your headache starts. You can take one or two more every four to six hours after that. Also ask about nonsteroidal anti-inflammatory drugs (NSAIDs) such as Aleve and Motrin. (SEE WHICH PAIN MEDICATION IS RIGHT FOR YOU? PAGE 272.)
- Take prescription drugs as directed.

Parkinson's Disease

"My husband has Parkinson's disease. He walks slowly and takes a drug called L-dopa. He has had this disease for about five years. I remind him that he should rest a few times a day. Resting seems to make him feel better. When he gets angry or frustrated, his symptoms get worse. So he exercises. When he stays active, his tremors are not as bad."

—Charlotte

Nearly one million Americans have Parkinson's disease. Most of them are age 50 or older. This disease is the slow breakdown of brain cells that make dopamine. Dopamine is a chemical that sends signals to nerve cells in the brain. These signals are important for movement. They let you move the way you want to move. When the cells break down, you make less dopamine. Then you lose control over how you move. Doctors do not know what makes the cells break down.

Signs of Parkinson's Disease

The symptoms of Parkinson's disease appear slowly. You may have it for years before you are diagnosed with it. Parkinson's disease makes you lose control of the muscles on one or both sides of your body.

Parkinson's disease appears in many ways. If you have this disease, you may have any of these problems:

- Difficulty chewing, swallowing, and talking

- Difficulty keeping your balance
- Flat speech patterns. You might not be able to vary the tone of your voice.
- Lack of facial expression. It can be hard to move your face muscles. Smiling or frowning can be hard if the disease is severe.
- Muscle stiffness. A stiff arm or leg can also be a sign.
- Resting tremors. Trembling hands are common. You may tremble less when you become active.
- Shuffling gait. Dragging your foot behind you when you walk is a classic sign of this disease.
- Slow movements

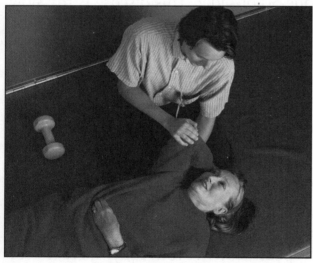

Physical therapy can help improve muscle control for people who have Parkinson's disease. Physical therapy is just one step you can take to control your symptoms.

- Stiff or stooped posture
- Unusual stillness while you sit or stand

How Your Doctor Knows if You Have Parkinson's Disease

There is no test for Parkinson's disease. But your doctor may order some tests to rule out other problems. These tests may include CT scans and MRIs. (SEE PAGE 173.) Or your doctor may do blood tests to rule out other diseases. Your doctor will also check to see if a drug, stroke, or brain tumor may be the cause of your symptoms.

How Parkinson's Disease Is Treated

Parkinson's disease gets worse with time. But it may be many years before it gets in the way of your daily life. It cannot be prevented or cured. Doctors are still looking for new ways to treat it. There are some new surgical treatments, but these are still in the trial stage. They are not yet routine.

Many drugs are used to treat Parkinson's disease. Levodopa (L-dopa) is one of the most common. You can take steps to help control your symptoms. Physical and occupational therapy can improve your muscle control. This treatment can also help you keep a positive outlook. Keeping a positive outlook may also help you avoid depression.

Self-Care: Parkinson's Disease

- Rest during the day. Being tired can make symptoms worse.
- Exercise. It can make it easier for you to walk.
- Try arts and crafts projects to improve the use of your hands and fingers. Call a senior center near you to see if it has groups that do crafts.
- Find things in your life that make you content. Meet with friends, visit family, or try your new hobby. Anything that makes you calm and happy can help ease your symptoms.

Stroke

"One night my mother was having trouble holding her fork. Her speech was slurred. She said she felt OK, but I was scared. I called her doctor. The doctor told me to bring her to the emergency room. I am glad I acted quickly. She was having a stroke."

—Margaret

When you have a stroke, the blood flow to a part of your brain stops. Stroke is a leading cause of impairment in older adults. It is the third leading cause of death after heart disease and cancer.

What to do about Stroke

Symptoms/Signs	Action
◆ **Sudden weakness or numbness on one side of body** ◆ **Finding it hard to talk, or being unable to talk** ◆ **Having a hard time understanding what is said** ◆ **Sudden loss of sight, especially in one eye, or losing part of your vision** ◆ **Double vision** ◆ **Sudden dizziness, especially with weakness in legs or arms, numbness, double vision, or loss of vision** ◆ **Severe headache pain and weakness in legs or arms, numbness, double vision, or loss of vision** ◆ **A transient ischemic attack, or TIA** (SEE WHAT IS A TIA? PAGE 186.)	 Call ambulance

Are You At Risk for a Stroke?

You are at risk for a stroke if you say "yes" to any of these questions:

- Are you older than 70? The risk of stroke doubles between ages 65 and 75. It doubles again between 75 and 85.
- Do you have coronary artery disease?
- Do you have diabetes? Diabetes that is not controlled can harm your blood vessels. Diabetes doubles the risk of stroke.
- Do you have high blood pressure? This can strain your blood vessels and make them weak.
- Are you a man? Men are at greater risk for a stroke.
- Have you had a stroke?
- Do you have a family history of stroke? You are more likely to have a stroke if one of your parents has had one.
- Are you African-American? African-Americans have a 50 percent greater risk of stroke than Caucasians do. Some of this is due to a greater risk of high blood pressure and diabetes.
- Do you smoke? Cigarette smokers are twice as likely to have a stroke as nonsmokers are.
- Do you have a high cholesterol level? (SEE PAGE 91.)

If you answered "yes" even once, follow the tips on How to Prevent Strokes. Also talk with your doctor about how to lower your risk.

How to Prevent Strokes

You can reduce your risk of a stroke.

- Stop smoking. (SEE PAGE 300.) Ask your doctor about help for quitting.
- Control your blood pressure. (SEE PAGE 90.) Have it checked often. Ask your doctor what you need to do if your blood pressure is high.
- Control your diabetes. (SEE PAGE 249.) Check your blood glucose each day. Have routine checkups with your doctor and dietitian.
- Control your blood cholesterol level. (SEE PAGE 91.) Have it checked regularly. If it is high, ask your doctor how to lower it.
- Eat well. Follow a healthy diet. (SEE EATING FOR YOUR HEALTH, PAGE 287.) Limit the amount of fat and cholesterol you eat.
- Make exercise a part of your routine. Physical activity helps your cir-

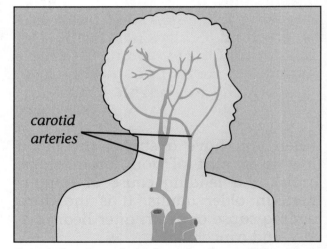

People have strokes when the flow of blood is stopped in one or more of the large arteries shown here.

culation and controls your weight. (SEE PAGE 291.)

- If you drink alcohol, do so in moderation. Get help if you think you may have a problem with alcohol. (SEE PAGE 285.)
- Watch your weight. (SEE PAGE 254.) Too much weight increases your risk of high blood pressure, diabetes, and heart disease. These conditions are all risk factors for stroke.

How a Stroke Is Treated

Emergency room care for a stroke is very important. Early care can reduce damage to your brain and limit the effects of the stroke. The doctor may give you anticoagulant drugs. These drugs thin your blood. That lets them keep blood clots from growing larger. The doctor may use other drugs to break up the clots. You might get a blood pressure drug like propranolol to treat a bleeding stroke. You might need surgery. The doctor could do a carotid endarterectomy. This surgery widens the carotid artery, the large artery in your neck. (SEE DRAWING, PAGE 184.) Your doctor may also suggest that you take aspirin to help lower your risk of a second stroke.

Strokes damage your brain cells. This damage may impair your ability to function normally. What kind of impairment and how severe it is can vary. It depends on what part of your brain is damaged. Brain cells destroyed by a stroke don't grow back. But the brain does adapt. The brain can make

Some people benefit from speech therapy after a stroke. Occupational therapy can help with things like dressing and bathing.

new nerve pathways or change existing pathways. Because the brain adapts, some functions that were lost may come back.

Therapy programs can help your brain relearn things right after a stroke. Physical therapy can help your muscles get stronger. It can also improve your balance and coordination. Speech and language therapy can help your language skills. Occupational therapy can improve coordination between your hands and eyes. This makes it easier to get dressed, cook, and bathe. The kind of therapy needed will differ from one person to the next. Some people can recover from a stroke completely in a few days or weeks. Other people may need months or years to get better. Many people who have a stroke do not recover completely. But most people who have a stroke are able to care for themselves.

What Is a TIA?

A TIA is a ministroke. TIA stands for transient ischemic attack. A TIA has the same symptoms as a stroke, but it lasts only a few minutes. A TIA can warn you that you have a high risk for a more serious stroke. Up to 40 percent of people who have a TIA have a stroke later. If you have a TIA, see your doctor right away.

Multi-Infarct Dementia

Multi-infarct dementia is a type of dementia caused by strokes. Dementia changes the way you act and think. One sign of dementia is a step-by-step loss of memory. Each stroke causes more loss of memory. The more loss there is, the less you are aware of it. Your personality can also change. You may cry or laugh for no reason. You may be depressed. Parts of your body might be paralyzed.

Multi-infarct dementia has some of the same signs as Alzheimer's disease. (SEE PAGE 172.) But Alzheimer's disease often comes on more slowly. Multi-infarct dementia can happen all at once. About 20 percent of people who have dementia have this form.

There is no way to treat this form of dementia. But if you stay fit and eat well, you can reduce your risk of having strokes. (SEE STAYING ACTIVE, PAGE 291, AND EATING FOR YOUR HEALTH, PAGE 287.) Doing these things lowers your risk of multi-infarct dementia.

Trigeminal Neuralgia

"One morning I felt a stabbing pain on the side of my face. I still had it that night, so I went to the doctor. I had trigeminal neuralgia. My doctor gave me a drug that took about a day to work."
—Emma

Trigeminal neuralgia is also known as tic douloureux, which is French for "painful twitch." It mostly affects women who are older than 50. It causes repeated, sharp, knifelike pains in one side of the face. It hurts so much that you can't help but wince each time you feel it. That is why people who have this condition seem to have a tic. A tic is a facial movement you can't control.

The trigeminal nerve supplies the face, teeth, mouth, and nose with feeling. It also allows you to chew. Trigeminal neuralgia is caused when the nerve does not work right. In rare cases it is caused by a tumor or blood vessel pressing on the nerve.

Certain actions may trigger the pain. It can start when you smile, talk, chew, blow your nose, or brush your teeth. The pain may be in your cheek, chin, gums, or lips. Pain in the forehead is rare but does occur. Attacks come and go. But as you age, the time between them may grow shorter.

Doctors treat this disorder with drugs that help prevent seizures. One drug is carbamazepine (Tegretol). Another drug is phenytoin (Dilantin). If these drugs don't work, your doctor may suggest surgery to ease the pain.

Chapter 12

Sexual Health Concerns

Intimacy comes from the closeness and affection that you share with a partner. Being intimate depends at least as much on your mind as on your body. You can feel close even if you don't have sex. Touching is one way to share affection. Hugging and kissing are other ways to share affection. You can show how close you feel by giving each other back rubs. You can hold hands.

Sex is good for both your physical and mental health. It is a fun and normal activity, no matter how old you are. People who are in fairly good health can enjoy sex for most of their adult lives.

This chapter deals with some concerns men and women have about sex. It suggests ways to solve problems that may arise. It also covers diseases that can be spread through sex.

Physical Changes and Sex

Your body changes as you age. Your heart and lungs may need to work harder to do the same job. Your muscles lose bulk and strength. Your skin becomes less elastic. All of these changes are normal. Some of them can affect your sex life.

People react to these changes in many ways. Some blame themselves when their sex life changes. Others think that something is wrong with their relationship. Some may think their sex life is over. But most of the changes in your body that affect sex are normal. You can adjust to these changes and continue to enjoy sex.

Changes in Desire and Intimacy

"My husband and I had gone two months without having sex. I thought he was mad at me. I thought that I was no longer attractive to him. At first I tried starting sex. But he was always tired or busy. I felt lonely and rejected. The tension was so bad that we finally had to talk. It was difficult. But talking did help. I guess we both needed to make some changes in the way we have sex. We had to work on treating each other better the rest of the time too."

—Jane

All people have different sexual needs. And those needs may change. For instance, your level of desire may not be the same as it was when you were younger. It may take you more time to have an orgasm. You may need to be touched more directly. Or you may not feel aroused as often as you once did. But you are not likely to lose your desire completely.

If you have less desire for sex than your partner does, talk about it with each other. Try to meet each other halfway. There is no normal level of desire. These kinds of problems can be confusing. You and your partner might want to think about getting help. (SEE WHEN TO GET PROFESSIONAL ADVICE ABOUT SEX, PAGE 192.)

Even if you don't have intercourse, you can still be close to your partner.

What to do about Sexual Problems

Symptoms/Signs	Action
◆ **Problems with desire** (SEE SELF-CARE: DESIRE AND INTIMACY.) ◆ **Problems with orgasms** (MEN: SEE SELF-CARE: SEXUAL CHANGES IN MEN, PAGE 190. WOMEN: SEE SELF-CARE: SEXUAL CHANGES IN WOMEN, PAGE 191.) ◆ **Problems with erections, or ejaculation** (SEE SELF-CARE: SEXUAL CHANGES IN MEN, PAGE 190.)	 Use self-care
◆ **Sexual problem that does not improve, even with self-care** ◆ **Pain or bleeding during sex** ◆ **Sexual problem caused by an illness, such as diabetes or heart disease**	 Call doctor

As you grow older, you may prefer to do other intimate things. You may like to touch, kiss, and cuddle. It can be exciting to give and receive pleasure in new ways. Just being together and talking can be intimate.

Self-Care: Desire and Intimacy

- Avoid alcohol. It can block sexual arousal.
- Avoid drugs that make you drowsy. Ask your doctor if the drugs you take could affect your sex life.
- Focus on your senses. It is easy to forget how good it feels to be caressed. You and your partner may need to get back in touch with that feeling. Relax and enjoy just touching each other.

Try this approach: Set aside time each day to give each other a massage. Take off your clothes. Explore and caress each other's body. But don't touch the breasts or the genitals. That might lead to intercourse before you are ready. Work slowly into intercourse. Caress each other in the ways you have practiced. All of this can help calm fears about sex. It can also help you respond better to your partner.

- Talk with your partner. Talking can improve your sex life. Tell your partner what excites you. Show your partner how you like to be touched. Talk about problems and tensions as they come up. Don't wait until problems seem too hard to deal with.

Intimacy is more than just having sex. It means feeling close to your partner. Talking, touching, or just being together can be intimate.

Sexual Changes in Men

"I knew that it was normal for men to have problems getting an erection sometimes. But it had never happened to me. Then it did, and I was too ashamed to talk about it, even with my wife. But I could see how much it hurt her. So I went to see my doctor. He checked me over and talked with both of us. He said my problem had nothing to do with how we feel about each other. It had a lot to do with my stress about retirement. Things are so much better now. It seems as if I never had a problem."

—Fred

To have intercourse, a man needs to have an erection. But some changes that occur with age can make it difficult to become erect. Older men often need the penis to be touched more directly to get an erection. Stroking can also help a man stay erect. Physical changes can also affect how a man ejaculates. Most problems can be treated.

About 10 million American men have a long-term problem with sexual function. Some problems that may affect your sex life include the following:

- problems with blood vessels (SEE ATHEROSCLEROSIS, PAGE 90.)
- problems with the prostate (SEE PAGE 222.)
- diabetes (SEE PAGE 249.)
- side effects from drugs

Ejaculation Problems

When a man is stressed, tired, or anxious, he may have trouble ejaculating. Diabetes and other conditions can also cause problems.

Early ejaculation is a problem for many men. It is also called premature ejaculation. This happens when semen comes out of the penis soon after stimulation starts. This can shorten foreplay or keep you from having intercourse. You may be able to overcome these problems by changing how you and your partner make love. Use the self-care tips for sexual changes in men.

Impotence

When a man can't get erect, or can't stay erect, it is called impotence. At some point in their lives, most men can't keep an erection. As you get older, your erection may be less firm than it once was. At times, you may lose your erection during intercourse.

Three things must occur to cause you to have an erection. First, you must be aroused through your thoughts and senses. Your senses include sight, hearing, touch, and smell. Second, your nervous system must respond. The nervous system sends a message from the brain to the penis. Third, your blood vessels must respond. They must relax so that blood can flow into the penis. If any of these responses is disturbed, you may not get an erection. As a rule, these problems don't last a long time.

Many long-term sexual problems have a physical cause. Your doctor can help. He or she might have you change one of the drugs you take. Your doctor might have you take a hormone that can help. Some people find that counseling helps.

Self-Care: Sexual Changes in Men

- Ask your doctor if any of the drugs you take can cause impotence.
- Ask your doctor about counseling.
- If ejaculating early is a problem, pause during the sex act. Change positions.
- Practice Kegel exercises. These strengthen the muscle around the urethra. Stronger muscles can lead to greater desire and stronger orgasms. You naturally squeeze these muscles any time you hold your urine. You squeeze them if you are waiting to get to a bathroom, for instance. Here's how to do the exercises:
  —Squeeze and relax the muscles. Do this 15 times in a row, two times a

day. You don't have to be urinating to do this. You can be driving, reading, or at work.

—Increase the number of squeezes you do. Work up to about 75 times, two times a day.

—When you can do 75 squeezes a day, hold the squeeze for a count of three. Then relax and repeat. These are harder to do. Try doing some long squeezes and some shorter ones.

—Continue doing Kegels for at least six weeks.

Sexual Changes in Women

"Sometimes it hurt when I had sex. That made me not want to have it. I kept making excuses to my husband. When I talked to my doctor, she asked me if my vagina was dry. Then she told me to try a lubricant. What an improvement! Now I use it each time we have sex."

—Doris

The average age that menopause starts is 50. (SEE PAGE 228.) During menopause, a woman's body starts to make less estrogen. Estrogen is a female sex hormone. When your estrogen level goes down, you may lose some of your desire for sex. That means your body may not respond during sex the way it once did. Menopause itself may make you cranky or depressed. These feelings of depression can also have an effect on your desire for sex.

Lack of Arousal

When you are aroused, blood rushes to your genitals. The increase in blood flow helps your vagina to open. It also makes your vaginal walls wet. The estrogen in your blood is what makes this happen. You can become aroused even when your estrogen level is low. But it may take longer, and the feeling may be less intense.

Vaginal Dryness

The vagina can become drier after menopause. The walls of the vagina become thin and less elastic. (SEE VAGINAL DRYNESS, PAGE 232.) If your vagina is dry, sex may hurt. Your vagina could become inflamed or infected. If sex hurts or makes you bleed, talk with your doctor. He or she may want you to take estrogen. This hormone can help thicken the vaginal walls. It can also help moisten the vagina. (SEE HORMONE REPLACEMENT THERAPY, PAGE 230.)

Self-Care: Sexual Changes in Women

- Talk with your doctor about hormone replacement therapy (HRT). HRT may help you with vaginal dryness as well as arousal problems. (SEE PAGE 230.)
- Talk with your partner about taking more time with each other. It may help to change the way you make love. This may help you become more aroused. (SEE SELF-CARE: DESIRE AND INTIMACY, PAGE 189.)

Medicines and Sexuality

"My doctor recently told me I have high blood pressure. He put me on a drug that lowers it. But when I wanted to make love with my wife, I could not get an erection. I was really upset. I called my doctor. He had me take a new drug. Now when we want to make love, I can."

—Sidney

Sometimes a drug you take can cause a problem with sex. A prescription drug or an over-the-counter drug can affect your sex life. Alcohol and other drugs can also have an effect. For instance, drugs for blood pressure and depression can cause a problem with a man's ejaculation or a woman's desire.

As you get older, your body becomes more sensitive to drugs. You may be more likely to have side effects from the drugs you take. Talk with your doctor if you think that a drug is affecting your sex life. Your doctor may want to change the prescription for the drug. Or the doctor may want to adjust the dose you take.

Always talk with your doctor before you take a new drug. Ask what side effects it could cause. Find out if the drug could cause a sexual problem. Sometimes you must take a drug that can cause sexual problems. If so, you may be able to be intimate with your partner in ways other than having intercourse. (SEE CHANGES IN DESIRE AND INTIMACY, PAGE 188.) Talk with your doctor for advice.

When to Get Professional Advice About Sex

If you have a sexual problem, talk about it with your partner. If that does not help fix the problem, or if you have concerns, talk with your doctor. At first you may find it hard to talk about sex. Many people do. Relax. Doctors know that people are often troubled about sex. Your doctor may review the drugs you take. Then he or she can see if a drug could be causing the problem. Your doctor can also check to see if your problems have a physical cause. Your doctor may have some helpful ideas. He or she may refer you to a counselor or specialist who treats sexual problems.

Talk with your partner about sex problems. If you have trouble talking, think about seeing a counselor.

Illness and Intimacy

"I love my wife dearly. But we stopped having sex after I had a heart attack. We were both afraid that I would have another one if we had sex. But we missed being that close to each other. We both felt as if something had gone from our lives. After a while, I built up my courage and talked with my doctor. I asked if I could have sex again. He said that it was safe. He also told me to talk with him anytime I have a question about sex and my health."

—Norbert

Many illnesses can keep you from enjoying sex. You may lose your desire for sex if you are ill or getting over an illness. Sickness can simply make you feel less attractive. Pain, such as from arthritis, can make it hard to move when you make love. Anxiety about your illness can make you lose your sexual desire. For instance, if you fear that sex will cause chest pains, you may try to avoid it as much as you can. Some conditions can affect how much energy you have. For instance, depression may have a major effect on your desire for sex.

If intercourse causes pain for you or your partner, it affects you both. You should talk with your doctor together. Then your doctor can help you find ways to have sex carefully. When you do, you can have sex without pain. (SEE WHEN TO GET PROFESSIONAL ADVICE ABOUT SEX, PAGE 192.)

Sexually Transmitted Diseases (STDs)

Sexually transmitted diseases are called STDs for short. STDs affect millions of Americans each year. AIDS is the most serious. But other STDs are more common. They include the following:
- chlamydia
- genital herpes
- gonorrhea
- hepatitis B
- syphilis

Age does not protect you against STDs. If you engage in risky sexual behavior, you could get an STD. This section tells you how to know if you are at risk for an STD. It tells you how to protect yourself from getting an STD. It also covers the signs of STDs and describes treatment.

Could You Be At Risk for an STD?
STDs are passed from one person to another during sex. Sex includes vaginal sex, oral sex, and anal sex. You are at risk for an STD if you have unprotected, or unsafe, sex. To protect yourself during sex, you need to follow the steps for how to have safe sex. (SEE PAGE 194.) You are at risk for an STD if you say "yes" to any of the following:
- Do you have unsafe sex with a partner who has an STD?
- Do you have unsafe sex with more than one person?

- Does your partner have unsafe sex with more than one person?

If you are at risk, be sure to talk with your doctor.

Some STDs can spread in other ways too. For instance, people who share needles and syringes are at risk for AIDS and hepatitis B. People who inject drugs may share needles.

Safe Sex: How to Prevent STDs

- Have a relationship in which you and your partner are faithful. Make sure that neither of you is infected. If you are unsure about either of these things, you should practice safe sex.
- Always use a latex condom when you have sex.
- Learn how to use a condom correctly. (SEE PAGE 196.) Condoms can break when people don't know how to use them the right way. Always use a water-based lubricant (with or without spermicide) on the outside of the condom. Don't use condoms made from lambskin. They can break easily. They also have tiny holes in them. The holes may let viruses and bacteria pass through.
- Always use spermicide with a condom. Some condoms have spermicide in them. You can buy spermicidal gel at the drugstore. Look for the words "nonoxynol 9" on the label. This spermicide guards against many STDs. But don't use the gel by itself. You need the condom, too.

- Use a barrier during oral sex with a female partner. You can use a dental dam. Or you can cut a condom lengthwise, then into a square. Place the cut condom between your mouth and the vagina.
- Protect yourself. Your risk of getting an STD increases when you have more than one partner.
- Avoid exposure to the blood of others. Don't share needles, tweezers, toothbrushes, or razors. If you have any body piercing done, be sure that the instruments have been sterilized.

If you think you may have an STD, see your doctor.

Acquired Immune Deficiency Syndrome (AIDS) and HIV

"HIV is the virus that causes AIDS. You can get HIV in specific ways. Sex is one way. If you have intercourse, protect yourself. Dirty needles can also spread the virus. If you inject drugs, don't share needles and syringes. You can't get HIV from toilet seats or casual contact."
—Immunologist

AIDS stands for acquired immune deficiency syndrome. AIDS is caused by a virus called HIV. The virus attacks and destroys the immune system. This is the system that helps you fight off disease. Once the immune system is

Talk With Your Partner About STDs

Don't be ashamed to talk with your partner about STDs. Unless you and your partner have had sex only with each other for many years, you could be at risk. It may be awkward at first to bring it up, but your health is worth it.

You may want to start the discussion by talking about ways you can practice safe sex. Or you may want to think about getting tested by your doctor. You could have an STD and not know it. You may not have any symptoms.

If your doctor has told you that you have an STD, tell your partner. Many times both of you will need to be treated. It is extremely important to tell your partner about an STD if she could get pregnant. An STD can spread from mother to child. An infected mother can spread some STDs while she is pregnant or breast-feeding. An STD can also spread to a baby when a woman gives birth.

If you know that you or your partner has an STD, you should take steps to keep from spreading it. Avoid sex until treatment for an active STD, such as gonorrhea, is completed. Then use a condom and spermicide together. Certain STDs, like genital herpes, cannot be cured but can be controlled. Talk with your doctor about how to prevent spreading these to your partner.

---

injured, people who have HIV have a hard time fighting infections.

Signs of HIV Infection

The first signs of HIV infection can be hard to spot, especially in older people. When people become infected with HIV, it can take years for symptoms to appear. In older adults, it may take less time. Once you have HIV, you can spread it to someone else before you know that you have it. The symptoms may look like signs of a less serious illness. And symptoms may go away in a few weeks. Some people who have HIV have no early signs. The first signs that you may have an HIV infection include the following:

- diarrhea
- fatigue
- fever
- joint aches and pains
- nausea and vomiting
- sore throat
- swollen glands

If you have any of these symptoms, don't panic. These are common for many illnesses. But if you are at risk and have signs, talk with your doctor.

Are You At Risk for AIDS?

About 1 out of 10 people with AIDS is older than age 50. Most of these people became infected with HIV through sex. Before 1985, some people received HIV-infected blood during a transfusion. These days, getting the HIV virus from a blood transfusion is extremely rare. Now all blood must be tested before it is used.

HIV can spread in only a few ways. You can get HIV if the blood, semen, or vaginal fluid from a person who is infected gets into your bloodstream. These fluids can get into your bloodstream if any of them touches a mucous membrane. Mucous membranes line the mouth, vagina, and rectum. HIV can also get into the blood through open sores or through broken or irritated skin. You are at high risk for getting HIV if you answer "yes" to either of the following questions:

- Have you had unsafe sex with someone who is infected with HIV?
- Have you shared needles or syringes to inject drugs?

If you answered "yes" to either of these questions, talk with your doctor. You are also at risk for HIV infection if you are at risk for other STDs. (SEE COULD YOU BE AT RISK FOR AN STD? PAGE 193.)

To be safe from AIDS, you need to protect yourself. When you have sex, practice safe sex. (SEE SAFE SEX: HOW TO PREVENT STDs, PAGE 194.) Practicing safe sex will help both you and your partner stay safe.

How AIDS Is Treated

Although there is no cure, AIDS can be treated. Some drugs can slow it down. New drugs are being developed that help people with AIDs to live longer, more healthy lives. If you have AIDS,

How to Put On a Condom

1. Make sure that the condom has a reservoir. Or you can leave at least half an inch of extra space at the top for semen.
2. Put on the condom when the penis is fully erect. Squeeze air from the tip of the condom, and roll it down to the base of the penis.

   You can use a lubricant to help keep the condom from tearing. Be sure to use only water-based lubricants. Oil-based lubricants such as petroleum jelly or baby oil can damage condoms. Then they are more likely to break.
3. Withdraw the penis soon after ejaculation, while the penis is still erect. Hold on to the base of the condom while withdrawing. This helps to avoid spilling the semen.

Use only latex condoms, and follow the instructions. Check the expiration date on the condom package. Don't use the condom if the expiration date has passed. Store condoms in a cool, dark, dry place. Heat can weaken them.

work closely with your doctor. Learn as much as you can about treatment. Treatment options for this disease change quickly.

Chlamydia

"Whenever I urinated, it would burn and hurt. I had a discharge from my penis. I knew something was wrong. I went to the doctor, who asked for a urine sample. The test said that I had chlamydia. The cure was simple and painless. I wish that I had talked with my doctor sooner."

—Bob

Chlamydia is an infection caused by bacteria. It can affect women and men. The disease can cause fever and pain in the abdomen. Bacteria can infect the genitals and the anus.

In women, the infection can inflame the cervix, vagina, and uterus. It can also cause a discharge from the vagina. This infection can be very serious for younger women. If bacteria infect the fallopian tubes, a woman may be unable to get pregnant. It also increases the risk of ectopic pregnancy. That means the embryo is not in the uterus. An ectopic pregnancy is dangerous for the mother and the child.

In men, chlamydia can inflame the urethra. The urethra is the tube that carries urine out of the body. (SEE DRAWING, PAGE 36.) The infection can also inflame the epididymis. This is the part of the body where sperm are stored. The infection can cause discharge from the penis or a burning sensation.

How Chlamydia Is Treated

If you have chlamydia, you and your partner need treatment. You will take antibiotics. The infection could come back unless you are both treated. After treatment, protect yourself by practicing safe sex. (SEE SAFE SEX: HOW TO PREVENT STDS, PAGE 194.) This can help keep you from getting an STD again.

Genital Herpes (Herpes Simplex 2 Virus)

"The skin around my vagina was very itchy. The next day, I saw some small blisters there. After the blisters broke, it hurt to urinate. So I went to my doctor. She told me that I have herpes."

—Ruth Ann

Genital herpes is a common STD. Many people who have it do not realize it. Genital herpes causes painful sores. The sores are filled with fluid. Women may have sores in or near the vagina, on the buttocks, and on or near the anus. In men, sores form on the penis, scrotum, buttocks, anus, and thighs. Sores may form on a woman's cervix and in a man's urethra. You may have a low fever and a headache. The glands in your groin may be swollen. The first time the sores appear they heal in about three weeks. After the first outbreak, sores will heal in two weeks. But there is no cure for herpes. Once you have the virus, you will always have it. You may have sores from time to time. After a while, you may have sores less often. Or you may not have them again.

You can spread genital herpes through sexual contact. The herpes virus may be most likely to spread when you have sores. But you can still spread it when you don't have sores. If you have genital herpes, you should practice safe sex. (SEE SAFE SEX: HOW TO PREVENT STDS, PAGE 194.) A drug called acyclovir can ease the pain. The drug may also make you less likely to spread the virus. An ointment that contains lidocaine may help ease pain where you apply it.

Gonorrhea

"John said he had something important to tell me. He went to the doctor without telling me. He has gonorrhea. He had a creamy discharge from his penis. He said it looked like pus. The doctor said that it spreads easily, so I probably have it. Now I need to take antibiotics. And I have been talking with John and our doctor to keep this from happening again."

—Martha

Gonorrhea is caused by bacteria. This disease spreads when you have sex. It can also spread if fresh, infected body fluids from one person touch the mucous membranes of another. These membranes line the mouth, vagina, and rectum. The eyes are also lined with mucus membranes. For instance, if an infected man wipes his penis with a bath towel, bacteria may be on that towel. If someone else dries his eyes with the towel, he could become infected.

Signs of Gonorrhea

Symptoms of this disease start within two to six days after contact with the bacteria. Men and women may feel pain when they urinate. The infection may also cause mild pain in the throat of people who have oral sex. The infection may cause pain in the rectum of a person who has had anal sex. A man may also see a pus-like discharge from the penis. However, signs of infection may be harder to notice in a woman. A woman may have pain in her abdomen. Or she may also have a cloudy discharge or bleeding from her vagina.

Sometimes the infected man or woman may not have symptoms from gonorrhea infection. He or she can spread it to others.

How Gonorrhea Is Treated

Your doctor can treat gonorrhea with antibiotics. Both you and your partner need treatment. You must take the drug just as your doctor tells you to. You may need more tests when your treatment ends. Without treatment, the infection can spread to other parts of your body. In men, it can inflame the prostate gland. (SEE PROSTATITIS, PAGE 224.) In women, it can inflame the uterus and ovaries.

Hepatitis B Virus (HBV)

"I went to give blood. When they tested my blood, I found out I had hepatitis B virus. My doctor told me to eat a healthy diet and not drink alcohol. I did and got better."

—Saul

Hepatitis B (HBV) is the most serious kind of hepatitis. It is named after the virus that causes it. HBV can inflame and scar the liver. This is called cirrhosis of the liver. If you have HBV for a long time it can also lead to liver cancer. HBV infection is most common in people between the ages of 15 and 35. Most of these infections are caused by sexual contact. But HBV can also be spread by sharing needles or razors. Body piercing can spread the virus too.

A few people become carriers of HBV. A carrier is someone who has the virus in his or her body but may show no symptoms. A carrier may not become ill but can spread HBV to another person.

Signs of HBV

Most adults don't get symptoms when they first have HBV. But any of the following may be a sign of HBV infection:

- fatigue
- fever
- joint or muscle aches
- loss of appetite
- nausea
- yellowish skin

The only way to know if you have HBV is to have a blood test for it.

How to Protect Yourself Against HBV

If you are at risk for hepatitis B, you should ask your doctor about the vaccine. (SEE HEPATITIS B VACCINE, PAGE 281.)

If you are exposed to the virus and have not had the vaccine, see your doctor right away. If you get an injection of a drug called hepatitis B immune globulin, you may not get the disease. But you need the drug within two days of being exposed to the virus.

How HBV Is Treated

The best way to treat HBV is to take good care of yourself. Eat a diet high in protein and carbohydrates. Get plenty of rest. And don't drink alcohol.

Most people who have HBV get better within six months. But it can take longer. Drugs such as steroids and interferon are used to treat HBV.

Syphilis

"A year ago, I had a sore on my penis that didn't hurt. Then later I thought I had the flu. Before Nancy and I got married, we had to have blood tests for syphilis. I'm glad we did. My doctor said the sores and flu were signs of infection. I took penicillin, and the infection went away."

—Donald

Syphilis is caused by bacteria. In its worst stage, the infection can affect your bones, brain, and heart. It can cause mental illness. These extreme symptoms are rare. But syphilis is more common in the United States today than it was 40 years ago.

Signs of Syphilis

The first and most common sign of syphilis is a sore on the genitals or rectum. Women are often less likely to notice these sores. Sores may also form on the tongue, lips, breast, or throat. Most sores are hard, red, and protruding. They may not hurt. Other symptoms may appear later, including:

- a rash anywhere on the body (the rash may come and go for months)
- enlarged lymph nodes that don't cause pain
- fever
- headache
- loss of appetite

How Syphilis Is Treated

If the disease is found in its early stages, doctors can use antibiotics to cure syphilis. If you have syphilis, you should avoid having sex until your doctor says it is safe to have it again. Avoid having sex until you have at least two blood tests that confirm that the infection is gone.

Chapter 13

Skin and Hair Concerns

Most people have treated their own skin and hair problems all their lives. You may be used to treating dry skin, rashes, and poison ivy. As you get older, you may have problems that you have not had before. Some skin and hair changes are a normal part of aging. For instance, it's normal for your hair to turn gray and for your skin to wrinkle. There's no reason to see your doctor about these changes. But you need to see your doctor for some conditions, such as moles that change shape or signs of shingles.

Your primary care doctor can offer advice and treatment for many skin and hair problems. He or she may suggest that you see a dermatologist or an allergist. Dermatologists treat skin problems. Allergists can help find out if a rash or an itch is an allergic reaction.

Age Spots

"At first I thought I was getting freckles. Then I realized that they were age spots."
—Barbara

Age spots are also called liver spots. These are blemishes that appear on the skin as you get older. They look like large freckles. Age spots are usually flat and brown with an even border or edge. Exposure to too much sun causes some age spots. They are often on the face and the backs of hands.

Most age spots are harmless, but watch them closely. Call your doctor if an age spot becomes very large, gets darker, develops an unusual shape, or has many colors. (SEE MOLES, PAGE 208, AND SKIN CANCER, PAGE 216.)

Some red spots on the skin are called cherry angiomas. They range in size from a pinhead to a ladybug. They may be on your face, scalp, trunk, neck, arms, or legs. They are rarely on hands or feet.

Bruises

"When I bruise, I just wait for it to turn green. My mom taught us as kids that this means it is healing."
—Helen

What to do about **Bruises**

Symptoms/Signs	Action
◆ **Skin that bruises easily when taking medicine**	Call doctor
◆ **Fever of 101 degrees or higher** ◆ **Bruise that becomes more painful**	See doctor

"Black and blue marks" are bruises. Most bruises occur when you hit something. A bruise appears when tiny blood vessels break. Broken blood vessels allow blood to seep under the skin.

New bruises are dark purple to black. As they heal, they turn green and yellow. Your skin may bruise more

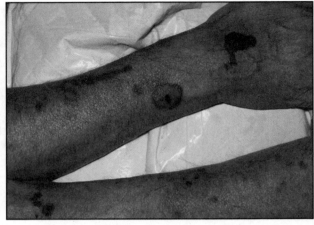

Large, bright purple patches on the forearms are called purpuras. These patches are common in older adults.

easily if you are taking aspirin or an anticoagulant (a drug to reduce blood clotting).

Purpuras. Older adults often have large, bright purple patches on their forearms. These bruises are called purpuras. They form when the forearms bump against objects and cause small blood vessels to break. They last for many weeks. These bruises often leave a brown area on the skin and can scar.

Self-Care: Bruises

- Apply an ice pack as soon as you can. This helps reduce pain and swelling. You can also use towels soaked in ice water.
- Raise and rest the part of your body that is bruised.

Dry Skin

"I always ignored my dry skin. But when my hands started cracking and bleeding, I knew I had to do something. So I called my doctor. "

—Arthur

By age 70, most people have dryness and itching on their lower legs, forearms, hands, and scalp. If you do not take care of dry skin, it can become red, cracked, and easily infected.

What to do about Dry Skin

Symptoms/Signs	Action
◆ Dry, chapped hands ◆ Regular exposure to intense sunlight	 Use self-care
◆ Itching that keeps you awake and does not improve with self-care ◆ Dry skin that is badly broken due to scratching	Call doctor
◆ Rough, scaly areas on parts of the body exposed to sun	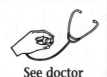 See doctor

Self-Care: Dry Skin

- Bathe only every other day. Too much soap removes the oil from your skin. In the winter, the air is driest, and your skin may dry out even more.
- Use cool or warm bath water, not hot water.
- Wash with bath oil instead of soap. (Be careful getting out. Oil can make the tub slippery.)
- Scrub gently when you use a washcloth so you don't irritate your skin.
- After bathing, use a cream or lotion on your skin. Try one like Lubriderm or Cetaphil. Put on the lotion while your skin is still damp.
- Wear rubber gloves while you do dishes or any time your hands are in water.

Eczema (Dermatitis)

"I kept scratching and scratching. But it didn't take away the itch. The more I scratched, the thicker my skin became, and the more it itched."

—Lucille

Your skin feels dry, and you may even have patches of red, flaky skin that itch. Your doctor calls it eczema, or dermatitis. Both words mean the same thing: Your skin is inflamed. There are several types of eczema.

What to do about
Eczema (Dermatitis)

Symptoms/Signs	Action
◆ **Mild itching or flaking**	Use self-care
◆ **Symptoms that don't improve after one week of self-care** ◆ **Sores that are crusting or weeping, or itching that is very bad**	Call doctor

Eczema related to dry skin is common. (SEE DRY SKIN, PAGE 203.) If your skin is very dry, it can itch, burn, crack, or scale. This can be a particular problem in the winter months.

Avoid scratching any type of eczema. When you scratch or rub again and again, your skin becomes thicker and more itchy. Scratching gives relief for only a short time. It can make the itching worse later.

Contact Dermatitis. You can get contact dermatitis if you are allergic to or irritated by something your skin touches. Your skin can become itchy and red. If your skin is irritated after contact with one of the following items, you may have an allergy to that item:
- hair dye
- costume jewelry
- things made of rubber or elastic
- household cleaners or bleach
- rubbing alcohol, paint thinner, or gasoline
- garden chemicals like fertilizer or insecticide

Seborrheic Dermatitis. If your face or scalp is itchy, red, and flaky, you may have seborrheic dermatitis. Your eyebrows can be affected. So can the skin from the sides of your nose to the corners of your mouth. This condition is common in older adults.

Atopic Dermatitis. If you have hay fever or asthma, you may get atopic dermatitis. This form of eczema can occur in childhood or later in life.

Self-Care: Eczema (Dermatitis)

- Wash skin gently in cool or warm water. Hot water dries the skin.
- Don't bathe every day if you have dry skin.
- Use only a soft cloth or your hands when washing. This helps avoid irritating the skin.
- Use a mild, cream-based soap like Dove or Camay.
- Use Vaseline or a lotion that contains lanolin after every bath or shower.
- Use a humidifier in your home during cold weather. This will add moisture to the air.
- Keep your nails short so you won't damage your skin more when you scratch.
- Wear soft clothes that don't scratch.

- Apply a cold, wet towel to itchy skin for quick relief.
- To relieve itching, apply a cream with hydrocortisone (such as CaldeCORT or Cortaid). You can buy this over the counter.
- When exposed to harsh chemicals, wear gloves and clothes that protect you.

Hair Loss

"Going bald didn't bother me since my brothers, my father—and even my uncles—are also bald."

—Francis

Losing hair is a natural process. People of all ages lose hair every day. A hair grows continually for three to four years. Then it falls out and a new hair grows in its place.

Baldness that runs in the family is called hereditary balding. Hereditary balding is the most common cause of hair loss. A person can inherit it from the mother's or father's side. If baldness runs in your family, you may or may not be affected.

Hereditary balding affects men and women. In men, the hairline moves back, away from the face. A bald spot often appears on the top or back of a man's head. Rather than having a bald spot, a woman's hair may just thin out over time.

Some drugs can cause or increase hair loss. Drugs for blood pressure, depression, and arthritis can cause hair loss while you are taking the drug.

What to do about Hair Loss

Symptoms/Signs	Action
◆ **Gradual hair thinning or loss** ◆ **Hair loss two to three months after surgery or major illness**	**Use self-care**
◆ **Sudden hair loss with scabs or scales and pain, soreness, or tenderness** ◆ **Bald spots that suddenly appear, rather than slow, even thinning** ◆ **Suspicion that a drug may be causing hair loss**	**Call doctor**
◆ **Bald spots with scaly spots, pus, or scabs**	**See doctor**

If you are treated for cancer with chemotherapy or radiation, you may lose most of your hair. Most of this hair loss is reversible. When you stop having the treatment, your hair will grow back.

Hair loss can be caused by some diseases, such as lupus and thyroid disease. Major surgery, a bad infection, or a high fever can cause you to shed hair. You may not start losing hair until

Most men who are older than age 60 have a bald spot on the top or back of their head.

three months after the illness or surgery. You may lose hair for several months.

A crash diet can cause hair loss. A fungal infection on the scalp can cause hair loss in one spot. This kind of infection can cause scaly bald spots. Hairstyles that pull hair tight can cause hair loss at the site of the tension.

Alopecia Areata. If you are losing hair in smooth, round patches, you may have alopecia areata. With this disorder, most of the scalp is normal and loses no hair. The bald spots usually fill in with new hair within a year. The cause of alopecia areata is not known.

If you have alopecia areata, medical treatment can speed up new hair growth. Ask your doctor about steroid lotions and scalp injections. Both can help treat this condition.

Self-Care: Hair Loss

If losing your hair bothers you, you can do some things to change the way you look:

- Wear a wig, toupee, hat, turban, scarf, or hairpiece.
- Color or perm your hair, but avoid too much bleaching. Bleaching can increase hair loss.
- Wash your hair daily with a gentle shampoo.
- Use a hair dryer and mousse to make your hair look thicker.
- Avoid curlers, braiding, ponytails, or anything that pulls on the hair.
- Try Minoxidil (Rogaine), a hair restorer you can buy over the counter. It helps hair grow in about one third of the people who try it. The hair may be fine and downy or as thick as normal hair. When you stop taking Rogaine, this new

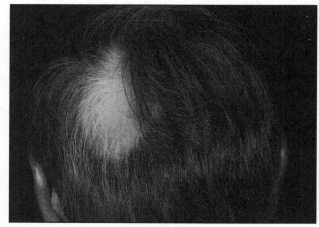

If you lose hair in smooth, round patches, you may have alopecia areata.

hair will fall out. So far, this treatment has been slightly more effective for women than it has been for men.

- Beware of radio and TV ads that promise easy cures for hair loss. Many claims are false, and the products can be costly.
- Ask your doctor about hair transplants. In these operations, hair is moved to the balding area from a part of the scalp where hair is thick. Hair transplants can be very expensive. They are rarely covered by health insurance.

Hives

"I ate some strawberries and broke out into a rash all over my body. It had never happened to me before. My doctor said it was hives."

—Marge

Have you ever suddenly broken out in itchy, pink lumps? Those lumps are called hives.

Hives occur when something tells small cells in the skin to release the chemical histamine. Histamine makes blood vessels release fluid, which then collects under the skin. This fluid produces itchy bumps that are called wheals, or hives. (SEE ALLERGIC REACTIONS, PAGE 333.) Some hives look like mosquito bites. Hives may be as large as a small peach. The cause of most hives is never found. Some people know that certain

What to do about **Hives**	
Symptoms/Signs	**Action**
◆ **Hives that respond well to self-care**	 Use self-care
◆ **Hives with no known cause** ◆ **Hives that don't respond to self-care** ◆ **Hives that form soon after you begin taking a new drug** (IF THIS HAPPENS, STOP TAKING THE DRUG RIGHT AWAY.) ◆ **Hives that make you very uncomfortable**	Call doctor
◆ **A big hive that forms at bite or sting site**	 See doctor
◆ **Hives over the whole body** ◆ **Difficulty breathing**	 Seek help now
◆ **Many hives with swelling around the face and in the throat and mouth**	 Call ambulance

foods or drugs give them hives. Some foods that may cause hives are:
- beans
- cheese
- chocolate
- corn
- eggs
- fish and shellfish
- fresh fruits (especially citrus fruits)
- milk
- peanuts (and other nuts)
- seasonings, such as mustard, ketchup, mayonnaise, or spices
- strawberries (and other berries)
- tomatoes
- wheat

Penicillin and sulfa are two drugs that can cause hives. But almost any drug can cause hives.

Hives usually last for a few hours. Hives that last for months are called chronic hives. It can be very hard to tell what is causing chronic hives.

Get help right away if your hives make it hard to breathe and swallow. If hives are on your lips or in your throat, you are having a serious reaction. In some cases, hives can make you go into shock and lose consciousness. (SEE ALLERGIC REACTION, PAGE 333.)

Self-Care: Hives

- Take an over-the-counter oral antihistamine, such as Benadryl.
- Many people use an anti-itch cream or lotion. These rarely help, but they are an option.

- Rub ice on hives, or take a cool shower for short-term relief.
- Soak in a lukewarm or cool bath with one cup of baking soda. Or use an oatmeal bath product such as Aveeno.
- If you are allergic to bee stings and insect bites, carry EPIPEN or AnaKit with you. Inject the drug as soon as possible after you have been bitten or stung. (SEE FIRST AID: ANAPHYLACTIC SHOCK, PAGE 335.)

Moles

"I'd always had the same mole. But when it got bigger, my doctor said I should have it removed."
—James

What to do about **Moles**	
Symptoms/Signs	**Action**
◆ **Skin growths or bumps that grow and/or change shape or color** ◆ **Rough, scaly areas on parts of the body exposed to sun**	 See doctor

As people grow older, a number of skin growths may appear. Most of these are not cancerous. Look at your body once a month. Look for changes in your skin. (SEE SELF-CARE: SKIN CANCER, PAGE 216.)

Small flesh-colored skin tags can be found around the neck, under the arms or breasts, and in the groin. (SEE PHOTO BELOW.) Most skin tags can be left alone.

Seborrheic keratoses look like warts. They are brown to black growths, are raised, and look as if they have been pasted on the skin. They often get irritated and crumble away.

Keratoses are harmless, but some people find them ugly and bothersome. They can often be left untreated. Treatment is usually quick and easy. But your health insurance may not cover this treatment.

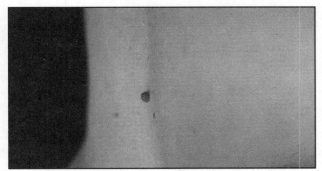

Skin tags are flesh-colored. They often appear on the neck, under the arms or breasts, and in the groin. Most skin tags can be left alone.

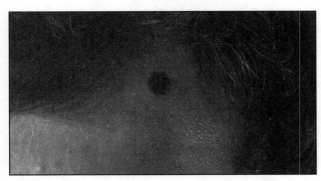

Moles are common. Become familiar with the moles on your body. If a mole grows or changes, show it to your doctor.

Poison Ivy, Poison Oak, and Poison Sumac

"I went for a walk in the woods. I didn't know what poison ivy looked like and ended up getting blisters."
—Patrick

Watch out for poison ivy, poison oak, and poison sumac. You may come near these plants when you pull weeds, garden, or walk in the woods. Wear rubber gloves, long sleeves, and long pants if you have to work near these plants.

What to do about Poison Ivy, Poison Oak, and Poison Sumac

Symptoms/Signs	Action
◆ Mild itching	Use self-care
◆ Rash that is swollen, hot, and filled with pus ◆ Very bad swelling from rash ◆ Rash that covers a large area or is on the face, eyes, or genitals	Call doctor
◆ Fever of 101 degrees or higher	See doctor

If your skin touches the broken leaves or stems of these plants, you may break out in an itchy, red rash. (SEE ALLERGIC REACTIONS, PAGE 333.) But you don't have to touch the plant to have a reaction. Dogs and cats can carry the poison on their paws or fur. Tiny, weepy blisters may pop up on your skin. Your reaction can range from a minor rash to large blisters and oozing. If you have a severe reaction, your doctor may give you a shot of cortisone or cortisone pills.

Poison ivy is a climbing woody vine or shrub. It has clusters of three leaves and light green berries.

In the west, poison oak is more common and grows as a shrub.

Self-Care: Poison Ivy, Poison Oak, and Poison Sumac

- If you think you have touched a poisonous plant, such as poison ivy, wash with soap and water as soon as you can. Wash all parts of your body that may have come in contact with the plant.
- Rinse off your pets, clothes, shoes, camping gear, and gardening gear.
- Put calamine lotion on the rash to ease irritation and itching.
- Take Benadryl or another over-the-counter antihistamine as soon as you can after touching a poisonous plant. It may help prevent an allergic reaction.
- If you get a rash, soak in a tub of lukewarm water mixed with baking soda or an oatmeal bath product (such as Aveeno). This will help relieve irritated skin and dry up the blisters.

Poison sumac is a tall shrub found in swampy, wet areas in the eastern United States. The plant has rows of paired leaflets.

Pressure Sores

What to do about Pressure Sores

Symptoms/Signs	Action
◆ A red area that does not return to its normal color after pressure is relieved	 Use self-care
◆ A red area that does not improve after you take steps to prevent sores ◆ A deepened area of the skin, a blister, or a dark area that looks like a scab	Call doctor
◆ Fever with a sore that has increased redness, milky oozing, or a foul odor ◆ Sore with increased pain or swelling	See doctor

Pressure sores are also known as bed sores or pressure ulcers. These sores are common in people who must sit or lie in bed for a long time. These sores can appear in the following ways:
- as a red area that does not turn white when you touch it
- as a crater in the skin surface
- as a blister, or a dark area that looks like a scab

Bed sores usually affect adults who have a hard time moving around. Older adults are at risk if they find it hard to change positions during sleep.

It doesn't take a lot of pressure for a sore to form. Just staying in one position for a long time can cause a sore. Older adults may get pressure sores if they sit in a chair all day and don't change position. (See DRAWING, PAGE 212.) This puts pressure on the soft tissue in the buttocks, and sores could form there.

People who have trouble moving around are at risk for bed sores. It doesn't take a lot of pressure for a sore to form.

Bed sores can also form when skin is pulled or stretched across a sheet. This causes one spot to rub again and again, and blisters may form. When the blisters open, they become bed sores. Older adults often have loose, folded skin. This skin is more sensitive to the pulling and stretching that can cause bed sores. If skin is wet, there is a greater chance that a sore will form.

A pressure sore may not look big. You cannot see the damage under the sore. Check the skin often for redness, blisters, craters, or dark areas. The earlier you find a bed sore, the easier it is to treat. Bed sores can be serious, so take steps to prevent them. Call your doctor right away if you think you have a bed sore.

Self-Care: Pressure Sores

Follow these steps to treat and prevent pressure sores:

- Use low-pressure mattresses, sheepskins, air mattresses, foam pads, or water-filled or gel-filled mattresses. These types of products can reduce the pressure on the area of the sore.
- Don't use donut-shaped cushions. These cushions decrease blood flow to the skin next to the center of the cushion.
- Your position should be changed every two hours to relieve pressure on your skin. Your back should be at a 30-degree angle to the bed. This helps avoid pressure on the bony parts of the ankles, heels, hips, and lower back.
- Sit at an angle rather than upright. This will relieve pressure on the buttocks.
- Eat a balanced, nutritious diet. And drink a lot of fluids. This can help the healing process.

Caring for Someone Who Has Pressure Sores

- If you think someone you are caring for has a pressure sore, call the doctor right away. If there is blood poisoning or a skin or bone infection from the sore, the doctor will prescribe antibiotics. The doctor can tell you how to clean and bandage the sore.
- Always wear gloves when you have any contact with the pressure sore. The bacteria can spread easily.
- To help the healing process, provide a balanced, nutritious diet. (SEE THE FOOD GUIDE PYRAMID, PAGE 288.)
- Help the person be as mobile as possible.

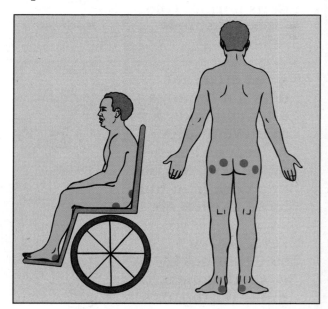

People who have to sit all day without changing position are most likely to get pressure sores. The dots in these drawings show where pressure sores form most often.

Rashes

"The location of a rash may give you a clue as to its cause. Is it where your pajamas' waistband touches your skin? If so, stop wearing those pajamas. Most rashes clear up on their own within a week or two."
—Dermatologist

What to do about **Rashes**

Symptoms/Signs	Action
◆ **Tolerable pain or itching**	Use self-care
◆ **Rash that lasts more than two weeks** ◆ **Fever of 101 degrees or higher**	Call doctor
◆ **Burning eyes and nose** ◆ **Expanding circular rash** ◆ **Swollen glands in groin** ◆ **Weeping blisters** ◆ **Swollen joints with chills, dizziness, or nausea** ◆ **Reddened skin that looks sunburned and feels like sandpaper** ◆ **Red streaks leading away from the rash**	See doctor

Many things cause rashes. A reaction to a chemical can cause a rash. (SEE CONTACT DERMATITIS, PAGE 204.) Symptoms include red swollen patches, raised red dots, itching, burning, and blisters that may weep or ooze.

Some rashes are related to strep, insect bites, hives, and Lyme disease. To find the cause of a rash, ask yourself these questions:

- Have I started a new medicine? If you have started one, call your doctor.
- Have I changed soaps, deodorants, cosmetics, or hair dyes lately? If you have made any of these changes, switch back, or try another.
- Does the rash appear where clothes are worn? If it does, the fabric may be causing the rash.
- Have I worn any new jewelry or used new lotion or nail polish? If you have, stop wearing it or using it.
- Have I been near plants such as poison oak, poison ivy, or poison sumac? If you have, see the section on poison ivy. (SEE PAGE 209.)

Self-Care: Rashes

- Gently wash the affected area with mild soap and water. Pat dry.
- To relieve itching, use calamine lotion or an over-the-counter hydrocortisone cream like CaldeCORT.
- Watch the rash for 24 hours to see if it spreads or changes.

Scrapes and Abrasions

"I scraped my hands when I fell leaving church. It hurt, but I was glad I didn't break my arm."

—Florence

What to do about **Scrapes and Abrasions**	
Symptoms/Signs	**Action**
◆ **Minor scrape**	 Use self-care
◆ **Scrape that you cannot clean easily (dirt or grit may be in the wound)** ◆ **Signs of infection, such as redness or pus**	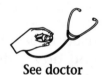 See doctor
◆ **Bleeding that cannot be controlled with self-care**	 Seek help now

Scrapes are usually caused when you fall onto your hands, knees, or elbows. Scrapes are common, so you may think they are not important. But if you treat scrapes and abrasions, you reduce the chance of infection and scars. Scrapes or abrasions happen when you injure or scrape the surface of the skin. Scrapes may hurt more than cuts because they can affect so many nerve endings.

You can treat most scrapes and abrasions at home. Call your doctor if one becomes infected. The signs of infection include redness and pus. (SEE SIGNS OF INFECTION, PAGE 344.)

Self-Care: Scrapes and Abrasions

1. Remove all dirt carefully.
2. Wash the wound for at least one minute with soap and warm water. Or rinse with hydrogen peroxide to clean the scrape completely.
3. To stop the bleeding, press firmly on the wound with gauze or a clean cloth.
4. If blood soaks through the gauze, don't remove it. Place a clean piece of gauze on top of the soaked one. You may have to apply pressure for 5 to 10 minutes.
5. Within 24 hours, remove the bandage and wash the area with mild soap and running water.
6. Wash the wound and change the bandages every day. Look for signs of infection such as redness or pus. (SEE PAGE 344.)

Shingles

"I remember when my grandmother had shingles. She said that she still felt the pain even after the rash had healed and gone away."
—Thomas

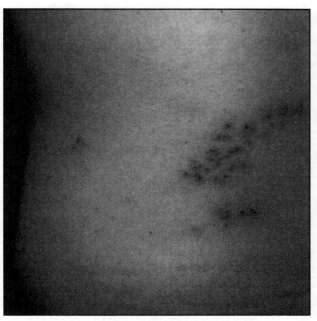

Shingles are small clusters of water blisters. The skin around them is painful.

What to do about **Shingles**

Symptoms/Signs	Action
◆ **Rash** ◆ **Fever that lasts longer than two to three days**	**Call doctor**
◆ **Rash that turns redder, has become swollen, or has pus** ◆ **Significant pain**	**See doctor**

Shingles is a painful skin rash caused by the virus herpes zoster. This is the virus that causes chicken pox in children. You can get shingles at any age, but it often affects adults over 50. Shingles are not catching.

The first sign of shingles is localized pain on one side of the body. A few days later, small clusters of water blisters form where the skin hurts. Shingles usually appear on the side of the chest or on the face. The blisters often spread in a line. After several days, the blisters will start to dry out and form scabs. The skin takes two to four weeks to heal completely. Even after the rash heals, your skin may still hurt for weeks or months.

Call your doctor if you think you have shingles. Your doctor may decide that you need a drug like Acyclovir. This drug usually eases the pain that comes with shingles. It also helps the blisters heal sooner. Acyclovir is most effective if you start taking it soon after you get shingles.

Self-Care: Shingles

- To ease pain, apply cool moist cloths soaked with a solution such as Domeboro. Do this 10 to 15 minutes at a time, five to six times a day.
- Take cool baths every three to four hours to relieve itching. Add 1/2 cup baking soda or 1/2 cup cornstarch to the water. Or use an oatmeal bath product, such as Aveeno. Follow the directions.
- To help stop itching, apply calamine lotion with a cotton swab. Or take an antihistamine such as Benadryl.
- Take mild to moderately strong painkillers like Tylenol with codeine.
- Wear light, loose clothing that does not press against the rash.

Skin Cancer

"I grew up thinking that a tan was healthy. Now I know that being in the sun can lead to cancer. I never go outside without wearing sunscreen and a hat."

—Irma

The good news about skin cancer is that it can be cured in 95 percent of cases. The bad news is that the number of skin cancer cases is increasing. And Americans are getting skin cancer at younger ages.

Skin cancer may or may not be easy to identify. You should do a skin self-exam once a month. Then it will be easier to notice any changes.

Self-Care for Skin Cancer: Examining Yourself

- After a shower or bath, see where birthmarks, moles, and blemishes are and what they look like.
- Be sure to check your entire body, including back, scalp, buttocks, and genitals. Use a mirror to check areas that are hard to see.
- If you are a man, pay special attention to your upper back when looking at your skin.
- If you are a woman, check your back, thighs, and calves. These are the areas where melanomas are most often found. (A melanoma is the most dangerous type of skin cancer.)
- Repeat this exam once a month.

During self-exams, look for small scaly areas on parts of the body that are exposed to sun, especially your face. Look closely at your ears, face, and the tops of your hands. These scaly areas could be actinic keratosis. This is not cancer, but it can develop into cancer. It may be easier to feel the scaly areas than to see them. Call your doctor if you feel any rough spots. These spots may need to be treated.

Who Is At Risk for Skin Cancer?

The most common skin cancer is basal cell cancer. It develops right where the sun hits. This includes the backs of the hands and neck, the face, and the tops of the ears. People who are bald or balding may develop skin cancer on the scalp. People who have light skin and blue eyes are at greatest risk for skin cancer. Dark-skinned people have less risk.

The risk of skin cancer is higher for light-skinned people who live in areas with higher levels of ultraviolet (UV) radiation from the sun. Places with more UV radiation include the southern United States, South Africa, and Australia. The risk of skin cancer is lower in areas where UV radiation is less intense. Places with less UV radiation include the northern United States, Canada, and northern Europe.

How to Protect Yourself From Skin Cancer

The best defense against skin cancer is always protecting your skin from the sun. This is especially important from 10 A.M. to 2 P.M. and in midsummer. (SEE HOW TO PREVENT SUNBURN, PAGE 218.) All forms of UV radiation add to a person's total lifetime exposure. Using sunscreen lowers the amount of exposure. But sunscreen does not prevent skin cancer. Benign (noncancerous) skin tumors are common in older adults. But call your doctor if you find a growth that concerns you.

Basal Skin Cancer. Areas that look like pearly or waxy bumps could be basal skin cancer. (SEE COLOR PHOTO AT END OF BOOK.) Most basal skin cancer is found on the face. This type of cancer grows slowly and rarely spreads to other parts of the body. As the cancer grows, the center can get soft. There may seem to be a small hole (indentation) in the center.

The ABCD Warning Signs of Skin Cancer

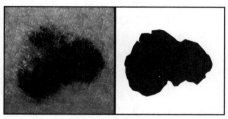

Asymmetry: *One side of the marking does not match the other.*

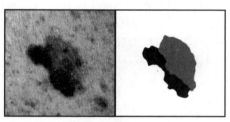

Border irregularity: *The edges are ragged, blurred, or notched.*

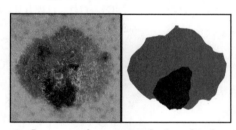

Color varies: *Watch for shades of red, brown, or black—or flecks of red, white, or blue.*

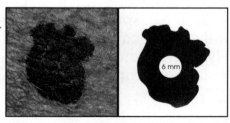

Diameter: *Skin markings should not increase in size or be larger than the size of a pencil eraser.*

Squamous Skin Cancer. Raised lumps that often look red and have a rough, scaly surface could be squamous skin cancer. (SEE COLOR PHOTO AT END OF BOOK.) Their borders are often irregular. When they are on the face and back of the hand, these cancers may bleed. But they rarely spread to other parts of the body. Still, this type of cancer spreads more often than basal skin cancer does.

Malignant Melanoma. Dark black spots that grow slowly are a sign of malignant melanoma. This type of melanoma is round at first. But as it grows, the edges may become uneven and irregular. It looks darker and bigger than other moles around it. (SEE COLOR PHOTO AT END OF BOOK.) Not all melanomas start out as a new black spot. Some develop from older moles.

If you have a mole that grows unevenly or looks darker than the moles around it, ask your doctor about it.

If you think you might have melanoma, you should see your doctor right away. It is important to find a malignant melanoma early and have it removed. Otherwise, it can spread to other areas of the body and can be fatal. Unfortunately, there is no effective drug therapy or chemotherapy for melanoma.

Sunburn

"I was confused about which number sunscreen to use. My dermatologist suggested a product with an SPF rating of 15. He said it is more important to reapply it after swimming, sweating, or being in the wind than to buy a product with a higher SPF."
—William

Ultraviolet (UV) rays from the sun can cause painful burns. If you stay in the sun too long and don't use sunscreen, you will probably get a sunburn. The sun can cause lasting damage to your skin. This damage can lead to premature aging and wrinkling, and it can also lead to skin cancer.

How to Prevent Sunburn
- When you are out, put on sunscreen or a sunblock.
- Cover up, or always use sunscreen if you are in the sun between 10 A.M. and 2 P.M. This is very important if you go out in the middle of the summer.
- Use a sunblock to protect your nose and lips. Some contain zinc oxide, which blocks all of the sun's rays.
- Use sunscreens with a sun protection factor (SPF) of 15 or higher. For the most protection, put on sunscreen

What to do about **Sunburn**

Symptoms/Signs	Action
◆ **Minor sunburn**	 Use self-care
◆ **Painful sunburn**	 Call doctor
◆ **Fluid-filled blisters** ◆ **Sunburn and purple blotches, or other skin that is discolored**	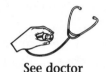 See doctor
◆ **Chills, nausea, or a fever of 102 degrees or higher** ◆ **Faintness, dizziness, or vision problems**	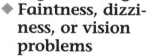 Seek help now

45 minutes before you go outside. Then put it on again often. Do this especially after swimming or exercise that makes you sweat heavily. (Sweating does not remove sunscreen, but towels do.)

- Wear a hat with a brim to protect your scalp and face.
- Before starting a new drug, talk with your doctor or pharmacist. Ask if the drug can cause you to react to sunlight. Some drugs can make you more sensitive to UV rays. These include Tetracycline and sulfa antibiotics. If you take these drugs, you can burn easily.

Self-Care: Sunburn

- Soak the affected area in cold water (not ice water). Or apply cold compresses for 15 minutes. This will reduce swelling and provide quick pain relief.
- If sunburn affects large areas of your body, soak in a cool bath. To soothe skin, add 1/2 cup of cornstarch, oatmeal bath product (Aveeno), or baking soda to the bath.
- Do not apply greasy lotions such as baby oil or ointment to sunburned skin. These products can make the burn worse.
- For relief, use over-the-counter creams or lotions, such as Solarcaine or Noxzema. Or use products that contain aloe vera.
- If you have a sunburn, stay out of the sun until your skin heals. Long exposure to the sun can lead to swelling and blistering.
- Take aspirin to help reduce inflammation.

Wrinkles

"I don't have as many wrinkles as my friends do. I think it's because I always wore sunscreen."
—Jane

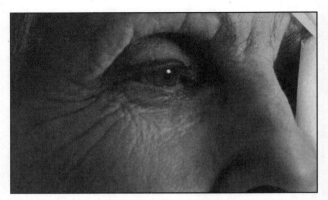

Wrinkles around the eyes are common with age. Staying out of the sun may protect you from wrinkles. Expensive creams and lotions usually don't have much effect on wrinkles.

Wrinkles are a normal part of the aging process. As skin ages, it loses its bounce and becomes less elastic. It starts to crinkle and sag. The lines around your eyes and mouth become deeper. Over time, these areas develop deeper, fixed wrinkles. If you want to keep wrinkles to a minimum, protect your skin from the sun as much as you can. (SEE SUNBURN, PAGE 218.) Watch out for products that promise to erase wrinkles or prevent aging skin. Most of these products cost a lot of money but don't offer much improvement.

Chapter 14

Special Concerns for Men

Before age 50, most men seldom see their doctor routinely. But as you age, things change. You are more likely to get diabetes, heart disease, or high blood pressure. Some of these conditions don't cause many symptoms. That means you need to go to your doctor just to make sure you are healthy. (SEE GUIDE TO PREVENTIVE SERVICES, PAGE 283.)

As you age, you may have problems when you urinate. Certain changes may affect your sex life. You may not want to talk with your doctor about these problems, but you should. Problems found early are easier to treat. Talk with your doctor about your symptoms and concerns. You may learn to prevent some problems.

Your doctor can treat most of your concerns. (SEE HOW TO MAKE THE MOST OF YOUR DOCTOR VISIT, PAGE 265.) Sometimes your doctor may suggest that you see a urologist. This is a doctor who treats urinary diseases.

This chapter covers some concerns men have as they reach 50:
- inguinal hernias
- prostate concerns, including enlargement and cancer

Inguinal Hernias

"I had a pain in my stomach and saw a bulge above my scrotum. I thought I had a tumor. So I was relieved when my doctor said it was a hernia."
—Edwin

An inguinal hernia occurs in your groin. It happens when the muscle that lines your abdomen gets weak. Then part of your intestine may bulge out through the inguinal canal. The inguinal canal is where your testes come down into the scrotum. (SEE DRAWING, PAGE 222.) The effect is a lot like an inner tube bulging through a weak spot in a tire. There may be no obvious cause for this hernia. You may get it from straining to move your bowels. Or you may get this kind of hernia from lifting heavy things.

Pain and other hernia symptoms may start slowly or quickly. Symptoms include the following:

- aches and pain in the abdomen that start and stop
- a feeling of pressure or weakness in the groin
- a bulge above or within the scrotum
- pain and tenderness in the lower abdomen and the scrotum

If you think you may have a hernia, call your doctor. Even if you are not in pain, your doctor may want to see you regularly. This way, he or she will know if the problem gets worse. If you have pain, your doctor may suggest surgery.

Strangulated Hernia. This happens when a hernia is pinched by the abdominal wall. The pinching cuts off the blood supply. This can cause the tissue of the intestine to swell and die. Dead tissue can become infected quickly. If the pain in your groin gets worse quickly, your hernia may be strangulated. This is an emergency. You should get medical care right away. Without treatment, a strangulated hernia can kill you within days.

Self-Care: Inguinal Hernias

- Don't do things that put strain and pressure on your abdomen. For instance, don't lift or push heavy objects.
- Use your legs if you have to lift things. Don't use your back to lift. (SEE POSTURES THAT PREVENT BACK PAIN, PAGE 154.)
- Don't strain to move your bowels. (SEE SELF-CARE: CONSTIPATION, PAGE 18.)

Prostate Concerns

The prostate is a gland about the size of a walnut. It is between a man's bladder and rectum. (SEE DRAWING, PAGE 224.) The prostate makes a part of the fluid that carries sperm out of a man's body. There are three main conditions that can affect the prostate:

- benign prostatic hypertrophy
- prostatitis
- prostate cancer

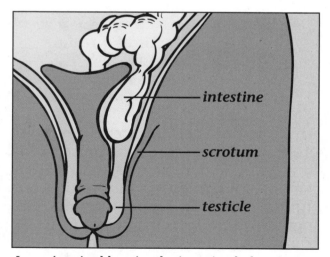

In an inguinal hernia, the intestine bulges into the canal where the testes drop into the scrotum.

Benign Prostatic Hypertrophy (BPH)

*"I started getting up three times
a night to use the bathroom.
My wife made me tell my doctor.
It was awkward. But my doctor
told me that many men my age
have the same problem. That
made me feel more at ease."*

—Ben

The prostate gland gets bigger in most men as they age. This starts to happen around the age of 40. An enlarged prostate gland is called benign prostatic hypertrophy, or BPH. "Benign" means harmless.

Your doctor will examine your prostate by doing a digital rectal exam. (SEE PAGE 226.) Not all men with an enlarged prostate have symptoms. That's why it is important to see your doctor for yearly exams.

When you have symptoms, it is often because your prostate is pressing on your urethra. The urethra is the tube that carries urine out of the body. (SEE DRAWING, PAGE 224.) Then it may be difficult to urinate. This may cause any of these symptoms:

- a hard time starting or stopping your urine flow (dribbling)

What to do about **Prostate Concerns**

Symptoms/Signs	Action	Symptoms/Signs	Action
◆ **Need to urinate in the middle of the night** (SEE PAGE 225.)	Use self-care	◆ **Weak or unsteady urine stream** ◆ **Pain or burning when you urinate** ◆ **Urine leaks (incontinence)**	Call doctor
◆ **Need to urinate during the night that does not improve with self-care** ◆ **Difficulty starting or stopping urination (dribbling)** ◆ **Frequent need to urinate** ◆ **Feeling as if your bladder is not completely empty after you urinate**	Call doctor	◆ **Pain or discomfort at the base of the penis, or between the scrotum and the rectum** ◆ **Fever, chills, or pain in the lower back or abdomen** ◆ **Urine that looks cloudy or has pus or blood in it**	See doctor

SPECIAL CONCERNS FOR MEN **223**

- a need to urinate often
- a need to urinate in the middle of the night
- pain when you urinate
- a weak or unsteady urine stream
- urine leaks (incontinence)

A blocked urethra can keep the bladder from emptying all the way. Then you may feel pressure. Or you may feel as if your bladder is still full after you urinate. Urine may build up if the urethra is blocked. If bacteria get into the bladder, they will grow more quickly when the bladder does not empty all the way. The bacteria may cause a urinary tract infection. (SEE PAGE 34.)

Working With Your Doctor to Treat BPH

A lot of men take care of their symptoms with self-care. For many men, BPH does not get worse over time. But if symptoms bother you, you may need treatment. Your doctor may suggest surgery or drugs.

Surgery can take pressure off the urethra. Discuss the risks and benefits of this surgery with your doctor. Only you and your doctor can decide if surgery is best for you. (SEE WHAT TO ASK IF YOU NEED SURGERY, PAGE 277.)

Prostatitis

"My urine sometimes looked cloudy. I didn't worry about that. Then I had pain when I urinated. That scared me, so I called my doctor. He told me that it was most likely just an infection. Knowing that made me a lot less nervous about going to see him."
—Greg

When the prostate swells or gets irritated, you have prostatitis. You may have this condition with or without an

The Prostate

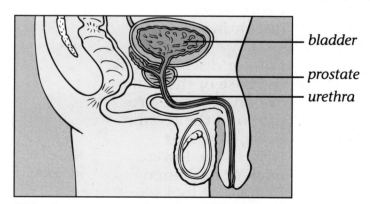

This shows a normal prostate. The prostate can become larger from BPH (SEE PAGE 223) or from prostatitis (SEE ABOVE).

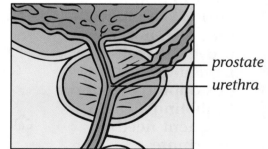

When the prostate is enlarged, it can squeeze the urethra, as shown here. This makes it more difficult to pass urine or semen.

infection. Prostatitis can be acute. That means it can be sudden and it can last a short time. Or it can be chronic. That means that the condition can last a long time.

Acute Prostatitis. Acute cases are often caused by an infection. You could have acute prostatitis if you have these symptoms:
- sudden fever or chills
- pain in the lower back or abdomen or around the base of the penis

If you have these symptoms, call your doctor. Your doctor may have you take antibiotics.

Chronic Prostatitis. This is most often caused by an enlarged prostate. You could have chronic prostatitis if you have any of these symptoms:
- a burning feeling when you urinate
- pain in and around the base of the penis
- pain or a heavy feeling between the scrotum and the rectum
- pus or blood in the urine

Self-Care: BPH and Prostatitis

The steps below will also help you prevent these conditions.
- Go to the bathroom as soon as you feel a need to urinate. Don't "hold it." If you wait to urinate, urine can back up and get infected.
- Drink six to eight glasses of water a day. Try to drink eight ounces of water each hour during the day. Fluids flush bacteria and old urine out of the bladder. Don't drink a lot of water right before bed. This may make you need to get up and urinate at night.
- Don't drink caffeine or alcohol. These make you urinate more. Caffeine is in coffee, tea, and colas.
- Soak in a hot bath to ease pain.
- Avoid drugs that have an antihistamine or decongestant in them. You may find either of these in cold and allergy drugs.
- Follow the self-care steps for urinary tract infections (SEE PAGE 38) and urinary incontinence (SEE PAGE 34).

Prostate Cancer

"Research on prostate cancer is ongoing. I tell my patients to ask a lot of questions about this kind of cancer. Then we can make decisions together."
—Family practice doctor

Prostate cancer is the most common cancer in older men. Yet doctors don't know all the facts about this cancer. One thing they do know is that there are often no early symptoms. That means this cancer is often found through screening.

Some men do have symptoms. If you have either of these symptoms, call your doctor:
- a sudden reduction in your normal urine flow
- a change in sexual function

Who Is At Risk for Prostate Cancer?

You are more likely to get prostate cancer if you say "yes" to any of these questions:

- Are you a man older than 50?
- Are you African-American?
- Has your father or brother had prostate cancer?

Screening for Prostate Cancer

Prostate cancer often grows slowly. It may not spread to other parts of the body. But in some cases it can grow quickly. It can then threaten your life. These are the two main tests for prostate cancer:

- digital rectal exam (DRE)
- prostate-specific antigen (PSA)

Talk with your doctor about which screening is best for you.

The DRE is the most common test used to find prostate cancer early. The PSA is a blood test. It will find cancer when the DRE may not. But it can miss about 1 out of 10 cases. If your doctor says you have a positive PSA, it does not mean that you have cancer. You could have a harmless prostate enlargement. (SEE PAGE 223.) You could have an inflammation. (SEE PAGE 224.) Only 1 out of 5 men with a positive PSA test has cancer. Many of the cancers found by PSA grow slowly. These cancers often do not cause health problems. If you have a positive DRE or PSA, work with your doctor. He or she will give you more tests.

How Prostate Cancer Is Treated

If prostate cancer is found early, a doctor may suggest one of these three treatments.

Watchful waiting. Your doctor may suggest that you do nothing to treat your cancer. Instead your doctor will say to watch your symptoms and tell him or her about any changes. The right treatment for many early prostate cancers is often no treatment at all. Since these cancers may progress slowly, many older men who have prostate cancer will die of something else. That's why not having treatment may be the right choice for older men. It might also be the right choice for men who have major health problems.

Radical prostatectomy. In this surgery, a surgeon removes the prostate.

Radiation therapy. This treats the prostate and the area around it. (SEE PAGE 16.) These treatments often last about six weeks.

Radical prostatectomy and radiation can cause impotence, loss of bladder control, and difficulty with urination. Talk with your doctor about your risks.

Since most early prostate cancers grow slowly, one of these treatments will help many men. Sadly, some prostate cancers grow quickly, even ones that are found early. When this happens, it may be too late for treatment to help.

Chapter 15

Special Concerns for Women

Women of all ages have special health concerns. This is true even when you can no longer have a child. During menopause, your hormone levels go down. This can bring new health concerns. Some of these concerns last long after you go through menopause.

Menopause marks more than the end of having children. For many women, it is a time when their lives change in many ways. They may take on new roles. Their relationships may change.

If you raised children, you may have time for other interests now. You may go back to school. You may advance in your job. You may take up hobbies or do volunteer work. You may find that much of your time goes to others. For instance, you may care for sick parents or an ill spouse. You may even raise grandchildren.

This time of change can be exciting. But it can be stressful too. You may feel scared, sad, or worried about your health. When you have concerns about your health, talk with your doctor. Your doctor will give you advice. Your doctor may also send you to a gynecologist or a nurse practitioner whose focus is women's health. Gynecologists prevent and treat problems in a woman's reproductive system.

This chapter is for women age 50 and older. It covers three main topics:
● menopause
● vaginal concerns
● cancers that affect only women

Menopause

"Last year our daughter Sue moved into her own apartment. At last we were empty nesters. I had always pictured this as the time when my husband and I would be able to enjoy life and each other. But then I began to have days when I felt moody and blue. I had trouble sleeping. I woke up sweating. I thought I was reacting to Sue's leaving. Then I realized I was going through menopause. Once I knew this was a natural change in my life, I began to relax."

—Marsha

When your ovaries no longer release an egg each month, you start making less of the hormone estrogen. After a while, your periods stop. Menopause is not a medical condition. But it is something most women go through in their 50s. The change in hormones can affect your health both during and after menopause.

How Menopause Starts

The average age when women have their last period is 51. Before your periods stop, you are likely to go through certain changes. These may include the following:

- regular periods that stop all at once
- bleeding more or less than usual during your periods
- a change in the length of time between your periods
- missed periods
- bleeding between periods

Periods that are not regular are common in the years before menopause. But bleeding that is not routine can also be a sign of cancer. (SEE ENDOMETRIAL CANCER, PAGE 241.) If your periods stop being regular, or if you bleed between your periods, see your doctor.

Changes during menopause can affect the way you think and feel. You may have mood swings. You may feel tired and cranky. Hot flashes may disturb your sleep. (SEE PAGE 232.) Then you may not get the rest you need. This lack of sleep may cause you to feel depressed. Of course, these feelings may be about other things in your life too. You can feel stress when your children leave home. Taking care of an aging parent can be hard. You may feel bad about getting older. You may feel sad that you won't have any more children. (SEE ANXIETY, PAGE 112, AND DEPRESSION, PAGE 114.)

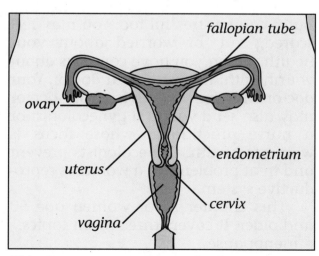

This shows a woman's reproductive system. Lower levels of estrogen may cause the vagina to become dry. (SEE VAGINAL DRYNESS, PAGE 232.)

What to do about **Menopause**

Symptoms/Signs	Action	Symptoms/Signs	Action
◆ **Hot flashes** (SEE PAGE 232.) ◆ **Vaginal dryness** (SEE PAGE 233.) ◆ **Leaking urine** (SEE SELF-CARE: URINARY INCONTINENCE, PAGE 34.)	Use self-care	◆ **Bleeding between periods or heavy bleeding that soaks a pad or tampon each hour for two to three hours in a row** ◆ **Irregular periods that don't return to normal within three months (for example: periods less than 20 days apart, periods more than 90 days apart, or bleeding for longer than 8 days)**	See doctor
◆ **Hot flashes, vaginal dryness, or incontinence not relieved by self-care** ◆ **Bleeding after sex** ◆ **Pain or burning during urination**	Call doctor		
◆ **Any vaginal bleeding after not having a period for six months or longer**	See doctor		

Can You Get Pregnant During Menopause?

You can still get pregnant once your periods seem to have stopped. Being pregnant has health risks for women older than age 50. If you think you might want to get pregnant, talk with your doctor.

If you don't want to get pregnant, use birth control for one year after your last period. Your options include the following:

- a vasectomy for your partner
- tubal ligation
- condoms
- a diaphragm
- birth control pills

You should not rely on the rhythm method. Your changing hormones make it hard to tell when you will be fertile.

How Hormone Changes Affect You

Reduced estrogen levels in your body can cause any of the following:

- vaginal dryness (SEE PAGE 232.)
- urine leakage, also called incontinence (SEE PAGE 32.)
- urinary tract infections (SEE PAGE 34.)
- hot flashes (SEE PAGE 232.)

Less estrogen also increases your risk of heart disease and heart attacks.

After menopause, you are more likely to get osteoporosis. (SEE PAGE 255.) This condition makes your bones more fragile and more likely to break. Taking preventive steps may help.

How to Prevent Health Problems During Menopause

- Exercise regularly. Walking is a good choice. (SEE PAGE 294.) It is a weight-bearing exercise. That means your legs carry your body's weight. This makes your bones stronger and helps prevent bone loss. Exercises such as swimming and biking don't prevent bone loss. But they can help prevent heart disease.
- Eat a low-fat diet. This will help prevent or slow heart disease. (SEE THE FOOD GUIDE PYRAMID, PAGE 288.)
- Get as much calcium each day as there is in four 8-ounce glasses of milk. You don't need to get all your calcium from milk. Cheese and yogurt are good sources. So are other milk products. If you can't eat milk products, take a calcium supplement such as Tums EX.

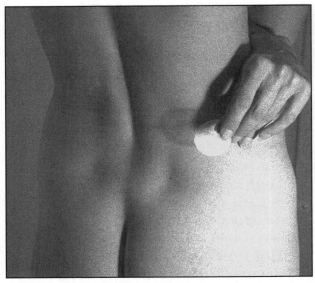

One form of HRT is a patch. Most women who use a patch wear it on their hip or stomach.

- Talk with your doctor about hormone replacement therapy.

Hormone Replacement Therapy

You may cope with menopause by using self-care. Or you may want help from your doctor. Hormone replacement therapy (HRT) is one option.

With HRT, your doctor prescribes hormones. This makes up for the lower levels in your body. If you stop HRT, do so slowly. If you don't, hot flashes and other problems may come back. If they do, they may be worse than before.

HRT comes in three forms:

- pills
- skin patch
- vaginal cream

Pills. This is the most common form of HRT. You will most likely take two types of hormones: estrogen and progestin.

Is HRT Right for You?

We are learning more about the effects of HRT. Decide with your doctor if you should use it.

You should consider HRT if any of these apply to you:
- You are thin and small-boned.
- You are Caucasian.
- You smoke cigarettes.
- You have a family history of osteoporosis.
- You have heart disease.
- You have a family history of heart disease.
- You have high cholesterol.
- You have high blood pressure.
- You have diabetes.
- You have frequent, uncomfortable hot flashes.
- You have vaginal itching or burning, or a milky or creamy discharge from the vagina.

You should not have HRT if either of these applies to you:
- You have had breast cancer.
- You have severe liver disease.

But if you have had your uterus removed, you will take only estrogen pills.

Skin patch. Most women who use the patch wear it on their stomach or hip. You change the skin patch once or twice a week. (SEE PHOTO, PAGE 230.)

Vaginal cream. Cream can ease dryness. You put it in your vagina. Doctors often start with creams that have a low dose of hormones. If that does not work, your doctor may give you a stronger cream. Or your doctor may tell you to use more of the low-dose cream.

HRT has many benefits:
- It can lower your risk of osteoporosis.
- It can reduce your risk of heart disease and heart attack.
- It can lower your total cholesterol level.
- It can ease or stop hot flashes.
- It can help treat urinary incontinence.
- It can help prevent urinary tract infections.
- It can ease vaginal dryness.

Some women have these side effects from HRT:
- sore or swollen breasts
- nausea
- headaches
- bloating
- vaginal bleeding

These side effects may be uncomfortable. But they don't make most women stop treatment. The side effects often go away a few weeks or months after you start taking them.

In the past, some women who took only estrogen got endometrial cancer. We now know that your risk of getting this type of cancer goes down when you take estrogen with progestin.

Some people worry that HRT may cause breast cancer. This has not been proven. But HRT is known to help prevent heart disease. After menopause, women are much more likely to die of heart disease than of breast cancer. So the advantage of protecting yourself from heart disease most often outweighs the disadvantages.

Hot Flashes

"When I began menopause, I would wake up in the night with hot flashes. It was hard to go back to sleep. It helped to turn down the heat and put layers of thin blankets on the bed. When a hot flash came, I threw off a few covers. When I felt chilled, I added a cover. I never had to get out of bed or fully wake up. Once I started to exercise and cut down on coffee, I didn't have as many hot flashes."

—Sophie

You may have hot flashes as your estrogen level falls. A hot flash is a warm, flushed feeling. It can last a few seconds or half an hour. The flush often starts around your chest. Then it spreads to your neck, face, and arms. After the flash, you may sweat. Then you may have chills. A hot flash can happen at any time. You may have more than one in a day. Or you may have only one a week. You can have hot flashes for as long as five years. Some women have them longer, but that is rare.

Self-Care: Hot Flashes

- Dress in layers and wear loose clothing. This will help you respond to a hot flash.
- Set the thermostat at 68 degrees or lower.
- Drink six to eight glasses of water a day.
- Exercise regularly. Thirty minutes of exercise three days a week can ease hot flashes.
- Avoid caffeine and alcohol. They can make hot flashes worse. They can also keep you up at night.
- Taking 800 IU of vitamin E every day may help. Look for this number on the bottle's label.

Vaginal Problems

Changes in your hormone levels cause changes in your vagina. These changes are normal but may be uncomfortable. You can reduce these effects.

Vaginal Dryness

"Sex was starting to hurt. I began to make up reasons to keep my husband away. I felt bad because we had always had a good sex life. I could enjoy sex again once I used the cream my doctor prescribed."

—Ellie

What to do about
Vaginal Dryness

Symptoms/Signs	Action
◆ Vaginal dryness or mild itching, burning, or discomfort ◆ Vaginal dryness with pain or discomfort during sex	 Use self-care
◆ Symptoms that do not improve with self-care ◆ Milky or creamy discharge ◆ Symptoms of a urinary tract infection, such as a frequent need to urinate or pain when you urinate ◆ Bleeding during sex	 Call doctor
◆ Pain in your lower abdomen with any of the symptoms above	 See doctor

As you age, your vagina can become dry. This is caused by lower hormone levels. Your vagina gets thinner and releases less fluid. Doctors call this vaginal atrophy.

Vaginal dryness can cause problems. Sex can cause bleeding and soreness. (SEE PAGE 191.) But if you don't have sex, the problem can get worse. Sex can improve blood flow. This will make the walls of your vagina more supple, which can ease discomfort. So having sex may mean that you will have fewer problems. Talk with your doctor. An estrogen cream or another form of HRT may help you. (SEE PAGE 230.)

Atrophic Vaginitis. When the walls of your vagina get thinner, you may be more likely to get infections. The most common problem is atrophic vaginitis. Symptoms of this include:
- itching
- burning
- a milky or creamy discharge
- pain when you urinate
- pain when you have sex

Atrophic vaginitis can occur with urinary tract infections. (SEE PAGE 34.) It can also occur with incontinence. (SEE PAGE 32.) The opening to the vagina may get narrow and rigid. This will make it harder to have sex. Your doctor may have you treat this problem with a vaginal cream. Or you may take pills.

Self-Care: Vaginal Dryness

- If your vagina is dry, use a water-soluble lubricant. Use products such as K-Y Jelly, Astroglide, or Replens. You can also use natural oils, such as almond oil, coconut oil, or vitamin E oil. Put these directly in the vagina.

- Don't use Vaseline or other petroleum jelly products. They can irritate your vagina, lead to infection, and damage condoms.
- Take time to enjoy foreplay. That makes dryness less of a problem. (SEE SELF-CARE: DESIRE AND INTIMACY, PAGE 189, AND SELF-CARE: SEXUAL CHANGES IN WOMEN, PAGE 191.)

Irritation and Infections of the Vagina

"I douched often. I thought it would get rid of the discharge I had. But the douches were only making it worse. My doctor told me that douches kill bacteria that my vagina needs to stay healthy."
—Sarah

A clear or cloudy discharge from your vagina is normal. It means that you have healthy bacteria in your vagina. Some douches and feminine hygiene sprays can kill these bacteria.

You may notice changes in the discharge from your vagina. The discharge may change color, smell, amount, or thickness. These changes could be a sign of a yeast infection. Or you could have bacterial vaginosis, trichomoniasis, or another sexually transmitted disease (STD). You can treat most yeast infections safely at home. You can buy cream or vaginal inserts over the counter. But you should see your doctor about other infections.

What to do about Vaginal Irritation and Infections

Symptoms/Signs	Action
◆ Itching with white vaginal discharge that looks like cottage cheese, or redness and swelling around the vagina (SEE SELF-CARE: YEAST INFECTIONS, PAGE 235.)	 Use self-care
◆ Symptoms that do not improve with self-care ◆ More than three yeast infections a year, or the first yeast infection in many years	Call doctor
◆ Yellow or greenish vaginal discharge with itching and burning when you urinate ◆ Pain during or after sex ◆ Sores in the genital area ◆ Pain in your lower abdomen with any of the symptoms above	See doctor

How to Prevent Vaginal Infections

- Clean your genital area with water each day.
- Wear cotton underwear. Cotton lets air flow. That can prevent bacteria and yeast from growing.
- Don't wear tight pants or panty hose. These block air flow.
- Don't douche. It can kill healthy bacteria.
- Don't use any of the following products. They can irritate you:
  —scented or deodorant soaps
  —harsh detergents
  —fabric softeners

Bacterial Vaginosis. This condition occurs when there is too much bacteria in your vagina. You may have these symptoms:

- increased discharge
- smelly discharge
- yellow or white discharge
- itching and burning when you urinate
- pain during or after sex

If you have these symptoms, see your doctor. Your doctor may prescribe medicine. You put some kinds of medicine in your vagina. Some medicine comes in the form of pills.

Sexually Transmitted Diseases (STDs). STDs include herpes, gonorrhea, and chlamydia. (SEE PAGE 193.) These diseases can cause irritation. Some cause a discharge that is not normal. Others can cause sores.

See your doctor if you think you have an STD. You can't treat it yourself. Your partner will also need treatment, or you could be infected again.

Yeast Infections. Yeast infections are often caused by a fungus. You may get a yeast infection if you take antibiotics. Diabetes can also make you more likely to get one. You could have a yeast infection if you have any of the following symptoms:

- strong itching and burning
- thick, white discharge that looks like cottage cheese
- a clear discharge
- red and swollen vagina and labia (the folds of the vagina)

There are many treatments for yeast infections. You can buy some over the counter. Other treatments must be prescribed by a doctor.

It is rare that yeast infections are spread between a man and woman during sex. If your male partner has genital itching, he can use an over-the-counter antifungal cream. Infections can be spread between two women during sex. If your female partner has an infection, you both need treatment.

Self-Care: Yeast Infections

- You should call your doctor if you have symptoms of an infection for the first time. Also call if you have symptoms for the first time in many years. When you call, your doctor may want to see you.

- Use antifungal vaginal cream or suppositories. You can buy these without a prescription. They include Gyne-Lotrimin, Monistat, and Mycelex. Follow the directions. Be sure to use all the medicine, even if you feel better before you finish it. Relief from your symptoms does not always mean that the infection is gone.
- Place a cool, wet washcloth on the area around the vagina. This may soothe your itching and any burning feeling.
- Soak in a tub of warm water. You can add baking soda. Or you can use an oatmeal bath product such as Aveeno. Don't use bubble baths, vaginal sprays, or douches unless your doctor says you should. All of these can irritate your vagina.

Women's Cancers

Some types of cancers occur only in women. They include the following types of cancer:
- cervical cancer
- endometrial cancer
- ovarian cancer

Breast cancer occurs mostly in women, though some men get it. Some of these cancers can be treated easily. Others need more care.

Breast Cancer

"Breast cancer runs in my family. Both of my sisters have had it. That made me scared so that I didn't want to check. But the people I love told me I had to be very careful. So I do a breast self-exam once a month. And since I turned 50, I have a mammogram once a year. I schedule it as close to my birthday as I can. That way I don't forget. So far, so good."
—Joanne

Breast cancer should be found early and treated right away. Then chances for survival are good. That's why you should know as much as you can about breast cancer. Know the risk factors. Know the symptoms.

Are You At Risk for Breast Cancer?

Some things can increase your risk of breast cancer. Getting older is one of these things.

The questions below can help you know if you are at risk for breast cancer. If you answer "yes" to any of these questions, tell your doctor.
- Did you give birth to your first child after age 30?
- Did your periods start before you were age 12?
- Did you start menopause after age 50?
- Has your mother or sister had breast cancer? Did they get it before they went through menopause?

- Have you had cancer anywhere in your body?
- Have you had a breast biopsy? Tell your doctor, even if no sign of cancer was found.
- Have you never had children?

How Breast Cancer Is Diagnosed

A lump in your breast can be breast cancer. Or it can be benign, which means it is harmless. It can also be a cyst. A cyst is a harmless sac of fluid. There are three ways to find breast lumps:

- breast self-exams
- clinical exams by a doctor
- mammograms

If you or your doctor finds a lump in your breast, you will need more tests to tell if you have cancer. Not all lumps mean you have cancer.

Breast self-exams. Frequent breast self-exams can let you find breast cancer in its early stages. Most doctors suggest you do a breast self-exam once a month. If you find breast cancer early, it is easier to treat. To learn how to do a breast self-exam, see below and page 238.

Breast Self-Exam: How to Look for Changes

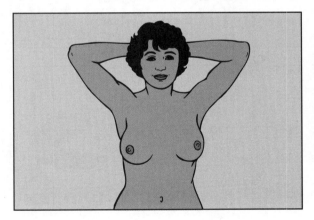

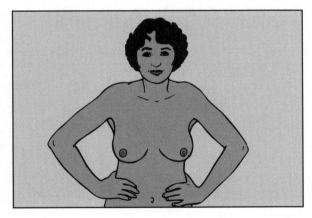

In a mirror, look for changes in the shape of your breasts. You may want to do this after you get out of the shower. Raise your arms above your head and clasp your hands together. Keep your elbows bent. Look for skin changes on both breasts, such as dimpling or a rash.

While you are still looking in a mirror, unclasp your hands and lower your arms. Put your hands on your hips and pull your shoulders and elbows forward. Lean a bit toward the mirror. Look again for any changes in your skin or changes in the shape of your breasts.

Your breasts may feel lumpy, swollen, or tender. The best time to do a breast self-exam is one week after your period starts. If you no longer have a period, do a breast self-exam on the same day each month. For instance, try the first day of each month.

A breast self-exam has two parts: feeling for lumps and looking for lumps or other changes. Self-exams will teach you the feel of your breasts. It will also teach you their shape and size. That way it is easier to tell if a change in your breasts is normal or not. Look for these warning signs:

- fluid leaking from the nipple
- change in the shape or the outline of your breasts, or strange swelling

Breast Self-Exam: How to Feel for Lumps

This is how to feel for changes in your breast.
- Start at the outer edge of the breast.
- Move your fingers firmly in small circles about the size of a dime.
- Work in a spiral toward the nipple.
- Check your other breast in the same way.

Call your doctor if you find anything that concerns you when you feel or look for lumps in your breasts.

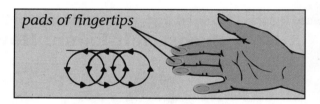

pads of fingertips

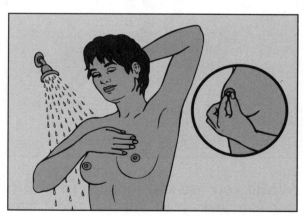

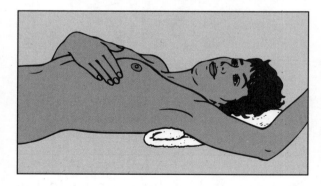

In the shower: Place one hand on the back of your head. Use the other hand to feel for lumps or changes. Use the method described above. Then gently squeeze each nipple to check for any discharge.

Lying down: Place a rolled towel or a pillow under one shoulder. Put your hand on that same side over your head. Use your other hand to examine your breast. Use the steps listed above. Check your armpit too. Use baby oil or lotion to help your fingers move more smoothly.

- changes in the color or texture of your skin
- dimpling, puckering, crusting, or rash, especially around the nipple
- new lumps, or any changes in the size or the shape of lumps you already have

Clinical exams by a doctor. Your doctor will do a breast exam and ask about your history of breast cancer at your yearly exam. Notice how hard your doctor presses on your breasts to check them. You should use the same amount of pressure for a self-exam. You may want to show your doctor how you do your self-exam. Ask if you do it the right way. If you have felt any lumps, ask your doctor to check them.

Mammograms. The best way to find breast cancer early is to have a mam-

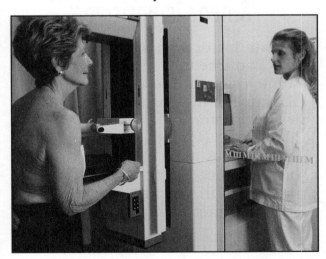

Mammograms have improved a lot. Now mammograms can find smaller cancers. They also use a lower dose of X-ray. The chance that the radiation in 10 mammograms will cause breast cancer is only 1 in 25,000.

mogram each year. This is a low-dose X-ray of your breast. It shows breast cancers when they are still very small. Sometimes it can find a tumor as early as two years before anyone can feel it.

If you are not at high risk for breast cancer, the American Cancer Society suggests the following schedule for mammograms:

- every one to two years between ages 40 and 50
- once a year after age 50

If you are at high risk, ask your doctor how often you need a mammogram. If you feel a lump that a mammogram did not show, have your doctor check it.

How Breast Cancer Is Treated

There are three methods to treat breast cancer. Your doctor may suggest any of the following methods.

- surgery
- radiation therapy
- chemotherapy

Each of these treatments has side effects. Your doctor can tell you what to expect. (SEE COMMON WAYS CANCER IS TREATED, PAGE 16.) Most women with breast cancer can be cured.

Surgery. Doctors often advise you to have surgery to remove a breast tumor. There are two main types of surgery. A mastectomy removes the whole breast. A lumpectomy takes only the part of the breast where the cancer is. In both, the surgeon takes samples of lymph nodes from the armpit. The samples can show if you need more treatment.

Radiation therapy. In most cases, your doctor will order this after you have had a lump removed.

Chemotherapy. You may have this treatment once or twice a month for six months to a year.

Cervical Cancer

"Pap smears protect you from cervical cancer. They're quick and painless and could save your life."
—Gynecologist

Women of any age can have cancer of the cervix. The cervix is the narrow end of the uterus. (SEE DRAWING, PAGE 228.) This cancer often starts slowly. Routine Pap smears are the best way to find it.

Are You At Risk for Cervical Cancer?
Ask your doctor how often you need a Pap smear. (SEE GUIDE TO PREVENTIVE SERVICES, PAGE 283.) If you answer "yes" to any of the following, tell your doctor. You may need a Pap smear more often.
- Have you never had a Pap smear?
- Has it been five years or longer since you had a Pap smear?
- Do you have HIV?
- Have you ever had an abnormal Pap smear?

How Cervical Cancer Is Diagnosed
The screening test for cancer of the cervix is a Pap smear. It is a simple test.

The doctor scrapes a few cells from your cervix. These cells are checked later in a lab.

After you have a Pap smear, your doctor will say the results are positive or negative. Negative means that all your cells look healthy. Positive means that some of your cells do not look normal. If you have a positive test, it does not mean that you have cancer. It just means that your doctor needs to look at more cells.

Even if you are afraid of what your doctor may find, you should have a Pap smear. Your doctor can treat any cells that are not normal. But if you don't get a Pap smear, your doctor can't find these cells. And cells that are

What If Your Pap Smear Is Positive?

If your doctor says you have a positive Pap smear, it means you have some cells that are not normal. Your doctor may call this dysplasia. It is common to have some cells like these. Having a positive Pap smear does not mean that you have cancer. Some cells that are not normal get better by themselves. Sometimes you may need treatment.

Make sure you keep all follow-up visits with your doctor. That way you will know how your treatment is working.

not normal and that are not found can lead to cancer.

If cancer of the cervix is not treated, it can get worse. It can spread to other parts of the body. Then it is called invasive cervical cancer. It is found mostly in women between ages 40 and 60.

How Cervical Cancer Is Treated

Doctors treat this cancer in three ways:
- surgery
- chemotherapy
- radiation

Doctors may use more than one type of treatment. (SEE COMMON WAYS CANCER IS TREATED, PAGE 16.) If the cancer is only in the cervix, a doctor may suggest a hysterectomy. This removes your uterus.

Surgery with radiation is the normal treatment if the cancer has moved to nearby tissue. Your doctor may suggest chemotherapy if the cancer has spread to your lungs, liver, or bones.

Endometrial Cancer

"I didn't have my period for more than a year. Then all at once I started bleeding. My doctor told me to come in. I had cancer of the uterus and had a hysterectomy to remove the cancer. Now I've been cancer-free for seven years."
—Thalia

The lining of the uterus is called the endometrium. Cancer of this lining is called endometrial cancer. It is also known as uterine cancer. It is found most often in women between the ages of 50 and 70 who are past menopause. The most common sign of this type of cancer is abnormal vaginal bleeding after menopause.

Are You At Risk for Endometrial Cancer?

If you answer "yes" to any of the questions below, tell your doctor. He or she can help you know your risk of endometrial cancer.
- Have there been times when you did not ovulate?
- Did you start menopause after age 52?
- Have you taken estrogen but not progestin?
- Have you taken tamoxifen for more than a year? (Tamoxifen is a drug to treat breast cancer.)
- Have you never been pregnant?
- Are you more than 20 pounds overweight?
- Do you have high blood pressure?
- Do you have diabetes?

How Endometrial Cancer Is Diagnosed

To check for this cancer, your doctor may take cells from your uterus. A lab checks these. If your doctor wants more tests, you may have a hysteroscopy, a D&C, or both. Both tests can be done in a day surgery center or in a doctor's office.

In a hysteroscopy, your doctor uses a special tool to look inside your uterus. D&C stands for dilation and curettage.

In a D&C, the doctor scrapes cells from the cervix and lining of the uterus. A lab then tests the cells for cancer.

How Endometrial Cancer Is Treated

Doctors most often suggest a hysterectomy to treat this cancer. The uterus, tubes, and ovaries are usually removed.

Your doctor may advise radiation after surgery. Sometimes radiation is used instead of surgery. If the cancer has spread, you may need chemotherapy. (SEE COMMON WAYS CANCER IS TREATED, PAGE 16.) The doctor might also prescribe progestin.

Ovarian Cancer

"With ovarian cancer, think about your family. At your regular checkup, tell your doctor about any relatives who have had it."
—Family practice doctor

Ovarian cancer causes more deaths than any other cancer of the reproductive system. The number of deaths from other cancers has decreased over the years. But ovarian cancer has caused about the same number of deaths each year for 50 years. This may be because the cancer is often found too late to treat it.

Are You At Risk for Ovarian Cancer?

Your risk of ovarian cancer goes up as you age. If you answer "yes" to either of the following questions, tell your doctor.

- Have two or more women in your family had ovarian cancer?
- Has your mother, sister, or daughter had colon cancer, endometrial cancer, or breast cancer?

How Ovarian Cancer Is Diagnosed

There is no screening test for this cancer. That's why you should know your family history and watch for signs. The most common signs of ovarian cancer are the following:

- swelling, bloating, or discomfort in the lower abdomen
- indigestion
- loss of appetite
- weight loss
- vague stomach pain

The first step in evaluating these signs is to talk with your doctor. Your doctor will examine your abdomen and pelvic area. Your doctor may suggest other tests. These other tests may include an ultrasound to look at your ovaries. The best way for doctors to find this cancer is to check cells from the affected ovary. To get these cells, a surgeon must remove the whole ovary.

How Ovarian Cancer Is Treated

Surgery is the main treatment for this cancer. If the surgeon finds cancer in one ovary, both ovaries are often removed. The surgeon may also take out the uterus and the fallopian tubes. These are the tubes that lead from the ovaries to the uterus. (SEE DRAWING, PAGE 228.) After surgery, your doctor may suggest chemotherapy.

Chronic Health Concerns

A chronic health problem is one that lasts a long time. A chronic illness cannot be cured, but it can be treated. You may need medication. You may need to change your diet. You may need to be more active. When you have a chronic condition, your symptoms can come and go for the rest of your life.

The more you learn about your condition, the better you will be able to take care of yourself. You will feel more in control. And it will be easier to stay healthy. You can learn how to keep your illness from disrupting your life too much. You can learn to avoid other health problems that a chronic illness may cause. You may even improve your overall health.

You may have more than one chronic illness. Each chronic illness brings its own set of problems. Some people respond to this fact with fear. They may worry about each ache and pain. Or they may choose to ignore their symptoms. They may not see a doctor because they are afraid of what they will learn. Not seeing a doctor is never a good idea. If you face your symptoms, you can work with your doctor to treat your illness. That way you can avoid problems later on.

The following chapter covers some types of chronic illness. To learn more about your chronic illness, look at the list of resources in the chapter that starts on page 322. You may find an organization that can help you. Call and ask for more information. Ask about support groups near you. A support group can help you learn how to live with and care for a chronic condition.

Your doctor is another source of information. He or she may give you pamphlets or suggest some books. Be sure to read them.

How to Stay Healthy When You Have a Chronic Illness

Each chronic disease has its own signs and treatments. But no matter what condition you have, there are some basic steps you can take to improve your health.

- Eat meals that are well-balanced. A dietitian can help design a meal plan that is good for your health. He or she will help you learn good eating habits. (SEE THE FOOD GUIDE PYRAMID, PAGE 288.)
- Deal with stress. (SEE PAGE 130.) Chronic health problems can cause physical and mental stress. This stress can make you feel worse. A counselor can help you learn to manage stress. You may learn how to tell others what you need. You may learn how to resolve conflicts with more ease. Dealing with stress also means learning how to relax. (SEE HOW TO RELAX, PAGE 129.)
- Work with the people who are close to you. Your illness may cause them stress too. Your family may have to make adjustments. They may need to learn special skills to help you. A counselor can help you and your family talk things out.
- Stay active. (SEE STAYING ACTIVE, PAGE 291.) You need to keep moving to stay healthy. You need to keep moving no matter what problem you may have. Ask your doctor if some exercises might be better for you than others.

Chapter 16

Living With a Chronic Illness

Adults who are older than 50 have a fairly high chance of having a chronic illness. Here are some of the most common illnesses:

- arthritis
- cancer
- chronic obstructive pulmonary disease (COPD)
- dementia (SEE PAGE 171.)
- depression (SEE PAGE 114.)
- diabetes
- heart disease (SEE PAGE 89.)
- high blood cholesterol (SEE PAGE 91.)
- high blood pressure
- obesity
- osteoporosis

This chapter covers some of these conditions. Some are discussed in other parts of the book. This chapter was written for people who know they have a chronic condition.

When You Have Arthritis

"My knees bother me the most. When I wake up in the morning, the first thing I do is take buffered aspirin. In an hour, the stiffness is gone. I try to take a walk at least once a day. It seems to help."
—Denise

More than 30 million people in the United States have some form of arthritis. Arthritis causes inflammation and can lead to joint pain. An inflamed joint can be red, stiff, swollen, painful, or hot. Three of the most common types of arthritis are osteoarthritis (SEE PAGE 146), gout (SEE PAGE 149), and rheumatoid arthritis.

Most forms of arthritis can't be prevented or cured. But if you mix the right types of treatment, you can deal with the problems all types of arthritis cause. There are three goals for arthritis care:

- easing pain, inflammation, and stiffness
- maintaining your range of motion (how well your joint moves)
- preventing more damage to your joints

Doctors know many ways to treat arthritis. Your doctor may talk with you about drugs, diet, exercise, and surgery. He or she may also show you some special aids made to help people who have arthritis. Over-the-counter drugs are often the first treatment choice.

Over-the-Counter Pain Relievers

Acetaminophen and nonsteroidal anti-inflammatories can ease pain. Each type of drug works on the body in different ways.

Acetaminophen eases pain and fever. It has no effect on inflammation. This drug will not hurt your stomach. But it can hurt your liver if you take high doses. The best-known brand of this drug is Tylenol.

NSAIDs are nonsteroidal anti-inflammatory drugs. Aspirin and ibuprofen are two types of NSAIDs. These drugs can ease pain and fever. They also reduce inflammation. But they may also upset your stomach. (SEE WHICH PAIN MEDICATION IS RIGHT FOR YOU? PAGE 272.)

Special Aids That Can Help

Some special aids can give support to painful joints. You can use a cane or a walker to take some of the weight off your joints. A special pillow can help support your neck while you sleep.

Other aids can help you do work that is too painful to do on your own. A doorknob extender can help you turn a doorknob. Handle grips for silverware can help you hold a fork. Ask your occupational or physical therapist about aids that may help you.

Your Diet and Arthritis

There is no special diet or nutritional supplement that will ease arthritis pain. You may hear claims that a certain product or vitamin is helpful. Be careful of these claims. The best diet for arthritis is one that is based on the Food Guide Pyramid. (SEE PAGE 288.) Eating well helps you stay at a healthy weight. And that puts less stress on your joints.

Exercise and Arthritis

Exercise helps keep your joints moving. It strengthens the muscles around joints. Choose a type of exercise that will use the joint that hurts. Start by doing the exercise for a short time. Then build up slowly and exercise a bit longer.

Walking, biking, and water exercises may be the easiest to do if you have arthritis. Swimming is a good choice because it does not put much stress on your joints. Exercise in a heated pool is good for knee, hip, and foot problems. Before you begin an exercise program, talk with your doctor.

Surgery for Arthritis

Surgery can ease the pain of arthritis. It can mend joints that have been badly damaged. It can increase the range of motion in a joint. You can also have surgery to replace joints. As a rule, this type of surgery is very successful. (SEE HIP REPLACEMENT, PAGE 157, AND KNEE REPLACEMENT, PAGE 161.)

When you have arthritis, exercise may ease joint pain. Swimming or water aerobics are both good choices. They put little stress on your joints.

Self-Care: Arthritis

- Stay active. You can do any exercise as long as it does not cause more pain or swelling. If pain or swelling lasts more than 30 minutes, you may have done the wrong exercise. Or you may have done too much. A physical therapist can teach you how to exercise with care.
- Use hot and cold packs. Heat is best to treat the stiffness that comes with arthritis. A hot shower can relax muscles and ease pain. Taking a warm bath can also help. A cold pack can numb an area that hurts. Use hot packs or cold packs to ease pain as needed, especially after you exercise.
- If arthritis makes it hard for you to go about your daily tasks, think about getting outside help. (SEE LIVING AT HOME, PAGE 306.)
- Take basic steps to stay well. (SEE HOW TO STAY HEALTHY WHEN YOU HAVE A CHRONIC ILLNESS, PAGE 244.)

When You Have Cancer

"When I was diagnosed with cancer, I thought my life was over. But my doctor has helped me understand my options. She also told me how important it is to take good care of myself. The treatment I had seemed to work. I can't say I'm cured, but I do enjoy the life I have. In a few more years, my doctor says, we'll know if the cancer has gone away."

—Bob

Cancer starts when cells become abnormal. Once this happens, the cells divide and multiply at a rapid rate. The abnormal cells then form a tumor. The cancer can spread to other parts of the body.

You may want to learn more about certain types of cancer. If so, look up cancer in the index of this book. Then you can find a specific type.

How Cancer Is Treated

You will have to decide with your doctor how your cancer will be treated. What treatment is best for you will depend on what type of cancer you have and how far along it is. (SEE COMMON WAYS CANCER IS TREATED, PAGE 16.) To learn about working with your doctor, see page 261 in chapter 17. If your doctor says that surgery is a way to treat your cancer, use the list of questions on page 277. It will help you plan for surgery.

The Chronic Nature of Cancer

Cancer is not often thought of as a chronic illness. Most cancer is found and then treated. For instance, if a breast tumor is found, the tumor is removed. Then there may be a time of follow-up treatment to get rid of any cancer cells that may still be present. After that, there is no more treatment, except for routine checkups. But sometimes cancer comes back. Then the cancer may seem to be chronic. For instance, with leukemia, there may be times when you have symptoms and times when you don't.

The time when you have no symptoms is called remission.

At times, the side effects from long-term cancer treatments can feel like a chronic illness. Some cancer treatments can cause fatigue. (SEE PAGE 117.) Some treatments may cause you to vomit and have nausea.

When You Have COPD

"I just found out I have chronic bronchitis. Now I know why I've had a bad cough every day. My doctor said I can control the disease if I do what he says. I have to quit smoking. I also have to drink a lot more water. He says I need eight glasses a day."

—Nick

Chronic obstructive pulmonary disease (COPD) is lung disease. Emphysema and chronic bronchitis (SEE PAGE 99) are two parts of COPD. When you have either of these, air has a hard time getting in and out of your lungs. Smoking is the most common cause of COPD. But over time, polluted air or chemical fumes may also cause harm. A few people have a rare form of emphysema that can be inherited.

Your doctor may treat COPD with one or more of the following methods:
- Antibiotics can treat an infection caused by bacteria. Proper treatment is vital since the infection can make it hard to breathe.

- Bronchodilators are drugs that make it easier to breathe and help stop wheezing. They can ease your congestion. Bronchodilators relax the muscles of the bronchial tubes.
- Corticosteroids are drugs that ease inflammation. They also reduce mucus in the lungs.
- Oxygen therapy may be used to increase the oxygen in your blood. Some people think of oxygen as a "last hope." But it is just one more form of treatment. Oxygen gives you energy. Having more energy can improve the quality of your life.

Self-Care: Chronic Obstructive Pulmonary Disease

- Quit smoking. If you need help, see page 300 and talk with your doctor.
- Do not go where there is a lot of polluted air or indoor smoke.
- Build strength in your upper body. If the muscles in your upper body are strong, you will find it easier to breathe. Ask your doctor for exercises you can do.
- Call your doctor at the first sign of a cold or influenza. You may need further treatment.
- Have a flu shot. (SEE PAGE 105.)
- Have a pneumonia shot. (SEE PAGE 109.)
- Drink lots of fluid. Drinking six to eight glasses of clear fluid a day will help keep your lungs moist.

Liquids also keep your bronchial tubes clear of mucus. Then you can breathe with more ease.
- Eat smaller meals, but eat more often. A full stomach can make it harder to breathe.
- Exercise your lungs. Ask your doctor to show you some exercises that improve breathing.
- Exercise to make your heart stronger. Just 30 minutes of aerobic exercise a day will help your heart fight problems that come with COPD. Aerobic exercise includes walking, biking, and swimming.
- Take basic steps to stay well. (SEE HOW TO STAY HEALTHY WHEN YOU HAVE A CHRONIC ILLNESS, PAGE 244.)

When You Have Diabetes

"I was shocked when the doctor said I had type II diabetes. At first I thought it would be hard to deal with. But I found out that if I exercise and watch what I eat, I do just fine."
—Naomi

Diabetes occurs when the body is not able to use food for the energy it needs. Here's how your body usually gets energy:
1. You eat food.
2. Your body makes a sugar called glucose from the food.
3. The glucose travels to all parts of your body through your blood vessels.

4. Insulin helps glucose enter each cell of your body. Insulin is a hormone made in the pancreas.
5. The glucose gives your body energy.

When you have diabetes, you have a problem with the fourth step. It could be that your body can't make enough insulin. Or you may have insulin, but your body can't use it in the right way. Both problems result in the same thing: Glucose increases in your blood. The main sign of diabetes is a level of glucose that is higher than normal.

Diabetes can lead to heart and kidney disease. It can also cause nerve damage and blindness.

The Types of Diabetes

There are two forms of diabetes. They are called type I and type II. You may know type I diabetes as juvenile diabetes. This type most often starts in people younger than 30. But it can occur in anyone at any age. With type I diabetes, the pancreas stops making insulin.

Type II diabetes is the form that most often starts in adults older than 40. With type II diabetes, the pancreas makes insulin but the body does not use it as well as it should. As a result, the blood sugar level rises.

You may be able to control type II diabetes if you watch what you eat and increase your amount of exercise. You may need to take pills or insulin.

How Diabetes Is Treated

There is no cure for diabetes, but you can manage it. You can eat right, be active, and monitor your blood glucose. Keep in touch with your doctor. Find a nurse educator and a dietitian to help you manage your diabetes.

Plan meals and eat well. Planning healthy meals and eating well are good for everyone. (SEE EATING FOR YOUR HEALTH, PAGE 287.) Both activities are very important for people who have diabetes. A meal plan tells you what to eat and when to eat it. Work with a dietitian to form a meal plan that is right for you. It should fit your lifestyle and fill your nutritional needs. It should help you manage your weight.

Some meal plans are based on carbohydrates. This kind of meal plan allows you to choose from a wide variety of foods. You add up the carbohydrates you eat each day. A dietitian can help you with a meal plan and show you how to count carbohydrates.

Increase your activity. Daily activity helps your body use insulin better. It helps you burn calories. Routine activity also helps your heart and lungs work better, reduces body fat, and tones your muscles.

Monitor your blood glucose. No matter what kind of diabetes you have, it is important to monitor your blood glucose. The goal is to keep your blood glucose level as close to normal as you can. Normal blood glucose is less than 110 mg/dl when you have not eaten for 12 hours or before meals. It is under 140 mg/dl one to two hours after meals. If you keep your glucose level in the normal range, you will feel better. You also are less likely to have other problems. Blood glucose levels that are too high can lead to heart disease, kidney disease, blindness, or nerve damage.

Monitoring your glucose levels routinely helps you prevent two serious problems. If you take drugs for your diabetes, the drugs could cause your blood glucose level to dip too low. Doctors call this hypoglycemia, or low blood glucose. The second problem comes from having too much sugar in your blood. Doctors call this hyperglycemia, or high blood glucose.

Avoid hypoglycemia. If you don't take insulin or any other drugs for diabetes, you don't need to worry about having low blood sugar. If you do take insulin or other drugs, however, you could get a blood glucose level that is too low. If your blood glucose level is too low, you might have any of the following symptoms:
- confusion
- fast heartbeat
- feeling dizzy
- feeling sleepy
- feeling weak or shaky
- hunger
- sweating

What to Do if Your Blood Glucose Is Too Low

1. If your blood glucose is below 70 mg/dl, eat or drink something that has about 15 grams of carbohydrate. Then rest for 10 to 15 minutes. Any of the following things would be a good choice of what to eat:
   - 3 glucose tablets
   - 1 cup of skim milk
   - 8 to 10 jelly beans
   - 1/2 cup of fruit juice
   - 1/2 cup of a regular soft drink
   - 6 to 7 hard candies
2. Test your blood glucose again.
   - If it is above 70 mg/dl and you feel better, you can go back to what you were doing.
   - If it is still below 70 mg/dl, eat another snack with 15 grams of carbohydrate. Wait another 15 minutes. Test again.
3. If your blood glucose is still low after three tests, call your doctor.
4. If you often have hypoglycemia, talk with your doctor.

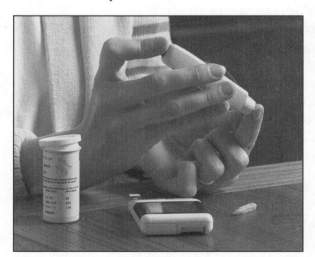

Monitoring your blood sugar level becomes routine when you have diabetes.

You could have low blood glucose and not know it. The only way to know for sure is to test your glucose level. If you often have low blood glucose, ask your doctor what you can do about it.

Avoid hyperglycemia. When your blood glucose level gets too high, you have hyperglycemia. Blood glucose is too high if it is over 240 mg/dl.

When you are sick, diabetes can get out of control quickly. Even the stress that results from being ill can cause your blood glucose level to rise quickly. Many common illnesses can cause very high blood glucose levels. These illnesses include:
- colds
- diarrhea
- fever
- flu
- nausea
- vomiting

When you are ill, be sure to keep close watch on your blood glucose level. Call your doctor if you find yourself in any of the following situations:
- You have a blood glucose level above 240 mg/dl for more than three days in a row.
- You vomit.
- You have diarrhea.
- You haven't been able to eat solid foods for more than a day.

You can have very high blood glucose levels and not notice any symptoms. That's why testing your blood glucose is so important. Testing is the only way to tell if your blood glucose is high.

Self-Care: Diabetes

- Control your weight. If you lose 10 to 20 pounds, your blood sugar will be easier to control.
- Be physically active. Regular activity can help control blood sugar levels. Start slowly and add to your activity each day. (SEE THE ACTIVITY PYRAMID, PAGE 294.)
- Follow your meal plan. A healthy meal plan is crucial when you have diabetes. A meal plan often spreads out the food you eat over a day. Your meals are smaller, but you can have snacks too. The goal is to eat less food at one time but to eat more often. This will help keep your blood glucose at a safe, steady level.
- Find ways to deal with stress. (SEE PAGE 128.) Increased stress can raise blood glucose levels, heart rate, blood pressure, and levels of adrenal hormones. Changes in blood glucose

Having diabetes can cause stress. Talking with a friend can help you deal with it.

levels can cause mood swings. These mood swings will create still more stress for you and those close to you. Exercise can reduce stress. Ask your doctor about stress management classes.

- Check your blood glucose levels. Your doctor will show you how to do this. He or she will also tell you how often you should do it.
- If your doctor prescribes pills or insulin, be sure you take it as directed.

When You Have High Blood Pressure

"For a while, my blood pressure was higher every time I went to the doctor. But he worked with me to change some things. Now that I exercise each day and have lost weight, my blood pressure is down to where it should be."

—Lee

High blood pressure is a major health risk. (SEE PAGE 90.) It can lead to heart disease, stroke, and damage to other organs, such as your kidneys. But blood pressure can be controlled. Working with your doctor to keep your blood pressure in the normal range is one of the most important steps you can take to better health.

Sometimes you can lower your blood pressure by changing what you eat and increasing how much you exercise. Work with your doctor and follow a plan to lower your blood pressure.

Self-Care: Lowering Your Blood Pressure

- Lose weight if you are overweight. (SEE PAGE 254.) Excess body weight can affect your blood pressure. A weight loss of 10 to 15 pounds can help control blood pressure.
- Stay physically active. (SEE PAGE 291.) Exercise can lower blood pressure. It also helps to control your weight and reduces stress.
- Cut the sodium in your diet. Canned foods are high in sodium. So are cheese, snack foods, and smoked meats and fish. Read the nutrition information on the label. Try to limit your sodium intake to no more than 2,300 milligrams a day (about a teaspoon of salt). This may help you control mild to moderately high blood pressure.
- Use alcohol only in moderation. If you drink alcohol, don't have more than two drinks a day. Alcohol can raise your blood pressure. (One drink is defined as 12 ounces of beer, 4 to 5 ounces of wine, or 1.5 ounces of 80-proof liquor.) Alcohol can also get in the way of some treatments for high blood pressure.
- Stay calm. Anxiety and stress can raise blood pressure. (SEE HOW TO RELAX, PAGE 129.)
- Take any prescribed medicine as you are told. Take it even if you feel fine.
- Don't smoke. If you have high blood pressure and you smoke, you are at greater risk for heart disease. For tips on how to quit, see page 300.

When You Are Overweight

"I have struggled with my weight all my life. I tried one fad diet after another. I finally just decided to eat a healthy diet, cut out junk food, and walk almost every day. I didn't believe I could, but I have lost some weight. The most important thing is that I feel better."

—Marge

You may think that as an older adult there is no point in losing weight. This is not true. Extra body fat can put you at risk for developing many diseases. Some of the more common ones include the following:

- type II diabetes (SEE PAGE 249.)
- heart disease (SEE PAGE 89.)
- high blood pressure (SEE PAGE 90.)

There is no such thing as a perfect weight or an ideal weight. Good health comes in many shapes and sizes. But there are guidelines for healthy weight ranges. (SEE BOX, PAGE 255.) The more your weight exceeds these ranges, the more likely you are to have weight-related health problems.

If you are overweight, it is not just because you eat too much. Your genes and upbringing also play a role. So do your emotions. There is no simple solution. You will have to learn to balance the calories in foods you eat with the calories your body uses. Use common sense when you eat.

How to Lose Weight Sensibly

Start by keeping a food diary for three or four days. Write down everything you eat and when you eat it. Most people don't know how much they eat. Just being aware of what you eat may help you eat less. You can also use this diary to see where and when you are eating extra calories and fat.

Make sure to eat healthy and balanced meals. Plan your meals using the Food Guide Pyramid. (SEE PAGE 288.) Limit the oil and fatty snacks you eat. Try to en-joy more fruits, vegetables, and grains. Choose lean meats and low-fat dairy products.

Keep moving. If you can, you should be active for at least 30 minutes each day. You can stay active in many ways. (SEE THE ACTIVITY PYRAMID, PAGE 292. ALSO SEE STAYING ACTIVE, PAGE 291.) Talk with your doctor before you begin an exercise program.

Cut out extra calories. Start with foods that are easy to do without. Set limits on other foods. You don't have to stop eating all of the foods you enjoy. Just eat smaller portions of the rich ones, and eat them less often. Be careful not to cut too many calories. Women should eat at least 1,200 calories each day. Men should have at least 1,500 calories each day.

Acceptable Weights for Men and Women

Height	Weight in Pounds
5'0"	97 to 128
5'1"	101 to 132
5'2"	104 to 137
5'3"	107 to 141
5'4"	111 to 146
5'5"	114 to 150
5'6"	118 to 155
5'7"	121 to 160
5'8"	125 to 164
5'9"	129 to 169
5'10"	132 to 174
5'11"	136 to 179
6'0"	140 to 184
6'1"	144 to 189
6'2"	148 to 195
6'3"	152 to 200
6'4"	156 to 205

From the *Dietary Guidelines for Americans*, fourth edition, 1995.

Lose weight at a healthy rate. Set small goals for yourself that you can reach. A weight loss of only 10 to 15 pounds can be good for you. Try to form habits that will help keep off the weight you lose. Most people have had their eating habits for a long time. But little by little, day by day, you can change them.

Stay away from fad diets and crash diets. They are almost never a good idea. In any case, don't try one without your doctor's guidance. Very low-calorie diets can harm your health. So can diets with strict limits on the kind of food you can eat.

When You Have Osteoporosis

"My daughter and I tacked down all the rugs in my house. She put handrails in my bathroom. She also set me up with a trainer to help me get stronger by lifting light weights. I never thought I would be in the gym at the age of 75. But I will do what it takes to keep from falling and breaking a bone."

—Jean

Osteoporosis means "porous bone." It means bones are thinner and weaker than they should be. Osteoporosis is the leading cause of fractures in older adults. It is most common in people older than 70 and in women who have gone through menopause.

There is no cure for osteoporosis. But you can learn to live with it. You will have to eat foods with calcium and vitamin D. You will also have to exercise each day. And you will have to learn how to go about your daily tasks safely so you won't break a bone. For instance, you should carry any object close to your body. And when you lift an object, you should squat, bending your knees. Then lift the object straight up. (See box, page 154.) You will also need to make changes in your home to reduce your chance of falling. (See page 294.)

Self-Care: Osteoporosis

- Do weight-bearing exercise. When you do things like walk, jog, or dance, you put healthy stress on your bones. This makes bones stronger. Exercise can also make you more steady on your feet.
- Make sure that you get enough calcium in your diet. Dairy foods are the best source of calcium. They also give you vitamin D and phosphorous. Both of these help your bones too. Some dark green leafy vegetables and fish have calcium. Breakfast cereals and orange juice with added calcium are also good choices. If you can't eat these foods, talk with your pharmacist about taking extra calcium. Most adults need at least 1,000 milligrams (mg) each day. Women who are past menopause and don't take estrogen need 1,500 mg per day. For women who take estrogen, 1,000 mg per day is recommended.
- Get enough vitamin D. The body needs vitamin D to absorb calcium. You can get more vitamin D by spending time in the sun. You can also drink more milk. If you don't get out in the sun, you might need a vitamin D supplement. Check with your doctor or dietitian before you take one. Too much vitamin D can harm you.
- Ask your doctor about drugs that can slow bone loss or help new bone to form.

Normal Bone versus Bone with Osteoporosis

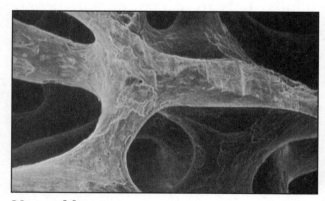

Normal bone
Normal bones are dense. Until the age of 35, our bodies can replace as much of the calcium in our bones as we use.

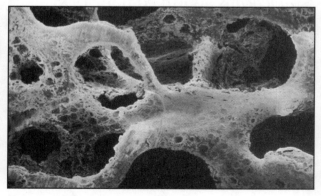

Bone with osteoporosis
When you have osteoporosis, your bones are porous. These bones break much more easily than normal bone.

Taking Charge of Your Health

Health experts think that talking with your doctor may affect your health more than medical tests do. Talking with your doctor can help you make smart choices about your health. You make these choices every day. You make a choice when you decide whether to exercise. You make a choice when you decide if you will drink alcohol or use other drugs. You make decisions about what you eat and how you deal with stress. These choices have a great impact on your health both now and over time.

This section deals with the role you play in taking charge of your health. Doctors are the medical experts. Your doctor can perform physical exams and order lab tests. These can show a lot about your health. But you have a lot to add. You know about your history and your symptoms. You also know your habits and how willing you are to change them.

When you take an active role in your health, you get better health care. You have an easier time keeping control of your own life. You get to make the decisions that affect the quality of your life. But to make good decisions, you need to know several things. You need to know how to work within the health care system. You need to know what options you have for treatment. You also need to know what options you have about where and how to live and for planning for the future. And to take an active role in your health, you also need to know how the things you do each day affect your health. You need to know how your actions will affect your life now and in the future. The chapters in this section help you learn all these things.

257

Here is a list of chapters in this section and what they cover:

Chapter 17:
Your Role as a Health Care Consumer
This chapter teaches you how to get the most from the health care system, such as how to choose a doctor and how to manage the drugs you take.

Chapter 18:
Preventive Health Care
This chapter teaches you how to decide with your doctor what preventive tests you need.

Chapter 19:
Making Healthy Lifestyle Choices
This chapter teaches you how to make healthy choices each day. It covers topics such as healthy eating, fitness, and safety. It explains ways you can change your habits for better health.

Chapter 20:
Your Future Health Concerns
This chapter gives you tips to help you figure out your options for long-term care. It also gives you forms you can use when you need to choose a place to live.

It is never too late to take a more active role in your health. It does not matter how old you are. It does not matter what your health history is. You may not think you can do a lot. But each small thing you do can make a difference. Start today to learn what you can do. Then each day you can do a little more.

Chapter 17

Your Role as a Health Care Consumer

You may not like to think about health care. It may worry or confuse you. You may be confused about which insurance plan to choose. You may not know how Medicare works. You may have concerns about the drugs you take or about surgery. As you get older, these feelings can get stronger.

Some people need several doctors, treatments, and drugs. As a health care consumer, it is up to you to stay informed about your choices. The more you know about how health care works, the better partners you and your doctor can be. Good health care happens when the following four parts of the system work together:
- you as the health care consumer
- your health care workers
- your drugstore
- your hospital

The Role You Play

Good health care starts with you. The choices you make every day affect your health. To get the best care, you need to do the following things:

Take care of your health. When you take steps to stay healthy, you can reduce your need for costly care. (SEE THE CHAPTER MAKING HEALTHY LIFESTYLE CHOICES, PAGE 285.)

Know the difference between self-care and medical care. You can care for some problems. Other problems need the care of a doctor. You can use the self-care sections in this book to know when to take care of a problem yourself. But sometimes you will need to see a doctor. For instance, to treat an ear infection you need to take antibiotics. Nothing you do by yourself can cure one.

It may cost more to treat a problem by yourself than to get the care you need. For instance, if you have a cold and you have emphysema, you need to see a doctor. A doctor's visit and a prescription drug may seem costly. But that care may cost less than if your condition gets worse and you need hospital care.

Be an active member of your health care team. You are the captain of your health care team. You choose the players. For instance, you decide what doctor to see. You also decide when to see the doctor. Ask questions and get the facts you need. You can make better choices about your health if you have the right information.

Keep medical records. Your health history can tell you a lot about your health care needs. Your family's history

---

Medical Resources

Keep this chart where you can find it easily. Tell friends and relatives where you keep it in your home.

Phone number

Doctor _____ _____

Doctor _____ _____

Hospital _____ _____

After-hours
medical care _____ _____

Pharmacist _____ _____

Poison control _____ _____

Local emergency squad _____ _____

Nearest hospital _____ _____

can tell you a lot too. Many health problems run in families. You should know about medical problems your brother, sister, or parents have had. Then you and your doctor can watch for signs of problems.

How to Keep a Health History

- Make copies of the form called Your Medical History. (SEE THE TEAR-OUT PAGE AT THE END OF THIS BOOK.) Fill out a form for yourself. Then fill one out for each member of your family.
- Keep these forms with your health records.
- Update these forms when your health changes.
- Take a copy of the form when you see your doctor.

You and Your Doctor

Your doctor might be a family practitioner or an internist. He or she might be a member of a group, work at a clinic, or have an office alone.

Choose a doctor who will listen to your concerns. This doctor should offer advice and give treatment when you need it. Your doctor should tell you about the risks of different treatments. He or she should explain those risks and help you decide what to do.

Each time you visit your doctor, ask questions and listen closely to the answers. Your doctor won't have all the answers. So he or she should be willing to ask other health care experts for help. Your doctor can help you choose health care providers who will give you specialized treatment. Your doctor can also help you understand what other doctors tell you. Your doctor can make sure that none of your treatments conflict with each other.

Finding a Doctor

"When my doctor retired, I asked him to suggest a new one for me. I thought it would be hard to get used to someone else, but my doctor knew what kind of person I work best with. I get along fine with my new doctor."
—Mildred

The best time to find a doctor is when you are in good health. Then you can take the time to look for a doctor you like and trust.

Make a list of traits you think are important in a doctor. Then talk with friends, family members, health specialists, and other doctors. Ask people for the names of doctors they like.

If your insurance plan has a list of doctors to choose from, find people who know those doctors. Ask them why they like their doctors. Compare what they say with your list of traits.

You can also check at the library to find the names of doctors who are board certified. These doctors have passed strict tests in their fields. Ask the

What You Should Know About Medicare

Do I qualify for Medicare?

Medicare is a federal health insurance program. You qualify for Medicare if you are at least 65 years old and a citizen of the United States. If you are older than 65 and are not a citizen, you still may qualify. You can qualify if you have been a legal resident for at least five years. You also may qualify if you are a person younger than age 65 but are disabled. To find out, call your local Social Security office.

How do I apply for Medicare?

You may already be enrolled. But to be safe, you should apply. The process is easy. To apply for Medicare, all you need to do is call the Social Security Administration. The toll-free number is 1-800-772-1213.

When should I apply?

The best time to apply is three months before you turn 65. That allows plenty of time for all the papers to be processed. Then you will be covered as soon as you turn 65.

What does Medicare cover?

Medicare has two parts. Part A is Medicare Hospital Insurance. Part B is Medicare Medical Insurance.

Part A. This part helps pay for some hospital expenses. You can ask your Social Security office to give you a full list of costs that Part A covers. The following is a partial list:

- care when you stay in the hospital
- care in a skilled nursing home if that home meets the requirements of the Medicare administration
- hospice care

If you are entitled to Social Security payments, you are eligible for Part A. You don't have to pay anything for Part A.

Part B. To enroll in Part B, you don't need to be entitled to Part A. Anyone who is older than 65 can enroll. If you want Part B, you must pay a small monthly fee for this coverage. You will also pay a $100 yearly deductible. This means that you must pay $100 of your medical costs each year before Medicare pays for any of them. You also pay 20 percent of the charges for services that Medicare covers.

Part B pays for some expenses for doctors. Your Social Security office can give you a full list of costs that Medicare pays. The following is a partial list:

- doctors' services in any location
- outpatient hospital care
- outpatient physical therapy
- some health services, such as speech therapy and home health care, or supplies that are not covered under Part A

What You Should Know About Medicare

Will Medicare pay all of my medical bills?

No. Medicare usually pays for 80 percent. You will be billed for the other 20 percent.

How can I pay for the charges that Medicare does not pay?

You have five options for paying for charges Medicare does not cover:

1. You can pay the remaining 20 percent of the charges out of your own pocket.
2. You can keep your health care coverage with an employer or a former employer.
3. You can buy private insurance to cover the extra cost. This is called Medigap insurance or Medicare supplemental insurance.
4. You can join an HMO that has a Medicare risk contract. With an HMO, you may need to use certain doctors and hospitals. But it is much easier to pay for health care when you belong to an HMO. You will also fill out fewer forms.
5. You can apply for Medicaid. If your income is low enough, Medicaid will help pay the medical costs that Medicare does not pay. When you qualify for Medicaid, you don't need to pay the monthly fee for Medicare Part B. You can also get free care in a nursing home. To see if you qualify, call a state or local Medicaid office. Your local Area Agency on Aging can help you find the office nearest you. Or call the Eldercare Locator at 1-800-677-1116 for help.

Is it true that doctors can ask for more money than Medicare will pay them?

It can be. Doctors deal with Medicare in one of two ways. Some take assignment. Others don't.

Taking assignment means that a doctor will accept what Medicare has decided is appropriate for that service. The doctor sends the bill to the government. For instance, Medicare may allow only $100 for an office visit. If the doctor takes assignment, Medicare pays $80. You or your insurance company pays $20.

If you go to a doctor who does not take assignment, the doctor may charge more than Medicare allows for a certain service. For instance, the doctor may charge $150. The doctor will file a claim. But Medicare won't send payment to the doctor. Medicare will pay you $80. This means that you must pay your doctor the $80 Medicare sent you, plus $70 to cover what the doctor charges.

How can I learn more about Medicare?

You can call the Social Security Administration. The toll-free number is 1-800-772-1213.

library staff for help. Think about other things, such as these:

Practice. Does the doctor practice at the hospital you prefer? Could you see other doctors in that doctor's group if you need to?

Insurance. Does the doctor accept your insurance plan? Will the doctor accept the amount that Medicare will pay?

Location and hours. How easy is it for you to get to the doctor's office? Does he or she have office hours that are good for you?

Service. What are the staff members like? Are they polite? Are they helpful?

Choose a doctor carefully. Then allow time for a relationship to grow. A lasting relationship with a primary doctor increases your chance of getting the best health care.

How to Interview a Doctor

Set up a meeting with anyone you might choose as your doctor. Check your insurance plan first to see if this meeting is covered. When you meet with the doctor, do the following things:
- Describe your health history to the doctor. Bring a copy of Your Medical History. (SEE THE TEAR-OUT PAGE AT THE END OF THIS BOOK.) Ask what kinds of tests and treatments the doctor thinks are

best for someone like you.
- Tell the doctor how much you would like to take part in decisions about your health.
- Find out what kinds of services the doctor offers. For instance, some offices have labs on-site.
- Find out how much the doctor knows about aging. Doctors who don't know much about aging might dismiss a problem as being related to old age. Then you won't get the kind of care you need.
- See if the doctor answers questions and listens. How willing is he or she to give advice? Above all, you need to find a doctor you can talk to.
- Think about how well your doctor will work with others. Your doctor may need to direct other people who are involved with your health care.

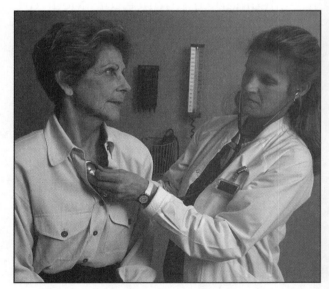

Choose your doctor carefully. The two of you need to work together as a team. Then you can be sure you get the best health care.

This may include dietitians, physical therapists, or counselors. You need to be able to trust your doctor as an expert and adviser.

Getting Ready to See the Doctor

"Most people take time to make a grocery list. But they don't take time to prepare to see the doctor. Before you go, make a list of what you want to talk about. Then you will get much more out of your visit."
—Health educator

Your most frequent contacts with your doctor are likely to be office visits. An office visit often lasts only 15 to 20 minutes. To get the most out of this short time, you need to plan. You can plan for your visit by doing the following things:

Make a list of your symptoms and concerns. Write down as many details as you can. Write down the most important ones first. Then you will be sure to ask about them. When you make your list, you should include these details:
- When did your symptoms start?
- Are your symptoms getting better or worse?
- Have you had this problem before?
- Have you tried treatments for this problem? If so, what? How well did treatments work?

Always bring your records with you. These records will help your doctor find the problem and prescribe the best treatment. You should bring the following records with you:
- A list of the drugs you use. Use the Personal Medication Chart. (SEE THE TEAR-OUT PAGE AT THE END OF THIS BOOK.) Be sure to include pain relievers, antacids, and laxatives. Also list any vitamins you take.
- A list of allergies you have. Include medicines, food, and environmental allergies.
- Any records you have of other health problems. Use the form called Your Medical History. (SEE THE TEAR-OUT PAGE AT THE END OF THIS BOOK.)
- A list of any treatments you have tried

How to Make the Most of Your Doctor Visit

At the doctor's office, use these guidelines to get all you can from the visit:

Be brief, clear, and honest when you talk with the doctor.
- Don't just say "I have been feeling sick lately." Tell the doctor what is bothering you. For instance, say "I have had a headache for three days."
- Have details ready. Don't just say "My back hurts." Say where it hurts. Say what the pain feels like. Tell your doctor what makes it hurt. For instance, "I feel a dull ache in my lower back when I garden."

- Tell the doctor the truth. Don't say that you are smoking less unless it is true. Or if you forget to take your pills, tell your doctor.
- Tell your doctor about changes in your life. Have you moved from your home? Has a close friend just died? Such changes can make you more likely to be ill.
- Tell your doctor about any changes in the way your body functions. You and your doctor need to find out if drugs you take are causing those changes. Even a drug you have taken for years can start to cause problems.

Be ready to listen and look.
- Bring your glasses with you. You may need to read something.
- If you use a hearing aid, wear it.
- Tell the doctor about any problems you have had with your vision or hearing.

Ask the doctor to be clear when he or she talks with you.
- If you are confused, tell your doctor.
- Ask the doctor to tell you things in a certain order:
  —First, have the doctor tell you about your health problem.
  —Next, ask what the medical terms and more common terms are for your problem.
  —Third, ask what tests or treatments your doctor thinks you need.
  —Last, ask what you should do differently.

Ask about drugs and other kinds of treatment.
- Tell your doctor about any side effects to drugs you have had in the past.
- Also ask about treatments that don't involve drugs. For instance, if you have high blood pressure, you may be able to lower it with exercise and weight loss.

Take special steps to remember what the doctor tells you.
- Take notes. Write down all the instructions your doctor gives you. When you leave the office, go over your notes and fill in any details.
- Talk about the visit with a friend or family member. Do this soon after the visit. It can help you remember what the doctor said.
- Bring a tape recorder to your appointment. Tape what your doctor tells you about how to take care of yourself. Tape your doctor's explanation of what is wrong.
- Bring a friend or family member to sit in on your talk with the doctor.

Ask the doctor to explain anything that is unclear.
- If the doctor says words you don't know, ask him or her to explain what they mean.
- If you are confused about a treatment, ask the doctor to describe it more clearly.
- Tell the doctor what you think he or she said. Then ask if you understood.

What to Ask When Your Doctor Prescribes a New Drug

- Why am I taking this drug?
- How long does it take for the drug to work?
- How much of the drug should I take at a time?
- When and how often should I take the drug?
- What should I do if I forget to take a dose?
- Is it OK to stop taking the drug when my symptoms are gone?
- Should I take this drug with food or on an empty stomach?
- Should I take other precautions while I take this drug?
- What are the most common side effects or allergic reactions that this drug causes?
- What side effects should I report?
- What should I do if I have an allergic reaction?
- Will side effects decrease after I use this drug for a while?
- What other drugs, foods, or activities should I avoid while I am taking this drug?
- When should I report back to the doctor?
- Do I need lab tests to keep track of changes?

After Your Doctor Visit

"People can prevent many health problems by going to their follow-up visits. Even if you feel OK, your doctor needs to check some things."
—Registered nurse

After you have been treated, a doctor may want to see you again. Be sure to keep a follow-up appointment. If you have problems before your next visit, call your doctor. If you are taking any drugs, watch for side effects. Report these right away. Then when you see your doctor, describe any problems you have had since your last visit. Describe any good or bad reaction that might be related to your drugs.

You and Your Drugstore

Your pharmacist is an important member of your health care team. He or she can help you choose the over-the-counter drugs that will work best for you. Your pharmacist can also make sure a new drug won't interact with any other drugs you take.

Pharmacists know a lot about how drugs work. They can answer questions about the prescription drugs you take. They can also tell you how to use them. If you have a question about any drug you take, ask your pharmacist.

Why Your Body Reacts to Drugs Differently as You Age

Aging affects how your body absorbs drugs and flushes them out. These changes can increase the chance of side effects from drugs.

As you age, your liver and kidneys are less efficient. These organs help flush drugs out of your body. When these organs don't work well, drugs stay in your body longer.

As you get older, your body tends to have less water in it. Some drugs are water-soluble. This means that they dissolve in water. Since you have less water in your body, it is harder for a drug to dissolve. That means that water will dilute some drugs less than it should. That makes their effect stronger.

As you get older, your body tends to have more fat. Some drugs are fat-soluble. This means that they dissolve in fat. The more body fat you have, the more of a drug your body may absorb. A drug may stay in your body for a longer time than it stays in someone else's body.

Choosing a Drugstore

"When I was younger, there was one drugstore in town. Now there is one on every corner and in every department store and grocery store."

—Ned

You should get your prescriptions from only one drugstore. Then the pharmacist can check your records each time you fill a prescription. If you always go to the same store, your file will be complete.

Find a store that has pharmacists who are willing to talk with you. See whether they are helpful when you ask questions in person and over the phone.

When you choose a drugstore, consider cost. Call around and compare prices. If your health plan covers the cost of drugs, find out which stores you can use.

Some drugstores have special services. These may include discounts for senior citizens, home delivery, and storing records on a computer. Some drugstores are open 24 hours. Choose one that offers you good service, fair prices, and convenience.

How to Work With Your Pharmacist

You and your pharmacist can work together best if you follow these steps:
- Tell your pharmacist about all the

drugs you take. Then he or she can help prevent bad side effects or inter-actions.

- Before you buy an over-the-counter drug, talk with your pharmacist. Ask him or her to help you answer your questions about the drug. (SEE YOUR GUIDE TO BUYING AN OVER-THE-COUNTER DRUG, PAGE 271.) Always ask how the drug will mix with other drugs you take.
- Tell your pharmacist about any past reactions or side effects you have had. If you are allergic to a drug, make sure that fact is written in your records at the doctor's office and at the drugstore.
- Ask your doctor and pharmacist if you can take generic drugs. Generic drugs cost less. They are safe and effective.
- If the label is hard to read, ask if your pharmacist has labels with large print.
- If childproof caps are hard for you to open, ask your pharmacist to use normal caps. You should get these caps only if there are no children in your home.
- Have your pharmacist answer your questions each time you get a new prescription. Make a copy of the list of questions you should ask. (SEE BOX, PAGE 267.) Bring a copy of this list with you to the doctor's office or to your drugstore.
- Ask your pharmacist for information about the drugs you take. Read it closely. Your pharmacist may give you a computer printout that can answer most of these questions.
- Follow instructions. Read the labels and ask your pharmacist about any-thing to watch out for.

Keeping Drugs Safe and Effective

"A lot of people don't read the directions on their prescription drugs. If you want to get the full benefit of a drug, take it exactly as it was prescribed."
—Pharmacist

Many things can affect the way your body reacts to drugs. Your body goes through changes as it ages. This affects your response to drugs. (SEE BOX, PAGE 268.) Drugs in the body are also affect-ed by the following things:

- alcohol
- caffeine
- diet
- genetic factors
- other drugs
- smoking
- viral infections

Some side effects are common and are not dangerous. Other side effects can signal that a drug may not be right for you. If you are having problems with a drug, call your pharmacist. Tell him or her the names of the drugs you take. Describe the side effects.

How to Manage the Drugs You Take

- The side effects listed below can cause problems when you drive. They can also cause you to have a fall. Tell your doctor if you are taking a drug that causes any of the following symptoms:
  - —blurred vision
  - —changes in the way your body works
  - —confusion
  - —dizziness
  - —light-headedness
  - —nausea
  - —sleepiness
  - —slow breathing or difficulty breathing
- Tell your doctor if you feel depressed. This is a side effect of some drugs. You may need a change in dosage or a different drug.

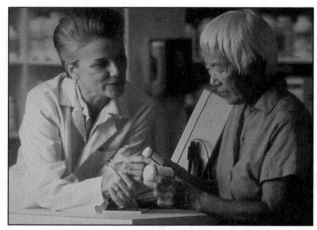

Your pharmacist can answer questions about prescription drugs. He or she can also help you choose an over-the-counter drug.

- Take your medicines when you are supposed to.
- Ask your doctor or pharmacist about what to do if you miss a dose. You might be told that you should take a dose as soon as you remember that you missed one. Or you might be told to double the next dose. It can be harmful to double the dose of some drugs. Don't decide on your own what to do.
- Keep all your medicines in the same place. Then you will be less likely to forget to take one.

Choosing Over-the-Counter Drugs

"I have never seen so many types of pain relievers. I could have stood in the drugstore reading boxes all day. Thank goodness for the pharmacist. She came right over to help me make the best choice."
—Elizabeth

You need to be careful with any drug you take. You need to be careful not to take too much and to watch for allergic reactions. This includes drugs you buy over the counter.

Over-the-counter drugs can cause problems when you are taking prescription drugs. For instance, an antacid can keep some antibiotics from working. And you should not take cough or cold medicines if you take drugs for high blood pressure, diabetes, or glaucoma.

Your Guide to Buying an Over-the-Counter Drug

Make copies of this guide and keep them handy. Always use this guide if you think you might take an over-the-counter drug.

Does the drug treat symptoms you don't have?	Yes	No
Could you treat your symptoms with home remedies?	Yes	No
Do you have any allergies that might cause a problem?	Yes	No
Do you have a chronic condition that this drug may affect?	Yes	No
Do the ingredients affect any other drug you are taking? (If you are not sure, ask your pharmacist.)	Yes	No
Are you allergic to any of the ingredients?	Yes	No
Do any warnings or cautions apply to you?	Yes	No

Did you answer "yes" to any of these questions? If so, this over-the-counter drug may not be the best choice for you. Talk with your doctor or pharmacist.

Over time, your reaction to a drug or a dosage of that drug can change. Be aware of your reactions. Let your doctor or pharmacist know if you notice any changes.

How to Use Over-the-Counter Drugs Safely

- Before you buy any type of drug, learn what you can about it. (SEE YOUR GUIDE TO BUYING AN OVER-THE-COUNTER DRUG, ABOVE.)

- Keep a list of any over-the-counter drugs you use. Use the Personal Medication Chart. (SEE THE TEAR-OUT PAGE AT THE END OF THIS BOOK.) Show this list to your pharmacist whenever you buy a new drug.
- You may want to keep notes about how to use an over-the-counter drug. Write down the name of the drug. Then write when to take the drug and any special instructions. List the dose and side effects to watch for.
- If you have questions or if the label is hard to read, be sure to talk with your pharmacist.

Which Pain Medication Is Right for You?

Use this table to decide what type of pain reliever is right for you. If you are not sure, talk with your pharmacist. Tell him or her what drugs you take and what medical problems you have.

	Dose	Use for Headache?	Use for Pain?	
Acetaminophen (Tylenol)	Adults: Take one or two 325 mg tablets, three to four times a day.	yes	yes	
Ibuprofen (Advil, Nuprin, Motrin IB)	Adults: Take one or two 200 mg tablets. Take with food. Don't take more than six tablets a day unless directed by a doctor.	yes	yes	
Aspirin	Adults: Take one or two 325 mg tablets every four hours. Take up to 12 tablets a day, unless a doctor tells you not to. Don't give to children.	yes	yes	
Ketoprofen (Orudis, Actron)	Adults: Take one 12.5 mg tablet every four to six hours. If you don't feel better, you may take a second tablet after one hour. Don't take more than six tablets in a 24-hour period.	yes	yes	
Naproxen Sodium (Aleve)	Adults: Take one 220 mg tablet every 8 to 12 hours. Start with two tablets, then take one tablet 12 hours later. Take no more than three tablets in 24 hours unless directed by a doctor. Adults over 65: Take no more than one tablet every 12 hours.	yes	yes	

Important Tips
• Don't use more than one type of pain reliever at a time. • Be careful with products that have more than one drug. Some may have caffeine. Some may mix poorly with other drugs. • Don't take aspirin when you are taking a cold medicine.

Use for Fever?	Use for Muscle/Joint Pain or Arthritis?	Use to Prevent Heart Attack or Stroke?	Side Effects and Other Things to Consider
yes	yes	no	Large doses can be harmful. If you regularly drink alcohol, talk with your doctor before taking this drug. Avoid if you have liver problems.
yes	yes	no	Don't take if allergic to aspirin. May cause stomach bleeding. Avoid if you have congestive heart failure, kidney problems, or ulcers. Avoid if you are taking diuretics or anticoagulants.
yes	yes	yes	May cause ulcers or stomach bleeding. Use enteric-coated aspirin to reduce stomach irritation. Older adults should use with caution. High doses can cause dizziness. Dizziness may lead to falls.
yes	yes	no	Can irritate stomach. Avoid if you have congestive heart failure, kidney problems, or ulcers. Avoid if you are taking diuretics or anticoagulants.
yes	yes	no	Can irritate stomach. Avoid if you have congestive heart failure, kidney problems, or ulcers. Avoid if you are taking diuretics or anticoagulants. If you have more than three drinks per day that contain alcohol, talk with your doctor before you use this drug.

How to Remember to Take Your Drugs

Try these tips for remembering to take your medicine properly and on time.

If You Take Many Drugs Every Day

The more drugs you take, the more you will need a system. Here are two methods that may help:

The Calendar Method

1. Keep a calendar in one place with all your drugs listed on it.
2. Write on it the time you are supposed to take each drug.
3. Write on it any special instructions.
4. Check off each dose as you take it.

The Pillbox Method

You can buy plastic pill containers at a drugstore. These containers can help you keep your drugs and your schedule straight. Before you use a pillbox, take these two steps:

1. Talk with your pharmacist. Make sure that it is safe to store pills out of the original container.
2. Label the new container clearly. Write down the name of the drug, how much to take, and when to take it.

If You Work or Travel Frequently

Make a card that lists your drugs and the times to take them. Keep this card in your wallet. Then you will have it when you are away from home.

If You Are Forgetful or If You Take Only a Few Drugs

Try to link other things with the times you take a drug. Here are some examples:

If you take a drug once a day: Take it right after you brush your teeth in the morning.

If you take a drug twice a day: Take it when you brush your teeth in the morning and again at night.

If you take a drug four times a day: Take it with each meal and when you go to bed. If you are supposed to take the drug on an empty stomach, take it one hour before each meal.

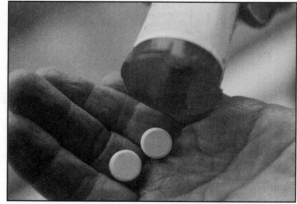

Be sure you follow your doctor's instructions when you take a drug. Take the drug when you are supposed to. And make sure that you take the drug for as long as the doctor has directed.

You and the Hospital

Sometimes you may need to stay at the hospital for tests or surgery. When you do, look at each choice. Think about how each choice could meet your needs. Talk with your doctor about what you want. Talk with your family. When you all work together, you can feel better able to make the best choice.

If Your Doctor Tells You to Go to the Hospital

"I remember the days when you had to stay in the hospital for some tests. Unless you stayed, insurance would not cover it. Things have changed. People have a lot more options now. You may be able to get a test done at the hospital and go home on the same day."
—Hospital administrator

People don't need to spend as much time in the hospital as in the past. Most tests and surgeries were once done in hospitals. Patients had to stay overnight. Now you can have many tests and surgeries done as an outpatient. This means that you can go home the same day you receive your treatment. Even when you must stay in the hospital, you may be able to go home sooner than you could have done in the past. If your doctor tells you to go to a hospital, make sure that you know why you need to go.

Ask your doctor questions to make sure that you understand all of your options. If you must stay in a hospital, find out as much as you can before you go. Find out what will happen when you are there. You may feel as if you won't have control when you are in the hospital. But you are still the consumer. You are the one buying the services of the nurses and doctors who treat you. Even in the hospital, you are the one who should make the decisions about your care.

What to Ask Before Going to the Hospital

- Why do I need to go to the hospital?
- What tests and procedures will I have done?
- Do I need to have the tests and procedures done at the hospital? Or can I have them done as an outpatient?
- What other treatment choices do I have?
- How much will I be involved in decisions about my treatment?
- Do the tests or procedures involve any risks?
- What will the tests tell us?
- How long will I be in the hospital?
- When can I return to my normal routine?
- How long will I be away from work or other activities?

If Your Doctor Says You Need Surgery

"Before we do any kind of transplant, we like to have the whole family come in. We show them pictures of the kidney and a video about what to expect. Then our health educators answer any questions that come up. You can tell the difference when you see how calm people are on the day of the surgery."
—Kidney specialist

If your doctor wants you to have surgery, you need to decide if it is worth the risks. You might have other options. Find out as much as you can. Learn as much as you can about what to expect. Then decide what you want to do.

Talk with your doctor. (SEE WHAT TO ASK IF YOU NEED SURGERY, PAGE 277.) If you think it may help, take a friend or family member with you to see the doctor. Ask if the doctor has booklets or videos about the surgery.

The first step is to find out whether the surgery is emergency or elective.

Emergency surgery. This is surgery needed to save your life or to prevent lasting damage. It is also called nonelective surgery. Nonelective means that you have little or no choice. You may not have time to consider other options. Emergency surgery is the only choice for conditions such as these:
- appendicitis
- blocked bowel
- uncontrolled bleeding from the stomach
- some injuries

Elective surgery. Most surgeries are elective. This means that you have some choice. You may have other options. One might be to use drugs to treat the problem. Physical therapy may be an option. At other times, surgery might be the only way to correct a problem.

Surgery is most often the right choice when it will do the following:
- ease or prevent pain
- restore or save a normal function
- correct a deformity
- save or prolong your life

Make sure that you do what you want. Don't let anyone pressure you. Don't have surgery if you don't need it or don't want it.

When You Should Ask for a Second Opinion

Get the facts. The more you know, the better you can decide about surgery. One way to get more facts is to ask another doctor. This is called getting a second opinion. It is sometimes called a review of treatment. Your health plan may want you to get a second opinion.

A second opinion can help you feel sure that you are making the right choice. You should get a second opinion if any of the following is true:
- The surgery is new or is a high-risk treatment. For instance, an organ transplant might be a risky surgery.

- Your symptoms are not bad and the outcome of the surgery is hard to predict.
- The surgery is often done even when it is not needed.

You might feel awkward asking for a second opinion. Most doctors want to help you make the right choice. If your doctor gets angry or won't help you, you should find a new doctor.

Your doctor may be able to give you the name of a second surgeon. Or you can ask for names from your health plan or your local hospital. Bring your medical records and X-rays with you. If you can't do this, have records and X-rays sent to the second doctor. Have this done before your visit. You can do this by signing a records release form. If the second doctor does not agree with the first, find out why.

Preparing for Surgery

Before you have elective surgery or go to the hospital, find out what your health plan covers. Find out what to do so that you will be covered. Make sure that you know these things:

- Do you need approval in advance from your health plan?
- Do you need a second opinion?
- Do you need a referral from your doctor?
- What copayments or what percentage of the bill do you need to pay?

Ask your surgeon or the office staff about fees and insurance. Find out if the doctor's office will fill out your insurance forms and send them in. If they won't, you will need to fill out the forms. Also ask if the doctor will accept the insurance payment as the full fee. This is called taking assignment. If the doctor won't accept, you must pay the difference.

What to Ask If You Need Surgery

- What is the surgery called?
- How is it performed?
- How long will the surgery take?
- Why do I need this surgery?
- How soon must I decide to have the surgery?
- How soon should I have the surgery?
- What will happen if I wait to have the surgery?
- What are the risks of this surgery?
- Will my other health problems affect the surgery? If so, how?
- What other treatment options do I have?
- Can I have outpatient surgery?
- What will happen if I don't have the surgery?
- Is not having treatment an option?
- What should I do if I don't have treatment?
- What complications may I have?
- What complications are common for my age and state of health?
- What can be done to prevent complications?
- How will this surgery help me?
- Are there any side effects of the anesthesia?
- Will I have tubes, catheters, or dressings after surgery?

- How long does it usually take to recover?
- Will I need help caring for myself after this surgery? If yes, for how long will I need help?
- When can I return to work and my normal routine?
- How often do you do this surgery?
- How often is this surgery done at your hospital?

How to Review Your Hospital Bill

"We're an insurance company. Many people count on us to review their hospital bills. They expect us to find any errors. But it is worth your time to check the bills. After all, you will have the most to gain. If there is an overcharge, you are the one who will have to pay."

—Insurance broker

Hospitals try to bill you correctly. But people do make mistakes. Ask the hospital billing office to explain unclear charges, terms, or tests. You can also ask the billing office for a copy of your bedside log or other records. Use these records to check your bill. If you need more facts, your doctor's office may be able to help you get them. It takes time to check hospital bills. But you need to do it. Don't be afraid to ask questions if things don't seem to add up.

How to Check a Hospital Bill

Take the following steps to find problems with a hospital bill:

1. Ask for an itemized bill. If you don't, most hospitals will send you only a summary.
2. Be sure that you were billed for the kind of room you had.
3. Be sure that you were charged for the right number of days. (Most hospitals don't charge for the day you were discharged.)
4. Make sure that you had each test and procedure listed on the bill.
5. Circle any charges that seem too high. For instance, $3 for a dose of acetaminophen (Tylenol) seems too high.
6. If you find a mistake, call the hospital's billing department. Ask them to correct it. If they won't, ask to speak with the department supervisor. Once the hospital agrees to correct the mistake, ask for a revised bill. Then send a copy to your health plan. If you have problems, call your health plan for help.
7. Before you pay your part of the bill, make sure that someone has answered your questions. Be sure that mistakes have been fixed. Find out if your health plan has paid its part. Don't be rushed into paying. You need to be sure that the bill is correct and that you know how much you owe.

Preventive Health Care

You may think disease prevention is only for younger people. But that is not true. After you turn 50, you have more risk for major health problems. You can prevent some of them with immunizations. You can find others early through health screenings. If you find a problem early, you can treat it. When you do, you will reduce the effect it will have on your life later. You need screening tests, even if you have a chronic health problem. They help to keep you healthy.

How often you need to see your doctor depends on your age, sex, and health history. Your doctor will consider these things when deciding what tests and immunizations you need. To help you prevent disease, your doctor may also suggest a change in your diet and exercise habits. You may also get advice about drinking and smoking. (See MAKING HEALTHY LIFESTYLE CHOICES, PAGE 285.)

This chapter tells you about screening tests and immunizations. The guide at the end of the chapter can help you know how often you should have both.

Having the Screening Tests You Need

"As with most things in life, there is no right answer for everyone. This is especially true when it comes to which health screening tests you need."
—Family practice doctor

Screening tests help doctors find a disease. How often you might need a certain test will depend on your health history. It will also depend on your family history.

As you get older, you become more at risk for a chronic disease. You are also at greater risk of getting cancer. So certain routine tests make sense. For instance, you may need to have your blood pressure checked. Or you may need a mammogram.

Doctors now know that there are some tests that you do not need on a regular basis. For instance, most people do not need routine urine tests or X-rays. Before you have a screening test, talk with your doctor about it. Make sure you know these things:
- what the test is for
- whether your insurance will cover it
- whether any risks are connected with it
- what you need to do to get ready for it

Keeping Your Immunizations Up-to-Date

"Last week my doctor asked when I had my last tetanus shot. I had no idea. She said I should keep track of the vaccines I get. She also said I would need booster shots from time to time."
—Annie

You may think that you don't need to get shots or immunizations. You may think they are just for children and people who travel abroad. But if you have never had vaccines before, you need them. And if you had vaccines as a child, you may need booster shots.

A vaccine helps keep you from getting a disease. It is made from a virus or a kind of bacteria that causes a disease. The vaccine is a weak or dead form of the disease agent. It does not cause the disease. But it tricks your body into thinking that you have the disease. Your body makes antibodies in response to the vaccine. These will protect you from the disease.

Antibodies are proteins your immune system makes. Each one fights a certain infection. For instance, if you have a measles shot, your body will make proteins that fight just the measles. Once you have antibodies for measles in your blood, you won't get measles. Some vaccines protect you for life. For others, you will need boosters.

Use the chart at the end of this book to keep track of your immunizations.

Older adults should stay up-to-date on their shots. To stay up-to-date, keep a record. List what vaccines you have had and when you had them. Use the tear out chart called Your Personal Health Record at the end of this book. If you think you need a booster or a new vaccine, talk with your doctor.

The vaccines listed here are the ones you should know about. If you plan to travel to a foreign country, talk with your doctor. There may be other vaccines you will need.

Hepatitis A Vaccine

The hepatitis A vaccine gives you short-term protection against hepatitis A. This disease is spread mainly by contaminated food or water. Hepatitis A can also be spread through direct contact with someone who has it. Most older adults don't need a vaccine for this condition. Your doctor may tell you to have it, though, if you are going to a country where sanitation is poor. This includes these areas:

- Africa
- Asia (except Japan)
- Eastern Europe
- Mediterranean basin
- Mexico
- Middle East
- South America and Central America

Your doctor may tell you that you need this vaccine if any of the following statements is true:

- You inject drugs.
- You have high-risk sexual behavior.
- You receive blood products.
- You are a health care worker.
- You are Native American or an Alaskan Native.

Hepatitis B Vaccine

Hepatitis B causes the liver to become inflamed. It can cause a range of problems. The virus can give you flulike symptoms. It may cause more serious problems too. Some people who have hepatitis B must stay in the hospital. The hepatitis B vaccine is advised only for adults who are at high risk. You are

Taking advantage of screenings and immunizations can help you maintain your health.

at high risk if any of the following statements is true:

- You inject drugs.
- You have high-risk sexual behavior.
- You travel to developing countries.
- You receive blood products.
- You are a health care worker.

Influenza (Flu) Vaccine

A flu shot can lower your risk of getting the flu. The shot is 75 percent effective in preventing the flu. You will need to get a flu shot each year. The flu vaccine has a few side effects, but they are rare. (SEE WHAT YOU NEED TO KNOW ABOUT THE FLU SHOT, PAGE 105.)

Pneumococcal Vaccine

One type of pneumonia is caused by pneumococcal bacteria. This vaccine prevents it. You need this vaccine only if you are at high risk. Most people need this shot only once. But if you are at risk, you may need the vaccine again. (SEE WHAT YOU NEED TO KNOW ABOUT THE PNEUMONIA SHOT, PAGE 109.)

Tetanus/Diphtheria Vaccine

Both tetanus and diphtheria are serious. But since vaccines have been around, these diseases have become less common. If you did not have three shots for these diseases as a child, you should get them now. Even if you got all three shots, you may need a booster shot. Everyone needs a booster shot every 10 years. The tetanus/diphtheria (Td) vaccine is quite safe. But the area around the shot may become sore or hard for one or two days. A worse reaction is very rare.

Varicella (Chicken Pox) Vaccine

Chicken pox is caused by a virus. It is easy to catch. In children, chicken pox is most often a mild illness. When adults get it, the symptoms can be much worse. This vaccine is advised for healthy adults who have no history of chicken pox and who have never been protected against it.

Recommended Preventive Services

You and your doctor should work as a team to decide about screening tests and immunizations. The guidelines that follow are based on recommendations from the U.S. Preventive Services Task Force and a thorough review of scientific evidence from many sources. (SEE GUIDE TO PREVENTIVE SERVICES, PAGE 283.) Work with your doctor to plan a preventive exam schedule that is right for you.

Guide to Preventive Services

Service	How Often		
	Ages 50–64	Ages 64–75	Age 75 and older
Blood pressure screening	Every two years		
Breast cancer screening: Breast self-exam	Each month, or as doctor suggests		As often as agreed upon with your doctor
Exam by doctor	Every one to two years	Every one to two years until age 69. After age 70, have an exam as often as agreed upon with your doctor.	As often as agreed upon with your doctor
Mammo-gram	Every one to two years	Every one to two years until age 69. After age 70, have screening as often as agreed upon with your doctor.	As often as agreed upon with your doctor
Cervical cancer screening: Pelvic exam and Pap smear	Every three years after you have three consecutive normal Pap smears in a five-year period	You may be able to stop having Pap smears at age 65 if: • You have had regu-lar, normal smears in the past. • Your doctor advises it, and you agree.	May not be needed if: • You have had regu-lar, normal smears in the past. • Your doctor advises it, and you agree.
Cholesterol screening	Every five years		Screening is not recommended. (After age 75, this screening does not predict risk well.)

Guide to Preventive Services

Service	How Often		
	Ages 50–64	**Ages 64–75**	**Age 75 and older**
Colon cancer screening: Fecal occult blood testing	Each year. Your doctor may suggest a sigmoidoscopy with this test or instead of it.		
Sigmoid-oscopy	Every three to five years. Your doctor may suggest a fecal occult blood test with this test or instead of it.		
Glaucoma screening	Ask your doctor how often you need this if: ● You are African American.	● You have a family history of glaucoma. ● You have diabetes or myopia.	
Influenza vaccine (flu shot)	Yearly if: ● You live in a chronic care facility. ● You have a chronic lung disease or kidney disease. ● You work in the health care field and see patients at high risk.	Each year	
Pneumo-coccal (Pneumonia) vaccine	If you have a chronic illness, ask your doctor if you should have this vaccine.	Once, at age 65	If your doctor suggests it, consider having another shot.
Tetanus/ diphtheria (Td) vaccine	Booster every 10 years		

Chapter 19

Making Healthy Lifestyle Choices

Scientists keep finding new ways to diagnose, treat, and prevent illness. But it is up to you to stay healthy. Healthy habits help you reduce your risk of many serious conditions.

Making healthy lifestyle choices may mean making changes in the way you live. You may need to stop smoking or eat less fat. But you don't have to make these changes all at once. This chapter shows you how to do it one step at a time.

Here is a list of changes you can make to improve your health. To learn more about any item, turn to the page number given.

- If you drink alcohol, drink only a moderate amount. (See page 287.)
- Eat a variety of healthy foods and balanced meals. (See page 287.)
- Exercise and stay active. (See page 291.)
- Make your home, your neighborhood, and your driving habits safer. (See Staying Safe, page 294.)
- If you smoke, quit. (See page 300.)

Alcohol Use and Alcoholism

"I used to meet my buddies every Wednesday for a few beers. On the weekend I'd drink with other friends. But my waist began to expand, so I cut down. I might have a glass of wine at a dinner party. But most nights, I just have seltzer and a twist of lime."

—Bill

You can drink alcohol and still have a healthy lifestyle. You might enjoy a glass of wine with dinner or a drink when you are out with friends. If your health permits it, this type of drinking is fine. The tips on moderate drinking can help you keep alcohol in its place. (See page 287.)

But alcohol abuse is not the same as enjoying a drink now and then. And it can be a problem for people of all ages. People who abuse alcohol keep drinking even when they know it has already hurt them and those they love. An alcoholic depends on alcohol. He or she may drink to keep from feeling strong emotions or even physical pain. An alcoholic may behave in abnormal ways and have health problems caused by drinking. When alcoholics try to stop drinking, they may have a physical reaction.

What Alcohol Does to Your Body

Even a small amount of alcohol can affect your body. Alcohol slows down your brain. It makes you less alert and impairs your judgment. When you have been drinking, you are more likely to fall or have an accident. Alcohol can also cause insomnia and nightmares. The older you are, the less alcohol your body can handle before you notice these reactions.

Heavy drinking can make you very sick. If you choose to drink alcohol, limit the amount you drink. For women, that means one drink a day. For men, that means two drinks a day. A drink is defined as 12 ounces of beer, 5 ounces of table wine, or 1.5 ounces of liquor such as gin or vodka. Heavy drinking can do any of the following harmful things:

- damage your brain, nervous system, liver, heart, kidneys, and stomach
- put you at increased risk for cancer of the throat, mouth, pancreas, liver, and stomach
- cause you to die 10 to 15 years before you would have if you did not drink too much
- hurt or even kill you if you mix

alcohol with drugs. Even aspirin taken with alcohol is risky. The combination could kill you.

Could You Have a Drinking Problem?

Not everyone who drinks is an alcoholic. Alcoholism is a disease that has symptoms. You may be an abuser of alcohol if you answer "yes" to any of the following questions:

- Do you drink alone more often now than you once did?
- Do you often drink too much?
- Do you eat only once in a while?
- Do you drink to calm your nerves or to forget your worries?
- Do you drink so that you will feel less sad or anxious?
- Have you hurt yourself or someone else while you were drunk?
- Do you need to drink more and more alcohol to get the feeling you want?

If you answered "yes" to any of the above questions, talk with your doctor or a counselor about getting help to stop drinking.

How Alcohol Abuse Is Treated

There are many ways to treat alcohol abuse. Your doctor can help you decide which treatment is best for you. Here are some of the options:

- Alcoholics Anonymous. AA offers support meetings with other people who have a problem with drinking. AA has a special group for older adults.
- Rehabilitation programs. You can

find these programs in hospitals, outpatient centers, and private clinics. Some of these programs are inpatient. That means you stay overnight. For others, you come in each day from home.

- Detoxification centers. Detoxification clears your body of the harmful effects of alcohol. This is called drying out.

How to Be a Moderate Drinker

Not everyone who drinks alcohol is an alcoholic. Most people can enjoy a drink now and then and still have a healthy lifestyle. Follow these guidelines.

- Cut down on the time you spend with people who drink a lot. If you avoid the time and place where you are likely to drink, you are less likely to abuse alcohol.
- Be sensible at parties. You can enjoy a glass of wine with dinner or a cocktail at a party. But have only one drink. Make your other choices nonalcoholic.
- Don't drink and drive. If you plan to drink when you are out, be sure to ask someone who is not drinking to drive you home.
- Don't drink alone. When you drink alone, it is easy to drink too much.
- Don't drink to avoid problems. If you are having trouble at work or home, talk to a friend, a member of the clergy, or a doctor that you trust.
- Feel free to say no. You don't need a reason for not drinking.

- Set a positive example for others. You can discourage alcohol abuse in others through your own healthy attitudes and actions.

Eating for Your Health

"Sometimes I don't feel like eating. I live alone and don't like to cook just for me. My doctor told me to have lunch at the senior center in my town. There is a lot more variety there than I have at home. Even better, now I eat with other people, and I have made new friends."
—Alice

The amount of food your body needs depends on your physical condition and on how active you are. One way to make sure you have a healthy diet is to use the Food Guide Pyramid. (SEE PAGE 288.)

By choosing a variety of foods from the Food Guide Pyramid, you eat a balanced diet. A balanced diet can help you keep a healthy weight and make you feel better. All you have to do is eat the proper number of servings from each food group in the pyramid. Most adults need at least the minimum number of servings each day from each food group listed in the pyramid.

How Health Problems May Affect What You Eat
Some chronic conditions call for a change in diet. These include:
- diabetes (SEE PAGE 249.)

The Food Guide Pyramid

Using the Food Guide Pyramid to improve your diet is easy. All you have to do is follow these three steps: Start from the bottom, eat a varied diet, and limit fats.

Step 1: Build your diet from the bottom up.

Most food in a balanced diet should come from grains, vegetables, and fruit. These foods give you energy. They also have fiber. Fiber can help keep your blood cholesterol level down. It can also help food move through your bowels easily. Most grains, fruits, and vegetables are also low in fat.

Step 2: Eat a variety of foods from each group.

No one food has all the nutrients you need. That is why you need to eat at least the minimum number of servings from each group.

Step 3: Limit the amount of food you eat from the top of the pyramid.

These foods include fats and sugar. You don't need much fat in your diet. Fats add calories and little else. Sugar gives you quick energy, but it fades quickly.

What Is a Serving?

The Food Guide Pyramid is based on servings. Use the following lists to help you know what a serving is. After a while, you will develop a sense of how much makes a serving.

Breads and Grains:
Examples of One Serving
- 1 slice bread or 1 dinner roll
- 1/2 bagel, bun, or English muffin
- 1/2 cup cooked cereal, rice, or pasta
- 3/4 cup to 1 cup dry cereal flakes
- 3 to 4 crackers

Vegetables:
Examples of One Serving
- 1/2 cup cooked or raw vegetables, such as carrots or green beans
- 1 cup leafy raw vegetables, such as fresh spinach or lettuce
- 3/4 cup vegetable juice

Fruits:
Examples of One Serving
- 1 piece fresh fruit, such as an apple, pear, banana, or melon wedge
- 1/2 cup fresh cut-up fruit, such as grapes or diced pineapple
- 1/2 cup cooked or canned fruit
- 1/4 cup dried fruit

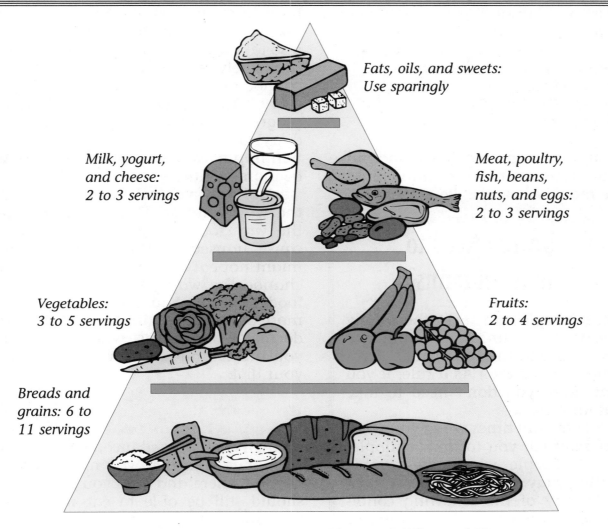

Fats, oils, and sweets:
Use sparingly

Milk, yogurt,
and cheese:
2 to 3 servings

Meat, poultry,
fish, beans,
nuts, and eggs:
2 to 3 servings

Vegetables:
3 to 5 servings

Fruits:
2 to 4 servings

Breads and
grains: 6 to
11 servings

Meat, Poultry, Fish, and Meat Alternatives: Examples of One Serving

- 2 to 3 ounces lean cooked meat, poultry, or fish (Do not eat more than 7 ounces in a day.)
- 1/2 cup cooked beans, such as kidney beans or black beans, 2 tablespoons of peanut butter, or 1 egg (Each of these is equal to one ounce of lean meat.)

Cheese, Milk, and Yogurt: Examples of One Serving

- 1 cup low-fat milk or low-fat yogurt
- 1 1/2 ounces natural cheese (Look for low-fat cheeses. These have 5 grams of fat or less per ounce.)

- gastrointestinal disorders (SEE CONSTIPATION, PAGE 17; DIVERTICULOSIS, PAGE 21; AND IRRITABLE BOWEL SYNDROME, PAGE 27.)
- heart disease (SEE PAGE 89.)
- hypertension (SEE PAGE 90.)
- obesity (SEE PAGE 254.)
- osteoporosis (SEE PAGE 255.)

If you have a chronic illness and make some changes in your eating habits, you may feel better. Be patient. It is hard to change what you eat. It may take you longer to plan meals. It might also take time to learn which foods you can safely eat. Focus on one small change at a time. Make little changes every day. It may help to track your progress on paper. Try keeping a log (or diary) of what you eat. As your nutrition improves, you will feel better and be more healthy.

Any drug you take can also affect the way you eat. Drugs can change the way food tastes. They can also cause nausea. If this happens, you might not eat enough. Drugs can also change the way your body uses the food you eat. You may need to eat more or less of certain foods. Ask your doctor or pharmacist whether a drug you are taking calls for a change in your diet.

Do You Need to Take Vitamins?

Most people can meet their daily needs for vitamins and minerals by following the Food Guide Pyramid. (SEE PAGE 288.) As a rule, if you eat right, you don't need to take vitamin pills.

There are times when your doctor may tell you to take a supplement. People who have trouble eating may need vitamins. People with any of the following conditions may need to take vitamins or minerals:
- osteoporosis (extra calcium)
- heart disease (vitamin E)
- alcoholism (multivitamins)
- digestion problems (multivitamins)

If you have a chronic illness such as heart disease or high blood pressure, talk with your doctor before you start taking any supplements.

How Your Budget Affects What You Eat

If you live on a fixed income and want to change your diet, you may need to change where and how you shop. You should still be able to eat what you like. You just need to buy wisely and make sure you choose foods that are good for you. It helps to plan. Write out a list of what you need before you go shopping. Use the food pyramid to help you plan. That way you will choose healthy food. Take the list with you to the store.

Choose your meats, vegetables and fruits, and dairy products first. If you need canned or boxed goods, look for what is on sale. Try the store brands. They are often a good buy.

If you find it very hard to pay for food, call your local Social Security Administration office. They can let you know if you are eligible for help. You can also call your local meals-on-wheels. This program is funded with federal dollars, and no one can be turned down.

How Your Emotions Affect What You Eat

Social and mental changes can affect your eating habits. If you feel sad or lonely, you might eat too much or too little. If you have lost a loved one, you might eat alone most of the time. You may not feel like shopping and cooking. This is common. But you should try your best to take care of yourself. Follow the tips below on how to enjoy meals to help rebuild your interest in food.

How to Enjoy Preparing and Eating Meals

Making healthy meals can be a challenge. This is especially true if you live alone or find it harder to get around than you once did. Many people think of meals as a time to relax and be with others. When people eat alone, they often eat quickly. They don't always eat right. If you are one of these people, try some of these ideas to improve your interest in food:

- Share a meal with a friend. Ask friends to come to your home or go out for lunch.
- Try new recipes. You can find new ideas in newspapers and magazines or on television.
- Make meal times special. Use your good dishes. Light some candles.
- Go to lunch and dinner events for seniors. These are often held in community centers, churches, synagogues, and schools.
- Get help if you can't fix your own meals. Check your local meals-on-wheels. If you live in an assisted living facility, find out more about the dining program.

Staying Active

"I've been less active since I retired. It seems the less I do, the more tired I feel. So I started walking each day after lunch. Sure enough, I felt better in a few days."
—Jack

An active lifestyle is a key to good health. Staying active has lots of benefits. It makes your muscles stronger and boosts your energy. It makes your heart and lungs work better. It improves your balance, and that means you are less likely to fall. It makes you feel good and reduces stress.

Physical activity is not another word for exercise. However, the two are closely related. Exercise involves movement that is planned and structured. Physical activity is any movement. You can be active in many ways. You can garden, walk, or do housework. You can also be active by doing exercise like jogging, swimming, or biking.

The Activity Pyramid

Use the Activity Pyramid to help you become more active. Everyone can gain by following the tips at the top of the pyramid. The top challenges you to walk away from a sedentary lifestyle. How you use the rest of the guide depends on how active you are now. Look for your activity level in bold print. Then follow the tips that are listed.

If You Are Not Active
Look at the bottom of the Activity Pyramid. Your first step is to add more activities from those listed there to each day. You should also do the following things:
- Try to spend more time being physically active each week.
- Cut back on doing things listed at the top of the pyramid.
- Think about what you do each day. Do you take as few steps as you can when you do chores? Do you drive when you could walk? You may be saving time, but you may also be cheating your health.

If You Are Somewhat Active
Look at the middle of the pyramid. Choose activities you think you will enjoy. Start off slowly. Work your way up to longer and more vigorous workouts. Keep these tips in mind:
- Do activities that you enjoy.
- Plan the time of day that you will be active.
- Set realistic goals.

If You Are Active at Least Four Days a Week
Look at the middle of the pyramid. Use the activities there to keep active. Here are some tips that will help to keep you interested:
- Try new activities.
- Change your routine if you get bored.
- Choose activities from the whole pyramid.

CUT DOWN ON

- Watching TV
- Playing computer games
- Sitting for more than 30 minutes at a time

2 TO 3 TIMES A WEEK

Leisure Activities

- Golf
- Bowling
- Softball
- Yard work

Flexibility and Strength

- Stretching and yoga
- Push-ups/sit-ups
- Weight lifting

3 TO 5 TIMES A WEEK

Aerobic Exercise
(20+ minutes)

- Brisk walking
- Cross-country skiing
- Bicycling
- Swimming

Recreation
(30+ minutes)

- Soccer
- Basketball
- Dancing
- Hiking
- Tennis

EVERY DAY
(or as much as possible)

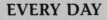

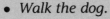

- Walk the dog.
- Take longer routes.
- Take the stairs instead of the elevator.
- Walk to the store or the mailbox.
- Park your car farther away than usual and walk.
- Add extra steps to your day.

Many doctors agree that being active for 30 minutes on most days of the week will help to keep you healthy. If you can't do that much at once, do a little at a time. If you take a short walk two to three times a day, it will add up.

What is important is to just get moving. Use the Activity Pyramid (SEE PAGE 292) to get started. Talk with your doctor about what is a safe activity level for you. This is especially important if you have heart disease or are at risk for it. (SEE PAGE 89.)

How to Start a Walking Program

Walking may be the closest thing to the perfect exercise. It's one of the best activity choices for almost anyone. You can do it indoors or outside. You can do it for the rest of your life. It doesn't usually cause injury. It helps burn calories for weight loss. And it's easy. Here are some tips for getting started:
- Wear comfortable shoes. A shoe designed for walking is best. Or choose a shoe with arch support, firm heel cup, and toe box with room to move.
- Walk with a friend. Walking is more fun and safer when you are with someone else. A friend can offer conversation, motivation, and relaxation.
- Make walking part of your daily routine. Some good times to walk are each morning, during a lunch break, while on an errand, or at the end of the day.
- Explore new routes. Any route can

become boring if you don't change it now and then.
- Have a backup plan for bad weather. For instance, check out a mall. Malls can be a nice place to walk, and some open early just for walkers.
- Pick up your pace. As you progress you can walk faster and add arm swings so that you are exercising more vigorously.
- Stick with it. With all of its benefits, walking is one of the best ways to build a lifelong program of activity.

Staying Safe

"Last spring, I fell. Luckily, I was more scared than hurt. That got me thinking about safety in my home. I put some nonskid strips in the shower. And I use a cane when it is icy outside."
—Marcy

To take good care of yourself, you need to do more than eat right, exercise, and cut down on alcohol. You also need to lead a safe life and be aware of your surroundings. You need to take steps to prevent falls, injuries, crime, car accidents, and fires.

How to Prevent Falls

Here are some tips to make your home safer. They won't cost a lot of money or take a lot of time.

Safety in the Bathroom

- Install grab bars on your bathroom walls. Put them near the tub and the toilet seat. Make sure that they are always fastened securely.
- Put nonskid strips or a rubber bath mat in your shower or tub.
- Use a bath stool when you shower or bathe. You can buy a stool at some drugstores. Make sure the legs of the stool have rubber tips that don't slip.
- Use only nonskid mats. Don't use throw rugs.

Safety on the Stairs

- Install sturdy handrails on both sides of your stairways.
- Keep all halls and stairways clean and free of clutter.
- Use nonskid strips on bare steps.
- Light all your stairways. Put light switches at the bottom and at the top of the staircase.
- Watch your step on carpeted stairs. Deep-pile carpet makes it hard to see each step.

Safety in and around Living Areas

- Keep wires and cords off the floor and close to the walls. Never stretch cords across walkways.
- Arrange your furniture so that you can walk easily through rooms.
- Keep your walkways and outdoor stairs clear and in good repair.
- Put in night-lights.
- Remove all loose rugs.
- Stand still for a moment when you get out of a chair or a bed.

Health Quiz: Personal Safety

This quiz is about your personal safety. Read each statement. Then circle the answer that applies to you.

I wear my seat belt when I drive or ride in a car.
Always   Sometimes   Never

I wear a helmet when I ride a bike or motorcycle.
Always   Sometimes   Never

I refuse to ride in a car if the driver has used alcohol or other drugs.
Always   Sometimes   Never

I follow "safe sex" practices or do not have intercourse. (SEE SAFE SEX: HOW TO PREVENT STDs, PAGE 194.)
Always   Sometimes   Never

I use sunblock when my skin is exposed to the sun.
Always   Sometimes   Never

If you answered "sometimes" or "never" to any of these statements, your safety may be at risk. Read each statement that you didn't say "always" to. Think about what keeps you from taking that action. Then take steps to follow all these simple safety guides each day.

Health Quiz: Home Safety

This quiz looks at how safe your home is. Read each statement. Then circle the answer that most applies to where you live.

1. I have a smoke detector in my home. It works and I check the batteries routinely.
   True   False

2. All poisonous items in my home are locked and stored where children can't reach them. Or children are never in my home.
   True   False

3. To prevent burns, I make sure my water heater is set no higher than 120 degrees.
   True   Don't Know   False

4. I don't have guns or weapons at home. Or I keep guns locked, stored, and unloaded where children can't get them.
   True   False

5. To prevent slips and falls, I have removed throw rugs from my house.
   True   False

6. To prevent slips and falls, I have made sure electrical cords are not on the floor where I walk.
   True   False

If you answered "don't know" or "false" to any statement, think about your safety habits. To make your home safer, follow the tips starting on page 294.

Make sure you are steady on your feet and not dizzy. (SEE PAGE 175.)

- Use a cane or a walker if you tend to get dizzy.
- Use a step stool that has a handrail to reach high shelves.
- Watch out for small pets. They can get underfoot and cause you to trip or fall.
- On wet or snowy walkways, wear boots or shoes that have rubber soles.
- Use a step stool with four legs. Don't use ones with three legs.

How to Prevent Crime

Do what you can to feel secure in your home and neighborhood. Take the following steps to protect yourself.

At Home
- Keep your doors and windows locked at all times, even during the day.
- Keep lights on in your yard and on porches.
- Make sure that your door hinges are located on the inside of the door.

That way someone trying to get in won't be able to remove them.

- Put dead-bolt locks on your doors.
- Put a peephole or wide-angle viewer in your door so you can see who is outside. If you don't know the person, ask for identification. Don't open the door until you see the person's ID card. Keep the door locked. Refuse to let in anyone who does not have proper identification.
- Trim tree branches or shrubs that hide your door and windows. Cut off any branches a thief could use to get in.
- Make a list of the valuables in your home. Keep the list in a safe-deposit box at your bank.
- Have valuables engraved with your driver's license or Social Security number. Take a photo of any items you can't have engraved.
- Join a neighborhood crime watch program.
- Ask your police department for more ideas.

On the Telephone

- Don't give your name or phone number to callers who have the wrong number. If they ask you what number they dialed, don't tell them. Just say, "Please look up the number and try again."
- Hang up on an obscene or crank caller. Contact the police and your phone company if you keep getting the calls.

On the Street

- Carry your money, credit cards, and wallet in an inside pocket.
- Don't carry a purse if you don't need one.
- Don't carry too much cash or any valuables with you.
- Stay alert. Stay away from dark parking lots or alleys.
- Don't walk alone if you can avoid doing so.

Basic Safety

- Watch out for con artists who say they can make you rich. They just want your money. It is OK to say you are not interested.
- Never take money from a bank or bank machine when a stranger wants you to. If you have any doubts, talk to someone you know and trust at the bank.

Trimming the bushes around your windows can make your home safer. It cuts down on hiding places for thieves. It also allows you to look out without obstruction.

How to Prevent Car Accidents

Car accidents are the most common cause of accidental death among people ages 65 to 74. As you grow older, you may not drive as safely as you should. You may not see as well. You may react more slowly. If you are in an accident, you are less likely to escape without injury. But wearing a seat belt can cut your risk of injury by more than half.

You can take classes to learn how to be a defensive driver. The AARP offers one such class. Call your local AARP to find out if they offer the 55 Alive program near where you live. This is a two-day class to improve the driving skills of people age 55 and older.

You should also change your driving habits as your health changes. For instance, you may want to stop driving at night if the headlights of other cars make it hard for you to see. The questions below can help you evaluate your current driving skills. For all drivers, it is a good idea to practice the following habits. They can help you avoid an accident.

Test Your Driving Habits

To test your driving habits, ask yourself the following questions.

Reaction Time
1. Do you tend to get too close to the car ahead?
2. Do you have close calls when the unexpected happens, such as when a car cuts you off?

Vision
3. Do you ever miss a turn because you can't read a street sign?
4. Is it hard to ignore dirt, raindrops, and the like on your windshield?
5. When you look straight ahead, do other cars suddenly seem to appear beside you?

Confidence
6. Do most cars seem to go faster than they should when you are on the road?
7. Do intersections bother you because there are too many things that you have to pay attention to at one time?
8. Is it hard to decide when to merge onto a busy highway?

Accidents
9. Have you had more close calls, or near-accidents, in the last year than you had before?

If you answered "yes" to any of these questions, talk with your doctor. Or call your state's motor vehicle office. You may want them to look more closely at how well you drive.

- Break up long drives. Stop every hour or two to get out of the car. As a rule, you should stay on roads that you know.
- Avoid driving when you are under stress.
- Concentrate on your driving. Don't daydream or look at the scenery.
- Don't eat or smoke while you drive.
- Don't talk on a car phone while you drive. If you need to make or take a call, pull off the road.

How to Prevent Fires and Burns

Burns are especially disabling to older adults because the body recovers more slowly. Here are some good practices to follow to prevent fires and burns:
- Be careful with all appliances. Only use space heaters that have emergency shut-off switches in case they tip over.
- Do not wear loose or flammable clothing when you cook. It is easy for bathrobes, nightgowns, and pajamas to catch fire.
- Install one good lock that you can quickly open from the inside. Some people get trapped behind hard-to-open doors.
- Plan how to escape in case of fire.
- Set the thermostat in your water heater to no more than 120 degrees. This will keep the water from scalding your skin. Take baths instead of showers. This will reduce your risk of burns even more.
- Use light bulbs with the correct

wattage in all lamps. Never use a bul higher than 60 watts unless otherwise noted on the lamp.
- Never smoke in bed or when you are tired.
- When cooking, turn handles on pots toward the back of the stove. This prevents knocking the handle and causing hot spills.
- Test the water temperature before you step into a bath or shower. If it is too hot for your finger, it is too hot for the rest of your body.

Quitting Smoking

"I smoked for 30 years. I really enjoyed it. But one day, my doctor told me I might live 15 years longer if I quit. I like living more than smoking, so I made up my mind to try. I set a date and got a nicotine patch. I was on my way. That was three years ago. Once in a while I miss smoking, but then I stop and think. I have lots of other things, like life, to look forward to."

—Lee

You may think you are too old to stop smoking. You may believe that stopping smoking won't make a difference. This is not true. No matter how old you are, you can benefit by quitting. Some of the health benefits start as soon as you put out your last cigarette. Here are some good reasons why you might want to get serious about quitting:
- Quitting smoking can improve your health almost immediately. You

don't have to wait years to benefit from stopping smoking. Within minutes, your blood pressure and heart rate return to normal. Your sense of taste and sense of smell improve within days.

- You will feel better. Within a week, your breathing and walking will be easier. You will have more energy.
- You may live longer. When you stop smoking, you decrease your risk of dying from heart disease (SEE PAGE 89) and from lung disease (SEE PAGE 97).
- You will increase your chances of enjoying what is important to you in the years to come. You may like traveling, spending time with grandchildren, or volunteering. Giving up smoking is taking a big step toward being as healthy as you can be.

How to Quit Smoking

Maybe you have tried to quit before. Most smokers try six times before they quit for good. You learned how to smoke, so you can learn how not to smoke. Remember that you learned this habit over months and years. Don't be discouraged. Consider some of the following things as you learn how to quit smoking. Some of them may work for you, others won't. Just keep trying.

- Pick a date to stop smoking. Write it down on a calendar. Then stick to it.
- Tell someone when you are quitting. Ask for his or her support.
- Find out about the nicotine patch or nicotine gum. Each can help you deal with withdrawal symptoms. Neither one is a "magic bullet." But gum or a patch will help you get through those first weeks after you quit. Your doctor or pharmacist can give you advice about them.
- Find a class or support group. Call the American Lung Association, the American Cancer Society, or your local hospital.
- Make your surroundings smoke free. Get rid of all of your cigarettes, matches, lighters, and ashtrays.
- Find ways to stay busy. Keep your mind off smoking by going for a walk, reading a book, or shopping.
- Discover places where no one smokes. Enjoy restaurants that have smoke-free sections. Spend time at movie theaters and shopping malls that are smoke free.
- Keep your hands and your mouth busy. Try chewing gum or sucking on hard candy. Or use flavored toothpicks. Learn a new hobby like woodworking or needlework.
- Live one day at a time. Focus on getting through today. Don't worry about tomorrow.
- Stay active. Being active will help control your weight. It can help ease stress and tension.
- Be good to yourself. Reward your success. You will save money by not smoking. Buy yourself a gift or save the money for a vacation.
- Stay with it. Keep trying to quit even if you slip up. Learn from your past experiences. Get right back to quitting by trying a different approach.

Chapter 20

Your Future Health Concerns

You may like to think that things will never change. You might think that you will always be healthy. We would all like to stay healthy. But things do change, including our health. Everyone needs to plan for those changes.

When you make plans for the future, think about how your health may change. Think about what might happen if you have a serious accident or become very ill. What kind of medical care would you want? Does your doctor know your wishes? Do your relatives and friends know what you want? You can take steps now to make sure that your wishes are carried out.

You should also think about how and where you will live. Many people want to stay in their own homes, and that makes sense. But over the years you may need help with chores or in dealing with money. Or you may need help just doing day-to-day tasks. You may also need to make your home safer. If you plan ahead and make a few changes now, you may be able to stay safe and comfortable at home for a long time.

You do have other options. Older people can live in many kinds of communities. Some places offer care for people who need it. It may help you to know what kind of services each place has. You may want to talk about all of these options with your friends, family, and doctor.

This chapter can help you think about your options. You may learn some new things that can help you lead a happy, healthy life.

Putting Your Affairs in Order

When you put your affairs in order, you organize personal, financial, and legal matters. Then you can feel assured that people will take care of important things if you can't. This part of the chapter gives an overview of some legal concerns, but mainly it focuses on your health and health care.

Personal Records

You should have a file that contains your papers and records. It can help a friend or relative in case of an emergency. Here is a list of the most important things that belong in this file:

- your full legal name
- your Social Security number
- your legal residence
- a description of how you wish to be buried or cremated
- any funeral arrangements you and your family have made

Financial Records

The amount of money you have matters when an illness strikes. Money may matter a lot if your living situation changes. Don't wait until there is a problem before you put a file together.

Your financial records file should contain all you need to know about your assets. Be sure that the file has details about the following:

- income and assets (pension funds, interest income, and other sources)
- investments (stocks, bonds, and property)
- bank accounts (checking, savings, and credit union)
- Social Security and Medicare records
- insurance, with policy numbers (life, health, and property)
- any safe deposit boxes you have (including their location)
- your most recent tax return (include a copy)
- a list of your debts (say when payments are due and to whom)
- deed to your house or mortgage information
- names and numbers of your credit cards and charge accounts
- your property tax records
- a list of valuable personal items, such as jewelry or family treasures, including their location

Talk with your family about your wishes for the future. Do this when you are well. Then your family will know what you want if there is an emergency.

Legal Matters

You should see a lawyer to discuss issues about your property. A lawyer can help you handle your property now. He or she can also make sure that your wishes are met after you die. When you meet with a lawyer, you may want to discuss creating a power of attorney, a will, and trusts.

Power of attorney. A power of attorney is a legal paper that lets someone else manage your funds while you are still alive and mentally well. The person you choose can sign your checks and pay your bills. This person can also take care of your real estate and legal affairs. If you become mentally incompetent, this arrangement is no longer valid. (SEE DURABLE POWER OF ATTORNEY, PAGE 304.)

Will. A will is a legal document that protects your dependents if you die. In a will, you appoint an executor. Your executor divides your property based on your will. He or she makes sure that your taxes are paid and takes care of medical bills and other expenses and debts. You may also choose a guardian for minors or developmentally disabled persons who are in your care.

Trusts. Trusts are property interests held for one person by another. A trust allows you to transfer ownership of your assets to someone while you are still alive. You will still continue to benefit from the property. For instance, you can transfer ownership of your house to a trust and still live in it.

Advance Directives

"You have the right to choose what kind of medical care you will and won't receive. You can protect this right by putting your choices in writing. Do this while you are still healthy."
—Nurse practitioner

What if you were hurt or sick and could not say what kind of care you wanted? Would a son, daughter, or friend know what you would want?

You can plan ahead for a time like this. The legal way to do this is to put your plan in writing while you are still healthy. This protects your right to receive the kind of medical care you would like.

The plan you write is called an advance directive. It tells your family and doctor the kinds of care you want and don't want. Then your wishes will be clear if you are hurt or become ill. An advance directive lets you accept or refuse care even when you are not physically or mentally able to do so.

A federal law says that health care centers must tell patients about advance directives. The law was passed in 1990. It is called the Patient Self-Determination Act. The law does not force you to write an advance directive. It states that the staff at any health care facility must tell you about this option.

There may come a time when you can't speak or write. If that happens, your doctor can use your advance directive to decide what care you will receive. But advance directives do not apply to home emergencies. If paramedics come to the scene, they are required to give full emergency care.

There are two main types of advance directives. One is the durable power of attorney for health care. The other type is the living will. Which one is best for you may depend on the laws in your state.

Durable Power of Attorney

When you give someone durable power of attorney, he or she is called your agent. Your agent can make choices about your health care when you can't.

Most people choose a relative or close friend as their agent. The person must be at least 18 years old. The person should be someone you trust to stand up for your wishes. In case the person is not around when needed, choose one or two other people to serve as alternates.

The durable power of attorney is good only if you are not able to speak for yourself. You don't have to be terminally ill. Your agent can make medical decisions for you anytime you are unable to do so. Consider this example. You are in a coma, but your doctor thinks you will live. In this case, your agent can speak for you. He or she can decide what care you should receive.

Before you sign the legal agreement for durable power of attorney, give it careful thought. Then tell your agent what kind of treatment you want. Be both broad and specific. What medical care, if any, would you want if you had

problems from surgery? If you had a chronic illness? If you became terminally ill? (See What You Need to Know About Your Treatment Options, page 305.)

The Living Will

At some point, you may become very ill. You may not be able to speak. Under certain conditions, a living will can speak for you. The living will is a legal document. A living will is good only if doctors say that you are unable to participate in health care decisions and that you have no hope of recovery. (See What You Need to Know About Your Treatment Options, page 305.)

In your living will, you should state if you would want to get food, fluids, or drugs through tubes if you could not take them by mouth. You should state whether you would want CPR (cardiopulmonary resuscitation). CPR can keep you alive if you stop breathing or if your pulse stops. Some people may not want to have CPR if they don't expect to live much longer.

You may also want to state whether you think treatment should keep you alive as long as possible. You might want to say when you believe life stops. Then let your doctor know what you believe. This may help him or her decide what kind of care you would want.

When you have a living will, you choose someone to act for you. This person is called your proxy. If you want your proxy to make medical choices, you must say so in your living will.

A doctor is the only one who can give orders based on a living will. Show your living will to your doctor.

What You Need to Know About Your Treatment Options

You may want to name an agent to have durable power of attorney. Perhaps you want a proxy who will be responsible for your living will. In either case, you will have to fill out certain forms. Before you do so, you need to know what your options are in life-or-death situations. Three kinds of treatment are often discussed in these forms. Be sure your agent or proxy knows how you feel about each type of treatment.

- Treatment that **supports** your life will keep your lungs and heart going when these organs can no longer work on their own. You may be given CPR or be placed on a respirator. A respirator is a machine that breathes for you.
- Treatment that **sustains** life keeps you alive longer. You may be fed through a tube. A kidney machine may be used to clean your blood.
- Treatment that **relieves suffering** keeps you as comfortable and pain-free as possible. It does not keep you alive longer. Strong drugs to ease pain and hospice care are forms of care that relieve suffering.

Your doctor must tell you if he or she will comply with it. Your doctor may not want to do as you wish. In that case, you might want to find a doctor who will.

Steps to Make an Advance Directive Legal

You need one form for the living will and another for the durable power of attorney for health care. These forms are easy to fill out. You can get them free from any hospital, home care agency, or senior citizen center. After you get the forms, follow these steps:

1. Read each form carefully.
2. Fill out all the information requested.
3. When you finish, sign the form in front of two witnesses. You may need to have a notary public sign the form.
4. Make copies for:
   - your doctor
   - your family members
   - your proxy (for a living will)
   - your agent and alternates (for durable power of attorney for health care)
5. Put the original form in a safe place where someone can find it easily.

The legal rules for advance directives differ from state to state. Read the form for your state before you file your forms and give out copies. Then check with local legal and health officials. Your lawyer can help. Or call a state hospital association or health department. They can tell you if you are complying with state law.

Living at Home

Most adults age 60 and older would like to live in their own homes until they die. Careful planning can make this possible. By taking some simple steps, you may be able to live without nursing-home care or other special care. It is important to think about the following:

- how you can make your home safe
- how you can make use of community services
- how you can use caregiving services

Making Your Home Safe

If you choose to stay in your home, take a good look at how safe it is. Check inside and outside for hazards. Make some simple changes in and around your home to prevent injuries. (See Health Quiz: Home Safety, page 296.)

Using Community Services

At some point, you may need someone to help you cook, clean, or provide home health care.

Look in the Yellow Pages under "Senior Citizens' Service Organizations" to find out who offers these services. Many of the groups listed offer a range of home services. You can also call any of the following:

- your local senior center
- your county or city social services department
- your local Area Agency on Aging
- local churches or synagogues
- the social service unit of hospitals near you

Some of the services you may need are listed below.

Chore services include major cleaning around your home, yard work, and minor house repairs.

Home care services deal with personal care and basic health care. Personal care includes feeding, bathing, and using the toilet. In some cases, home care also includes skilled nursing care. Physical, occupational, and speech or language therapy may be

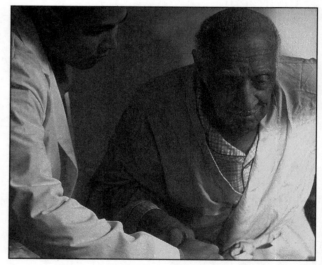

Home care services bring basic health care to you. Even if you have some mobility problems, you may be able to live at home.

When You Are Thinking About Being a Caregiver

The best caregiving does two things. It lets the person who receives care be as independent as possible. And it follows clear guidelines about how much the caregiver will do. Before deciding to be a caregiver, think about these questions:

- What kind of care does the person need?
- What kind of care does the person want?
- How well do you and the person get along?
- Will the person who needs care live with you?
- If the person will live with you, what will he or she be leaving behind? Will the person miss friends, family, activities, and belongings?
- What support networks will be available to you and the person you care for?
- Does the person who needs care have money or insurance to pay for the care?
- How much do you know about the medical condition of the person you may care for?

Include the person in decisions. Ask his or her opinion about future care. If both of you make a decision, your burden will be lighter. And your loved one can keep his or her dignity and some control.

Try not to make promises you can't keep. Instead, talk about what will work for both of you. Before you make a final decision, talk it over with your family or friends. Be sure to talk with the people who live with you. This may help avoid problems later.

offered. Social services such as counseling might be included. People may receive care for a few hours a week or for up to 24 hours a day.

Homemaker services help you with home duties. A homemaker may cook meals for you. He or she may also clean, shop, and do your laundry.

Home-delivered meals (also called meals-on-wheels) are hot, wholesome meals that are delivered to your home. The meals are delivered to people who are unable to cook and who have no one to cook for them. Some of the programs charge fees for these meals. But other programs offer the meal service for free.

Friendly visitors stop in to see people who are confined to their homes. Friendly visitors may write letters, make phone calls, play cards, or chat for a few hours. As a rule, they don't clean houses or provide personal care.

Emergency alert services bring support to you when you need it. If you purchase this service, you wear a transmitter. People often wear a button around their neck. If you are in urgent need of help, you push the button. This sends a signal to a response station or hospital. Someone there calls a neighbor who has agreed to help you in an emergency. If the neighbor is not home to find out how you are, the hospital or response station will send an ambulance. Costs vary for this service.

Senior centers are places where older people can meet. Many centers offer meals, games, entertainment, lectures, and more. Most of the services are free.

Getting Care From Family and Friends

Before you let someone become your caregiver, the two of you should discuss the kind of care you need. Think about what is hard for you to do. Do you need someone to go to the store for you? Do you need help to take your medicine? Will the person be able to do these things for you on a routine basis?

If you need a lot of care or full-time care, a friend or family member may ask you to move in with them. Or a friend or family member may want to move in with you. Before you take a step like this, consider these things. Think about what you are leaving behind. Think about how well you get along with the person you will be living with. Talk these things over. Discuss when a nursing home might become the best choice. Talking it out can help everyone avoid feelings of guilt later.

Living Away From Home

As you age, there may come a time when you can no longer live alone. Your health may be at risk or it may be hard for you to get around. Your income may change. You may feel that you are leaning too much on family and friends.

No matter where you live or how old you are, a sense of home is important. If you need to move, you may have many decisions to make. What are your options? You might think about the following:
- assisted living facilities
- continuing care communities
- nursing homes (These include residential care, intermediate care, and skilled nursing care facilities.)

Many people must decide about long-term care when they are in the hospital. These decisions are hard to make during a crisis. Here is some advice to help you make the right choice.

- Don't make permanent decisions. Think of each choice you make as a short-term solution. Even most stays in a nursing home are short. Most people go in and out of a nursing home three times before they need to make it their home.
- Don't make decisions alone. Work with other family members. Talk to the social workers in the hospital. They can often help you look at all your choices.

Assisted Living

"When my father was 80, he got sick. I had to find a place that would take good care of him. I looked at an assisted living center. It had a cozy living room, a dining room, a sunny kitchen, and a game room. I thought, 'I could live here.' It felt like being at home."
—Phil

Assisted living offers you a mix of home care and nursing home care. You may have your own apartment with a kitchen. Or you may eat meals in a dining room with others. Other shared areas might be sitting rooms, game rooms, and gyms.

In an assisted living facility, you can get help with your health care and housekeeping needs. You also can be with others your age and keep your independence.

At an assisted living program, the staff should help you keep your independence. They should take care of security, housekeeping, and laundry. They can also help you walk, bathe, dress, and take medicine. In case you are sick or are hurt, there is someone on call 24 hours a day. You can also take part in social activities. You may take day trips or go to plays, shows, or concerts.

Before you make a choice, visit several assisted living facilities. Visit each one more than once. Go at different times of the day. Before you make your first visit, write a list of questions. Bring it with you. (SEE CHOOSING AN ASSISTED LIVING FACILITY: A CHECKLIST, PAGE 310.)

Choosing an Assisted Living Facility: A Checklist

Make copies of this form. Bring a copy to each facility you visit.

Name of Facility _____

Address_____

Contact Person_____

Licensing and Management

1. Does the center meet local and/or state licensing laws? _____
2. Does the staff help with medicines for the people who live there? For instance, does the center store medicines? Does the staff keep records? Is the staff well trained? Are staff members supervised? _____

   _____
3. Is there a written care plan for each person who lives at the center?

   _____
4. How does the staff decide what each person needs? Does the staff include the person, his or her doctor, and the family in these decisions?

   _____

Contracts and Finances

1. Can the center or the person who lives there break the contract? How? What are the refund policies?_____
2. Are there any government, private, or corporate programs that can help people with the cost of services? _____
3. Do costs vary with levels of service? _____
4. May people who live there handle their own money matters with the staff's help? _____

Staff

1. Do staff members treat each other with respect? _____

Choosing an Assisted Living Facility: A Checklist

2. Are the staff members friendly? Did you get a warm greeting from a staff member?_____

3. Do staff members use the names of people who live there? _____

4. Is it easy for people to find the staff when they need to? _____
_____

Comfort and Safety

1. Is the floor plan easy to understand and follow? _____

2. Are there elevators? _____

3. Are there handrails in hallways and on staircases?_____

4. Are cupboards and shelves easy to reach? _____

5. Are the rooms well lit? Is there enough natural light? _____

6. Will it be easy to leave the center to visit friends and pursue interests? Is it near public transportation? _____

7. Is the lobby homelike and attractive? _____

8. Does the outside seem well kept, clean, and appealing? _____

9. Do the people who live there talk and laugh with each other? Do they seem happy? _____

10. Can you talk about the center and the staff with people who live there?
_____

Care and Services

1. Can people keep and take their own medicines? _____

2. Does a doctor or nurse visit the center often to give checkups? _____
_____

3. Does the staff give 24-hour help with the following needs?
   - ❑ dressing
   - ❑ eating
   - ❑ getting around
   - ❑ hygiene and grooming
   - ❑ bathing and toilet use
   - ❑ phone calls
   - ❑ shopping
   - ❑ laundry

(continued on next page)

Choosing an Assisted Living Facility: A Checklist (continued)

4. Does the center serve three wholesome meals, seven days a week? Can people who live there get snacks? _____

5. Are there shared places to eat? Do the menus vary each day and week?

   _____

6. Does the center provide housekeeping for living units? _____

   _____

7. Will the center drive people to doctors' offices, hairdressers, stores, and other such places? _____

8. Does the center offer social, recreational, and spiritual programs? _____

   _____

9. Are there pharmacy, barber/beautician, and physical therapy services on-site? _____

10. Does the center keep pets? _____

11. May people who live there keep their own pets? _____

Living Units

1. Do the units vary in size and type? _____

2. May people who live there smoke in their units? In public spaces? _____

   _____

3. May people bring their own furnishings? _____

4. Do all units have a phone and cable TV? How does the center bill for these services? _____

5. Can people lock their own doors? _____

6. Are the bathrooms private? Can people with walkers or wheelchairs use the bathrooms with ease? _____

7. Is there a 24-hour emergency-response system in the units? _____

8. Is there a kitchen in each unit? _____

Continuing Care Communities

> "We chose a continuing care community because we knew my husband might need more serious care at times. He has emphysema. This way, even if he has to go to the nursing-home wing, he will be just down the hall from me."
>
> —Josie

Continuing care communities can be pleasant, campuslike settings. Meals and personal care are provided. You can take part in social and cultural programs. You can stay active and live a full life. These places also help with your future health care needs. Many have a nursing home on site. If you should need more care at some time in the future, you could move from your private quarters into the nursing home. (SEE NURSING HOMES, PAGE 315.) Continuing care communities come in all sizes. They can be as small as one building or as big as a village.

Whatever the size, these places have a lot to offer. They also have drawbacks. One of them is cost. Entrance fees can be as high as $250,000. Maintenance fees are about $1,000 a month.

If you choose a continuing care community as your new home, make sure to get a written agreement from the management. It should clearly state these things:

- the type of care you will get
- the conditions under which you could be forced to move out and what care you would get instead
- your right to end the contract and to get a refund if you wish to move out

Before you take a tour of a continuing care community, make a list of questions. (SEE CHOOSING A CONTINUING CARE COMMUNITY: A CHECKLIST, PAGE 314.)

Most continuing care communities have activities for the people who live there. You may take pleasure from playing games or just from being with others.

Continuing care communities have private living areas. They also may have a nursing home on site. This way they can deal with your future needs.

Choosing a Continuing Care Community: A Checklist

Make copies of this form. Bring a new one to each continuing care community you visit.

Name of Facility _____

Address_____

Contact Person_____

1. Is the community accredited by the Continuing Care Accreditation Commission (CCAC)? _____

2. What is the community's mission? _____

_____

3. Suppose you decide to move after a few months. How much of your entrance fee will you get back? _____

_____

4. If you die, what part of your entrance fee will be returned to your estate? _____

5. When you apply, how much of a deposit is required? Can the deposit be refunded? _____

6. What is the monthly fee? What does it cover? _____

_____

7. Is there a waiting list? How long is the list? _____

8. What health care services does the place offer? How much do they cost? _____

9. What meal plans can you get? _____

10. What social and educational programs are offered?_____

_____

11. Can you get other personal services? _____

_____

12. Is the community financially stable? _____

Nursing Homes

"I truly did not want to give up my apartment. Then I broke my hip. I could not move out of my wheelchair by myself anymore. My doctors and I decided that a nursing home was the best option. I found one where I could set up my stereo in my room. They also have a library. I know this is what I need right now."

—Helen

A nursing home can be both a health care center and a home. Nursing homes offer nursing and personal care, room and board, and custodial services. Today, there are thousands of nursing homes in the United States. You will find three basic kinds:

- residential care
- intermediate care
- skilled nursing care

These may differ a bit from state to state. Each offers a certain standard of care. Some offer all three types of care. As a resident's needs change, he or she may be able to move from one home to another.

Residential care nursing homes offer meals and sheltered living. Residential care is best for people who don't need a lot of medical care. These homes can take care of your medicines. They can also watch out for medical problems. These homes may offer social and recreational events as well. Some also have spiritual programs.

Intermediate care nursing homes give you room, board, and nursing care. However, these homes don't provide care 24 hours a day. Many of these nursing homes have social and recreational programs. They may offer physical, occupational, or speech therapy. They may also offer other services to help meet your specific needs.

Skilled-care nursing homes provide 24-hour nursing care. These homes are staffed by registered nurses, licensed practical nurses, and nurse's aides. Skilled nursing homes are set up to meet the needs of people who need a lot of medical care.

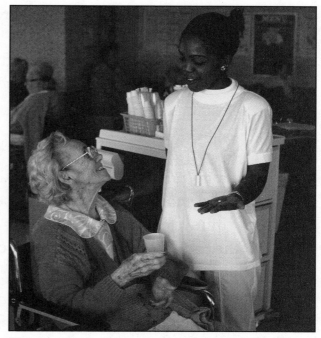

When you choose a nursing home, think of the kind of care you need. You can find a home that offers only residential care. Or you can find a nursing home that has skilled nurses on duty 24 hours a day.

Choosing a Nursing Home: A Checklist

Make copies of this form. Bring a new one to each nursing home you visit.

Name of Nursing Home _____

Address _____

Contact Person _____

Licensing and Reputation

1. Does the nursing home have a current state license? _____
2. Does the administrator have a current license? _____
3. Is the home certified for Medicare and Medicaid programs? _____
4. Does the home have good community standing? _____

   _____

5. Does the home have a list of references? _____

   _____

6. Does the local ombudsperson visit the home often? _____
7. Does the nursing home have current survey results from the state?_____

   _____

Staff

1. How long has the staff been working at the nursing home?_____
2. How long has the management been running the home? _____
3. How many residents are there for each nurse? _____
4. Do the management and health care staff have special training in geriatrics or long-term care?_____
5. Do people who live there seem to enjoy being with the staff? _____
6. Do staff members use the names of people who live there? _____
7. Does the staff quickly answer a person's call for help?_____
8. Is a registered nurse on-site 24 hours a day?_____

Choosing a Nursing Home : A Checklist

Comfort and Safety

1. Is the nursing home clean and free of odor? _____

2. Does the outside of the home seem well kept and in good repair? _____
   _____

3. Are there enough of the following safety features?
   - Handrails in halls and stairways? _____
   - Grab bars in the bathrooms? _____
   - Emergency call buttons throughout the building? _____
   - Smoke detectors?_____
   - Sprinkler systems? _____
   - Emergency lighting? _____

4. When floors are being cleaned, are warning signs set up? Are areas
   blocked off to prevent accidents?_____

5. Are there outdoor areas for residents to use?_____
   _____

6. Would your room have a storage area for your personal items? Could
   you get to this area easily? _____

7. Are the toilets located near enough to the bedrooms? _____
   _____

8. Is it easy to move around the home in a wheelchair? _____

9. Is the lighting good? Do people have the proper light to see what they
   are doing? _____

10. Are the noise levels OK?_____

11. Do people have personal items in their bedrooms, such as family
    pictures, furniture, or mementos?_____
    _____

12. Is the nursing home near where your family members live? _____

(continued on next page)

Choosing a Nursing Home: A Checklist (continued)

Care

1. Do the people who live there look well cared for? _____

2. Are most people dressed for the season and time of day? _____

3. Do staff and health experts seem to think about each person's needs and interests? _____

4. Would you or your family be able to help write your care plan? _____
_____

5. Does the nursing home work with a local hospital? _____
_____

6. Does the nursing home limit the use of physical restraints?_____
_____

7. Does the nursing home limit the use of medication for restraining residents? _____

8. Do the meals look and taste good? (Eat some of the food to find out.)
_____

9. Does the home ask people what they like or don't like to eat?_____
_____

Services and Costs

1. Are routine and emergency medical care ensured?_____
_____

2. Are there private places to visit with family and friends? _____
_____
_____

3. Are there places where you can meet with other people who live there?
_____

Choosing a Nursing Home: A Checklist

4. Can the staff transfer people to a hospital in an emergency? _____
_____

5. Will your doctor visit the home? _____

6. How close is the home to a hospital? _____

7. How much does it cost to live in the home? What does the cost cover?
_____
_____

8. What are the ways you can pay? _____

9. Is there a council for residents? Does the council have an effect on the
home life of residents? _____
_____

10. What extra services can you get? (For instance, is there physical, occupational, or speech therapy? Are there social services?) What are the costs
of these services? _____
_____

11. Does the home have special services that meet your needs? (For instance,
are there special care units for people who have dementia or respiratory
problems?) _____

12. Are there many activities you can do there? _____
_____

13. Do the activities meet your needs and interests? _____
_____

14. Does the home have contact with community groups, such as Boy Scouts,
Girl Scouts, or pet therapy programs? _____
_____
_____

How to Choose a Nursing Home
Visit the home. This is the most important step in choosing one.

- Ask for a tour.
- Use the checklist that starts on page 316.
- After your first visit at the home, drop in with no warning. Try this at night or during other off-hours. If no one expects you, you may get a clearer picture of what the home is really like.
- To find out more, call your local ombudsperson. This person checks out complaints made about nursing homes and then works to fix the problems. Ombudspersons are not allowed to suggest one nursing home over another. But they can tell you about the nursing homes in their area. You may be able to find an ombudsperson in the Yellow Pages. Look under "Nursing Homes—Referrals and Information."

Stay Informed About Your Choices

You have options when it comes to housing and care. Talk with other people your age. Ask them what they like and what they don't like about where they live. Borrow books about housing from your library. Visit different places near you to learn about your options.

Write to the directors of these places to find out more. What do programs cost? How independent can you be? How good is the medical care? Ask about anything that concerns you.

Above all, be honest with yourself. You may want to stay as independent as you can. But you may need access to 24-hour care. To find the place that is best for you, think about what you want and what you really need.

Chapter 21

Where to Get Help

To take care of your health, you need answers to your questions. This chapter tells you where you can look to find help.

One of the most useful sources is Eldercare Locator. This program is a service of the National Association of Area Agencies on Aging. The people there cannot answer your questions. But they will give you a number to call in your area. Then you can get answers. The Eldercare Locator number is 1-800-677-1116. Write this number down. Keep it near your telephone.

Before you call Eldercare Locator, have a pencil ready. Write down the number they give you for the agency or organization that can help you. When you call that agency, tell them what you want to know or what help you need. It is a good idea to ask for booklets or other reading materials they may have that might answer your questions.

Consider a Support Group

If you have a serious illness or have gone through a trauma, a support group may help you. You can find a support group for many things. There are support groups for people with arthritis, women with breast cancer, and people who have a family member with Alzheimer's disease. There are also support groups for people who have lost a loved one. In meetings, people who attend share their feelings and talk about what they have learned. They share information on resources, treatments, doctors, and hospitals.

It is not hard to find a support group. You can begin by asking your doctor to suggest one in your area. You can also call the Office of Disease Prevention and Health Promotion National Health Information Center to ask about groups. The toll-free number is 1-800-336-4797.

Advance Directives

American Association of Retired Persons (AARP)
Legal Council for the Elderly
601 E St. NW
Washington, DC 20049
1-202-434-2120

Choice in Dying
10th Floor, 200 Varick St.
New York, NY 10014
1-800-989-WILL (1-800-989-9455)

Aging

Administration on Aging
330 Independence Ave. SW
Washington, DC 20201
1-202-619-0724

American Association of Retired Persons (AARP)
Health Advocacy Services
601 E St. NW
Washington, DC 20049
1-202-434-2277

American Geriatric Society
Suite 300, 770 Lexington Ave.
New York, NY 10021
1-212-308-1414

American Medical Association
515 North State St.
Chicago, IL 60610
1-312-464-4507

National Association of Area Agencies on Aging (Eldercare Locator)
Suite 100, 1112 16th St. NW
Washington, DC 20036
1-800-677-1116

National Council on the Aging, Inc.
Suite 200, 409 3rd St. SW
Washington, DC 20024
1-202-479-1200

National Institute on Aging
Room 5C 27, Building 31
31 Center Dr.
Bethesda, MD 20892-2292
1-301-496-1752

Alcohol and Other Drugs

Alcoholics Anonymous (AA)
P.O. Box 459
Grand Central Station
New York, NY 10163
1-212-870-3400

National Clearinghouse for Alcohol and Drug Information
P.O. Box 2345
Rockville, MD 20852
1-800-729-6686

National Council on Alcoholism and Drug Dependence
12 West 21st St.
New York, NY 10010
1-212-206-6770
Automated line: 1-800-NCA-CALL
(1-800-622-2255)

National Institute on Drug Abuse
1-800-662-HELP (1-800-662-4357)

Alzheimer's Disease

Alzheimer's Association
919 North Michigan Ave.
Chicago, IL 60611-1676
1-800-272-3900

Alzheimer's Disease Education and Referral Center
P.O. Box 8250
Silver Spring, MD 20907-8250
1-800-438-4380

Arthritis

Arthritis Foundation
1330 West Peachtree St.
Atlanta, GA 30309
1-800-283-7800

Cancer

American Cancer Society
2200 Lake Blvd.
Atlanta, GA 30319
1-800-227-2345

National Cancer Institute
9000 Rockville Pike
Bethesda, MD 20892
1-800-422-6237

Diabetes

American Diabetes Association
National Service Center
1660 Duke St.
Alexandria, VA 22314
1-703-549-1500
For customer service questions:
1-800-DIABETE (1-800-342-2383)

International Diabetes Center
3800 Park Nicollet Blvd.
Minneapolis, MN 55416-2699
1-612-993-3393

National Diabetes Information Clearinghouse
1 Information Way
Bethesda, MD 20892-3560
1-301-654-3327

Digestive Concerns

National Digestive Disease Information Clearinghouse
2 Information Way
Bethesda, MD 20892-3560
1-301-654-3810

Driving Safety

American Association of Retired Persons (AARP)
55 Alive Program
601 E St. NW
Washington, DC 20049
1-202-434-2277
1-800-424-3410

Exercise

American College of Sports Medicine
P.O. Box 1440
Indianapolis, IN 46206
(Write to get the "Fit Over 40" brochure. Send a self-addressed stamped envelope.)

American Council on Exercise
P.O. Box 910449
San Diego, CA 92191-0449
1-800-825-3636

President's Council on Physical Fitness and Sports
Suite 250, 701 Pennsylvania Ave. NW
Washington, DC 20004
1-202-272-3421

Eye and Ear Concerns

Foundation for Glaucoma Research
Suite 830, 490 Post St.
San Francisco, CA 94102-9950
1-415-986-3162
Automated line: 1-800-826-6693

National Eye Health Education Program
National Eye Institute
2020 Vision Place
Bethesda, MD 20892
1-800-869-2020 (for publications only)

National Eye Institute
Information Office
Room 6A32, Building 31
MSC 2510
31 Center Dr.
Bethesda, MD 20892-2510
1-301-496-5248

Self Help for Hard of Hearing People, Inc.
Suite 1200, 7910 Woodmont Ave.
Bethesda, MD 20814
1-301-657-2248
1-301-657-2249 (TDD)

Headaches

American Council for Headache Education (ACHE)
Suite 200, 875 Kings Hwy.
Woodbury, NJ 08096
1-800-255-ACHE (1-800-255-2243)

National Headache Foundation
2nd Floor, 428 West St. James Place
Chicago, IL 60614
1-800-843-2256

Heart and Lung Concerns

American Heart Association
1-800-AHA-USA1 (1-800-242-8721)

American Heart Association
Stroke Connection
7272 Greenville Ave.
Dallas, TX 75231
1-800-553-6321

American Lung Association
1740 Broadway
New York, NY 10019-4374
1-800-LUNG USA (1-800-586-4872)

Courage Stroke Network
3915 Golden Valley Rd.
Golden Valley, MN 55422
1-612-520-0524

National Heart, Lung, and Blood Institute
Information Center
P.O. Box 30105
Bethesda, MD 20824-0105
1-301-251-1222

National Stroke Association
Suite I, 96 Inverness Dr. East
Englewood, CO 80112-5112
1-800-STROKES (1-800-787-6537)

Mental Health

National Institute of Mental Health
Room 7-C02, 5600 Fishers Lane
Rockville, MD 20857
1-301-443-4513

National Mental Health Association
1021 Prince St.
Alexandria, VA 22314-2971
1-800-969-6642

Nutrition

American Dietetic Association
Suite 800, 216 West Jackson Blvd.
Chicago, IL 60606-6995
1-800-366-1655

Osteoporosis

National Osteoporosis Foundation
Suite 500, 1150 17th St. NW
Washington, DC 20036
1-202-223-2226

Parkinson's Disease

American Parkinson's Disease Association
1250 Hylan Blvd.
Staten Island, NY 10305
1-800-223-2732

United Parkinson's Foundation
833 West Washington Blvd.
Chicago, IL 60607
1-312-733-1893

Smoking

American Cancer Society
2200 Lake Blvd.
Atlanta, GA 30319
1-800-227-2345

American Heart Association
1-800-AHA-USA1 (1-800-242-8721)

**Centers for Disease
Control and Prevention**
Office on Smoking Health
Mail Stop K-50
4770 Buford Hwy. NE
Atlanta, GA 30341-3724
1-770-488-5677

Travel

**The International Association for
Medical Assistance to Travelers**
417 Center St.
Lewiston, NY 14092
1-716-754-4883

Emergency Care

Don't wait for an emergency to happen before you read this section. Read it now. Then you can be ready to help yourself or someone else if you need to.

Where to Get Help: Emergency Rooms

If your life is in danger from a sudden illness or accident, go to an emergency room. Also go if you think your health will be at greater risk if you don't go. As a rule, insurance plans pay for visits that are true emergencies. You don't need to speak with a plan doctor first. You don't need to go to a hospital that is part of your health plan. Go to the nearest hospital, and go in the fastest, safest way.

Emergency room care is needed for anyone who has any of the following problems:

- chest pain, or can't catch his or her breath (These can be signs of a heart attack.)
- trauma from a car accident
- bleeding that can't be stopped
- loss of consciousness after an injury

Emergency care may be needed in other situations. If you are not sure what to do, call your doctor.

When an Emergency Room May Not Be Best

You can get treatment for almost any health problem in an emergency room. But an emergency room is not always

327

the best place to go. Here are two reasons why.

People with routine problems get treated last. Routine problems include sore throats, earaches, and bad colds. The doctors in the emergency room are trained to treat problems that can threaten your life. They care for these problems first. When they care for routine problems, they do it quickly. Unlike family doctors, they don't have time to teach you about prevention. And they don't follow up to see how the treatment works.

Your insurance plan may not pay for your visit. As a rule, if you go to an emergency room for routine care, insurance won't pay. You will have to pay the bill. But if your doctor tells you to go to an emergency room, most insurance plans will pay for it.

Here are some problems that most often do *not* call for a trip to the emergency room:
- a bruise or a cut that does not need stitches
- cold, flu, or fever
- earache
- headache
- stomach pain from constipation
- sore throats or strep throat
- sprain

These are only examples. Each case is unique. Sometimes you may need help but are not sure what to do. In that case, first think about your present health and your health history. For instance, you may have a chronic illness that could make even a minor problem worse. Then you may need emergency care. If you are still not sure what to do after some careful thought, call your doctor.

After-Hours Help (When It Is Not an Emergency)

If possible, it is always best to see or talk with your own doctor. You should see or talk with your own doctor even for things such as stitches or treatment of minor broken bones. But sometimes you may not be able to reach your doctor. Here are two ways to get help at such times.

Call the after-hours phone number. Most clinics have doctors who take calls after the clinic has closed for the day. When you call, you may first reach the answering service. Tell the person who answers the phone that you need to speak with a doctor. You may not get your own doctor. But the doctor who helps you will tell your doctor about your call.

Go to an urgent care center. These centers have normal daytime hours. They also have evening and weekend hours. An urgent care center has doctors that can treat all nonemergencies. Ask your insurance company for a list of approved centers.

Chapter 22

First Aid and Urgent Care

In a true emergency, always get medical help at once. The "What to do about" boxes in this chapter tell you when and who to call for help. But in any emergency, you also need to know what to do until help arrives. To know what you need to do, use the advice under the first aid headings in this chapter.

But remember, first aid does not take the place of getting proper medical treatment. Use the first aid guidelines in this chapter only to keep yourself or someone else safe in an emergency until medical help comes.

To be ready to give help when a person needs it, you should learn first aid. First aid classes teach you how to know an emergency when you see one. They help you learn about injuries. They also teach you how to give help. If you know these things, you are more likely to stay calm when you need to help yourself or someone else.

When you have first aid skills, you may be able to keep an injured person alive. You can also keep an injury from getting worse before help comes. To find a class in first aid, check the local chapter of the American Red Cross. Some adult education programs also offer classes in first aid. Colleges may have them too.

The first aid advice in this chapter tells you about basic first aid techniques. But these techniques are only a small part of what you would learn from a first aid class.

You should always call for help first in any emergency. Then use what you know about first aid until help arrives.

Preparing for an Emergency

Preparing for an emergency means being ready to get help as well as to give it. To get help quickly, you need to have the right phone numbers. Use the Medical Resources form (SEE PAGE 260) to list the phone numbers you may need. Put them near your phone in a place where you can see them. Take the time to get the number for the local emergency squad. In many places, this number is 911. In other places, you need to call the police or fire department. You can find these numbers in the front pages of your phone book.

Take the time to find out the phone number for the emergency squad near you. Not every area has 911.

If you are away from home, you can call the operator for help. Make sure everyone who lives with you, even a young grandchild, knows how to call for help.

How to Call for Help

1. Tell the person you have called for help where you are. Also tell the person what phone number you are calling from.

2. Stay calm. Take a deep breath. Explain in clear words what the emergency is. If more than one person is involved, say how many.
3. Say where the emergency is. Give an address if you can.
4. Don't hang up until the person on the other end tells you to.
5. If you can, have someone meet the emergency team to show them where to go.

To be ready to give help during an emergency, you need the right supplies. You can use some of the everyday supplies you have on hand for self-care of minor problems. (SEE BOX ON PAGE 331.) But it is also a good idea to have a first aid kit.

How to Make Your Own First Aid Kit

Store your first aid kit on a top shelf where children can't reach it. Don't store it in a hot, cold, or damp place in your house. To make your own first aid kit, start by placing a copy of this book in a small tote bag. Or you can use a sturdy box that is easy to carry. Add the following things to the bag or box:

To Clean Wounds
- bottle that can be filled with water
- bulb syringe to rinse eyes or wounds
- cotton swabs
- soap
- sterile cotton balls

When You Don't Have a First Aid Kit

When you don't have a first aid kit, you can make do with what you have on hand.

- Use a clean dish towel or hand-kerchief as a bandage or sling.
- Use a diaper or sanitary napkin as a compress, bandage, or padding for splints.
- Use rolled-up magazines or papers to make a splint. Or use an umbrella as a splint.
- Use a table leaf or an old door as a stretcher. (Don't move a person with head and neck injuries unless his or her life is in danger.)

- sterile eye wash and/or plastic cup
- tissues
- tweezers

To Cover Wounds

- a variety of adhesive bandage strips
- adhesive or paper dressing tape
- butterfly bandages
- elastic roll bandages, 2 or 3 inches wide
- safety pins
- sharp scissors
- sterile eye patches
- sterile gauze pads, 4 by 4 inches
- sterile nonstick tape
- stretchable gauze, one roll
- triangle-shaped bandage to use as a sling or dressing cover

To Protect the Care Giver

- airtight packages of hand wipes
- throw-away latex gloves

For Emergency Care

- antihistamine tablets for allergic reactions
- antiseptic ointment such as Neosporin
- aspirin for adults and acetaminophen for children under age 16
- medicine your doctor has prescribed for emergency situations, such as:
  —adrenaline or epinephrine, for asthma or allergy emergencies
  —insulin and sugar, for diabetes
  —nitroglycerin, for heart problems
- blanket
- candle and waterproof matches
- flashlight with the batteries removed to prevent corrosion, and a fresh pack of batteries
- instant cold packs
- paper and pen so you can write down important information
- syrup of ipecac to induce vomiting

What to Do in an Emergency

Preparation helps, but no one is ever fully prepared for an emergency. It can help to follow some basic guidelines. Here are the main things you need to remember.

1. Be sure someone calls for help.

Why You Should Learn CPR

CPR stands for cardiopulmonary resuscitation. When you learn CPR, you learn a skill that may save a person's life. You use CPR when someone is not breathing or does not have a heartbeat. With CPR, you can keep oxygen in the person's blood and keep blood moving so oxygen gets to the brain and other organs.

You should not try to learn CPR from a book. You need to take a class to learn the right method and timing.

It is not a good idea for you to try to learn CPR from a book. You need to follow certain steps in an exact order for CPR to work. You also need to act quickly and go through the steps at the right pace.

The American Heart Association (AHA) approves classes and teachers for CPR. In these classes, you practice on dummies. A trained teacher will show you how to tell when someone needs CPR. The teacher coaches you to make sure you know how to do the right thing at the right time. Call your local AHA chapter to find out where and when classes are taught in your area. You can also call the American Red Cross.

If you took a class a long time ago, call about a refresher course.

2. Ask for permission before you try to help someone. You can assume you have permission if the person is not conscious. You can also assume you have permission if the person is so badly hurt he or she can't give it. If the person is a child, ask the guardian for permission. In most cases, you don't have to worry about legal problems later if you help in good faith and don't do anything wrong on purpose.

3. Protect yourself from the injured person's blood. Always wear latex gloves when you give first aid. When blood from an injured person gets on broken skin, it can spread disease. You may have cracked skin or scratches and not know it. If you don't have latex gloves, use plastic wrap, several layers of gauze pads, or something else—such as a piece of clothing—to make a barrier between you and the person's blood.

4. Stop any bleeding. (SEE CUTS AND WOUNDS, PAGE 342.)

5. Treat the person for shock. (SEE PAGE 353.)

Emergency Situations

If you know someone has a certain problem, such as a heart condition, read about it now. Don't wait for an emergency. Taking the time now means you will be familiar with the proper steps to take. And the few seconds you save may save a life.

Allergic Reactions

You can get a new allergy at any time. Some allergies have only mild symptoms. You might not even know you have an allergy unless your doctor tells you. Other allergies can put your life in danger. When you have an allergic reaction, try to remember what might have caused it. What did you touch or

What to do about **Allergies**

Symptoms/Signs	Action	Symptoms/Signs	Action
◆ **Mild reactions that are like a cold**	Use self-care	◆ **Chest tightness, wheezing, and an itchy, bumpy rash** (SEE FIRST AID: ANAPHYLACTIC SHOCK, PAGE 335.)	Seek help now
◆ **Mild rash** (SEE SELF-CARE: RASHES, PAGE 213.)	Use self-care + Call doctor	◆ **Widespread rash from an insect sting** (SEE FIRST AID: ANAPHYLACTIC SHOCK, PAGE 335.) ◆ **Vomiting or diarrhea**	Apply first aid
◆ **Runny nose, watery eyes, and sneezing that last more than 10 days**	Call doctor	◆ **Rapid heart beat, flushed face or skin, turning blue around lips** ◆ **Swollen lips, tongue, or throat** ◆ **Choking or difficulty swallowing** ◆ **Difficulty breathing**	Call ambulance

Do You Have an Allergy?

You can be allergic to almost anything. The thing you are allergic to is called an allergen. Common allergens include pollens, molds, drugs, insect bites, animals, make-up, foods, and dust. You might have allergy symptoms only at certain times of the year. Or you could have allergy symptoms all year round.

You should suspect that you have an allergy if you have:
- a family history of allergies
- hives or rashes (SEE HIVES, PAGE 207, AND RASHES, PAGE 213.)
- itchy throat and eyes (SEE BURNING, DRY, AND IRRITATED EYES, PAGE 50.)
- sneezing or a runny nose
- sore throat or a dry cough (SEE SORE THROATS, PAGE 143.)
- wheezing (SEE WHEEZING, PAGE 110.)

If you have an allergy, wear a medical alert bracelet. This bracelet will let others know how to treat you safely if you are unable to talk. It is very important to wear this bracelet if you are allergic to any drugs. Ask your doctor how to get one.

eat? What medicines did you take? Did an insect bite you? Tell your doctor.

Anaphylactic shock is the most severe allergic reaction. It often occurs within 15 minutes after you are exposed to the cause of the allergy.

This type of shock puts a person's life in danger. It narrows the airways and makes it hard to breathe. It can also make blood pressure drop.

Self-Care: Allergic Reactions

- Avoid exposure to allergens.
- Wash pets regularly.
- Vacuum your home carefully twice a week to control dust.
- Consider installing air conditioning and air cleaning devices in your home. Have heating and cooling systems professionally cleaned twice a year.
- Remove unnecessary carpeting, paper, and cloth materials from your home.
- Use nonprescription antihistamines carefully.
- Lubricate your nasal passages with nasal saline rinses.

Signs of Anaphylaxis

The signs of anaphylactic shock include the following:
- dizziness or fainting
- drop in blood pressure
- hives or swelling all over the body
- loss of bowel and bladder control
- loss of consciousness
- nausea
- shock
- shortness of breath
- stomach cramps
- swelling of the throat that makes it hard to swallow
- vomiting

- weakness
- wheezing

If someone has these signs, call for an ambulance at once.

First Aid: Anaphylactic Shock

1. Have someone call an ambulance.
2. Use an EPIPEN if you have one. (An EPIPEN is a syringe that injects epinephrine, which is like adrenaline.) If you don't have an EPIPEN, give the person a double dose of Benadryl.

Burns

Any hot surface can cause a serious burn. So can steam, hot liquids, and certain chemicals. The longer the skin touches something that is hot, the worse the burn may be.

What to do about **Burns**			
Symptoms/Signs	**Action**	**Symptoms/Signs**	**Action**
◆ **Burn affects only the outer layer of skin. There may be some pain and redness but little swelling.** (SEE FIRST AID FOR MINOR BURNS, PAGE 336.)	Apply first aid	◆ **Burn is large or has a lot of blistering.** (SEE FIRST AID FOR MINOR BURNS, PAGE 336.)	See doctor + Apply first aid
◆ **The victim has not had a tetanus shot in the last 10 years.**	Call doctor	◆ **Burn causes an open wound. Damaged skin is red, white, or charred black. There may be little or no pain.** (SEE FIRST AID: MAJOR BURNS, PAGE 337, AND FIRST AID: SHOCK, PAGE 353.)	Call ambulance + Apply first aid
◆ **Burn is small, red, and painful. It swells and has some blisters.** (SEE FIRST AID FOR MINOR BURNS, PAGE 336.)	Call doctor + Apply first aid		

Kinds of Burns

Doctors let us know how bad a burn is by giving it a number. The higher the number, the worse the burn and the more layers of skin it affects. Our skin has three layers.

First-degree burns are slight and affect only the top layer of skin. Symptoms include redness, pain, and minor swelling.

Second-degree burns affect the two top layers of skin. These burns cause redness, pain, swelling, and some blisters. Second-degree burns are often the most painful burns. You can treat most second-degree burns at home if only a small amount of skin is burned. (See First Aid for Minor Burns, below.) But you should see your doctor if any of the following happens:

- The burn covers more than one square inch of skin.
- The burn causes a lot of blistering.
- The burn is on the hand or face.

Third-degree burns destroy all three layers of skin. They may go deep below the surface of the skin. The burned skin may be red, white, or charred black. Depending on the

First Aid for Minor Burns

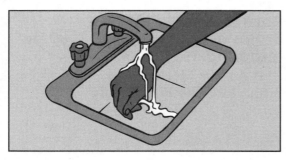

1. Soak small burns in cold water. Don't use ice water or snow unless that is all you have. For burns that are quite mild, a cold wet compress may be all that is needed.
2. Don't use water on a burn that occurred in cold air.
3. You may treat burns with an over-the-counter burn product with aloe vera in it to ease pain. To reduce the chance of infection, don't break blisters. Allow them to heal on their own.
4. Protect the burn with a clean, light gauze bandage. Tape the bandage to skin that has not been burned.
5. Watch for signs of infection. (See page 344.) Call your doctor if they occur.

amount of nerve damage, there may be no pain, or there may be severe pain. The wound may weep or ooze large amounts of clear liquid from damaged blood vessels in the area. You should see a doctor right away for all third-degree burns.

First Aid: Major Burns

1. If a person's clothes are on fire, put out the flames with a blanket, towel, rug, or coat. Wrap it over the flames. Press down to keep air from reaching the flames. The person may struggle or try to run. Make the person lie down on the floor.
2. Pull away bits of clothing that may be smoldering. Leave alone any cloth that sticks to the skin but is not burning. Emergency room workers can take off these stuck pieces safely.
3. Wrap the person loosely in a clean sheet. The sheet should cover the entire burned area. Don't put butter, first aid creams, or antiseptics on the burn. These can cause infection. Don't break blisters that form on the burn.
4. Call for an ambulance.
5. Treat the person for shock. (SEE FIRST AID: SHOCK, PAGE 353.)

6. If the burned person is conscious and is not vomiting, try to get him or her to drink warm water. The water will replace fluids lost from the burn.
7. Emergency care is needed. If there is no ambulance and the person can be moved, take him or her to an emergency room. Don't let the person drive.

Carbon Monoxide Poisoning

Carbon monoxide is a harmful gas that you can't see or smell. It comes from any of the following sources:
- exhaust fumes of car engines
- heating systems that don't work as they should
- fires

When you breathe in carbon monoxide, your blood can't get the oxygen it needs. If you don't get away from the carbon monoxide, its effects will kill you. The first symptoms of this poisoning are mild. You should suspect carbon monoxide poisoning if you have a headache, dizziness, or fatigue. These symptoms will often go away when you are in the open air.

Before you start first aid, leave the area where there is carbon monoxide.

What to do about Carbon Monoxide Poisoning

Symptoms/Signs	Action
◆ **Headache, tiredness, weakness**	 Use self-care
◆ **Headache, feeling dizzy or tired, and weakness that does not go away after a few hours in fresh air**	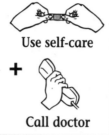 Use self-care + Call doctor
◆ **Nausea and difficulty thinking**	 Seek help now + Apply first aid
◆ **Rapid breathing and heartbeat, disturbed vision, confusion** ◆ **Loss of consciousness**	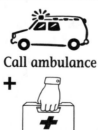 Call ambulance + Apply first aid

Self-Care: Carbon Monoxide Poisoning

- If you feel tired or have headaches, open a window. If that makes you feel better, you should check your home for carbon monoxide. (SEE HOW TO PREVENT CARBON MONOXIDE POISONING, PAGE 339.)
- Call your gas company. Ask them to check your house if you think carbon monoxide is there. Checking your home is important if you often have headaches or nausea or feel tired at home but feel better when you go out.

First Aid: Carbon Monoxide Poisoning

If you find someone who has passed out and you think carbon monoxide may be present, you should follow these steps:

1. Move the person into fresh air as quickly as you can. Do this even before you start first aid. Before you go into the area, take a few deep breaths. Then hold your breath. Drag or pull the person to open air. If you can, shut off any open source of carbon monoxide fumes.

How to Prevent Carbon Monoxide Poisoning

- Avoid breathing the smoke from a fire.
- Buy a carbon monoxide detector for your home. This device looks and works the way a smoke detector does. If you have only one carbon monoxide detector, put it in your bedroom or near it. If the alarm goes off, leave your home.

   Many hardware stores sell detectors. Some drugstores also sell them. Call the local office of the American Lung Association. Someone there may be able to tell you where to buy detectors at a discount. Don't use carbon monoxide "sensor cards." They don't work well.
- Don't use a charcoal grill in an enclosed space.
- Don't leave your car running in a closed garage. And don't drive with the trunk or tailgate of your car or van open.
- Have the exhaust system on your car checked to make sure that it does not leak.
- Have your gas company check all the heat sources in your home at least once every two years. Some heat sources give off carbon monoxide. These include the following:
   —fireplaces
   —furnaces
   —kerosene heaters, gas space heaters, and wood-burning stoves that are not vented
   —other appliances that are not vented well, such as hot-water heaters

2. Don't stay in the house. Get out if you think that carbon monoxide is in the house.
3. Call for an ambulance if the person is not conscious. Also call if the person is very ill.
4. Check for breathing and pulse. If there is none and you know how to do CPR, start CPR right away. Continue until help arrives.

Chest Pain

Chest pain has many causes. Some chest pain might be an emergency. (SEE WHAT TO DO ABOUT CHEST PAIN, PAGE 82.) If you think you are having a heart attack, call an ambulance. Don't drive yourself to the hospital. If you have a heart problem, bring your medicines with you.

Choking

If you are around a person who is choking, you need to act at once. Choking puts a person's life in danger.

A person who is choking and can't cough needs the Heimlich maneuver.

If a person can speak, cough, or breathe, air is still getting through his or her airway. Don't get in the way of the person's efforts to get out an object that is causing the choking. You should follow the self-care tips for this kind of choking.

What to do about **Choking**	
Symptoms/Signs	**Action**
◆ **The person can cough, speak, or breathe**	Use self-care
◆ **The person can't cough, speak, or breathe**	Call ambulance + Apply first aid

Heimlich Maneuver: When the Person Is Standing or Sitting

1. Have someone call for an ambulance.
2. Stand behind the choking person so you can wrap your arms around him or her.
3. Place the thumb side of your fist against the person's stomach, just above the navel.
4. Grip your fist with your other hand. (SEE CIRCLE IN DRAWING AT LEFT.) Press your doubled fist into the person's abdomen with a quick upward thrust.
5. Repeat the thrust until the object comes out of the airway or the person loses consciousness.
6. Don't squeeze the person's ribs with your arms. Use only your fist in the abdomen. Each thrust should be a separate and distinct movement.

If the person can't speak, breathe, or cough, his or her airway is blocked. The person may clutch his or her throat. In these cases, follow the first aid steps for choking.

Self-Care: Choking

- Try to cough. This will help you get out the object that is stuck.
- If someone else is choking, let the person cough. Don't get in the way of his or her efforts to get out the object that is stuck.

- Take slow, deep breaths. This will help relax the muscles around your windpipe.

First Aid: Choking

When an object is stuck in someone's throat and causes choking, you can help by using the Heimlich maneuver. The Heimlich maneuver will free the object so the person can breathe again. First have someone call for an ambulance. Then follow the steps in the appropriate box on page 340, 341, or 342.

Heimlich Maneuver: On Yourself

1. Make a fist and place the thumb side of it on your stomach just above your navel.
2. Grasp your fist with your other hand. (SEE CIRCLE IN DRAWING AT LEFT.) Press inward and upward with a quick motion.
3. If this does not work, press your upper abdomen over any firm surface, such as the side of a table or the back of a chair.
4. Repeat this single thrust until the object comes out of your airway.

Heimlich Maneuver: On an Infant Who Is Awake

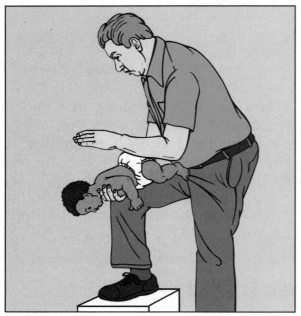 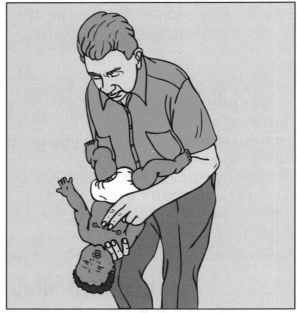

1. Have someone call an ambulance.
2. Rest the baby facedown on your forearm. Support the baby's head by firmly holding the jaw.
3. With the heel of your hand, give four quick blows to the baby's back. Aim between the shoulder blades. If the baby is still choking, go on to step 4.
4. Turn the child over onto his or her back.

5. Measure down one finger-width below the infant's nipples. Place two fingers there in the center of the chest on the breastbone.
6. Push forward and downward. Do these thrusts more gently than you would on an adult.
7. Repeat steps 5 and 6 if you need to.
8. If the Heimlich maneuver does not remove the object, do CPR if you know how.

Cuts and Wounds

First aid is enough to treat many simple wounds and minor puncture wounds. A puncture wound is a small but deep hole. A sharp object—such as a pin, nail, or tooth—can cause a puncture wound. More serious wounds may need a doctor's care. Call your doctor if you have a wound caused by a dirty or rusty object such as a nail or shovel. A deep cut can damage muscles, tendons, blood vessels, ligaments, or nerves. See your doctor if you have a deep cut.

What to do about Cuts and Wounds

Symptoms/Signs	Action	Symptoms/Signs	Action
◆ Bleeding that stops within 10 minutes when you apply direct pressure ◆ Minor puncture wound or shallow cut	Use self-care	◆ Cut that is deep or so irregular that the edges can't be held together with a bandage ◆ Deep cut that is located on the face, chest, abdomen, back, hand, finger, knee, or elbow ◆ Puncture wound that is in a joint ◆ A wound that may have something in it	See doctor + Apply first aid
◆ Cut or wound that does not heal in 10 to 14 days ◆ Signs of infection, such as redness or pus	Call doctor		
◆ Wound that breaks skin and you have not had a tetanus shot in the last 10 years ◆ Loss of more than three tablespoons of blood in 24 hours ◆ Numbness or weakness	See doctor	◆ Wound that spurts or gushes blood ◆ Inability to move fingers or toes normally	Seek help now + Apply first aid
◆ Cut or wound that was caused by a dirty object and you have not had a tetanus shot in the last five years	See doctor + Apply first aid	◆ Signs of shock: shallow breathing, nausea, or confusion (SEE FIRST AID: SHOCK, PAGE 353.)	Call ambulance + Apply first aid

Do You Need Stitches?

You may need stitches for some cuts. Call your doctor if you have any of the following:

- bones or muscles that are showing or are damaged
- deep cut on an elbow, knee, finger, or other part of the body that bends
- deep wound that won't stay closed, even with a bandage
- wound that is dirty or has an uneven edge
- wound on the hand, face, or other area where you want to avoid scars

Signs of Infection

Early signs of infection include the following:

- swollen lymph nodes
- increased redness or swelling around the wound
- pain that increases where the wound is located

If you show any of these signs of infection, call your doctor for advice. If the infection is not treated, you might start to have other, more serious symptoms. If you have any of the following more serious symptoms, you need to see your doctor:

- pus draining from the wound
- red streaks spreading from the wound toward the heart
- fever of 101 degrees or more

Self-Care: Minor Cuts and Wounds

Minor cuts hurt only the skin and the fatty tissue beneath it. Most minor cuts heal without lasting damage.

1. Wash the wound right away with soap and warm water. Wash out all the dirt and debris.
2. You can use an ointment like Neosporin on and around the wound. It kills bacteria and will help keep the bandage from sticking to the wound.
3. Cover the wound with a bandage.
4. Remove the old bandage once a day. Clean the wound. Then put on a new bandage.
5. Call your doctor if you have any sign of infection. Also call if the wound does not heal within two weeks.

First Aid: Cuts and Wounds

1. Stop the Bleeding
- Cover the wound with a gauze pad or a thick, clean cloth.
- Press hard enough on the wound to stop the bleeding. Don't ease the pressure and don't change cloths. Just add a clean cloth over the first one you used.
- Raise the wound above the heart unless doing so causes more pain.
- Get medical help at once if blood spurts from a wound.

And get help if bleeding won't stop after 10 minutes of pressure.

2. **Clean the Cut or Wound**
   - Wash the cut with soap and water, or use hydrogen peroxide.
   - Make sure that no dirt, glass, or other debris stays in the wound.

3. **Bandage the Wound**
   - Cover the wound with a sterile bandage. Put the bandage across the wound, not down the length of it. This will keep the wound closed. Butterfly bandages are a good choice. (SEE DRAWING, BELOW.)
   - Use tape to hold the bandage in place. Don't use tape directly on the wound.
   - If the cut is on the face, it does not need a bandage. Clean it and put on a light coat of antibiotic ointment, such as Neosporin.

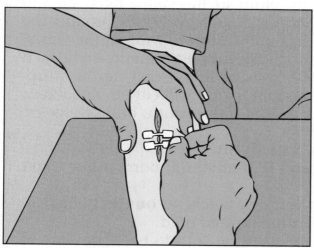

Use butterfly bandages to keep the edges of a wound together. Place the first one across the center of the cut. Then add bandages along the whole length.

Fractures

A fracture is a break, crack, or chip in a bone. If you fracture a bone, you will need a doctor's care.

Signs of a Fractured Bone
These are signs of a fractured bone:
- tenderness over a bone
- shooting pain

What to do about **Fractures**	
Symptoms/Signs	**Action**
◆ **Bone that seems to be broken**	Call doctor **+** Apply first aid
◆ **Limb that is crooked** ◆ **Inability to use the limb or bear weight**	See doctor
◆ **Limb or part of a limb is cool, blue, or numb** ◆ **Bone protruding through the skin**	Seek help now
◆ **Possible head or neck injury** ◆ **Unable to move patient safely**	Call ambulance

- visible deformity
- increased pain when you move
- a bone protruding through the skin

If you suspect that you have fractured a bone, you should call your doctor. Ask if you should go in to the doctor's office to be checked. You should also call your doctor if you have any pain or stiffness that lasts more than two to three days.

How a Fracture Is Treated

Your doctor may want to take an X-ray of the bone. Some small fractures are easier to see by X-ray 7 to 10 days after they occur. Some fractures need casts. Casts often stay on for three to eight weeks. If you have a wrist or ankle cast, move your fingers, elbows, shoulders, and toes often. This keeps your muscles from getting stiff. Pain and weakness often go away in 6 to 12 months.

How to Use a Splint

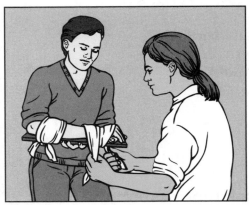

Using a Rigid Splint

1. Use a board or stiff object to keep the broken limb from moving. The splint should be longer than the bone so that it extends past the bone at both ends.
2. If you can, line the splint with something soft. Gauze works well.
3. Hold the limb to the splint by wrapping long strips of gauze or cloth around the limb and splint. Start to wrap at the end of the limb that is farthest from the body, such as the fingers or toes. Don't tie the wrapping too tightly or it will cut off blood flow.
4. Check for feeling, warmth, and skin color.

Using a Soft Splint

If you can't find anything hard, make a soft splint.

1. Use a blanket, pillow, or any soft object to support the injured area.
2. Tie with strips of cloth to hold the limb to the splint.
3. Check for feeling, warmth, and skin color.

First Aid: Fractures

1. If the bone pokes through the skin, wrap the injury with clean white bandages or sheets.
2. Use a splint to keep the bone from moving. (SEE BOX, PAGE 346.)
3. If there is bleeding, apply pressure to stop it. (SEE FIRST AID: CUTS AND WOUNDS, PAGE 344.)
4. Treat for shock. (SEE FIRST AID: SHOCK, PAGE 353.)

Frostbite and Hypothermia

Frostbite and hypothermia both result from cold weather. But the way to respond to each is different.

Frostbite

Frostbite occurs when skin and the tissue below it freeze. The hands, feet, ears, and nose are the most common areas for frostbite. Frostbite makes your skin look white or grayish-yellow. The spot feels hard to the touch. It may be very

What to do about Frostbite and Hypothermia

Symptoms/Signs	Action	Symptoms/Signs	Action
◆ Numb skin	Use self-care	◆ Loss of consciousness ◆ Stiff muscles and bluish skin ◆ Person is confused and speech is slurred ◆ Nausea, dizziness, or vomiting ◆ Pale, cold, clammy skin ◆ Fast pulse and fast breathing	Call ambulance + Apply first aid
◆ Blistered skin ◆ Headache ◆ Shivering that won't stop	Call doctor + Apply first aid		
◆ Cold, white, or grayish-yellow skin	Seek help now + Apply first aid		

cold and numb. Frostbite may also make the skin hurt, tingle, or sting. As the skin thaws, it hurts and becomes red.

Self-Care: Frostbite

1. If you think you may have frostbite, get out of the cold right away.

How to Prevent Frostbite and Hypothermia

The best way to avoid frostbite and hypothermia is to stay warm.
- Change out of wet or damp clothes as soon as you can.
- Don't drink alcohol. It makes your body less able to hold heat and makes you less able to tell when you are cold.
- Call your gas or electric company if you can't afford to pay your bill. There may be programs that can help you. In many places, landlords and utility companies can't legally shut off gas or electric service during cold months.
- Dress warmly for bed. Cover up with blankets.
- In cold weather, dress warmly. Wear several layers of clothes that fit loosely. Wear a hat and gloves when you are outside.
- Wear clothes that draw sweat away from your skin. Silk, wool, and polypropylene do this.

---

2. Warm the skin by putting it in water that is barely warm. Don't use hot water.
3. Don't rub the skin. Rubbing can cause harm.
4. If the skin stays numb, get medical help at once.

Hypothermia

Hypothermia occurs when your body temperature drops after being exposed to cold or dampness. If your body temperature drops too low, you are in grave danger. You must act right away.

Your body temperature can drop without your being aware of it. You can get hypothermia even when it is not very cold outside. With cold weather and wind, you can lose vital body heat in a few hours. The colder it is, the faster this happens. And as you age, you don't warm up as quickly as you did.

If you have hypothermia, you will probably need medical attention. Call your doctor even if your only symptoms are shivering and cold pale skin.

First Aid: Hypothermia

Take these steps until help comes:
1. Get out of the cold. If you can, go to the emergency room.
2. If you are trying to help someone who is unconscious, first see if the person is breathing and has a pulse. If not, and you know how to do CPR, start CPR at once.
3. Take off any clothes that are damp or wet. Put on warm, dry clothes.

4. Wrap a blanket around you, but don't use an electric blanket. It might cause burns. If you have someone with you, lie next to the person, under a blanket if you can. The person's body heat will help warm you.
5. Don't rub your arms, legs, or body. Rubbing can cause more injury.

Head Injuries

Head injuries are frightening, but most are minor. A head injury can make your scalp bleed. The bleeding should stop within 10 minutes when you apply pressure. (SEE FIRST AID: CUTS AND WOUNDS, PAGE 344.) But any head injury should cause concern.

What to do about Head Injuries

Symptoms/Signs	Action	Symptoms/Signs	Action
◆ A slight bump or knot that causes minor discomfort	Use self-care	◆ Bloody or clear liquid that drains from the nose or ears ◆ Fever that rises above 100 degrees	Seek help now
◆ Bleeding from the scalp that lasts more than 10 minutes, even when pressure is applied	See doctor + Apply first aid	◆ Neck or back injury (SEE FIRST AID: HEAD INJURIES WITH NECK OR BACK INJURY, PAGE 350.)	Call ambulance + Apply first aid
◆ Bad headache or neck pain	Seek help now + Apply first aid	◆ Seizures ◆ Confusion, dazed look, or person is hard to awaken ◆ Difficulty walking or talking ◆ Blurred vision or pupils that are not the same size ◆ Difficulty breathing ◆ Loss of consciousness	Call ambulance
◆ Headaches that get worse ◆ Vomiting	Seek help now		

You need to watch someone with a head injury for 24 hours. Be alert for any signs of problems. Have a doctor look at any bump that causes head pain or neck pain. Don't move someone who has a head injury and might also have a neck or back injury. Call for an ambulance.

Call an ambulance for someone who has a head injury with a neck or back injury. Don't move that person.

Self-Care: Head Injuries

- Use an ice bag to ease the swelling of a bump.
- Don't take any medicine before you talk with your doctor.
- Limit activity for 24 hours.
- Wake a child every hour or two to make sure that he or she is responsive.
- Wake an adult every few hours to check breathing and responsiveness. Ask for the person's name, age, and address to make sure he or she is not confused.
- Call your doctor right away if the person has any of the following problems:
  —bleeding that won't stop
  —confusion
  —headache
  —inability to be awakened
  —vomiting

First Aid: Head Injuries

1. If the head is bleeding, apply pressure to the wound.
2. Clean and bandage the wound.
   (SEE FIRST AID: CUTS AND WOUNDS, PAGE 344.)

First Aid: Head Injuries with Neck or Back Injury

1. Call for emergency medical help right away. Then stay with the person.
2. Don't move anyone with a head, neck, or spine injury unless you think he or she is in danger. If you can, wait for professional help.
3. If you must move the person to keep him or her safe, use these steps:
   - Be careful not to move the head, neck, or back.
   - Use a heavy towel or scarf to make a collar around the neck.
   - Slide a wide and rigid board under or behind the person. A table leaf or a door will do. Whatever you use should give solid support from the head to the buttocks. If you can, have several people work as a team. They should support the head and neck and keep both level with the back.
   - Use broad straps to secure the person to the board. Wide belts or ties will work.
4. Treat for shock. (SEE PAGE 353.)

Heat-Related Problems

Heat exhaustion and heatstroke are two problems caused by hot and humid weather. People with heart, lung, or kidney disease are more likely to suffer from these problems. People who take any of the drugs listed below may also be more likely to experience these problems:

- blood pressure drugs
- diuretics
- heart drugs
- sedatives
- tranquilizers

These drugs can prevent sweating. Your body needs to sweat to stay cool.

Signs of Heat Exhaustion

You don't have to exert yourself to get heat exhaustion. If you are not used to heat, even a temperature in the 80s can cause it.

You should suspect heat exhaustion if you notice any of these warning signs:

- excessive thirst
- headache
- heavy sweating
- loss of appetite
- nausea
- pale, moist skin
- vomiting
- weakness

Signs of Heatstroke

Heatstroke puts a person's life at risk. A person with heatstroke needs med-

What to do about **Heat Exhaustion and Heatstroke**	
Symptoms/Signs	**Action**
◆ **Headache** ◆ **Thirst, heavy sweating, or nausea**	 Use self-care
◆ **Weakness or dizziness** ◆ **Rapid pulse and breathing** ◆ **Red, dry, hot skin and lack of sweating** ◆ **Fever of 103 degrees or more** ◆ **Difficulty breathing** ◆ **Confusion or strange behavior, delirium** ◆ **Loss of consciousness**	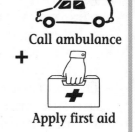 Call ambulance + Apply first aid

ical care right away. You should suspect heatstroke if you see any of the following signs:

- body temperature goes up swiftly
- red, dry, and hot skin
- a strong, rapid pulse
- confusion
- strange behavior
- loss of consciousness

Self-Care: Heat Exhaustion

When you have symptoms of heat exhaustion, you should take the following steps. You also need to watch for signs of heatstroke.

1. Lie down in a cool, shady place.
2. Drink half a glass of cold water every 15 minutes.
3. Try a cool compress to ease a headache.
4. If you don't feel better within half an hour, call the doctor's office for advice.
5. Get help for heatstroke if needed.

How to Prevent Heat-Related Problems

Here are some ways to avoid problems when the weather is hot and humid:

- Ask your doctor if the drugs you take put you at risk for heat-related problems.
- Don't drink alcohol or beverages that have caffeine in them.
- Drink a lot of fluids, even if you are not thirsty. When the weather is quite humid, drinking fluids is important. Sweat on your skin can't evaporate to cool you off when there is a lot of moisture in the air. Ask your doctor how much you should drink each day. This may depend on the medicines you take. It may also depend on how healthy you are.
- Eat light. Avoid eating hot, heavy foods. Don't use the oven in hot weather.
- Wear loose-fitting clothes. Lightweight and light-colored cotton is best.
- Find an air-conditioned place to spend at least part of the day. You may go to a library, a shopping mall, or a movie. Or visit a friend who has air conditioning at home.
- Get used to the heat a little at a time. Go outside at first for only brief periods. Work your way up to spending more time outside.
- If you don't have air conditioning, open your windows at night. Close windows and curtains in the morning. Do this before the day gets hot. Use electric fans to move the air.
- If you have air conditioning, set it below 80 degrees.
- On hot days, take cool baths or showers throughout the day.
- Stay out of the heat, especially in the afternoon.
- Wear a wide-brimmed hat or use an umbrella for shade.

First Aid: Heatstroke

Call for help right away if someone has heatstroke. While you wait, do the following things:
- Wrap the person in wet sheets.
- Fan the body by hand or with an electric fan.
- Give the person water if he or she can drink.

Shock

Any major illness or injury can cause shock. A person in shock will die without medical treatment. Get help right away.

When a person is in shock, the heart can't send enough oxygen to the

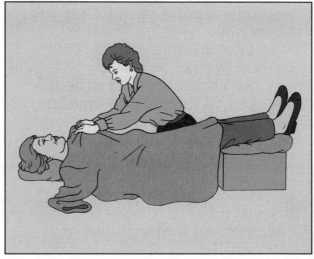

Lay the shock victim flat with feet raised. Cover the person.

rest of the body. The brain, heart, kidneys, and other organs slow down. Then the person can die.

Shock

What to do about **Shock**	
Symptoms/Signs	**Action**
◆ **Nausea and vomiting** ◆ **Pale, clammy skin** ◆ **Rapid, weak pulse** ◆ **Shallow breathing** ◆ **Shivering and coldness in limbs**	 Call ambulance **+** Apply first aid

First Aid: Shock

1. Call for an ambulance and say that the person is in shock.
2. If you suspect a neck or back injury, don't move the victim. (See First Aid: Head Injuries with Neck or Back Injury, page 350.)
3. Try to find the cause of shock and tell the medical team when it arrives. Also, check for a medical alert tag.
4. Make sure the victim has an open airway and is breathing. If the person is not breathing or does

not have a pulse, start CPR if you know how.

5. Stop any bleeding. (SEE FIRST AID: CUTS AND WOUNDS, PAGE 344.)

6. Lay the victim flat and raise the feet 8 to 12 inches. Use anything you have for support. Don't raise the feet if you think there is injury to the head, neck, back, or leg. Also, don't raise the feet if the person is having trouble breathing.

7. Give first aid for the illness or injury.

8. Cover the victim with a blanket or coat. Don't apply direct heat.

9. If the victim vomits or is drooling, turn the head to one side so that fluids can drain.

10. Keep checking the person's breathing and pulse until help comes. If the person is not breathing or does not have a pulse, start CPR if you know how.

Stroke

Strokes occur with no warning. But once a stroke has occurred, there may be several signs of it. (SEE WHAT TO DO ABOUT STROKE, PAGE 183.)

Index

A

AA (Alcoholics Anonymous), 286, 322
Abdominal pain, 11–12
  chlamydia with, 197
  depression and, 115
  diarrhea with, 20
  fever with, 103
  gastritis with, 23
  gonorrhea with, 198
  indigestion with, 26, 27
  ovarian cancer with, 242
Abrasions, 214
Acetaminophen
  abdominal pain and, 12
  for arthritis, 246
  for colds, 102
  decision chart for, 272–273
  for fever, 103
  for headaches, 181
  for heartburn, 25
  for hemorrhoids, 25
  for muscle cramps, 162
  side effects with, 273
  for sore throat, 144
  for toothaches, 141
Achilles tendon
  exercises for, 164
  inflammation of, 148–149
  shinsplints and, 163
Acquired immunodeficiency syndrome. See AIDS.
Advance directives, 303–305, 322
Advil. See Ibuprofen.
African-Americans

glaucoma and, 59
heart attacks and, 87
prostate cancer and, 226
stroke and, 184
Age spots, 201–202
Aging, 1–8
  depression and, 115
  drug effects and, 268
  exercise and, 5, 291–294
  hair and, 6, 201
  hearing loss with, 47
  insomnia and, 121
  organizations for, 322
  sexuality and, 7, 187
AIDS, 194–197
  cervical cancer and, 240
  safe sex and, 193–194
Airplane ears, 40–41
Alcohol
  abdominal pain and, 12
  aspirin with, 286
  bronchitis and, 100
  diarrhea and, 21
  drug interactions with, 269, 286
  dry mouth with, 134
  effects of, 286
  gastritis from, 23
  grieving and, 120
  heat exhaustion and, 352
  hypertension and, 253
  insomnia and, 123
  moderation with, 287
  palpitations with, 94
  problems with, 286
  prostate problems and, 225

rectal pain and, 30
sexual concerns with, 189, 192
stroke and, 185
throat cancer and, 144
Alcohol abuse, 285–287
  depression and, 115
  fatigue and, 117
  help with, 322–323
  vomiting from, 31
Allergy(ies), 333–335
  asthma with, 98
  drug, 271
  flu shot, 105
  pinkeye from, 54
Alopecia areata, 206
Alzheimer's disease, 171–174
  anxiety with, 113
  depression and, 115
  memory loss with, 127
  multi-infarct dementia vs., 186
  organizations for, 323
Amebic dysentery, 19
Anaphylactic shock, 333–335
Aneurysm, 178
Angina, 83–86
  decongestants and, 41
  insomnia and, 121
Angioplasty, 85
Ankle, pain in, 148–149, 161
Antibiotics
  for ear infections, 42, 44
  hearing loss with, 48
  for lung disease, 248
  for peptic ulcers, 23
  for pneumonia, 108
  sunburn and, 219

Antihistamines. See also
Decongestants.
    bad breath from, 132
    bronchitis and, 100
    dry mouth with, 134
    labyrinthitis and, 177
Anus. See also Rectum.
    itching of, 13, 29
    pain in, 28–30
Anxiety, 112–114
    dizziness with, 176
    fatigue and, 117
    hypertension and, 253
    medical conditions
      with, 113
Appetite loss, 12
    constipation with, 17
    depression and, 115
    heat exhaustion and,
      351
    ovarian cancer with,
      242
    syphilis and, 200
Arthritis, 245–247. See
also Osteoarthritis.
    balance problems
      with, 176
    dry eyes with, 50
    fatigue from, 117
    insomnia with, 121
Aspirin
    abdominal pain and, 12
    alcohol with, 286
    for arthritis, 48, 246
    for back pain, 154
    for colds, 102
    decision chart for,
      272–273
    dosage for, 272
    for fever, 103
    gastritis and, 23
    for headaches, 181
    hearing loss from, 48

    for phlebitis, 94
    side effects with, 273
    for sore throat, 144
    for sunburn, 219
Assisted living facilities,
   309–312
Asthma, 98
    anxiety with, 113
    insomnia with, 121
    wheezing with, 110
Atherosclerosis, 90
    sexual concerns with,
      190
Athlete's foot, 74–75
Atopic dermatitis, 204
Atrophic vaginitis, 233

B

Back. See also Vertebrae.
    diagram of, 150
    exercises for, 152–153,
      155
    head injury with,
      349, 350
    herniated disk and, 155
    osteoarthritis of, 146
    pain in, 150–154
      brace for, 155
      stress and, 128
Bacterial infections
    colds with, 101
    pneumonia and, 107
    vaginal, 234, 235
Bad breath, 132–133
Baldness, 205–207
Bandages, 345
Basal skin cancer, 217
Bathroom safety, 295
Bed sores, 211–212
Bell's palsy, 174
Birth control, 229
Bleeding, 342–345

    head, 349–350
Blindness. See Vision
   concern(s).
Blisters, fever, 135–136
Blood clots, in leg, 94, 161
Blood pressure. See
   Hypertension.
Bloody stools, 12–14, 20
    colon cancer and, 15
Bowel, blocked, 276
BPH (benign prostatic
   hypertrophy), 223–225
Brain
    aging of, 4–5
    alcohol and, 286
    ways examined, 173
Brain disorder(s), 171–186
Breast cancer, 236–240
    ovarian cancer and,
      242
    screening for, 283
Breathing difficulty
    from allergies, 333
    with diarrhea, 20
    from drugs, 270
    with head injury, 349
    with panic attack, 113
    with shock, 353, 354
    from sore throat, 143
Breathing exercises, 129
Bronchitis, 98–100
    chronic, 99, 248–249
    influenza with, 104
    pneumonia with, 99,
      108
    wheezing with, 110
Bronchodilators, 249
Bruises, 202
Bunions, 67
Burns, 299, 335–337
Bursitis, 145–146
Bypass heart surgery,
   85–86

C

Caffeine
  anxiety and, 112, 114
  bronchitis and, 100
  diarrhea and, 21
  drug effects and, 269
  dry mouth with, 134
  fatigue and, 118
  heart disease and, 89
  heat exhaustion and, 352
  hot flashes and, 232
  insomnia and, 122–123
  muscle cramps and, 162
  pain relievers with, 123
  palpitations with, 94
  prostate problems and, 225
  stress and, 130
Calcium
  dietary, 5–6
  muscle cramps and, 162
  osteoporosis and, 256
  supplements of, 230
Calf stretch, 163
Calluses, foot, 75–76
Cancer, 247–248. See also specific types.
  anxiety with, 113
  basal cell, 217
  fatigue from, 117
  lip and mouth, 133, 286
  malignant melanoma, 218
  organizations for, 323
  squamous cell, 218
  treatment of, 16
Canker sores, 135–136
Carbon monoxide poisoning, 337–339

Cardiologist, 81
Cardiopulmonary resuscitation (CPR), 304, 332
Cardiovascular disease. See Heart disease.
Caregivers, 307
Carotid artery, 184, 185
Carpal tunnel syndrome, 169–170
Cataracts, 57–58
Cervical cancer, 240–241, 283
Chemotherapy, 16
  and baldness, 205
  for breast cancer, 240
  for colon cancer, 16
  and dry mouth, 134
  for endometrial cancer, 242
  for ovarian cancer, 242
Chest pain, 82–83, 339
Chicken pox, vaccine for, 282
Chlamydia, 197
Choking, 340–342
Cholecystectomy, 22–23
Cholesterol, 91
  cardiovascular risks from, 87
  gallstones and, 22
  screening for, 283
  stroke and, 184
Chondromalacia patella, 159–160
Chronic illness, 243–256
Chronic obstructive pulmonary disease (COPD), 248–249
Cirrhosis, 199
Cluster headaches, 179–180
Colds, 101–102. See also Flu.

bad breath and, 132
  hoarseness with, 142
  hyperglycemia with, 252
  insomnia with, 121
Cold sores, 135–136
Colitis, 13, 15
Colon, spastic, 27–28
Colon cancer, 14–17
  bloody stools with, 13
  ovarian cancer and, 242
  screening for, 15–16, 284
Community services, 306–308
Compression fracture, 155
Computed tomography (CT), 173
Condoms, 194, 196
Conductive hearing loss, 46
Confusion, 35, 151, 270
Congestive heart failure, 122, 161
Constipation, 17–19, 26, 113
Contact dermatitis, 204
Continuing care communities, 313–314
Contraception, 229
COPD, 248-249
Corticosteroids. See Steroids.
Cough. See also Lung concern(s).
  bloody, 99, 109
  bronchitis with, 98–99
  colds with, 101–102
  lung cancer and, 106
  pneumonia with, 108
  productive, 98
  vaporizer for, 10

Antihistamines/Cough

Cough medicine, 117, 270
Counseling
    for chronic illness, 244
    for depression, 116
    for grief, 120–121
    for sexual concerns,
        190, 192
CPR, 304, 332
Cramps, 162, 334
Crime prevention,
    296–297
Crohn's disease, 13
Crying, 115, 120
CT scan, 173, 182
Cuts, 342–345. See also
    Hemorrhage.
Cystitis, 34
Cysts
    breast, 237
    eyelid, 55

D

Dairy products
    in Food Guide Pyramid,
        289
    muscle cramps and,
        162
    osteoporosis and, 230,
        290
D&C (dilation and curet-
    tage), 241–242
Deafness. See Hearing,
    loss of.
Decongestants, 102
    anxiety and, 112, 114
    drug interactions with,
        270
    earaches and, 41
    insomnia and, 123
    prostate problems and,
        225
Dehydration

aging and, 268
burns and, 337
diarrhea with, 20
dizziness and, 178
dry mouth from, 134
fever and, 103
heat exhaustion and,
    351
signs of, 30
Dementia, 245. See also
    Alzheimer's disease.
    memory and, 126–127
    multi-infarct, 186
Dental health, 131
Dentures, 136–138
Depression, 114–117, 245
    caused by drugs, 115,
        270
    grieving and, 120
    insomnia with, 121,
        122
    intimacy and, 193
    loneliness and,
        123–125, 128
    menopause and, 228
    Parkinson's disease
        with, 182
    stress and, 128
Dermatitis, 203–205
Desire, 188–189. See also
    Sexual concerns.
Detoxification centers,
    287
Detrusor instability, 32
Diabetes, 249–253
    body fat and, 254
    cardiovascular risks
        from, 87
    diarrhea with, 20
    diet for, 287
    drug interactions and,
        270
    dry mouth with, 134

endometrial cancer
    and, 241
eye concerns with, 56
fatigue from, 117
foot concerns with, 64,
    77
hormone replacement
    therapy and, 231
organizations for, 323
plantar warts and, 77
retinopathy from, 58
sexual concerns with,
    188, 190
stroke and, 184
urinary tract infections
    with, 36
vomiting with, 31
Diaphragm (birth con-
    trol), 229
Diarrhea, 19–21
    allergies with, 333
    back pain with, 151
    hyperglycemia with,
        252
Diet, 287–291
    abdominal pain and, 12
    arthritis and, 246
    bad breath and, 133
    calcium in, 5–6
    cholesterol and, 22, 91
    chronic illness and, 244
    colon cancer and, 15
    constipation and,
        18–19
    diabetes and, 252
    diarrhea and, 21
    drug effects and, 269,
        290
    dry mouth and, 134
    emotions and, 291
    fatigue and, 118
    fatty foods in, 22
    food diary for, 254

gallstones and, 22
hair loss from, 206
headaches and, 178
heartburn and, 24
heart disease and, 89, 91
hives and, 208
indigestion and, 27
insomnia and, 123
lung disease and, 249
mouth sores and, 136
muscle cramps and, 162
osteoporosis and, 230, 256, 257
recommended calories for, 254
rectal pain and, 30
stress and, 128
urinary tract infections and, 38
Digestive concern(s), 11–31
alcohol and, 286
diet and, 290
Digital rectal exam (DRE), 16, 226
Dilation and curettage (D&C), 241–242
Diphtheria vaccine, 282, 284
Diuretics
bad breath from, 132
hearing loss with, 48
heat exhaustion and, 351
insomnia and, 121
Diverticulitis, 18, 21–22
Diverticulosis, 21–22
Dizziness, 175–178
anaphylaxis with, 334
back pain with, 151
caused by drugs, 270
frostbite with, 347

heat exhaustion with, 351
panic attack with, 113
Doctor, working with, 261-267
Dramamine, 178
DRE. See Digital rectal exam.
Driving
accidents, 298–299
dizziness while, 178
drinking and, 287
quiz, 298
vision problems and, 8, 298
Drugs. See also specific types.
aging and, 268
anticoagulant, 185
anticonvulsant, 186
antidepressant, 114, 116, 174
antipsychotic, 174
anxiety and, 112–113
arthritis, 246
bad breath from, 132
baldness from, 205
constipation from, 19
depression and, 115, 270
diet and, 290
edema from, 89
fatigue from, 117
hearing loss from, 48
heat exhaustion and, 351
hives from, 208
insomnia and, 121, 123
management of, 270
memory aids for, 274
missed dose of, 270
muscle relaxant, 117, 150

over-the-counter, 270–273
prescription for, 267
questions about, 267
seizure, 186
sexual concerns with, 189, 190, 192
side effects from, 270
storage of, 269
sunburn from, 219
Drug abuse, 194. See also Alcohol abuse.
Drugstore, 267–269
Dry skin, 203
Dysentery, 19

E

E. coli, 34
Ear concern(s), 39–48. See also Hearing.
dizziness and, 176–178
infection of, 42, 104, 177–178
Earwax buildup, 41–42
hearing loss from, 46
Eczema, 203–205
Edema, 88–89, 149, 157
leg pain with, 161
Ejaculation problems, 190
EKG (electrocardiogram), 85
Eldercare Locator, 321
Elective surgery, 276
Electrocardiogram (EKG), 85
Embolism, 109–110
Emergency alert services, 308
Emergency care, 327–354
Emergency surgery, 276
Emphysema, 248–249
insomnia with, 121

Endarterectomy, carotid, 185
Endometrial cancer, 241–242
Erection problems, 190
Estrogen
    edema from, 88, 89
    endometrial cancer and, 241
    during menopause, 229
    migraines and, 180
    replacement therapy, 230–232
    sexual concerns and, 191
    for urinary tract infections, 36
Exercise(s), 5, 8, 291–294
    Achilles tendon, 164
    aging and, 5, 8
    arthritis, 246–247
    back, 152–153, 155
    breathing, 129
    chronic illness and, 244
    depression and, 116
    diabetes and, 250, 252
    fatigue and, 118
    hypertension and, 253
    insomnia and, 122
    jaw, 140
    Kegel, 33, 190–191
    knee, 160
    leg, 163
    lung disease and, 249
    muscle cramps and, 162
    neck, 166
    organizations for, 324
    osteoporosis and, 256
    Parkinson's disease and, 183
    stress and, 130
    swimming as, 246–247
    toe tap, 163
    walking for, 294
    weight-bearing, 5
Exercise stress test, 85
Eye. See also Vision.
    burning, 50–51
    chemicals in, 52–53
    diagram of, 50
    discharge, 51
    floaters, 62
    foreign object in, 52–53
    infections of, 54
        headaches from, 178
    irritation of, 50–51
    itchiness of, 50–51, 55
    pus from, 54
Eyeglasses, 5
Eyelid cyst, 55

F

Facial nerve, 174
Fainting, 175–178. See also Dizziness.
    anaphylaxis and, 334
    carbon monoxide poisoning and, 338
    head injury with, 349
    panic attack with, 113
Falls, prevention of, 294–296
Farsightedness, 61
Fat
    body, 254
    cholesterol and, 22, 91
    drugs and, 268
Fatigue, 117–118
    from cancer treatment, 248
    from carbon monoxide poisoning, 338
    from drugs, 270
    from heat exhaustion, 351
    from hepatitis, 199
    and sexual concerns, 190
    and stress, 128
Fear. See Anxiety.
Fecal occult blood test, 284
Feet. See Foot.
Fever, 102–103
    back pain with, 151
    bronchitis with, 99
    dehydration with, 30
    diarrhea with, 20
    earache with, 40
    head injury with, 349
    hepatitis with, 199
    hyperglycemia with, 252
    influenza with, 104
    pneumonia with, 108
    sore throat with, 143
    urinary tract infection with, 35
    vomiting with, 31
Fever blisters, 135–136
Financial records, 302
Fingers. See Hand.
Fire safety, 299. See also Safety.
First aid, 329–354
First aid kit, 10, 330–331
Flat feet, 68–69. See also Foot concern(s).
    aging and, 6
    shinsplints and, 163
Floaters, 62. See also Vision concern(s).
Flossing, 131, 132
    toothaches and, 140–141
Flu, 104–105. See also Colds.

hoarseness with, 142
hyperglycemia with, 252
insomnia with, 121
self-care for, 102, 105
shot for, 105, 249, 281, 284
stomach, 104
Fluoride supplements, 131
Food Guide Pyramid, 288–289
Foot
  athlete's, 74–75
  calluses on, 75–76
  coldness in, 128
  corns on, 76
  numbness in, 161
  pain, 65–66
    prevention of, 66
    self-care for, 66
  referred pain from, 150
  swollen, 149
  ulcers on, 77
Foot concern(s), 63–80
Foreign object, in eye, 52–53
Fractures, 345–347
  osteoporosis and, 255
  stress, 71
Frostbite, 347–348
Fungal infections
  foot, 74–75
  pneumonia as, 107
  toenail, 79–80
  vaginal, 234, 235

G

Gallbladder disease, 22–23
  chest pain with, 83
Ganglions, 170
Gas, 26–27
Gastritis, 23–24

Generalized anxiety disorder, 112
Genetics
  aging and, 3
  drug effects and, 269
Genital herpes, 194, 197–198
Genital itchiness, 235
Giardiasis, 19
Gingivitis, 139. See also Gums, disease of.
Glaucoma, 58–59
  drug interactions and, 270
  screening for, 284
Glucose
  digestion and, 249–250
  monitoring of, 250–251
Gonorrhea, 195, 198
Gout, 149
Grieving, 114, 118–121
  stress and, 128
Groin
  hernia, 221–222
  pull, 156
Gums. See also Teeth.
  dentures and, 137
  disease of, 139
    bad breath from, 132
    doctor for, 131
    infection of, 141

H

Hair
  aging and, 6, 201
  gray, 3, 6
  loss of, 205–207
Halitosis, 132–133
Hammertoe, 68
  corns with, 76
Hamstring
  exercise for, 153

pulled, 156
Hand
  numbness in, 169
  osteoarthritis in, 146
  pain in, 168–170
HBV (hepatitis B virus), 194, 199
Headaches, 178–181
  carbon monoxide poisoning and, 338
  depression and, 115
  frostbite and, 347
  heat exhaustion and, 351
  hormone replacement therapy and, 231
  insomnia with, 122
  nausea with, 179, 180
  organizations for, 324
  stress and, 128
  stroke and, 183
  syphilis and, 200
Head injuries, 178, 349–350
Health history, 261
Health maintenance organizations (HMOs), 263
Healthy lifestyles, 285–300
Hearing, 47. See also Ear concern(s).
  aging and, 5
  aids, 45–46
    MRI and, 173
  loss of, 44–48
    anxiety and, 113
    dizziness with, 176
    loneliness with, 123–124
Heart attack, 86–88. See also Heart disease.
  heartburn vs., 24
  intimacy after, 193
  shoulder pain with, 167

Heartburn, 24–25. See also Indigestion.
    from hiatal hernia, 26
    from indigestion, 26–27
    and insomnia, 122
Heart disease, 81–96. See also Heart Attack.
    aging and, 4
    alcohol and, 286
    anxiety and, 113
    body fat and, 254
    chronic illness and, 245
    depression and, 115
    diet and, 290
    dizziness with, 176
    fatigue from, 117
    insomnia with, 121–122
    organizations for, 325
    sexual problems with, 188
    stroke from, 184
Heart palpitations, 93–94
Heat exhaustion, 351–353
Heatstroke, 351–353
Heel spurs, 65
    self-care for, 70
Height
    compression fracture and, 155
    loss of, 6
Heimlich maneuver, 110, 340–342
Helmet, cycling, 295
Hemorrhage, 342–345
    from head, 349–350
    shock and, 354
Hemorrhoids, 25–26
    bloody stools with, 13
Hepatitis, 12, 194, 199. See also Jaundice.
    fatigue from, 117
    signs of, 199, 281

vaccines for, 281
Hernia
    hiatal, 26
    inguinal, 221–222
    strangulated, 222
Herniated disk, 150, 155
Herpes
    cold sores from, 136
    genital, 194, 197–198
    zoster, 215–216
Hiatal hernia, 26
High blood pressure. See Hypertension.
Hip
    fracture of, 157
        home safety and, 294–296
    osteoarthritis of, 146
    pain in, 156–158
        referred, 150
    replacement of, 157
Histamine, 207. See also Antihistamines.
HIV. See AIDS.
Hives, 207–208, 334
HMOs, 263
Hoarseness, 141–142
    throat cancer and, 144
Homemaker services, 307
Hormone replacement therapy (HRT), 230–232
    sexual concerns and, 191
Hospital(s), 275–278
Hot flashes, 232
    hormone replacement therapy for, 231
    panic attack with, 113
Housemaid's knee, 158
HRT. See Hormone replacement therapy.
Human immunodeficiency virus. See AIDS.

Humidifiers, 10, 102, 144
Hunchback, 155
Hyperglycemia, 252
Hyperopia, 61
Hypertension, 90–93, 253
    body fat and, 254
    decongestants and, 41
    diet and, 290
    dizziness with, 176
    drug interactions and, 270
    drugs for
        depression and, 115
        dry mouth with, 134
        fatigue from, 117
        sexual concerns with, 192
    endometrial cancer and, 241
    eye concerns with, 56
    headaches from, 178
    heart attack and, 87
    heat exhaustion and, 351
    insomnia with, 121
    screening for, 283
    self-care for, 253
    sodium and, 253
    stroke and, 184
Hypoglycemia, 251–252
Hypothermia, 347–349
Hysterectomy, for cancer, 241-242
Hysteroscopy, 241

I

IBS (irritable bowel syndrome), 18, 27–28
Ibuprofen
    abdominal pain and, 12
    for back pain, 154
    decision guide for, 272

for colds, 102
for toothaches, 140, 141
Ice, for muscle injuries, 147
Immunization(s), 280–282, 284
  flu, 105, 249
  pneumococcal, 109, 249
Impotence, 190, 226
Incontinence, 32–34, 230
Indigestion, 26–27. See also Heartburn.
  ovarian cancer with, 242
Infection, signs of, 344
Influenza. See Flu.
Ingrown toenails, 78–79
Inguinal hernia, 221–222
Insect bites, 334
Insomnia, 121–123, 286
Insulin, 250-251
Intestines, ulcers of, 23
Intimacy, 188–189, 193
Iron pills, black stools from, 12, 13
Irritable bowel syndrome (IBS), 27–28
  constipation with, 18
Itching. See also Rash(es).
  eczema, 203–205
  eye, 50–51
  genital, 235
  rectal, 13, 29
  vaginal, 233, 234
Ivy, poison, 209–210

J

Jaundice, 22
Jaw exercises, 140
Joint(s), 145–170

aging and, 5–6
temporomandibular, 139–140
Joint mice, 160–161

K

Kegel exercises, 33, 190-191
Ketoprofen, decision chart for, 272–273
Kidneys
  alcohol and, 286
  diagram of, 37
  diseases of, 35, 36
  drug excretion and, 268
Knee
  exercises for, 152, 160
  gout in, 149
  housemaid's, 158
  osteoarthritis in, 146, 160–161
  pain in, 158–161
  replacement of, 161
  swelling in, 159
Kyphosis, 155

L

Labyrinthitis, 177–178
LactAid, 28–29
Lactose intolerance, 28
Language problems
  Alzheimer's disease and, 172
Laparoscopy, for gallstones, 22–23
Laryngitis, 141–142
Laxatives, 18
Leg(s)
  blood clots in, 161
  exercises for, 163
  gout in, 149
  pain in, 161–164

restless, 164
swelling in, 88–89, 157
Legal concerns, 303
Levodopa, 182
Lifestyles, 285–300
Lifting
  correct method of, 154
  injuries from, 155
  osteoporosis and, 255–256
Light-headedness. See Dizziness.
Lip cancer, 133
Liver
  alcohol and, 286
  drugs and, 268
Living facilities, 309–312
Living wills, 304–305
Loneliness, 123–125
Lumpectomy, 239
Lung cancer, 106–107
Lung concern(s), 97–110
  organizations for, 325

M

Macular degeneration, 59–60
Magnetic resonance imaging (MRI), 173, 182
Mammograms, 239, 280, 283
Mastectomy, 239
Meals-on-wheels, 307
Medicaid, 263
Medical records, 260–261
  for doctor visit, 265
  of immunizations, 280
Medical supplies, 10
Medicare, 262–263
Medications. See Drugs.
Medigap insurance, 263

Melanoma, malignant, 218

Memory, 126–127
  Alzheimer's disease and, 171–172
  learning and, 5
  short-term, 5

Meningitis, 167

Menopause, 228–232
  breast cancer and, 236
  endometrial cancer after, 241
  osteoporosis and, 255
  sexual concerns with, 191

Men's health concern(s), 221–226

Mental health, 111–130
  aging and, 7–8
  chronic illness and, 244
  organizations for, 325

Mental imagery, 129

Middle ear infections, 42

Migraines, 180

Milk products. See Dairy Products.

Minoxidil (Rogaine), 206–207

Moles, 208–209

Mood changes, 115

Morton's neuroma, 70–71

Mouth, 131–136

MRI (magnetic resonance imaging), 173

Mucous membranes, 3

Multi-infarct dementia, 186

Muscle(s)
  cramps in, 162
  pulled, 148
  relaxants for, 117, 150
  spasms of, 162

Myocardial infarction.
See Heart attack.

Myopia, 61

N

Napping, 122

Naproxen sodium, decision chart for, 272–273

Nearsightedness, 61

Neck, 164–167
  trauma to, 349, 350

Nerve, disorders, 171–186

Neuralgia, trigeminal, 186

Neural hearing loss, 47–48

Nipple, discharge from, 238

Nitroglycerin, 85, 86

Nonsteroidal anti-inflammatory drugs (NSAIDs). See also specific types.
  for arthritis, 246
  decision chart for, 272–273
  gastritis and, 23
  for headaches, 181
  heartburn and, 25
  for phlebitis, 94

Nose infections, 178

NSAIDs. See Nonsteroidal anti-inflammatory drugs.

Nursing homes, 315–320

Nutrition. See Diet.

O

Obesity, 290

Occupational therapy, after stroke, 185

Oncologist, 131

Ophthalmologist, 49

Optic nerve, 50

Optometrist, 49

Oral cancer, 133

alcohol and, 286

Orgasm, 188

Orthopedist, 145

Osteoarthritis, 146, 150
  chronic, 246
  knee, 160–161
  neck, 164–166
  spinal stenosis with, 156

Osteoporosis, 255–256
  diet and, 230, 290
  hormone replacement therapy for, 231
  menopause and, 230
  stress fractures and, 71

Otolaryngologist, 131

Ovarian cancer, 242

Overflow incontinence, 34

Over-the-counter drugs, 270–273

Overuse injury
  carpal tunnel syndrome as, 169
  hip, 157
  knee, 158
  shoulder, 168
  wrist, 169

Oxygen therapy, 249

P

Pacemaker, 173

Pain. See also specific types.
  living will and, 305
  referred, 150
  response to, 5

Pain relievers. See also specific types.
  caffeine in, 123
  choice of, 270–271
  decision chart for, 272–273
  fatigue from, 117

Palpitations, 93–94. See also Heart disease.
  anxiety from, 113
Panic attacks, 113. See also Anxiety.
Panic disorder, 83
Pap smears, 240
  recommendations for, 283
Paralysis
  back pain with, 151
  from Bell's palsy, 174
Parkinson's disease, 181–183
  depression with, 115
  insomnia with, 121
  organizations for, 325
Pelvic exam, 283
Pelvic-floor exercises, 33
Pelvic tilt exercise, 152
Peptic ulcers, 23–24
  black stools from, 13, 23
  chest pain with, 83
Pepto-Bismol, 21
  black stools from, 13
Periodic limb movements, 164
Periodontal disease, 131, 139
  bad breath from, 132
Periodontist, 131
Personality changes
  aging and, 4
  with Alzheimer's disease, 172
Personal records, 302
Pets, loneliness and, 124
Pharmacist, 267–269
Phlebitis, 94–95, 161
Physiatrist, 145
Physical therapy
  for carpal tunnel

syndrome, 170
  for joint problems, 145
  for Parkinson's disease, 182
  for stroke, 185
Physician. See Doctor.
Piercing, body, 194, 199
Pinkeye, 54
Plantar fasciitis, 65, 69
Plantar warts, 77
Plaque
  bad breath from, 133
  gingivitis and, 139
Pleurisy, 107
Pneumococcal vaccine, 109, 249, 281–282
  recommendations for, 284
Pneumonia, 107–109
  bronchitis and, 99, 100
  shot for, 109, 249, 281–282
    recommendations, 284
  wheezing with, 110
Podiatrist, 63
Poisoning, 296
  carbon monoxide, 337–339
Poisonous plants, 209–210
Positional vertigo, 177
Posture, back pain and, 154
Potassium, muscle cramps and, 162
Power of attorney, 303, 304
Pregnancy
  chlamydia and, 197
  ectopic, 197
  hemorrhoids and, 25
  menopause and, 229
  varicose veins and, 95

Prepatellar bursitis, 158
Presbyopia, 61–62
Pressure sores, 211–212
Preventive health care, 279–284
Prostate, 222–226
  gonorrhea and, 198
  sexual concerns with, 190
  urination and, 36
Prostate cancer, 225–226
Prostatitis, 224–225
PSA (prostate-specific antigen) test, 226
Pseudoephedrine, 114
Psychiatrist, 111
Psychologist, 111
Psychotherapy. See Counseling.
Pulmonary embolism, 109–110
Puncture wound, 343
Purpura, 202
Pyorrhea, 139. See also Gums, disease of.

Q

Quadriceps stretch, 158

R

Radiation therapy, 16
  for breast cancer, 240
  for cervical cancer, 240
  for colon cancer, 16
  dry mouth after, 134
  for endometrial cancer, 242
  for prostate cancer, 226
  for throat cancer, 144
Rash(es), 213. See also Itching.
  from allergies, 333, 334

on breast, 237
from syphilis, 200
Records
   financial, 302
   immunization, 280
   medical, 260–261, 265
   personal, 302
Rectum. See also Colon.
   bleeding from, 13
   blood from, 12
   exam
      for colon cancer, 16
      for enlarged
        prostate, 223
      for prostate cancer,
        226
Referred pain, 150
Refractive vision prob-
   lems, 60–62
Relaxation technique(s),
   129, 130
   anxiety and, 114
   back pain and, 154
   bath as, 122
   dizziness and, 178
   fatigue and, 117
   headaches and, 181
   meditation as, 94
   palpitations and, 94
Restless legs, 164
Retinopathy, diabetic, 58
Retirement
   mood changes with,
      114
   planning for, 8
Rheumatoid arthritis, 246
Rheumatologist, 145
RICE method, 147
Rotator cuff injuries, 168

S

Sadness, 114, 115. See
  also Depression.

grieving and, 120
Safe sex, 193–194, 295
Safety, 294–299, 311
Salt water gargle, 102,
  144
Sciatica, 151, 155
Scrapes, 214. See also
  Wounds.
Screening tests, 279–280,
  282–284
   for colon cancer, 15–16
   for prostate cancer, 226
Seat belts, 295
Seborrheic dermatitis, 204
Seborrheic keratoses, 209
Second opinion, 276–277
Sedatives
   Alzheimer's disease
      and, 174
   fatigue from, 117
   grieving and, 120
   heat exhaustion and,
      351
Seizures
   drugs for, 186
   head injury with, 349
Senior centers, 308
Sensory neural deafness,
  47–48
Sexual concerns, 187–200,
  221
   aging and, 7
   after prostatectomy,
      226
   with vaginal dryness,
      232
Sexually transmitted dis-
  eases (STDs), 193–200,
  234
Shingles, 215–216
Shinsplints, 161, 163–164
Shock, 353–354
   anaphylactic, 333–335

back pain with, 151
burns with, 337
head injury with, 349
wounds with, 343
Shoes
   shinsplints and, 163
   walking, 294
Shoulder pain, 167–168
Sigmoidoscopy, 16, 284
Sinuses
   diagram of, 180
   infection of
      bad breath and, 132
      headache from, 180
      toothache from, 140
Sitz bath
   for hemorrhoids, 25
   for urinary tract infec-
      tion, 38
Skin cancer, 6, 216–218
Skin concern(s), 6,
  201–220
   breast changes and,
      237, 239
   feet and, 72–77
   frostbite as, 347–348
   heat exhaustion and,
      351
   jaundice as, 199
   shock and, 353
   sunburn as, 6, 218–219
Skin patch hormone
  replacement, 230, 231
Skin tags, 208–209
Sleep disturbance. See also
  Insomnia.
   alcohol and, 123
   fatigue from, 117
   stress and, 128
Sleepiness. See Fatigue.
Sleeping pills. See
  Sedatives.
Smoke detector, 296

Smoking. See Tobacco use.
Smoking cessation programs, 299–300
Sociability, 7, 124
    withdrawal vs., 112–113, 172
Social Security Administration, 262–263
Sodium, hypertension and, 253
Sores
    genital, 197, 199
    mouth, 135–136
    pressure, 211–212
Sore throat, 143–144
Spasms, 162
    drugs for, 150
Spastic colon, 27–28
Speech problems
    Parkinson's disease and, 182
    stroke and, 176
    therapy for, 185
Spermicide, 194, 195
Spine. See Vertebrae.
Splints, 346
Sprains, 148
Squamous skin cancer, 218
STDs. See Sexually transmitted diseases.
Stenosis, spinal, 156
Steroids
    for Bell's palsy, 174
    for carpal tunnel syndrome, 170
    depression and, 115
    edema from, 88, 89
    for lung disease, 249
Sties, 55
Stitches, 344
Stockings, support, 96
Stomach. See also

Digestive concern(s).
    alcohol and, 286
    flu, 104
Stomachache. See Abdominal pain.
Stools
    bloody, 12–14
    cancer test with, 14, 16
    impacted, 17
    light, 31
    tarlike, 12, 23
    thin, 15, 17
Strains, 148
Strangulated hernia, 222
Strep throat, 143–144
Stress, 128–130
    anxiety and, 114
    cardiovascular risks and, 88
    chronic illness and, 244
    diabetes and, 252–253
    headaches from, 178
    hypertension and, 253
    management of, 129
    neck pain and, 165
    palpitations with, 94
    sexual concerns with, 190
    vomiting from, 31
Stress incontinence, 33–34
Stress test, 85
Stretching, 147
    back, 152–153
    calf, 163
    neck, 166
    quadriceps, 158
Stroke, 183–186, 354
    depression with, 115
    headaches from, 178
    hypertension and, 93
    memory loss with, 127
Substance abuse. See Alcohol abuse.

Suicide, 114, 115. See also Depression.
Sunblock, 295
Sunburn, 6, 218–219
Support groups, 243, 321–326
Surgery, 276-278
    for cancer, 16
Swelling
    knee, 159
    leg, 88–89, 149, 157
        pain with, 161
    throat, 334
Swimmer's ear, 42–44
Syphilis, 199–200

T

Tartar, 139
Taste, aging and, 5
Teeth. See also Gums.
    brushing of, 139
        toothaches and, 140–141
    care of, 131
    chipped, 138
    concerns with, 136–141
    grinding of, 140
    loss of, 138
    pain in, 140–141
Telephone safety, 297
Temporomandibular joint (TMJ) problems, 139–140
Tendinitis, 146
    Achilles, 148–149
    carpal tunnel syndrome and, 169
    RICE method for, 147
Tendons
    injury to, 148
    shoulder, 168
Tension headaches, 180
Testosterone, 88, 89

Tetanus shot, 282
  for burns, 335
  recommendations for, 284
Tetracycline, sunburn and, 219
Therapy. See also Counseling.
  occupational, 185
  oxygen, 249
  physical, 145, 170, 182, 185
  speech, 185
Throat, 141–144
  swollen, 334
Thrombophlebitis, 94–95
Thyroid problems
  anxiety with, 113
  constipation and, 18
  fatigue from, 117
TIA (transient ischemic attack), 183, 186
Tinnitus, 47. See also Ear concern(s).
Tiredness. See Fatigue.
TMJ (temporomandibular joint) problems, 139–140
Tobacco use.
  asthma and, 98
  bad breath from, 133
  bronchitis and, 99, 100
  cardiovascular risks from, 87
  cataracts and, 57
  drug effects and, 269
  dry mouth with, 134
  ear infections and, 42
  effects of, 4
  fatigue and, 118
  heartburn and, 25
  hoarseness with, 142
  hormone replacement therapy and, 231

hypertension and, 253
lung cancer from, 106
lung disease from, 249
organizations for, 326
quitting of, 299–300
sore throat with, 144
stress and, 128
stroke and, 184
throat cancer and, 144
wellness and, 2
Toenails, 78-80
Tongue brushing, 133
Tonsils, 132, 142
Tooth. See Teeth.
Toothaches, 140–141
Tranquilizers
  fatigue from, 117
  heat exhaustion and, 351
Transfusions, AIDS and, 196
Transient ischemic attack. See TIA.
Transplants, 276
Traveling, medical assistance, 326
Tremor
  panic attack with, 113
  Parkinson's disease with, 181
Trichomoniasis, 234
Trigeminal neuralgia, 186
Trusts, 303
Tubal ligation, 229
Tunnel vision, 56
Tylenol. See Acetaminophen.

U

Ulcerative colitis, 13, 15
Ulcers
  bleeding, 23
  foot, 77

insomnia with, 122
peptic, 23–24
  black stools from, 13, 23
  pressure, 211–212
Urethritis, 34
Urge incontinence, 32
Urgent care centers, 328–329
Urinary incontinence, 32–34
Urinary tract infections (UTIs), 34–38
  atrophic vaginitis and, 233
  chlamydia and, 197
  enlarged prostate and, 224
  fatigue from, 117
  insomnia with, 122
  menopause and, 230
  vaginal dryness with, 233
  vaginal hormone cream and, 231
Urination, 32–38
  back pain with, 154
  burning with, 225, 229
  dark, 12
  difficult, 226
  pain with, 198, 233
Urine tests, 37, 280
Urologist, 221
Uterine cancer, 241–242
UTIs. See Urinary tract infections.

V

Vaccines. See Immunization(s).
Vagina
  bleeding from, 198, 229
  discharge from, 233, 234

chlamydia with, 197
gonorrhea and, 198
hormone replace-
   ment therapy
   and, 231
dryness of, 7, 191,
   232–234
infections of, 233–236
Vaporizer, 10, 102, 144
Varicella vaccine, 282
Varicose veins, 95–96
Vasectomy, 229
Vertebrae. See also Back.
curving of, 155
stenosis of, 156
Vertigo, 176
Viral infections, 101–102
pneumonia as, 107
Vision, 50
blurred
   cataracts and, 57
   from drugs, 270
   head injury with,
      349
   pinkeye with, 54
   sunburn with, 219
loss of, 113
tunnel, 56
Vision concern(s), 49–62
aging and, 5
Bell's palsy and, 174
driving and, 8, 298
gonorrhea and, 198
headache and, 179
organizations for, 324
stroke and, 183
Vitamin B12 deficiency,
   113
Vitamin D, osteoporosis
   and, 256, 257
Vitamin supplements, 290
Vocal cords, 141-142, 144
Volunteer work, 7

Vomiting, 30–31
allergies and, 333, 334
back pain with, 151
bloody, 12, 31
constipation with, 17
heat exhaustion and,
   351
hyperglycemia with,
   252
shock and, 353, 354
urinary tract infection
   with, 35

W

Walking program, 294.
   See also Exercise(s).
Warts, plantar, 77
Water. See also
   Dehydration.
fluoridated, 131
lung disease and, 249
need for, 134
Weight control, 254–255
arthritis and, 246
back pain and, 152
cardiovascular risks
   and, 88
diabetes and, 252
fatigue and, 118
hypertension and, 253
stroke and, 184–185
Wheezing, 110
colds with, 101
influenza with, 104
Whiplash injury, 165, 167
Wills, 303
living, 304–305
Withdrawal
drug, 112–113
social, 7, 172
Women's health
   concern(s), 227–242

sexual changes and,
   191
Wounds, 342–345
head, 349–350
shock from, 354
Wrinkles, 3, 6, 220
Wrist pain, 168–170

X

X-ray
for fractures, 346
routine, 280

Y

Yanuzzi card, 60
Yeast infections, vaginal,
   235–236
Yoga, 94

Credits

Institute for Research and Education
HealthSystem Minnesota

Editor in Chief: Paul E. Terry, Ph.D.,
Institute for Research and Education

Medical Editors: David Abelson, M.D.;
Joseph Alfano, M.D.; Allan Kind, M.D.;
Linda Peitzman, M.D.
Park Nicollet Clinic

Managing Editor: Lisa Harvey, M.P.H.

Writers: Lisa Bartels-Rabb, M.S.J.; Suzanne
Bennett, M.P.H.; Tom Brandes, M.A.; Scott
Glickstein, M.D.; Lisa Harvey, M.P.H.;
Jeanne Mettner, M.A.; Susan S. O'Donnell;
Paul E. Terry, Ph.D.; Kathy Tingelstad

Production and Research: Julie Broberg;
Jessica Grossmeier; Linda Olson

Medical Reviewers

Allergy: David Graft, M.D.; William
Schoenwetter, M.D.; Richard Sveum, M.D.

Cardiology: Steve Benton, M.D.; Sue
Hanson, R.D.; Mark Haugland, M.D.; Joni
Hoffman, R.N.; Richard Madlon-Kay, M.D.;
Philip Ranheim, M.D.; George Strauss, M.D.

Dermatology: Spencer Holmes, M.D.;
Michael McCormick, M.D.; Louis Rusin,
M.D.; Victoria Vanroy, M.D.

ENT: David Buran, M.D.; Gerard
O'Halloran, M.D.

Family Practice: Donald Abrams, M.D.;
Barbara Benjamin, M.D.; Alan Carter,
M.D.; Susan Carter, M.D.; Janet Frost, R.N.;
John Haugen, M.D.; Mark Hench, M.D.;
Jeanne Hesse, M.D.; Bonita Hill, M.D.; Julie
Hudson, R.N.; John Kaintz, M.D.; Michael
Lano, M.D.; Douglas Lowin, M.D.; Joseph
Lukaska, M.D.; Alston Lundgren, M.D.;
Jean Lundgren, M.D.; Donald Lynch, M.D.;
Rosa Marroquin, M.D.; Charles McCoy,
M.D.; Kenneth Olson, M.D.; Carolyn
Torkelson, M.D.; David VonWeiss, M.D.

Gastroenterology: Matthew Bagamery,
M.D.; Michael Levy, M.D.; Michael
Newcomer, M.D.

Geriatrics: Nancy Carlson, LSW; Michael
Dukinfield, M.D.; Jennifer Olson, M.D.;
Robert Sonntag, M.D.

Infectious Diseases: Leslie Baken, M.D.;
Paul Carson, M.D.; Pat Dahlman, R.N.

Internal Medicine: Avis Baumann, R.N.;
Jane Oh, M.D.; Linda Pietz, R.N.; Barbara
Steigauf, R.N.; Anthony Woolley, M.D.

Mental Health: Barry Cosens, M.D.; Susan
Czapiewski, M.D.; Ranson Pinck, Ph.D.;
Gretchen Van Hauer, M.D.

Neurology: Daniel Freking, M.D.; Sandra
Hanson, M.D.; Debra Heros, M.D.; Eric
Shenk, M.D.

Nutrition: Joan Bissen, R.D. Susan Deno,
R.D.; Sue Hanson, R.D.

OB/GYN: Dale Akkerman, M.D.; Janet
Claxton, N.P.; Barbara Davenport, N.P.;

Deborah Meade, R.N.; Mario Petrini, M.D.; Leslie Pratt, M.D.; Lois Satterberg, N.P.; Deborah Thorp, M.D.

Occupational Medicine: David Parker, M.D.

Oncology: J.P. Carlson, M.D.; Steven Duane, M.D.; Charles Murray, M.D.

Ophthalmology: Robert Campbell, M.D.; Timothy Diegel, M.D.; Rodney Dueck, M.D.; Richard Freeman, M.D.; Jeffrey Freund, COMT; Anne Towey, M.D.; Anton Willerscheidt, M.D.

Orthopedics: Renner Johnston, M.D.; Matthew Putman, M.D.; Gregg Strathy, M.D.; Thomas Youngren, M.D.

Pharmacy: Richard Bleck, R.Ph.; Scott Bryngelson, R.Ph., Roger Mickelson, R.Ph.

Podiatry: Judy Hopkins, C.M.A.; Anthony Pojman, M.D.

Pulmonary Medicine: A. Stuart Hanson, M.D.; Kathleen Hornsby, R.N.; Kevin Komadina, M.D.; Richard Woellner, M.D.

Rehabilitation Medicine: Ann Brutlag, M.D.; Robert Gorman, M.D.; George Kramer, M.D.; Mary Kruse, M.S., ATC; Daniel Kurtti, M.D.

Rheumatology: Scott Glickstein, M.D.; Eric Schned, M.D.; John Schousboe, M.D.

Urgent Care: Shelly Barton, R.N.; Paul Bearmon, M.D.; Carol Manning, M.D.; Linda Peitzman, M.D.; Mary Ratz, M.D.; Suzanne Schaefer, M.D.; Omri Shochatovitz, M.D.; Susan Vitalis, M.D.

Urology: Steven Bernstein, M.D.; Clyde Blackard, M.D.; William Borkon, M.D.;

Sharon Reiter, R.N.; William Sharer, M.D.; Erol Uke, M.D.; Kevin Zhang, M.D.

Specialty Reviewers: Gail Amundson, M.D.; Dale Anderson, M.D.; Deborah Boal, R.N.; Hyacinth Campbell-Roberts; Pat Drury; Stacie Emberley; Mary Figueroa, M.D.; Lisa Fish, M.D.; Jinnet Fowles, Ph.D.; Marion Franz, R.D.; Robert Green, M.D.; Stanley Greenwald, M.D.; Carol Hersman, R.N., M.A.; Judy Kelloway, Ph.D.; David J. Knutson; Thomas Kottke, M.D.; James Li, M.D.; Janet Lima; Sheila McCormick, R.N.; Gordon Mosser, M.D.; Jeanne Nelson, M.D.; Joseph Nelson, L.P.; Jane Norstrom, M.A.; Steven Powless, M.D.; Ira Rabinowitz, D.M.D.; James Reinertson, M.D.; Michael Rethwill, M.D.; Lee Simso, M.D.; Peter Smars, M.D.; Leif Solberg, M.D.; Paul Spilseth, M.D.; Linda Strohmayer, R.N.; Susan Sullivan, Ph.D.; James V. Toscano

Mosby Consumer Health

Editor in Chief: Sandy McDowell

Art Director: Nancy Olson

Layout & Electronic Production Director: Maritza Medina

Copy Chiefs: Jules Verdone; India Koopman

Senior Editor: Joseph Saling

Associate Designer: Lynn Whittemore

Layout & Production: Scott D. Hadley; Kay Jones

Associate Editors: Jennifer Hicks; Gina Skurchak

Illustrators: Nancy Olson; Joan Orme

Photography

Amethyst/Custom Medical Stock Photo, Inc., 209

Ayres, Bruce/Tony Stone Images, 270, 306

Barber, Patricia, RBP/Custom Medical Stock Photo, Inc., 96 (bottom right)

Barros & Barros/The Image Bank, Inc., 114, 173, 185, 321

Beaton, Bruce, 63, 245, 251

Berwin, Derek/The Image Bank, Inc., 119

Bittorf, Andreas /The University of Erlangen, 202

Bokelberg, Werner/The Image Bank, Inc., front cover (upper left), 111, 187

Caliendo,Marilee, RBP/Custom Medical Stock Photo, Inc., 96 (bottom left)

Cralle, Gary/The Image Bank, Inc., 309

Glaser, K., & Associates/Custom Medical Stock Photo, Inc., 247

Gordon, Larry Dale/The Image Bank, Inc., 302

Gupton, Charles/Tony Stone Images, 313

H.M.S. Images/The Image Bank, Inc., 125

Habif, Thomas P., M.D./*Clinical Dermatology*, Third Edition, 1996, St. Louis, Mosby–Year Book, Inc., 206, 217, 385

Hamilton, David W./The Image Bank, Inc., front cover (bottom right), 6, 130

Henley, John/The Stock Market, Inc., 257

Huang, Ken/The Image Bank, Inc., front cover (center right), 227

Janeart/The Image Bank, Inc., 116

Kinne, Russ/Comstock, Inc., 215

Kuhn, Chuck/The Image Bank, Inc., 252

LeDoux, Ronald G., D.P.M./Calgary Podiatry Centre, 68, 75

Lewin, Elyse/The Image Bank, Inc., front cover (center left and bottom left), 1, 192, 301

Magnatone Quality Hearing Instruments, 45

Martin, Butch/The Image Bank, Inc., 9

Martin/Custom Medical Stock Photo, Inc., 136

Miller, Peter/The Image Bank, Inc., 97

Niedorf, Steve/The Image Bank, Inc., 4

Olson, Nancy, 39, 49, 57, 58, 59, 62, 76, 81, 145, 201, 206, 230, 329, 386, 387, 388

Park Nicollet Medical Foundation, 55

PhotoDisc, Inc., 11, 131, 171, 182, 220, 221, 239, 243, 259, 264, 274, 281, 285, 297, 315, 327

Pierce, Larry/The Image Bank, Inc., 3

Romanelli, Marc/The Image Bank, Inc., 7, 189

Schleichkorn, H., RBP/Custom Medical Stock Photo, Inc., 209

Science Photo Library/Custom Medical Stock Photo, Inc., 67, 74, 135, 256

Steinmark, L./Custom Medical Stock Photo, Inc., 279

Satushek, Steve/The Image Bank, Inc., 8

Yanuzzi, Lawrence A., M.D., 60

Your Medical History

Name _____ Date of birth _____ Blood type _____

Acute Diseases

Disease	Date of Illness	Disease	Date of Illness	Disease	Date of Illness
Chicken pox	_____	Mononucleosis	_____	Sinus infection	_____
Ear infection	_____	Mumps	_____	Strep throat	_____
German measles (rubella)	_____	Polio	_____	Whooping cough	_____
		Scarlet fever	_____	Other	_____
Hepatitis	_____	Sexually trans-			_____
Measles	_____	mitted disease	_____		_____

Chronic Diseases

Disease	Date Diagnosed	Treatment
Arthritis	_____	_____
Asthma	_____	_____
Blood disorder	_____	_____
Cataracts	_____	_____
Diabetes	_____	_____
Epilepsy	_____	_____
Gastrointestinal disorder	_____	_____
Glaucoma	_____	_____
Heart disease	_____	_____
High cholesterol level	_____	_____
High blood pressure	_____	_____
HIV	_____	_____
Kidney disease	_____	_____
Mental illness	_____	_____
Ulcers	_____	_____
Other	_____	_____
	_____	_____

Family Medical History

Have any of your blood relatives had any of the following conditions? (This includes your mother, father, brothers, sisters, grandparents, aunts, or uncles.)

Disease	Relationship	Cause of Death	Age at Death
Allergies	_____	_____	_____
Anemia or other blood disorder	_____	_____	_____
Arthritis	_____	_____	_____
Asthma	_____	_____	_____
Bowel disorder	_____	_____	_____
Cancer	_____	_____	_____
Cataracts	_____	_____	_____
Diabetes	_____	_____	_____
Eczema	_____	_____	_____
Emphysema	_____	_____	_____
Epilepsy	_____	_____	_____
Glaucoma	_____	_____	_____
Heart disease	_____	_____	_____
High cholesterol level	_____	_____	_____
High blood pressure	_____	_____	_____
Liver disease	_____	_____	_____
Lung disease	_____	_____	_____
Nervous system disorder	_____	_____	_____
Thyroid disorder	_____	_____	_____
Ulcer	_____	_____	_____
Other	_____	_____	_____
	_____	_____	_____
	_____	_____	_____
	_____	_____	_____
	_____	_____	_____
	_____	_____	_____

cut on dotted line

Personal Medication Chart

Make copies of this form as you need them.

Prescription Drugs

List any prescription drugs you have taken in the past four weeks. Also list any prescription drugs you have on hand to use as needed. List them even if you have not taken them recently. Add new drugs as your doctor prescribes them.

Drug _____

Purpose _____

Dose _____

Instructions _____

Date started _____

Drug _____

Purpose _____

Dose _____

Instructions _____

Date started _____

Drug _____

Purpose _____

Dose _____

Instructions _____

Date started _____

Drug _____

Purpose _____

Dose _____

Instructions _____

Date started _____

Over-the-Counter Drugs

List any over-the-counter drugs you have taken in the past four weeks. Also list any over-the-counter drugs you have on hand but have not taken recently. Add the names of new over-the-counter drugs to the list as you buy them.

Drug _____

Purpose _____

Dose _____

Instructions _____

Date started _____

Drug _____

Purpose _____

Dose _____

Instructions _____

Date started _____

Drug _____

Purpose _____

Dose _____

Instructions _____

Date started _____

Drug _____

Purpose _____

Dose _____

Instructions _____

Date started _____

Your Personal Health Record

Make copies of this form as you need them.

Use this form to record the dates and results of preventive exams, immunization dates, and doctor recommendations. Having your own written records may help you know when to see your doctor and how to keep yourself healthy.

Preventive Exams	Date of Exam (month/year)	Results	Date of Next Test (month/year)
Blood pressure	_____	_____	_____
Cholesterol	_____	_____	_____
Colorectal screening	_____	_____	_____
Fecal occult blood test (FOBT)	_____	_____	_____
Sigmoidoscopy	_____	_____	_____
Mammogram	_____	_____	_____
Pap smear	_____	_____	_____
Other _____	_____	_____	_____
_____	_____	_____	_____

Immunizations	Date of Immunization (month/year)	Date Next Due (month/year)
Influenza	_____	_____
Pneumococcal	_____	_____
Tetanus diphtheria	_____	_____
Other (if at risk)	_____	_____
	_____	_____
	_____	_____

Preventive exams recommended by your doctor: _____
_____
_____

Health habit follow-up recommended by your doctor: _____
_____
_____

cut on dotted line

Color Plates

Types of Skin Cancers

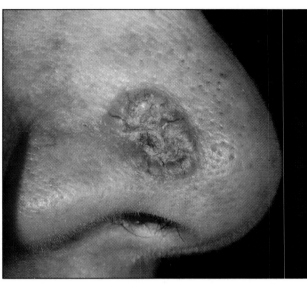

Basal cell cancer often has an open sore that bleeds. It may also crust and scale. (SEE PAGE 217.)

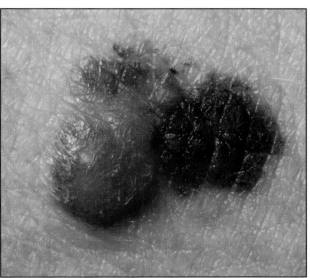

Malignant melanoma often has an uneven border with different colors in the same mole. (SEE PAGE 218.)

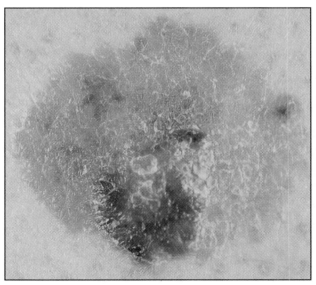

Malignant melanoma in a later stage. (SEE PAGE 218.)

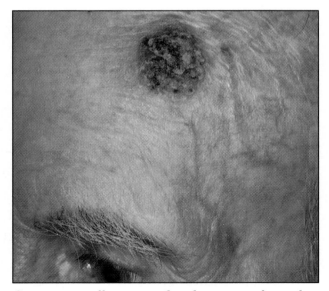

Squamous cell cancer often has a rough, scaly surface. The base may be red. (SEE PAGE 218.)

Skeletal System

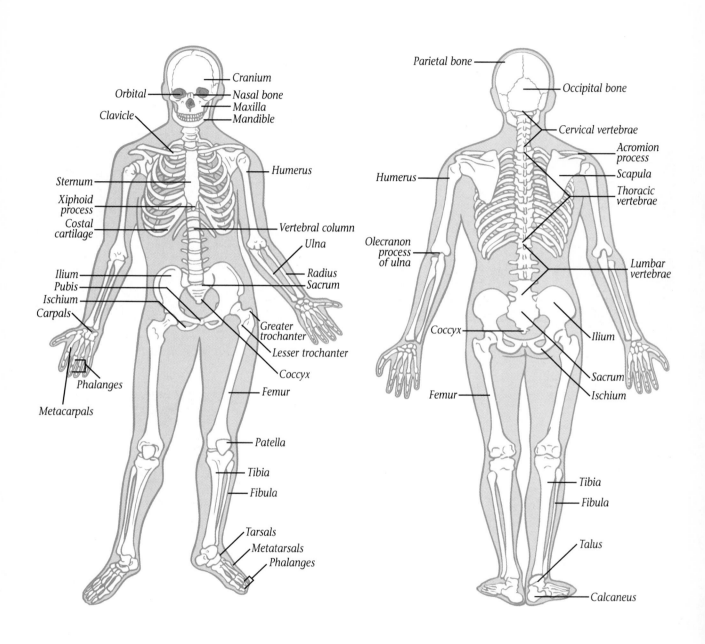

Front View

- Cranium
- Orbital
- Nasal bone
- Maxilla
- Mandible
- Clavicle
- Humerus
- Sternum
- Xiphoid process
- Costal cartilage
- Vertebral column
- Ulna
- Radius
- Sacrum
- Ilium
- Pubis
- Ischium
- Carpals
- Greater trochanter
- Lesser trochanter
- Coccyx
- Phalanges
- Femur
- Metacarpals
- Patella
- Tibia
- Fibula
- Tarsals
- Metatarsals
- Phalanges

Back View

- Parietal bone
- Occipital bone
- Cervical vertebrae
- Acromion process
- Humerus
- Scapula
- Thoracic vertebrae
- Olecranon process of ulna
- Lumbar vertebrae
- Coccyx
- Ilium
- Femur
- Sacrum
- Ischium
- Tibia
- Fibula
- Talus
- Calcaneus

Muscular System

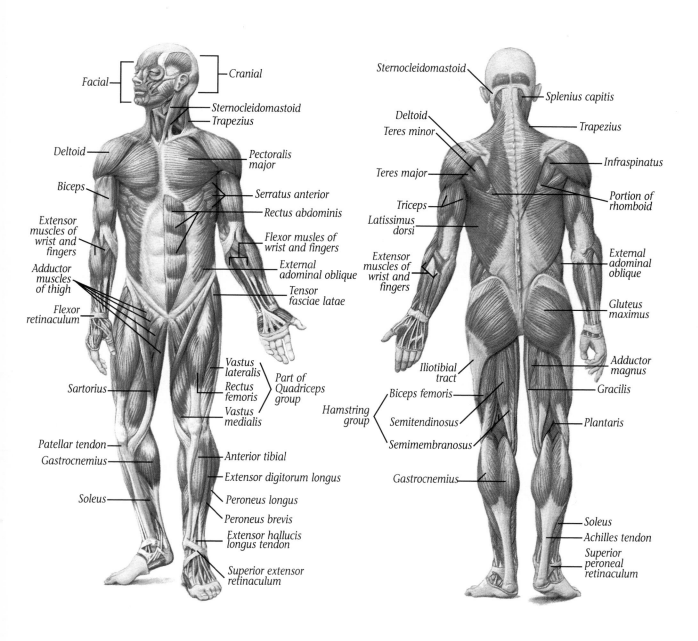

Front View

Facial

Cranial

Sternocleidomastoid

Trapezius

Deltoid

Pectoralis major

Biceps

Serratus anterior

Rectus abdominis

Extensor muscles of wrist and fingers

Flexor musles of wrist and fingers

External adominal oblique

Adductor muscles of thigh

Tensor fasciae latae

Flexor retinaculum

Sartorius

Vastus lateralis

Rectus femoris

Part of Quadriceps group

Vastus medialis

Patellar tendon

Gastrocnemius

Anterior tibial

Extensor digitorum longus

Soleus

Peroneus longus

Peroneus brevis

Extensor hallucis longus tendon

Superior extensor retinaculum

Back View

Sternocleidomastoid

Splenius capitis

Deltoid

Teres minor

Trapezius

Teres major

Infraspinatus

Triceps

Portion of rhomboid

Latissimus dorsi

Extensor muscles of wrist and fingers

External adominal oblique

Gluteus maximus

Adductor magnus

Iliotibial tract

Gracilis

Biceps femoris

Hamstring group

Semitendinosus

Plantaris

Semimembranosus

Gastrocnemius

Soleus

Achilles tendon

Superior peroneal retinaculum

Mosby Consumer Health